American Indian Studies
University of Wisconsin - Madison
315 Ingraham Hall
1155 Observatory Drive
Madison, WI 53706

A BIBLIOGRAPHY OF CONTEMPORARY

North American Indians

Other Books from Interland

A BIBLIOGRAPHY OF CONTEMPORARY

North American Indians

Selected and Partially Annotated with Study Guide

WILLIAM HODGE

INTERLAND PUBLISHING INC.
New York
1976

Copyright © 1976

Interland Publishing Inc.
799 Broadway
New York, New York 10003
tel. (212) 673-8280

Cover design and typography by Judith Woracek

Library of Congress Cataloguing in Publication Data

Hodge, William H.   1932–

A Bibliography of Contemporary North American Indians.

Includes index.
1. Indians of North America—Bibliography.   I. Title.

Z1209 2.N67H6   [E77]   016.970'004'97   75-21675

ISBN 0-87989-102-5

Library of Congress Catalog Card Number 75-21675
International Standard Book Number 0-87989-102-5

For Dorie

Acknowledgments

I have had considerable assistance over the years in preparing this bibliography and study guide. Fellow anthropologists in several countries have been generous with their resources. Those who have been especially helpful include: John H. Bodine; Donald M. Bahr; John F. Martin; Kenneth M. Stewart; Keith H. Basso; Theodore E. Downing; Jerrold E. Levy; Thomas Weaver; Bernard L. Fontana; William Willard; Robert F. Heizer; Leslie A. White; Triloki N. Pandey; Fred Eggan; W. H. Oswalt; Eleanor B. Leacock; Weston La Barre; Charles M. Hudson, Jr.; Joseph B. Casagrande; Alan P. Merriam; June Helm; Alice B. Kehoe; Frank C. Miller; R. F. Spencer; M. Estellie Smith; Morris E. Opler; E. A. Kennard; Ernest L. Schusky; Henry F. Dobyns; John Price; Jim Howard; and Nancy O. Lurie.

My chairman and colleagues of the Department of Sociology-Anthropology, University of Wisconsin-Oshkosh, graciously allowed me to arrange my teaching schedule so that uninterrupted periods of time for thinking and writing were available. The Reference Services of the University Library and the Oshkosh Public Library gave prompt and efficient assistance. Mr. Jerry Carpenter of the Interlibrary Loan Service of the University Library through patient and resourceful effort was able to provide many items not immediately and locally available. The Department of Indian Affairs and Northern Development in Ottawa, Ontario, were exceedingly generous in discussing how they met their administrative responsibilities throughout Canada. Dr. Stewart Raby, head of the Indian Claims Commission of Canada, and his staff provided invaluable assistance by supplying information on a wide variety of aspects of the Canadian Indian experience. They also supplied a large variety of materials on the native peoples of Canada. A large number of Bureau of Indian Affairs personnel and those from other federal offices have provided prompt and informed assistance with respect to information on Indians and Eskimos within the United States. Many tribal governments, off-reservation Indian organizations, and Indian newspapers have given me valuable assistance. My wife has been helpful in a number of ways. To all these friends go my deepest thanks. I, of course, assume responsibility for errors of commission and omission.

The excerpt on pp. 8–10 is reprinted from *North American Indians in Historical Perspective* by Eleanor Leacock and Nancy Lurie, (eds.), © 1971 by Random House. Reprinted by permission.

The material on pp. 3–4 is used with the permission of Gordon Willey. This material originally appeared in "New World Pre-History" published in *Science*, volume number 131, pages 73 through 86, issue of 8 January 1960. © January 8, 1960 by the American Association for the Advancement of Science.

Foreword

The present age is one of the recurring times in history when public as well as scholarly interest in the Native Americans is at a high point. The Indians, by dramatic presentations of their plight, have captured the minds and stirred the consciences of the American people. This national attention paid to the Indians is reminiscent of similar periods of concern about the Indians' welfare in the 1880s and 1890s and in the 1920s. Present-day interest, however, goes deeper than that of past times of agitation and deeper than the superficial treatment that is possible in the mass media. There is today a strong desire to study the Indians, their culture, and their place in American society at some depth, as the increasing number and wide diffusion of scholarly studies clearly indicate. And this is a desire both on the part of Indians themselves, who want an accurate knowledge of their own heritage, and on the part of white citizens, who are coming to realize more and more the contributions made to America by the Indians.

There has long been public interest, of course, in the more romantic aspects of the Indians' past. The encounter with the aboriginal peoples in the New World was a dramatic experience for the Europeans who came for trade and settlement, and continuing interest in Indian cultures as they existed before contact with white civilization has tended to obscure the fact that the Indian groups are living, growing, and changing communities today.

William Hodge's bibliography on North American Indians is important because, like any extensive bibliographic tool, it helps us to order and organize the massive outpouring of writings on Indians that marks our age. It is necessary to find a competent guide through the mass of materials lest they crush us by their volume. But the bibliography is especially useful because it concentrates on contemporary Indians and their communities. As the compiler notes in his introduction, large numbers of Indians now live in urban centers, and their conditions should interest us as much as those of the more traditional groups, who are closer to the stereotypes that many whites still have of the Indians. Although he presents plenty of material to give adequate background information on the earlier history of the Indians, his intent is to direct us toward materials that will contribute to an understanding of the Indians in our own society.

Bibliographies generally tend to be cold, impersonal lists. They are often produced today by a staff of workers, in a more or less mechanical way, following guidelines and principles of selection set up to insure some sort of uniformity. In an ultimate form they are spewed forth in computer printouts from stored data keyed to set categories by faceless workers. It may well be that the accumulation of knowledge in our time and the almost uncontrollable proliferation of published works in every field make this necessary and inevitable.

William Hodge offers here quite a different sort of work. It is, if one may so speak, a personal bibliography, one that reflects the mind and experience of one man, a scholar and teacher, who quite evidently has lived with the items he sets down in his guide and in his bibliographical lists. The categories are those that he has found useful as he grew in knowledge of the subject matter, and he enthusiastically wants to share that knowledge with other seekers down his pathways.

His interests are broad ranging. He is concerned with the work of anthropologists in their study of Indian cultures, with migration patterns, with social organization and social control in Indian communities, with contemporary images of the Indian and with "professional Indians," with education, and with city living—as well as with government relations and historical accounts. His sections on government documents—both of the United States and of Canada—contain a vast array of data, which would be hard for the uninitiated to dig out by themselves from official depositories. Many of the items in the bibliography are papers read at meetings and mimeographed studies. These may be difficult to lay one's hands on, but they help to show the directions that investigations are taking, and they give a sense of immediacy to the bibliography.

The study guides included at the beginning of the volume set forth the plan of the whole work and help to place the specifically Indian materials in a broad sociological and anthropological perspective which will prevent their being treated in a vacuum. The lists, too, are of tremendous value. Some persons may desire more precision in classification and more complete annotations. Such niceties will not be the main interest of most who pick up this bibliography. These users will delight in the mountain of information to which they are directed and will be continually grateful that someone has had the patience to assemble the lists and the willingness to share his findings with all of us.

FRANCIS PAUL PRUCHA
Marquette University

Contents

xii

Introduction

Why This Book Was Written:

I compiled the bibliography and prepared the study guides because of my neighbors back in my home town of Coffeyville, Kansas. When I was growing up there, it was—and still is—a small place. For me there were only two things about the town that were really interesting. In 1892, some forty years before I was born, the Dalton gang had tried to rob the local bank and found the experience to be fatal. They were buried in an old cemetery on the edge of the town with a hitching rack over their graves as a marker. I used to bicycle out there occasionally and think about these men.

As absorbing as this subject was, some of our neighbors intrigued me even more. These were self-contained, independent people who worked at the same sort of jobs that other residents in town did. Most of the time, they were pleasant and helpful to everyone. Their houses and yards were well kept and, like all the rest of us, they fished, hunted, and sometimes worried about tornados and why there was either too much rain or none at all. But in many ways they were different from the other people. They were usually more willing than the rest to visit and joke with a naive kid like me who often talked too much and probably asked too many questions. Most weekends, vacations, and holidays they would drive south to Oklahoma and visit friends and relatives in such places as Anadarko, Bokchito, Caddo, Chickasha, Hominy, Lenapah, Oologah, Tahlequah, and Pawhuska. I often sat on their front porches when they came back from these trips and they would tell me where they had been and what they had done there. They made the rolling prairies, the winding creeks, the biting gales of winter, and everything else found on our southern plains sound important. If I asked them, which I often did, they would get out such things as moccasins, breast plates, and eagle feather dance bustles. They told me how they had been made and something about their uses. They also taught me more about living than either they or I realized at the time. These neighbors were American Indians: Cherokees, Creeks, Kiowas, Comanches, Poncas, plus many from other tribes that I have since forgotten.

None of them as individuals were perfect, and all of them had their worries, but they were comfortable to be around and I was lucky to have them as friends. They often said, "If it isn't fun, try not to do it." In the years since then I have generally found this to be good advice. I prepared this bibliography and appreciation of contemporary American Indian life because it was fun to do. I hope that those who use the book will find the experience to be enjoyable and instructive.

American Indians Today:

Before discussing the structure of this work, it would be useful to consider briefly my conception of the general nature of contemporary Indian life, since the outline to be presented below has been considerably influenced by my impressions in this area.

I would estimate that at least 60% of American Indians now are full or part time residents of cities. Obviously, the urban milieux of these people assumes great importance. However, attention must also be given to Indians who live on reservations or in other kinds of rural communities, because for most Indians urban and rural living are part of one pattern of life or one system. Both kinds of residence must be considered if either is to be understood. Much stress should also be devoted to the examination of modern Indian life as movement *per se.*

One of the central integrating aspects of all Indian life is travel. Travel is conceived as a necessity to gain that which makes life possible, but also as a great good in itself. To be Indian is to constantly seek new vistas and challenges, but then to return home. Indians would agree with Robert Frost who defined home as "a place where, if you go there, they got to take you in."

I believe that this perpetual wandering and camping is a very old endeavor for Indians. It is as old as North American cities themselves. From Jamestown, Virginia, to the concrete wilderness of Los Angeles, Indians have come, looked, briefly lived in cities, and then moved on to be replaced by others of their kind. Throughout this process, most have remained Indians, first, last, and always.

This desire for travel used as a frame of reference and placed in sharper focus centers around the interrelationships between three variables: migration, residence, and behavior as they relate to fluctuations in resources. Fluctuations in resources, in turn, are correlated with a variety of social and cultural changes, the instability of resources, and an expanding population. These changes cannot always be readily predicted by those most closely influenced by such developments. Hence, Indian life is based upon varieties of subsistence patterns as they vary through time, and consequently assumes a plastic effervescent kind of texture characterized above as movement, travel, or migration.

The Indian population has been increasing at a significant rate for at least the past fifty years. The resources that Indians have had to rely upon within the confines of their reservations and/or rural communities during this period have either remained constant or decreased in magnitude. The various modes of subsistence such as pastoralism or limited dry and wet farming supplemented by a modicum of hunting and gathering have proven to be woefully inadequate to support the increasing population numbers. Accordingly, wage labor and some form of welfare support have been relied upon with greater frequency, both generally being sought outside the home. The utilization of wage labor and welfare imply some form of migration, often to an urban area, on the part of individuals or individuals as members of families.

How This Book Is Organized:

In arranging the materials in this book, I was faced with two central operational problems: first, what is implied by the terms "traditional" and "contemporary"? Second, what valid criteria are to be used in choosing references for the selected, annotated bibliography? Definitive answers to these questions are difficult to provide.

The term contemporary as used here refers to an indefinite period of time beginning about the last quarter of the 19th century and stretching into the future. The beginning of this era virtually marks the end of the military conquest of all of the native peoples on the North American continent. Many groups, of course, were not only subjugated but destroyed by European influences well before this time. However, by 1875, almost all native Americans were well launched upon a course of stabilized, permanent socio-cultural pluralism within the larger white society. I view this as a central aspect of contemporary Indian existence. The "contemporary" begins at the time when a particular group becomes economically and politically subordinated within the larger society. Further, it is possible to separate the "traditional" from the "contemporary" only in a relative conceptual sense here because by the time it was possible for adequate accounts of an aboriginal people to be made, much of the pre-European contact life had disappeared or been changed almost beyond recognition. In the cultural areas of the Southwest, the Great Basin, California, the Northwest Coast, the Subarctic, and the Eskimo-inhabited regions, this was especially the case. This situation is also true with respect to folklore, arts and crafts, and music and dance. The concepts of past and present or traditional and contemporary cannot assume the same meaning as they do with respect to European civilization. Hence in moving from the traditional to the contemporary, the transition is not abrupt but a matter of a gradual shift of degree, with respect both to time and place. Changes were initiated when European-native contact first began. Areas more remote from Europeans were affected only in an indirect sense or not at all. The structure of this study guide then is the result of a very general and loose kind of organization where ease of presentation is stressed at the expense of an inclusive, but less satisfactory classification system.

The past, present, and future are all categories which have very different meanings when used as a frame of reference for Indian behavior rather than that of whites. It is for this reason that some attention is given here to Indian life prior to 1875. In many respects, Indian life is blended into a single, timeless and inseparable whole, which is perhaps why contemporary Indian life has a vividness that so many non-Indians find attractive.

The second operational problem centers around the general nature and potential applications of this book with regard to similar works. There are now some useful general bibliographies on American Indian life that are available, e.g. G. P. Murdock's *Ethnographic Bibliography of North America,* 3rd Edition (a 4th edition should be ready in late 1975), and the shorter reading lists included as parts of the six or seven better textbooks on American Indians. It is not the intent of this book to either duplicate or compete with these efforts. Instead, I hope to present a body of material organized in such a way as to supplement helpfully the work of others. I attempt to do this by focusing on contemporary Indian life as I have defined it here and by not including materials unless they meet one or more of the following criteria: 1) They have not been published, e.g. state and federal reports such as committee hearings, position papers, procedural guides, tribal government documents, etc; 2) For one or a combination of reasons, they have not been widely circulated; 3) They contain significant amounts of ethnographic data which also have immediate implications for important theoretical questions now current within the society sciences; 4) Their chief focus is upon current Indian activity.[1]

Some overlap with other bibliographic works occurs and is inevitable. There are undoubtedly critical omissions because it is impossible for a single individual to learn of all the books, papers, reports, and magazine articles that pertain to modern American Indian life. I would regard it as a personal favor if such omissions were called to my attention by the readers.

The bibliography is partially annotated because: 1) A few of the references listed are not available to me; 2) The nature of others is obvious from their title; 3) Some of the materials while being of interest are not as important as others, and space here is limited.

The bibliography is selective because: 1) Some available items known do not meet the criteria stated above; 2) It is unrealistic for me to assume that I have found all available, relevent information.

It is my sincere hope that this book will be of use not only to professional anthopologists and those who deal with Indians in an official capacity, but that it will encourage others with only a casual interest in American Indians as they are now to learn and appreciate more about current Indian life. Native Americans have much to tell others about the art of living. Their wisdom can make a vital contribution to the survival of humanity.

---

[1] A small fraction of the items in this bibliography are unpublished, exclusive of the federal documents of the United States and Canada. Information concerning the majority of the former sources may be obtained by contacting the authors, many of whom are listed in one or more of the following directories:

1. *Guide to Departments of Anthropology 1975-76.* To be obtained from the American Anthropological Association, 1703 New Hampshire Avenue NW, Washington, D.C. 20009.

2. *Fifth International Directory of Anthropologists.* To be cbtained from: The University of Chicago Press, 11030 Langley Avenue, Chicago, Illinois 60628.

3. *Guide to Departments of Sociology and Anthropology in Canadian Universities 1973-74.* To be obtained from: The Canadian Sociology and Anthropology Association, Postal Box 878, Montreal, Quebec, Canada.

4. *American Men and Women of Science, 12th edition. The Social and Behavioral Sciences. Volumes 1 and 2.* New York: Jaques Cattel Press/R. R. Bowker Company, 1973.

5. Many dissertations can be obtained from: University Microfilms, Ann Arbor, Michigan.

Study Guide for
Indian Life Prior to 1875

A two-part study guide is now presented. The first part stresses Indian life prior to 1875; the second section is devoted to activities after that time. In my opinion, Indian life in one time period can be understood only with reference to the other.

Rationale:

The general aim of the guide is to illustrate something of the depth and complexity of the Native American experience through time and space. In space, interest is confined largely to an area reaching from the southern borders of the United States to the Arctic Circle. In time, only limited attention is given to the insights supplied by archeologists. A time span covering more than 25,000 years is encompassed within a limited canvas. Central emphasis is given to American Indian life from the time of 18th century European contact to about 1875. The coverage of various peoples within these limits is unequal out of necessity since some cultures are better known to anthropologists and historians than are others. Considerable effort has been made to supply materials which will allow you to focus along the lines of your own interests.

Introduction:

It is suggested that you read or review a good introductory textbook in anthropology before beginning your study. Frequent references to such a book will also be helpful as you learn about Indians. There are a number of good texts available. Three of these are:

1

Harris, Marvin. *Culture, Man and Nature. An Introduction to General Anthropology.* New York: Thomas Y. Crowell Co., 1971.

Barnouw, Victor. *An Introduction to Anthropology. Vol. I. Physical Anthropology; Vol. II. Ethnology.* Homewood, Illinois: The Dorsey Press, 1971.

Beals, Ralph L., & Hoijer, Harry. *An Introduction to Anthropology,* 4th edition. New York: Macmillan Co., 1971.

It is also recommended that you read a good, general, brief treatment of the native peoples of the New World as soon as possible. One such book is:

Josephy, Alvin M., Jr. *The Indian Heritage of America.* New York: Bantam Books, 1969.

The conscientious student will need to refer frequently to a major reference work concerned with a description and analysis of the cultural, geographical and linquistic dimensions of native life:

Kroeber, A.L. *Cultural and Natural Areas of Native North America.* Berkeley: University of California Press, 1953.

The materials discussed below will be more meaningful if this preliminary preparation is made. You would also benefit from exposure to the following:

McNickle, D'Arcy. "Indian, North American." *Encyclopedia Britannica.* Vol. 12, pp. 62–79. 1969.

Eggan, Fred. "Indians, North American." *Encyclopedia of the Social Sciences,* Vol. 7, pp. 180–200. Edited by David L. Sills. New York: Macmillan Co. and Free Press, 1968.

Curtis, E.S. *The North American Indian.* Norwood, Mass.: The Plimpton Press, 1926. 24 volumes.
A work of valuable first-hand accounts of Western Indians with priceless early photographs. A significant resource.

Field, T.W. *An Essay Towards an Indian Bibliography.* New York:18 ; reprint edition, New York: Gales Research Co., 1967.

"A very old reference work listing and annotating thousands of sources on the American Indian from the author's personal library. A very useful source for the pre-1873 literature and a refreshing reminder of the deep roots of scholarly interest in the American Indians." Professor Fred Eggan, University of Chicago.

Murdock, George P. *Ethnographic Bibliography of North America,* 3rd Edition. New Haven: Human Relations Area Files, 1960.

A new edition may be available soon.

British Parliamentary Papers. Shannon: Irish University Press, 1969.

The intrepid student will find this a rich source of largely unexploited material concerning the native peoples of Canada. There are approximately 7,000 volumes for the period 1800 to 1925. "For the modern researcher, the basic problem is to extract from the sessional set the material relevant to his particular project—material which might easily be scattered throughout hundreds of volumes. The indexes provide some guidelines, but not enough to make identification a simple task." p. 5 (from an advertisement issued by the Irish University Press.)

The Hudson's Bay Company Archives.

An invaluable source of material giving detailed continuous accounts of Canadian Indians having contact with this pioneer firm. Included are descriptions of the country and the fur trade kept in the form of day-by-day post journals, district reports, account books, and correspondence files. Records begin in 1670 and continue to the present. The Archives are located in London, but microfilm copies of the material can be found in the Public Archives of Canada in Ottawa.

Part I. Some of the Beginning As We Know It.

North, Central and South America are one unit with regard to cultural and social development. The archeological data concerning the New World is extremely complex. They are difficult to assess and to summarize. Because this guide concerns itself largely with cultures in the ethnographic present, some sort of summary treatment is necessary. Hence, the discussion is concerned with the universal themes of man's existence as they have been expressed in "New World Prehistory." These themes are *technology, environmental adaptation, subsistence,* and *settlement.* A consideration of these variables provides a good background to the understanding of societies and cultures in pre-Columbian America.

Initially, it is necessary to consider some of the major problems confronting the archeologist who studies the themes mentioned above. The problems can be stated in the form of eight basic questions.

1. Who were the earliest inhabitants of the New World? Were they food gatherers having a subsistence technology similar to peoples of the Old World during lower and middle Paleolithic times?

2. Where and when did the American big game hunting specialization of the

Pleistocene arise? What were its relationships to the possible earlier food gatherers that were just mentioned? What were its relationships to the big game hunting tradition of the Old World? What happened to this pattern?

3. What were the origins and relationships of the specialized food-collecting subsistence patterns of the post-Pleistocene? Did Asiatic diffusions and migrations play a part in these developments, especially in the Arctic and Boreal zones?

4. Where and when were food plants first domesticated in the New World and what was the effect of plant domestication on society and culture?

5. What is the history of pottery in the New World?

6. When and where did sedentary village life based upon farming arise in the New World and what was the history of the spread of this pattern in native America?

7. What was the nature of sedentary village life in the New World in those places where plant cultivation was poorly developed or lacking? At what time period was such village life found? To what extent were such cultures and societies dependent upon the diffusion of ideas and elements from the village farming pattern?

8. When and how did the native civilizations of Nuclear America come into being? What were their relationships *within* the Nuclear sphere?

For obvious reasons, definitive answers to these questions cannot be given here. All the facts are not in, and will not be in for a very long time, if ever. But it is possible to discuss at least in a general way what is known about these various questions at present.

A definition of three concepts is essential:

1. *Food gathering:* applied to subsistence patterns where gathering of wild food plants or hunting of animal life lacked both regional specialization or technological diversification.

2. *Food collection:* implies both specialization and diversification in the taking and using of wild plant and animal foods.

3. *Nuclear America:* refers to the southern two-thirds of Mexico, all of Central America, and Andean and Coastal Columbia, Ecuador, plus Peru with adjoining portions of Bolivia. Nuclear America was the center of native American agriculture and the locus for at least two pre-Columbian centers of civilization.

REFERENCES:

There are two relevant basic references:

Willey, Gordon R. "New World Prehistory." *The Smithsonian Report for 1960.* (Publication 4455). Washington, D.C.: Smithsonian Institution, 1961. pp. 551–575.

Much of the material in the early paragraphs of this section has been taken from this source.

Willey, Gordon R. *An Introduction to American Archaeology, Volume One. North and Middle America.* Englewood Cliffs, New Jersey: Prentice-Hall, Inc., 1966.

Additional useful materials are available in:

Struever, Stuart, editor. *Prehistoric Agriculture.* American Museum Sourcebooks in Anthropology. Garden City, New York: Natural History Press (Doubleday), 1971.

Especially useful are the papers of Caldwell, Struever, and Fowler.

Quimby, George I. *Indian Life in the Upper Great Lakes, 11,000 B.C. to A.D. 1800.* Chicago: University of Chicago Press, 1960.

Jennings, Jesse D. *Prehistory of North America,* second edition. New York: McGraw-Hill, 1974.

Chapter 9, "Summation," is of special interest since it includes a discussion of the following topics: Needed Research; Trends; Increments in Theory; Other Trends; Language; The Future; Recapitulation.

In addition to the above, there is a large and growing body of literature concerning the possible role of trans-Atlantic and trans-Pacific contacts in the cultural development of the New World. The most important references here are:

Meggers, Betty J., Evans, Clifford, & Estrada, Emilio. "Early Formative Period of Coastal Ecuador: The Valdivia and Machalilla Phases." *Smithsonian Contributions to Anthropology, Vol. I.* Washington, D.C.: Government Printing Office, 1965.

This significant work discusses the supposed spread of ideas and people from Japan to Ecuador.

Ford, James A. "A Comparison of Formative Cultures in the Americas. Diffusion or the Psychic Unity of Man." *Smithsonian Contributions to Anthropology, Volume XI,* Washington D.C.: Government Printing Office, 1969.

Ford takes up where Meggers, Evans, and Estrada leave off with regard to diffusion and the part it plays in the cultural development of North America. However, a number of archeologists, e.g. Bischof and Lathrap, have recently begun to question seriously some of the basic conclusions in the Meggers, Evans, Estrada and Ford works.

Edwards, Clinton R. "Aboriginal Watercraft on the Pacific Coast of South America." *Ibero-Americana* 47. Berkeley and Los Angeles: University of California Press, 1965.

Edwards, Clinton R., "New World Perspectives on Pre-European Voyaging in the Pacific." *Center Reprint No. 6.* Milwaukee: Center for Latin American Studies, University of Wisconsin-Milwaukee, September, 1969.

Edwards, Clinton R., "Possibilities of Pre-Columbian Maritime Contacts Among New World Civilizations." *Pamphlet No. 8.* Latin American Center Pamphlet Series. Milwaukee: Center for Latin American Studies, University of Wisconsin-Milwaukee, February, 1970.

The following work discusses trans-Atlantic as well as trans-Pacific contact:

Riley, C.L., *et al. Man Across the Sea. Problems of Pre-Columbia Contacts.* Austin: University of Texas Press, 1971.

One brief paper provides a very useful discussion of the nature of diffusion *vis-a-vis* cultural development:

Harris, Marvin, & Morren, G.E.B. "The Limitations of the Principle of Limited Possibilities." *American Anthropologist* 68 (February 1966): 122–127.

Alvin M. Josephy, Jr. provides a useful general bibliography to early man in the Americas: (*Op. cit.*, 370-375.)

FILM RESOURCES;

There are a number of sources which provide lists of films concerning American Indians which are suitable for classroom use. The most extensive and readily available are:

"Educational Films on the American Indian." *The North American Indians. A Sourcebook.* Edited by R. C. Owen, J. J. F. Deetz, and A. D. Fisher. New York: Macmillan Co., 1967. pp. 718–744.

There are 251 films listed. Section I provides 23 titles which have to do with prehistory.

Extension Media Center. "Anthropology Films List." Berkeley: University of California, n.d.

1970 Catalog Educational Motion Pictures. Bloomington: Audio-Visual Center, Indiana University. Also cf. 1974 Supplement—Cumulative.

LANGUAGES-LINGUISTICS:

One or all of the following should be studied initially:

Burling, Robbins. *Man's Many Voices. Language in Its Cultural Context.* New York: Holt, Rinehart & Winston, Inc., 1970.

Fromkin, Victoria, & Rodman, Robert. *An Introduction to Language.* New York: Holt, Rinehart & Winston, Inc., 1974.

Gudschinsky, Sarah C. *How to Learn an Unwritten Language.* New York: Holt, Rinehart & Winston, Inc., 1967.

Three older, general works should then be perused:

Powell, J. W. "Linguistic Families of America North of Mexico." *Seventh Annual Report, Bureau of American Ethnology. 1885–1886.* pp. 7–142. Washington, D.C.: Government Printing Office, 1891.

Report of Committee of American Anthropological Association. "Phonetic Transcription of Indian Languages." *Smithsonian Miscellaneous Collections* 66.6 (Publication 2415). City of Washington: Smithsonian Institution, 1916. (Reprint)

Boas, Franz. "Handbook of American Indian Languages Parts 1 & 2." *Bulletin 40. Bureau of American Ethnology.* Washington, D.C.: Government Printing Office, 1911.

The introductory essay by Boas is essential reading.

The following is also useful:

Map of North American Indian Languages. Compiled by C. F. Voeglin and F. M. Voeglin. American Ethnological Society. Prepared and Printed by Rand McNally & Co. 1966.

"This map reflects classificatory consensus reached by the First Conference on American Indian Languages and levels of confidence reported in *Anthropological Linguistics,* Vol. 6, no. 6 (1964), and vol. 7, no. 7 (1965) Languages of the World; *Native American Fascicles One and Two* and boundaries as given by Driver, Cooper, Kirchoff, Massey, Rainier and Spier, where their *Indian Tribes of North America* shows boundaries between phyla of languages which are not included in the 1944 map, Publication no. 20, American Ethnological Society now issued (1966) as *Revised Publication No. 20, American Ethnological Society,* based on American Geographic Society and Army Map Service Sheet. 1 D, 8-52, 102887 (Alaska, Canada, and Greenland); edition 1-AMS, 4-59, 102886 (United States, Southern Canada, and Newfoundland); edition 2-AGS, AMS, 3-58, 144496 (Mexico, Central America, and the West Indies)."

It is suggested that the paper by Karl Teeter listed in the Contemporary Study Guide also be consulted.

Part II. Some Essential Dimensions of Indian Life Then and Now.

In this section, a dual approach is taken to the difficult question of accounting for the similarity and diversity of Indian peoples by reading the two basic references below:

Oswalt, Wendell H. *This Land Was Theirs,* 2nd edition. New York: John Wiley & Sons, 1973.

Leacock, Eleanor, & Lurie, Nancy O., editors. *North American Indians in Historical Perspective.* New York: Random House, 1971.

Throughout the discussion in both books, there are two central explanatory themes: history and ecology. History is viewed as a series of specific and sometimes unique experiences which happen to groups living at a particular time and place. Ecology is regarded as the interaction between a given group and the natural and social habitat where it exists.

An excellent historical summary statement concerning Indian-White interaction within the United States is contained in: Billington, Ray Allen. *Westward Expansion. A History of the American Frontier. Fourth Edition.* New York: Macmillan Publishing Co., Inc., 1974.

For Indian-White interaction within Canada, consult: Patterson, E. Palmer, II. *The Canadian Indian: A History Since 1500.* Don Mills, Ontario: Collier-Macmillan Canada, Ltd., 1972.

To provide a general, overall frame of reference, the chart on pp. viii–ix of Leacock and Lurie, "Changes in Indian-White Relationships in North America in Historical Perspective" should be studied. Chapter 1, written by Leacock, provides good material. She discusses (pp. 9–12) the expansion of Europe in North America. Then she characterizes five phases of Indian history.

PHASE I:

> Late precontact with its manifold adaptation to varying types of environment. . . . These adaptations have been generally described in terms of nine "culture areas," the Southeast, Northeast, Plains, Southwest, Great Basin, California, Northwest Coast, Subarctic, and the Eskimo area. The culture areas concept has its limitations, yet it still has a powerful descriptive utility.

> *SOUTHEAST:* The culture of agricultural peoples had reached a peak in the development of town life and in elaborate ceremonial centers that had apparently declined by the 16th century.

> *NORTHEAST:* Village life based on horticulture faded off into the nomadism of the northern hunters.

PLAINS: In precontact times an extension of the eastern agricultural areas, although also the home of some buffalo hunters. In later historic times the Plains became the center of a culture type based on horse nomadism, generally thought to represent the way of the "typical Indian."

SOUTHWEST: Food-producing villagers had experienced a cultural decline from an earlier period, and where people practicing simpler forms of gardening or subsisting by hunting and gathering also dwelt.

GREAT BASIN: Between the Rocky Mountains and the Sierras where peoples depended on hunting and the gathering of nuts and other wild vegetable foods.

CALIFORNIA: Agriculture was not practiced but in some parts of the area dependable supplies of acorns and other foods enabled a relatively settled village life. California has an extremely complex Indian cultural history.

NORTHWEST COAST: Plentiful resources enabled a richer life for fishermen than did early agriculture.

SUBARCTIC: Inhabited by hunters of caribou, moose, and other game.

ESKIMO AREA: Shows an ingenious adaptation of its people to the exploitation of sea mammals along the Arctic coasts.

PHASE II:

Commences with early contacts, either directly with explorers, missionaries, and traders, or indirectly with goods traded through neighboring tribes. The extent to which a reintegration of Indian institutions followed these first contacts has often been underestimated. It has been all too common for anthropologists to assume that information gathered by anthropologists from elders about life styles that stretched back to the beginning of the 19th century and even earlier represented pre-Columbian society. Cases in point are the assumptions that individualized patterns of fur trapping in the north woods and the virtually total dependence on the buffalo in the Plains were aboriginal. Indian-white contacts during this phase, which extended over several generations for most Indian societies, were relatively equal and commonly of a mutually beneficial nature. The common Indian preference for contractual relationships with whites—as reflective of interacting but not merging societies—may well stem from this early period. So also may concepts of the "golden age" that Indians still dream of recapturing, with modifications appropriate to modern conditions.

PHASE III:

was the period of large-scale settlement and of serious conflict and other pressures. Disruption and at times virtual annihilation were caused by new diseases as well as warfare. However, in great sections of the North, in place of settlement, permanent trading posts were established upon which Indians and traders were mutually dependent. Thus there was less disruption in this area and a continuation of the essential features of the second phase.

PHASE IV:

was a period of relative stabilization and the institution of government controls, in most cases involving the establishment of reservations. During this phase a recurrent assertion of the Indian desire for independence took the form of religious revitalization and the belief in many of the cults such as the Ghost Dance which culminated in the "Sioux outbreak" of 1890-1891. Ghost Dancers believed that on a stated day the white man would be swallowed up by the sea or otherwise destroyed and Indian lands regained. Military reprisals by the United States against the more militant Indian cults brought home the futility of hoping to prevail over whites. With the creation of reservations or the Indian withdrawal into areas the whites did not covet, adaptations became increasingly directed toward maintaining social boundaries through passive resistence, manipulating white sources of power, and continuing to make selective adaptations from white culture in order to survive as Indian enclaves.

PHASE V:

The recent period which has been marked by the emergence of a new sense of national consciousness and common purpose and by attempts to achieve effective political organization and the viable social and cultural reintegration of Indian institutions within the context of contemporary industrial society.

Following the presentation of these five phases, the remainder of the chapter, pp. 12-28, is devoted to an examination of the basic trends in Indian social history.

Attention is now turned to specific Indian cultures from each of the nine culture areas described earlier. Materials are taken from Oswalt, Leacock and Lurie, and other sources.

SOUTHEAST:

Oswalt, Wendell H. "Chapter 12, The Eastern Cherokee. Farmers of the Southeast." In *This Land Was Theirs,* pp. 501-528.

Gearing, Fred. "Priests and Warriors. Social Structures for Cherokee Politics in the 18th Century." *Memoir 93.* American Anthropological Association 64:5. Pt. 2. October, 1962.

Oswalt, Wendell H. "Chapter 13, The Natchez. Sophisticated Farmers of the Deep South." In *This Land Was Theirs,* pp. 529-558.

Swanton, John R. "Indian Tribes of the Lower Mississippi Valley and Adjacent Coast of the Gulf of Mexico." *Bulletin 43, Bureau of American Ethnology.* Washington, D.C.: Government Printing Office, 1911.

With regard to readjustment after 17th century European contact:

Leacock and Lurie. "Chapter 4. Creek into Seminole," pp. 92–128. By W. C. Sturtevant.

NORTHEAST:

Oswalt, Wendell H. "Chapter 11. The Iroquois. Warriors and Farmers of the Eastern Woodlands." pp. 445–498.

To be used in conjunction with this chapter is the following map:

Map of Ho-De-No-Sau-Nee-Ga or the People of the Long House. Compiled 1851 by Lewis H. Morgan and Ely S. Parker, A Seneca Sachem From Several French Maps of 1720 or Earlier, Showing Ancient Trails, Lakes, Villages and Principal Locations With Their Aboriginal Names. Redrawn 1962 by Eber L. Russell, Historian, Perrysburg, New York With Additions of Villages, Trails, and Springs From More Than Fifty Years of Research. (Available from: Iroqrafts Ltd., R.R. #2, Ohsweken, Ontario, Canada NOA 1MO).

This is followed by:

Leacock and Lurie, Chapter 5. "The Iroquois in History." By W. N. Fenton, pp. 129–168.

Because of their crucial historical position and the wealth of useful data available, considerable attention is given to the Chippewa. A good introduction is:

Landes, Ruth. "The Ojibwa of Canada." In *Cooperation and Competition Among Primitive Peoples,* pp. 37–126. Edited by Margaret Mead. New York: McGraw-Hill, 1937.

Hickerson, Harold. "The Chippewa of the Upper Great Lakes: A Study in Socio-political Change." In Leacock and Lurie, pp. 169–199.

If these readings have only wetted your appetite for a more detailed consideration, it is recommended that the following sequence of materials dealing with the Ojibwa and neighboring groups be used:

Copway, G., or Kah-Ge-Ga-Gah-Bowh, Chief of the Ojibway Nation. *The Traditional History and Characteristic Sketches of the Ojibway Nation.* London: Charles Gilpin, 1850.

A quaint and obviously subjective account of an Ojibway's appreciation of his position and surroundings.

Carver, J., Esq. *Travels Through the Interior Parts of North America, in the Years 1766, 1767 and 1768.* London: Walter and Crowder, 1778; reprint edition, Toronto: Coles Publishing Co., 1974.

Much of the information concerns Indians west of the Mississippi. This work should be used only in conjunction with other authenticated sources.

Long, J. *Voyages and Travels of an Indian Interpreter and Trader, Describing the Manners and Customs of the North American Indians; with an Account of the Posts Situated on The River Saint Laurence, Lake Ontario, &c., to which is added A Vocabulary of the Chippeway Language. Names of Furs and Skins, in English and French. A List of Words in the Iroquois, Mohegan, Shawanee, and Esquimeaux Tongues and a Table Shewing the Analogy between the Algonkin and Chippeway Languages.* London: Robson *et al,* 1791.

Kinietz, W. Vernon. *The Indians of the Western Great Lakes 1615-1760.* Ann Arbor: Ann Arbor Paperbacks, University of Michigan Press, 1965.

Hickerson, Harold. *The Chippewa and Their Neighbors: A Study in Ethnohistory.* New York: Holt, Rinehart and Winston, 1970.

A careful reading of this book will yield not only an increased knowledge of the Chippewa, but insights into the methodology of the ethnohistorian.

Hodge, G. Stuart *et al. Art of the Great Lakes Indians.* Flint: Flint Institute of Arts, 1973.

The zealous and/or professional scholar may want to explore:

Schoolcraft, Henry R. *Historical and Statistical Information Respecting the History, Condition and Prospects of the Indian Tribes of the United States: Collected and Prepared Under the Direction of the Bureau of Indian Affairs, Per Act of Congress of March 3d, 1847.* Six Volumes. Reprint edition, New York: AMS Press, Inc., 1973.

An index simplifies the use of these materials. One of the best is:

Nichols, F. S., compiler. "Index to Schoolcraft's "Indian Tribes of the United States." *Bulletin 152, Bureau of American Ethnology.* Washington, D.C.: Smithsonian Institution, 1954.

While not complete, the following is useful. Use of an index here is also a necessity.

The Jesuit Relations and Allied Documents: Travels and Explorations of the Jesuit Missionaries in New France, 1610-1791. Edited by R. G. Thwaites. Cleveland: The Burrows Brothers Company, 1896-1901. 73 volumes.

McCoy, James C. *Jesuit Relations of Canada, 1632-1673, a Bibliography.* Introduction by Lawrence C. Wroth. Paris: 1937; reprint edition: New York: Burt Franklin, 1974.

PLAINS:

If man is to live, he must eat. To eat, he must enter into an elaborate series of mutual relationships with his environment. The study of man-environment interaction can be called cultural ecology. Cultural ecology suggests, among other things, that the requirements of a particular kind of food production strongly influence other aspects of a given way of life. Accordingly, an understanding of the nature of essential foods, the forms of life which support them, and the effective means of subsistence production are important for acquiring comprehensive insights into the questions of group survival, maintenance, and change.

The Plains area has long been recognized by many anthropologists as an ideal place to study the interrelationships between man, the land, and the forms and processes which support both. Essential reading concerning these questions begins with a careful study of:

Forde, C. Daryll. *Habitat, Economy and Society. A Geographical Introduction to Ethnology.* Fifth edition. London: Methuen and Company, Ltd., 1946.

The Introduction and Part IV, "Habitat and Economy" contain the essentials of Forde's argument.

A more recent and classic discussion should be studied next:

Oliver, S. C. "Ecology and Cultural Continuity As Contributing Factors in the Social Organization of the Plains Indians." *University of California Publications in American Archeology and Ethnology* 48:1, pp. 1–70. Berkeley: University of California Press, 1962.

To acquire a deeper understanding of cultural ecology with respect to Plains people, the student should then consult:

Baker, H. G. *Plants and Civilization.* Belmont, California: Wadsworth Publishing Co., Inc., 1965.

Leeds, Anthony, & Vayda, Andrew P. *Man, Culture and Animals. The Role of Animals in Human Ecological Adjustments. Publication No. 78 of the American Association for the Advancement of Science.* Washington, D.C.: 1965.

The opening chapter, "Anthropologists and Ecological Problems" by A. P. Vayda and a concluding chapter, "Functional Analyses in the Symposium Man, Culture and Animal," by Paul W. Collins provide the beginnings for systematic study.

Since grass is the basic and most important life support system on the Plains, a general understanding of its specific nature and significance can be gained by reading:

Wedel, Waldo R. "The Central North American Grassland: Man-Made or Natural?" *Studies in Human Ecology. Social Science Monographs III.* Washington, D.C.: Pan American Union, 1957. pp. 39-69.

A thoughtful discussion is supplemented by an excellent bibliography.

Additional attention should then be given to a series of materials concerning food, its production, and the relationship of both to the Plains area.

Roe, F. G. *The North American Buffalo. A Critical Study of the Species in its Wild State.* 2d edition. Toronto: University of Toronto Press, 1970.

This work is the definitive study of the buffalo.

Roe, F. G. *The Indian and the Horse.* Norman: University of Oklahoma Press, 1955.

An invaluable work.

Will, George F., & Hyde, George E. *Corn Among the Indians of the Upper Missouri.* Lincoln: Bison Books, University of Nebraska Press, 1964.

Holder, Preston. *The Hoe and the Horse on the Plains. A Study of Cultural Development among North American Indians.* Lincoln: University of Nebraska Press, 1970.

Two sub-varieties within the category of "Plains" cultures are considered next: the nomadic buffalo hunting Cheyenne and the prairie, village-dwelling Omaha. Basic sources for the Cheyenne are:

Hoebel, E. A. *The Cheyennes. Indians of the Great Plains.* New York: Holt, Rinehart, & Winston, 1960.

Powell, Peter J. *Sweet Medicine. The Continuing Role of the Sacred Arrows, the Sun Dance, and the Sacred Buffalo Hat in Northern Cheyenne History. Vol. I and II.* Norman: University of Oklahoma Press, 1969.

Grinnell, G. B. *The Fighting Cheyennes.* Norman: University of Oklahoma Press, 1955.

Eggan, Fred. "The Cheyenne and Arapaho Kinship System." In *Social Anthropology of North American Tribes, Enlarged Edition,* pp. 35-98. Edited by F. Eggan. Chicago: University of Chicago Press, 1972.

Next read a classic study on a prairie, village-dwelling group, the Omaha.

Fletcher, Alice C., & La Flesche, Francis. *The Omaha Tribe. Vol. I and II.* Lincoln: Bison Books, University of Nebraska Press, 1972. (Initially published as the *27th Annual Report of the Bureau of American Ethnology to the Secretary of the Smithsonian Institution, 1905-1906.* Washington: Government Printing Office, 1911).

Then read Chapter 7 from Leacock and Lurie:

Weltfish, Gene. "The Plains Indians: Their Continuity in History and Their Indian Identity." pp. 200-227.

Then, consult the following:

Catlin, George. *Letters and Notes on the Manners, Customs, and Conditions of North American Indians.* New York: Dover Publications, 1973. (Originally published in 1844).

The introduction to this edition reads in part: "Crow, Blackfoot, Pawnee, Sioux, Comanche, Mandan, Choctaw, Cheyenne, Winnebago, Creek, Assiniboin; wild prairies teeming with buffalo; the sacred site of *Catlinite* stone—all were subjects of Catlin's letters and paintings. For eight years (1832-39) George Catlin ventured among the Indians of the North American Plains capturing in verbal and visual pictures every facet of their lives . . .

Catlin's book is an adventure. It is an adventure of the painter who was called 'the great white medicine man' for his ability to paint. It is an adventure of a self-taught painter who vowed: '. . . nothing short of the loss of my life shall prevent me visiting their country, and of becoming their historian.' It is a story of the great mysteries of the many tribes of Indians he visited—the mysteries of costume, posture and myth, the mystery of weapons, hunts and manly games, the mystery of a life still close in connection with the Great Spirit, with the buffalo and with the traditions of thousands of years, all which would soon be destroyed . . ."

Catlin's work is some of the best writing ever done on the American Indian.

SOUTHWEST:

Two groups living side by side for some time are considered: the Navajo and the Hopi. The literature on both groups is very large. The following sources are suggested:

NAVAJO:

Downs, James F. *The Navajo.* New York: Holt, Rinehart & Winston, 1972.

Downs, James F. "Animal Husbandry in Navajo Society and Culture." *University of California Publications in Anthropology, Vol. I.* Berkeley & Los Angeles: University of California Press, 1964.

Kluckhohn, Clyde. *Navaho Witchcraft.* Boston: Beacon Press, 1962. (Originally published in 1944).

Reichard, Gladys A. *Navaho Religion. A Study of Symbolism.* New York: Bollingen Series 18. Pantheon Books, 1950.

HOPI:

Oswalt, Wendell. Chapter 10, "The Hopi, Farmers of the Desert." pp. 397–443.

Titiev, Mischa. *Old Oraibi.* Papers of the Peabody Museum of American Archaeology and Ethnology, 22:1. 1944. (Kraus Reprint Corp., 1968).

Titiev, Mischa. *The Hopi Indians of Old Oraibi. Change and Continuity.* Ann Arbor: University of Michigan Press, 1972.

Simmons, L. W. *Sun Chief. The Autobiography of a Hopi Indian.* New Haven: Yale University Press, 1942.

Aberle, David F. "The Psychosocial Analysis of a Hopi Life-History." *Comparative Psychology Monographs* 21 (December 1951). Berkeley: University of California Press.

With regard to cultural reintegration, consult:

Leacock and Lurie. Chapter 8. "The American Southwest." By E. P. Dozier. pp. 228–256.

The ambitious student could read with great profit:

Spicer, E. H. *Cycles of Conquest. The Impact of Spain, Mexico and the United States on the Indians of the Southwest, 1533–1960.* Tucson: University of Arizona Press, 1962.

GREAT BASIN:

Downs, James F. *The Two Worlds of the Washo.* New York: Holt, Rinehart & Winston, 1966.

An excellent discussion of European impact on selected Basin peoples is in:

Leacock and Lurie, Chapter 9. "The Ute and Paiute Indians of the Great Basin Southern Rim." By Morris K. Opler. pp. 257–288.

CALIFORNIA:

Oswalt, Wendell. Chapter 8. "The Yurok. Salmon Fishermen of California." pp. 307-346.

Oswalt, Wendell. "The Cahuilla. Gatherers in the Desert." pp. 175-214.

Baumhoff, Martin A. "Ecological Determinants of Aboriginal California Populations." *University of California Publications in American Archaeology and Ethnology* 49:2, pp. 155-236. Berkeley: University of California Press, 1963.

With regard to cultural integration or European impact and Indian response, cf.

Leacock and Lurie. Chapter 10. "California" by J. F. Downs. pp. 289-316.

NORTHWEST COAST:

Oswalt, Wendell. Chapter 9. "The Tlingit. Salmon Fishermen of the Northwest." pp. 347-396.

de Laguna, Frederica. "Under Mount Saint Elias: The History of Culture of the Yakutat Tlingit. Parts I-III." *Smithsonian Contributions to Anthropology, Vol. 7.* Washington, D.C.: Government Printing Office, 1972.

SUBARCTIC:

Oswalt, Wendell. Chapter 2. "The Chippewyan. Hunters and Fishermen of the Subarctic." pp. 35-78.

Helm, June. "The Lynx Point People: The Dynamics of a Northern Athapaskan Band." *National Museum of Canada Bulletin No. 176.* Ottawa: Queen's Printer and Controller of Stationery, 1961.

Helm, June, & Lurie, Nancy O. "The Dogrib Hand Game." *National Museum of Canada.* Ottawa: Queen's Printer and Controller of Stationery, 1966.

These two items, while concerned with contemporary situations, present these Indians much as they were 100 years ago.

For cultural reintegration:

Leacock and Lurie, Chapter 12. "The Hunting Tribes of Subarctic Canada." pp. 343-375.

ESKIMO AREA:

Oswalt, Wendell. Chapter 4. "The Kuskowagamiut. Riverine Eskimos." pp. 123-172.

Damas, David. "Igluligmiut Kinship and Local Groupings: A Structural Approach." *National Museum of Canada Bulletin No. 196.* Ottawa: Queen's Printer and Controller of Stationery, 1963.

Valentine, V. F., & Vallee, F. G. *Eskimo of the Canadian Arctic.* The Carleton Library no. 41. Toronto: McClelland and Stewart Ltd., 1968.

Ruesch, Hans. *Top of the World.* New York: Harper and Row, 1950. (Novel)

Metayer, Maurice, editor and translator. *I. Nuligak. The Autobiography of a Canadian Eskimo.* Richmond Hill: Simon & Schuster of Canada, Ltd., 1971.

For cultural reintegration:

Leacock and Lurie. Chapter 13. "The Changing Eskimo World." By C. C. Hughes. pp. 375–417.

Part III. Folklore—Arts & Crafts

FOLKLORE:

A good general reference is:

Georges, Robert A., editor. *Studies on Mythology.* Homewood, Illinois: The Dorsey Press, 1968.

> This is a helpful selection of eleven essays on folklore. The introductory paper by Franz Boas, "The Growth of Indian Mythologies" is of special interest.

Alan Dundes has written two papers that lend themselves well to this area of study:

> "African Tales Among the North American Indians." *Southern Folklore Quarterly* 29 (September 1965): 207–219. (Also available as a Bobbs-Merrill Reprint BC-70).

> "North American Indian Folklore Studies." *Journal de la Société des Americanistes* 56 (1967): 53–79.

Judith Ullom has compiled a brief but interesting annotated bibliography which contains 152 items:

> *Folklore of the North American Indians.* Washington, D.C.: Library of Congress, 1969.

ARTS & CRAFTS:

There are a number of general books in this area. Two of these are:

Fraser, Douglas. *The Many Faces of Primitive Art. A Critical Anthology.* Englewood Cliffs, N.J.: Prentice-Hall, 1966.

Jopling, Carol F., editor. *Art and Aesthetics in Primitive Societies. A Critical Anthology.* New York: E.P. Dutton & Co., Inc., 1971.

One or both should be carefully read before using the publications listed below.

Feder, Norman. *American Indian Art.* New York: Harry N. Abrams, Inc., 1965.

This is the best single work now available on the subject.

Whiteford, A. H., et. al. *American Indian Art: Form and Tradition.* Minneapolis: Walker Art Center, 1972.

In addition to a large number of good color photographs, there are twelve thoughtful essays on various aspects of the subject.

Three classic works on crafts of the Southwest are:

Fontana, B. L., et al. *Papago Indian Pottery.* Seattle: University of Washington Press, 1962.

Adair, John. *The Navajo and Pueblo Silversmiths.* Norman: University of Oklahoma Press, 1944.

Bunzel, Ruth L. *The Pueblo Potter. A Study of Creative Imagination in Primitive Art.* New York: Dover Publications, 1972. (Columbia University Press, 1929).

Study Guide Contemporary American Indians

How It Was Made—What It Is—How To Use It.

The entries in the bibliography constitute the resources of the study guide. Most of them were gathered informally over a period of sixteen years in the course of routine work, first as a graduate student and then as a professional anthropologist and university instructor. During this period, given my teaching obligations and my early, long-established interest in Indians, all sources concerning contemporary Indian life were recorded on index cards and kept in loose alphabetical order.

As the needs of the classroom, research, and writing dictated, this *ad hoc* bibliography was consulted. Time passed and my interest in the subject grew in proportion to the extent of the resources. However, the more entries that were added, the more difficult it became to use the bibliography effectively. Sheer number was only a part of the problem. The highly varied nature of the items made any sort of conventional system of classification impractical. At the end of ten years, I suffered from an embarrassment of riches, and the accumulation of six additional years resulted in an impossible kind of congestion. I was faced with the dilemma of not being able to take advantage of what had been gathered at considerable time and expense and yet could obviously not bring myself to throw away this valuable resource. Clearly, something had to be done. The study guide is an attempt to resolve the conflict.

The positive receptions which four abbreviated unpublished forms of the bibliography were given acted as additional inducement to bring the project to maturation. In response to a brief notice in *Current Anthropology* 9 (April–June 1968): 236, more than 500 requests from around the world were received and answered.

As a first step in organization, each item was checked for accuracy. New index cards were made using the following as a guide:

Turabian, Kate L. *A Manual for Writers of Term Papers, Theses and Dissertations.* Fourth Edition. Chicago: University of Chicago Press, 1973.

21

When this task was finished, it was noted that more than half of the entries tended to group themselves into an order generally comparable to the table of contents of a textbook on cultural anthropology. The prominent exceptions to this order were the documents of the Canadian and United States governments, current Indian newspapers, and newsletters, and other bibliographies. Additional categories of materials with smaller numbers of entries also appeared: Other Bibliographies and Resources; Anthropologists and Indians; History/General Information; Contemporary American Indian Images/Professional Indians; Education; Arts and Crafts: Supplies; Museums Having Displays and Publications Concerned with American Indians: Prehistory, History, and Contemporary Periods. In all, the items in the bibliography sorted themselves into the twenty-seven categories listed in the Table of Contents.

Where appropriate, entries are cross-indexed by tribe, state, area of the country (Northwest, Southwest, etc.), or regional grouping (Plains, Pueblos, etc.). This index appears at the end of the bibliography.

The categories themselves are presented in a logical order. Since there are a number of other bibliographies, they should be consulted. The kind of interaction that takes place between anthropologists and Indians significantly influences the kinds of results produced by research. It is helpful to have a general overview firmly rooted in historical processes of the modern Indian situation before examining its particular dimensions, etc.

The general nature of each category is now discussed and a kind of summary or assessment provided concerning their contents. Such an assessment is not intended to be definitive. Rather, it is hoped that such a characterization will enable the reader to quickly determine the nature of the available material especially with respect to its relevance to his given interests. All references are referred to by their number assigned in the bibliography. The more significant works are indicated by an asterisk in the bibliography.

I. Other Bibliographies and Resources

There are 66 items in this category. There is considerable internal variation which centers around the initial and intended purpose of each. 1 is an extensive formal publication which is the result of several years' preparation on the part of professional anthropologists and their graduate student assistants. It is concerned with publications on native Canadian peoples produced during the decade 1960–1970. 3 was obsolescent at its completion, given the highly ephemeral nature of Indian newspapers. Probably not more than 50% of the items are being produced at the time of this writing. 8 and 9 are intentionally limited and designed primarily for public school teachers with a nominal interest in native peoples. 10, 14, 45, 46, 47, 48, and 49 are intended for university classroom use, and are extremely difficult to obtain. They overlap considerably with many of the other items in this category. If time and resources are limited, primary attention should be given to 1, 2, 5, 11, 12, 20, 26, 28, 35, 56, and 63.

II. Anthropologists and Indians

There are 70 items in this category. 69, 116, and 117 are concerned with the pueblo of Zuni which has always been a field area requiring considerable sensitivity and tact on the part of the anthropologist. 70 and 80 are written by anthropologists who are also Indians. None of the items listed give the reader the means to determine in a precise fashion what influence field conditions and the social and personal background of the anthropologist had in the formulation of specific questions, the analysis of data, and the given conclusions reached. The various sources do indicate that research on American Indians is a difficult procedure whether the anthropologist is an Indian or non-Indian, largely because most American Indians are suspicious of all outside contacts. Hence, they attempt to insulate themselves in various ways from such influences. Experience has usually shown their fears to be well grounded. Finally, the various writings do indicate that anthropologists are becoming aware of the burgeoning Indian resentment toward them, and they attempt to take some account of this in their design of research and in their own conduct during and after field work. The items listed here will repay a careful reading since there are many valuable suggestions offered concerning future research.

III. History—Overview

There are 58 items in this category. In the initial phases of any serious study, it is necessary for the student to emulate Stephen Leacock's horse and attempt to dash in several different directions at once. 160, mentioned in the previous guide, should be reviewed. With this information newly honed, additional insights can be supplemented by studying 141, 163, 166, 173, 187, and 188. 178 deserves a careful, thoughtful reading. The central import of this material centers around two known historical facts and a probable assumption about the future: a) Indians have lived in North America for a very long time; b) today, native peoples in North America continue to pursue their lives in many distinctively native ways; and c) Indians will form a significant part of North American life for the indefinite future. Some of the material is polarized in that it attempts to describe the Indian situation as consisting only of mistreated subservient natives who are continually plagued and victimized by a hostile, implacable non-Indian world. 145, 146, 149, 176, 177, 180, 183, 191, and 196 must be included here. 161, 164, 165, 167, 170, 175, 177, 182, 190, 194, and 195 tend to be more dispassionate, while discussing specific and general Indian problems. The remainder of the items are factual, with 147, 153, 168, and 185 being the most helpful. All these items should be continually referred to as more specific materials are considered.

IV. Contemporary American Indian Images—Professional Indians of Various Kinds

There are 39 items here. The Images and professional Indians are included together because available information suggests that much of the public conception concerning Indians stems from the character of professional Indians, now and in the past. Professional Indians are defined as those who make a significant part of their living by performing as Indians before the public. In this context their behavior may or may not reflect some aspects of that of the non-professional Indian. Prominent kinds of professional Indians in the past have been Wild West Show performers and medicine show entertainers. Examples from the present include television and movie personalities, a number of folk singers, and others who perform in various ways in a public situation, e.g. artists, craftsmen, Indian politicians who may coincidently hold graduate academic degrees, etc. The references listed here suggest, among other things, that the non-Indian public likes to regard the American Indian as someone who lived in the past and has either vanished or is happily in the process of disappearing. North American whites do not enjoy or easily tolerate diversity of an ethnic nature. Since there is a slowly increasing realization that Indians may not go away, many whites are now in the process of convincing themselves that while all Indians may not evaporate, those who do remain will closely resemble themselves. The items included in this section of the bibliography have to do with the inherent nature and dynamics of this situation. Most of them are entertaining as well as informative. The most substantial sources are: 203, 205, 217, and 224. 199 and 210 are of largely clinical interest, while the remainder occupy an intermediate position between the two extremes.

V. Material Culture-Food Getting-Food Habits-Arts & Crafts-Artists

There are 60 items in this section. To a large extent, contemporary Indians have made white technology their own while modifying selected aspects to serve particular purposes. References concerning situations closely derived from an aboriginal baseline include: 239, 241, 242, 246, 261, 265, 273, 278, 280, 281, 282, 284, and 288. Technology and art farther removed from pre-Columbian times and even stemming directly from non-Indian sources are considered in: 238, 240, 244, 245, 247, 248, 252, 266, 287, 290, 291, and 295. 286 is an unusual and interesting study of an art form as it is related to various aspects of social structure. 246, 264, 265, 276, 277, 285, and 293 are concerned with food and food preparation. Far more work, however, should be done along the lines indicated by Ethel Nurge, 277, especially with respect to the relationship between modern nutritional factors and behavior.

VI. Social Organization

68 items make up this section. Social organization as conceived by anthropologists consists of patterned forms of interpersonal relations. As Murdock *et al, Outline of Cultural Materials,* 4th Revised Edition, Second Printing with Modifications. New Haven: Human Relations Area Files, Inc., 1965, state:

Society is a structure of interpersonal relationships, i.e., sets of reciprocally adjusted habitual responses between pairs of interacting individuals. These tend widely to become culturally defined or standardized in terms of polar statuses. A social group arises whenever a number of specific individuals are linked, each to every other by relationships of the same general types, e.g., friendship, kinship or coresidence. Groups likewise reveal a marked tendency to become culturally standardized. p. 78.

Principal emphasis within this category is centered upon Indians as they live within a world of relatives. The various authors are concerned with how blood kinsmen and in-laws support and compete with each other in the process for survival as a subordinate part of a white dominated society. The literature on competition, particularly in the form of community factionalism, is extensive. 303, 307, 308, 313, 318, 321, 322, and 356 consider this question. However, far more attention is given to the description of factions rather than the processes which have produced and maintained them. Leadership is another area which has received attention. 312, 340, 355, and 366 are concerned with the nature of leadership, how leaders emerge, and what factors work to promote or impede their effectiveness as leaders. The nature and structuring of families/households are considered in 302, 345, 346, 349, 353, 359, and 361. Groups as wholes and their boundaries are analyzed by 306, 309, 317, 325, 333, 342, 344, 354, 359, 362, and 363. Other topics considered are social class, social disorganization, social networks, inter-communities ties, kinship systems and kinship terminology. More attention could be given to the nature and significance of the interrelationships which exist between these and other factors not considered.

For helpful supplementary reading, consult:

Needham, Rodney. *Remarks and Inventions: Skeptical Essays About Kinship.* London: Tavistock Publications Ltd., 1974.

Boissevain, Jeremy. *Friends of Friends. Networks, Manipulators and Coalitions.* Oxford: Basil Blackwell, 1974.

Lofland, John. *Analyzing Social Settings. A Guide to Qualitative Observation and Analysis.* Belmont, California: Wadsworth Publishing Company, Inc., 1971.

Schusky, Ernest L. *Variation in Kinship.* New York: Holt, Rinehart, & Winston, Inc., 1974.

VII. Population Dynamics

There are 27 items in this category. Population dynamics is concerned with the numbers of people within given groups and their distribution throughout space and time. The reasons behind fluctuation in either instance are considered. Implicit within this category is the problem of the definition of native ethnic identity which in some situations remains more or less constant and in others varies in response to a wide variety of conditions. Migration and its associated cultural and social variables are also of importance. A careful reading of these selections leaves one with the impression that Indian populations, for a variety of reasons, are difficult to enumerate. For the past fifty years, the Indian population has been increasing. Comparatively high birth rates are associated with high levels of infant mortality and shorter life expectancies than is the case with the remainder of the population. The future direction of Indian population levels is difficult to predict. 377, 378, 379, 380, 384, and 387 deserve special attention because of the kinds of questions raised, the related methodology, and the conclusions reached.

VIII. Reservations/Rural Areas As Communities

There are 257 items in this category. The more comprehensive community descriptions include: 399, 415, 417, 427, 440, 442, 457, 464, 466, 484, 493, 518, 539, 548, 550, 557, 558, 560, 567, 568, 582, 583, 586, 587, 590, 599, 603, 604, 611, 614, and 629. Almost all descriptions of communities suffer from the failure to take into account the effects of migration on community structure. In addition, the relations between Indian populations and their non-Indian counterparts are seldom systematically explored. There are many instances where the existence of a distinct Indian community *per se* is questionable. Rather, Indians could often be more accurately viewed as being closely integrated with segments of the non-Indian population. Closer attention needs to be given to the similarities as well as the differences between non-Indians and Indians.

The following should be carefully read:

Hillery, George A., Jr. *Communal Organizations. A Study of Local Societies.* Chicago: University of Chicago Press, 1968.

Keesing, Roger M. *Kin Groups and Social Structure.* New York: Holt, Rinehart & Winston, Inc., 1975.

Bell, Colin, & Newby, Howard. *Community Studies.* London: George Allen and Unwin Ltd., 1971.

IX. Linguistics—Languages

25 items are included here. Far more has been done in this area. Systems of writing are also considered. 642 and 643 probably should be read first. The selections listed here should be studied in conjunction with the following germinal paper:

Teeter, K. V. "American Indian Linguistics." *Annual Review of Anthropology, Vol. I,* pp. 411–424. Edited by B. J. Siegel, A. R. Beals, and S. A. Tyler. Palo Alto, California: Annual Reviews, Inc., 1972.

X. Stability and Change in Culture

241 entries make up this section. 659, 670, 674, 686, 708, 710, 713, 725, 731, 732, 739, 748, 754, 756, 748, 759, 776, 797, 803, 813, 834, 837, 841, 842, 853, 854, and 857 are of primary importance. None of these entries adequately deal with the conceptual problems inherent in the consideration of change and stability or persistence. More subtle questions such as the rate and direction of change are for the most part, also ignored. Studies are focused on either the individual or group levels. Emphasis is given to a kind of journalistic description, that is none the less valuable. Obvious is the highly variable nature of change and persistence from one situation to another with respect to processes or cause. The highly miscellaneous nature of this conglomeration prevents further useful commentary.
Essential collateral reading would include:

Bailey, F. G., editor. *Debate and Compromise. The Politics of Innovation.* Oxford: Basil Blackwell, 1973.

Zaltman, Gerald, Duncan, Robert, and Holbek, Jonny. *Innovations and Organizations.* New York: John Wiley and Sons, Inc., 1973.

Martindale, Don. *Social Life and Cultural Change.* New York: D. Van Nostrand Co., Inc., 1962.

XI. Migration Patterns

There are 37 items in this category. Of central importance are: 907, 915, 919, 921, 929, 936, 937, and 939. One principal conclusion emerges from the study of these items. Relatively little is known about the migration patterns of American Indians, in part because there is so little systematic knowledge of non-Indian migration. The subject by its very nature does not lend itself readily to analysis.

XII. City Living

There are 109 items in this category. Those of principal interest include: 952, 985, 986, 1018, 1022, 1034, 1035, and 1040. Again, the depressing and challenging conclusion emerges that far too little is known about the nature of Indian urban life. The materials presented here should be read in conjunction with one or all of the following items:

Foster, George M. and Kemper, Robert V., editors. *Anthropologists in Cities.* Boston: Little, Brown and Co., 1974.

The introduction, "A Perspective on Anthropological Fieldwork in Cities" is especially important.

Friedl, John, and Chrisman, Noel J. *City Ways. A Selective Reader in Urban Anthropology.* New York: T. Y. Crowell Co., 1975.

Topic headings are: The City as A Unit of Analysis; Urban Analysis: Scope and Method; Categories of Urban Dwellers; Specialized Communities; Urban Adjustment: The Continuity of Social Relations; The Culture of Poverty.

Southall, Aidan, editor. *Urban Anthropology. Cross-Cultural Studies of Urbanization.* New York: Oxford University Press, 1973.

P. C. W. Gutkind's "Bibliography on Urban Anthropology" pp. 425-489, is of particular interest.

XIII. Economics

There are 32 items in this category. The most important references are: 1053, 1054, 1060, 1061, 1063, 1068, 1071, 1073, 1075, and 1084. All the items are concerned with the various ways that Indians use money and other units of value within traditional and non-traditional milieux. Helpful collateral readings are:

Firth, Raymond, editor. *Themes in Economic Anthropology. A.S.A. Monograph 6.* General Editor: Michael Banton. London: Tavistock Publications, 1967.

Belshaw, Cyril S. *Traditional Exchanges and Modern Markets.* Englewood Cliffs, N.J.: Prentice-Hall, Inc., 1964.

A brief summary of the relations of western and non-western economies and problems.

Cook, Scott. "The Obsolete 'Anti-Market' Mentality: A Critique of the Substantive Approach to Economic Anthropology." *American Anthropologist* 68 (April 1966): 323–345.

Cook, Scott. "Maximization, Economic Theory, and Anthropology: A Reply to Cancian." *American Anthropologist* 68 (December 1966): 1494–1498.

XIV. Anthropology of Development

There are 76 items in this category. The most important are: 1088, 1097, 1098, 1099, 1111, 1118, 1131, 1132, and 1162. Most of this material is concerned with how government funds can be used to "improve" native communities of various kinds. Criteria for improvement are either implicit or nonexistant. Essentially, the concern of various government agencies amounts to the effort to make Indians no longer dependent upon public charity in various forms. Such attempts consist of poorly planned and sporadic donations of monies which usually result in increased dependence upon welfare. Useful parallel readings are:

Foster, George M. *Applied Anthropology.* Boston: Little Brown & Co., 1969.

Clifton, J. A., editor. *Applied Anthropology. Readings in the Uses of the Science of Man.* Boston: Houghton Mifflin Co., 1970.

Downs, James F. *Cultures in Crisis.* Beverly Hills, California: Glencoe Press, 1971.

Niehoff, Arthur H., editor. *A Casebook of Social Change. Critical evaluations of attempts to introduce change in the five major developing areas of the world.* Chicago: Aldine Publishing Co., 1966.

Foster, George M. *Traditional Societies and Technological Change.* Second edition. New York: Harper and Row, 1973.

XV. Personality and Culture (Including Folklore)

There are 162 items in this section. Of compelling interest are: 1164, 1166, 1167, 1168, 1170, 1175, 1186, 1190, 1191, 1193, 1198, 1203, 1216, 1219, 1224, 1225, 1236, 1240, 1244, 1248, 1251, 1257, 1261, 1263, 1267, 1270, 1279, 1280, 1284, 1302, 1304, 1313, 1320, and 1325. The entries in this section are generally of a higher quality than those of some of the other categories. They could be read with profit in conjunction with:

Kaplan, Burt, editor. *Studying Personality Cross-Culturally.* New York: Harper & Row, 1961.

Central topics are: Culture and Personality, Theory and Research; Social Theory and Personality; The Methodological Issues in the Cross-Cultural Study of Personality; Problems of Cross-Cultural Research; Approaches to Cross-Cultural Personality Study.

Barnouw, Victor. *Culture and Personality.* 2nd edition. Homewood, Illinois: The Dorsey Press (in preparation).

Dundes, Alan, editor. *The Study of Folklore.* Englewood Cliffs, N.J.: Prentice-Hall, Inc., 1965.

Topics included are: What is Folklore?; The Search for Origins; Form in Folklore; Transmission of Folklore; The Functions of Folklore; Selected Studies of Folklore; Suggestions for Further Reading in Folklore.

XVI. Formal Education

There are 58 items in this category. Of principal interest are: 1331, 1348, 1351, 1354, 1357, 1367, 1378, 1380, and 1383. All materials require supporting references. For this necessary perspective, one useful starting point is:

Gearing, Fred. "Anthropology and Education." In *Handbook of Social and Cultural Anthropology,* pp. 1223–1249. Edited by John J. Honigmann. Chicago: Rand McNally & Co., 1973.

XVII. Political Organization (Including Politicians & Tribal-Federal Government Relations).

There are 224 items in this category. Essential reading includes: 1385, 1406, 1407, 1408, 1412, 1416, 1418, 1419, 1428, 1429, 1430, 1431, 1433, 1435, 1456, 1471, 1475, 1479, 1490, 1498, 1504, 1512, 1520, 1526, 1528, 1536, 1546, 1548, 1552, 1556, 1560, 1565, 1568, 1572, 1578, 1579, 1582, 1585, and 1603. For a number of reasons, this area has attracted more attention than many of the others. Parallel reading could include:

Bailey, F. G., editor. *Gifts and Poison. The Politics of Reputation.* Oxford: Basil Blackwell, 1971.

Bailey, F. G. *Stratagems and Spoils. A Social Anthropology of Politics.* Oxford: Basil Blackwell, 1969.

Cohen, Abner. *Two-Dimensional Man. An essay on the anthropology of power and symbolism in complex society.* London: Routledge & Kegan Paul Ltd., 1974.

Chapter headings are: 1. Introduction: the bizarre and mystical in modern society; 2. Power relations and symbolic action; 3. The dialectics of politico-symbolic interdependence; 4. Political man—symbolist man; 5. Symbolic strategies in group organization; 6. 'Invisible' organizations: some case studies; 7. Conclusions: symbolic action in the politics of stratification.

Balandier, Georges. *Political Anthropology.* New York: Vintage Books, 1970.

XVIII. Social Control

There are 50 items in this category. Of greatest interest are: 1611, 1614, 1617, 1625, 1630, 1631, 1636, and 1646. Supplementary reading should begin with:

Nader, Laura, and Yngvesson, Barbara. "On Studying the Ethnography of Law and Its Consequences." In *Handbook of Social and Cultural Anthropology.* Edited by John J. Honigmann. Chicago: Rand McNally and Company, 1973.

Additional references are supplied by the accompanying bibliography.

XIX. Music—Dance

There are 54 references listed here. Most important are: 1661, 1663, 1664, 1668, 1669, 1671, 1674, 1675, 1677, 1698, 1705, 1711, 1714, and 1715. This area, like all others associated with American Indian life, is complex. Unfortunately, readily available literature is scarce. The most accessible and useful publications are:

Nettl, Bruno. "North American Indian Musical Styles." *Memoirs of the American Folklore Society,* Vol. 45. Philadelphia: 1954.

Driver, Wilhelmine. Chapter 12. "Music and Dance." In *Indians of North America,* 2nd edition, revised. By H. E. Driver. Chicago: University of Chicago Press, 1969.

Powers, William. *American Indian Hobbyist.* Vol. 7, Parts 1-6. 1960.

Part 1, "American Indian Music: An Introduction." Part 2, "The Language." Part 3, "The Social Dances." Part 4, "War Dance Songs." Part 5, "Contemporary Music and Dance of the Western Sioux." Part 6, "The Sioux Omaha Dance."

Ibid: Volume 8, 1961. Part 7. "The Rabbit Dance."

The above articles were "written for the student without musical training who wishes to learn to 'sing Indian' ". *The American Hobbyist* is no longer being published.

There are three sources of reasonably good phonograph records of American Indian Music:

Folkways/Scholastic. 906 Sylvan Avenue, Englewood Cliffs, New Jersey 07632.

Indian House, Bro-Dart, Inc., Audiovisual Division-West. 15255 East Don Julian Road, City of Industry, California 91749.

Indian Records, Inc. P.O. Box 47, Fay, Oklahoma 73646.

All of these firms supply free catalogs.

It must be stressed, however, that it is extremely difficult to study Indian music and dance using only written materials and phonograph records. There is no substitute for attendance at various dance and music functions.

XX. Religion

There are 129 entries in this category. The most important are: 1717, 1718, 1722, 1724, 1725, 1727, 1728, 1729, 1730, 1733, 1739, 1740, 1741, 1746, 1747, 1752, 1753, 1760, 1768, 1769, 1780, 1782, 1787, 1804, 1807, 1808, 1809, 1812, 1820, 1822, 1833, 1837, 1838, 1844, and 1845. Helpful collateral readings include:

O'Dea, Thomas F. *The Sociology of Religion.* Englewood Cliffs, New Jersey: Prentice-Hall Inc., 1966.

Malefijt, Annemarie de Waal. *Religion and Culture. An Introduction to Anthropology of Religion.* New York: The Macmillan Company, 1968.

XXI. Health—Disease—Poverty

There are 47 entries in this category. Of significant interest are: 1849, 1850, 1856, 1867, 1872, 1873, 1874, 1875, 1879, 1880, 1883, 1888, 1891, and 1892. Useful collateral readings are:

Valentine, Charles A. *Culture and Poverty, Critique and Counter-Proposals.* Chicago: University of Chicago Press, 1969.

Pindborg, J. J. *Pathology of the Dental Hard Tissues.* Philadelphia: W. B. Saunders Company, 1970.

Metress, James F. *A Guide to the Literature on the Dental Pathology of Post Pleistocene Man. Supplementary Monograph 1.* Toledo Area Aboriginal Research Club Bulletin, 1974. Mimeo.

> Pp 1-12 and p. 59 have references to prehistoric and current American Indian populations.

Harvey, A. McGehee *et al,* editors. *Principles and Practice of Medicine,* 17th edition. New York: Appleton, Century Crofts, 1968.

Holvey, David N., editor. *Merck Manual of Diagnosis and Therapy,* 12th edition. Rahway, N. J.: Merck, Sharp, Dohme, Research Laboratories, Merck and Co., 1972.

Hamlon, John. *Principles of Public Health Administration.* 5th edition. New York: Mosby and Co., 1969.

Burton, Lloyd E., and Smith, Hugh H. *Public Health and Community Medicine.* Baltimore: Williams and Wilkins, 1972.

XXII. Canadian Government Documents

There are 90 entries in this category. Most important are: 1896, 1900, 1901, 1907, 1913, 1918, 1925, 1926, 1935, 1947, 1948, 1950, 1955, 1965, 1966, 1967, 1968, 1974, 1981, 1982, and 1984. Item 1 in this bibliography should be consulted.

/

XXIII. United State Publications

There are 426 entries in this category. Of particular interest are: 1990, 1994, 1995, 1996, 2000, 2004, 2005, 2016, 2046, 2047, 2048, 2049, 2050, 2051, 2052, 2056, 2057, 2058, 2059, 2061, 2064, 2065, 2068, 2073, 2076, 2078, 2080, 2081, 2082, 2083, 2091, 2092, 2094, 2095, 2096, 2097, 2105, 2106, 2118, 2124, 2126, 2127, 2129, 2135, 2136, 2137, 2146, 2147, 2156, 2166, 2167, 2170, 2189, 2208, 2209, 2210, 2211, 2212, 2213, 2214, 2215, 2216, 2217, 2218, 2221, 2224, 2226, 2227, 2228, 2229, 2236, 2238, 2239, 2241, 2265, 2285, 2286, 2287, 2290, 2291, 2292, 2293, 2299, 2301, 2304, 2305, 2316, 2328, 2350, 2351, 2355, 2374, 2375, 2388, 2390, 2391, 2394, 2405, and 2411.

The titles of some items in this section may closely resemble each other. However, their contents differ sufficiently to warrant separate listings.

The materials from the federal government provide ample but awkward sources of material. The greatest single obstacle in their use is sheer numbers. One source,

Kenneth Turan of *The Washington Post,* 12/26/74, has estimated that twenty billion pages a year of federal documents are printed covering a vast array of subjects. Between 2% to 3% are stored in the National Archives. What is presented here is a very small sampling of an immense universe. Those who are interested in keeping abreast of some of the materials produced are advised to regularly consult:

> *Monthly Catalog of U.S. Government Publications Issued by the Superintendent of Documents.* Washington, D.C.: Government Printing Office.

Finally, students with an interest in Indian-federal relations should bear in mind the observation of Charles Royce made almost a century ago:

> The social and political relations that have existed and still continue between the Government of the United States and the several Indian tribes occupying territory within its geographical limits are, in many respects, peculiar.

> "Cessions of Land by Indian Tribes to the United States: Illustrated By Those in the State of Indiana." *First Annual Report of the Bureau of Ethnology 1879–1880.* Washington, D.C.: Government Printing Office, 1881, p. 249.

XXIV. Current Newpapers, Newsletters, Magazines

This section was compiled by writing in July, 1974, to each organization listed in the *American Indian Media Directory 1974 Edition* and asking for a sample copy of their publication. The organizations that were able to respond to my request are those that are listed. It is significant that approximately 50% of the items listed in the 1974 Directory could not be supplied because they were no longer being published.

There are 95 items in this category. The most useful are: 2412, 2415, 2429, 2434, 2438, 2444, 2446, 2458, 2465, 2473, 2496, 2503, and 2506.

XXV. Arts and Crafts—Supplies

There are 40 entries in this category. Of greatest interest are: 2509, 2510, 2512, 2522, 2528, 2536, 2537, and 2548.

XXVI. Some Museums Having Displays/Publications Concerned with American Indians—Prehistory, History, and Contemporary Periods

There are 36 entries in this category. The institutions most likely to be helpful are: 2552, 2554, 2558, 2559, 2562, 2564, 2566, 2567, 2573, 2578, 2579, 2581, 2583, and 2585.

XXVII. Maps

There are 9 entries. All are extremely important.

It is suggested that the reader of this book use a common sense approach. If he is interested in a specific area of activity, e.g. religion, he should consult the various items listed under that category. In addition, he should examine the categories which seem to have a direct functional relationship to a particular interest. If his needs are not satisfied, he should next consult one or more of the entries given in the "Other Bibliographies and Resources" category. If adequate materials for his purpose are still lacking, he can be reasonably certain that he is concerned with an aspect of contemporary Indian life about which not enough is known.

If the reader initially knows little or nothing about the subject but would like to develop a broad, comprehensive understanding and has access to a well endowed library, he should begin his reading with Category II, "Anthropologists and Indians" and continue through Category XXI, "Health, Disease and Poverty," drawing on the other sections as required. The best kind of preparation for either direction taken would be to work through the steps set out in the Study Guide for Indian Life Prior to 1875.

Index

Bibliography

THE MOST SIGNIFICANT ITEMS IN THE BIBLIOGRAPHY ARE
INDICATED WITH AN ASTERISK IN THE MARGIN

I. Other Bibliographies and Resources

* 1. Abler, Thomas S., and Weaver, Sally M. *A Canadian Indian Bibliography,
   1960-1970.* Toronto: University of Toronto Press, 1974.

* 2. Brugge, David M., *et al. Navajo Bibliography.* Window Rock, Ariz.:
   Navajoland Publications, Navajo Tribal Museum, 1967.

3. Bush, Alfred L., and Fraser, Robert S. *American Indian Periodicals in the
   Princeton University Library. A Preliminary List.* Princeton, N.J.: Princeton
   University Library, 1970.

   271 newspapers, newsletters, etc. listed.

4. Canada. Citizenship Branch, Department of State. *A Bibliography on
   Attitudes of Native Indian People Towards Non-Indian Society in Canada.*
   Ottawa: 1967. Mimeo.

* 5. Canada. Group Development on Native Peoples, Department of State. *A
   Preliminary Review of the Literature on Metis Peoples.* Ottawa: 1971.
   Mimeo.

6. Canada. Legal Services. Dept. of Indian Affairs and Northern Development.
   *Bibliography of Periodicals and Articles on Law Related to Indians and
   Eskimos of Canada.* Ottawa: n.d. Mimeo.

   Aboriginal Rights, Alberta, Arts & Crafts, Band Government, British
   Columbia, Citizenship, Courts, Culture, Enfranchisement, Eskimos,
   Federal Policies, Fishing & Trapping, General Information, Government
   Relations, History, Housing, Human Rights, Hunting Rights, Indian Act,
   Indian Affairs, Indian Associations, Indian Lands, Labrador, Land
   Tenure, Law, Legal Status, Liquor, Manitoba, Medical Services, Metis,
   Newfoundland, N.W.T., Ontario, Prairie Provinces, Quebec, Reservations,
   Saskatchewan, Speeches, Statistics, Treaties, U.S.A., Urban Life, White
   Paper.

7. Canada. The Library. Dept. of Indian Affairs and Northern Development. *Indians of Canada, A Reading List for Junior High School Students.* 1968.

8. Canada. The Library. Dept. of Indian Affairs and Northern Development. *Indians of Canada, A Reading List for Senior High School Students.* 1968.

9. Canada. Northern Co-Ordination and Research Centre. Dept. of Northern Affairs and National Resources. *Yukon Bibliography.* Preliminary Edition Compiled by J. R. Lotz, YRP1. Ottawa: 1964.

   155 pages of items.

10. Center for Urban Affairs. *The North American Indian: A Selected Bibliography of Materials to be Found in The Center for Urban Affairs' In-House Library as of November, 1972.* East Lansing: Michigan State University. Ditto.

* 11. *CIS. Congressional Information Service.* Washington, D.C.: CIS Publisher, 1974.

   Begins in 1970 and supposedly is the first comprehensive, detailed guide to the information output of the U.S. Congress. Contains two reference systems: the "CIS System" for Congressional publications and legislation, and the "ASI System" for statistical publications of the U.S. Government: Congress, the Executive agencies and other statistics-producing programs. This organization claims to have "a total documents acquisition program." The five years CIS/Microfiche Library costs $15,500.

* 12. Dockstader, F. J. *The American Indian in Graduate Study: A Bibliography of Thesis and Dissertations.* New York: Museum of the American Indian, 1957.

13. Dobyns, Henry F. "Native American Publications of Cultural History." *Current Anthropology* 15 (September 1974): 304–306.

14. Driver, H. E. "Bibliography on Indians in the U.S. in the 20th Century for Anthropology 670." Bloomington: University of Indiana, 1971. Mimeo

15. Freeman, J. F. *A Guide to Manuscripts Relating to the American Indian in the Library of the American Philosophical Society.* Philadelphia: The American Philosophical Society, 1966.

   An indexed listing of manuscript materials available in the A.P.S. arranged by tribes, language families, and areas. Many items pertain to contemporary situations.

16. Gibson, Gordon D., compiler. "A Bibliography of Anthropological Bibliographies: The Americas." *Current Anthropology* 1 (January 1960): 61–75.

   Bibliographies of J. A. Jones, L. F. Schmeckbeir, etc. are of interest.

17. Graves, T. D. "Annotated Bibliography of Research Reports Navajo Urban Relocation Research." Institute of Behavioral Science. Boulder: U. of Colorado, n.d.

18. Harding, A. D. & Bolling, P. *Bibliography of Articles and Papers on North American Indian Art.* New York: Kraus Reprint Co., 1969.

Disappointing since art and technology are merged. Not really worth reprinting.

19. Hargrett, Lester. *A Bibliography of the Constitutions and Laws of the American Indians.* Cambridge: Harvard University Press, 1947.

Excellent.

* 20. Haywood, Charles. *A Bibliography of North American Folklore and Folksong.* Vol. 2: *The American Indians North of Mexico, Including the Eskimos.* Second Revised Edition, New York: Dover Publications, Inc., 1961.

Organized by culture area, tribe, and topic.

21. Heider, Karl G. *Films for Anthropological Teaching.* 5th ed., American Anthropological Association, 1972.

22. Henry, Jeannette, editor. *Index to Literature on the American Indian, 1970.* San Francisco: The Indian Historian Press, 1972.

23. Henry, Jeannette, editor. *Index to Literature on the American Indian, 1971.* San Francisco: The Indian Historian Press, 1972.

24. Henry, Jeannette, editor. *Index to Literature on the American Indian, 1972.* San Francisco: The Indian Historian Press, 1974.

25. Hippler, A. E. *Eskimo Acculturation. A Selected Annotated Bibliography of Alaskan and Other Eskimo Acculturation Studies.* Institute of Social, Economic and Government Research. College, Alaska: University of Alaska, 1970.

* 26. Hodge, F. W., editor. *Handbook of the American Indian North of Mexico.* Bureau of American Ethnology Bulletin 30, 2 vols. Washington, D.C.: Smithsonian Institution, 1907-1910.

This older source, representing the pooled knowledge of the leading students of the American Indian of the day, remains a standard reference work. It is the closest thing to an encyclopedia or dictionary of American Indian life.

27. *The Human Relations Area Files.* New Haven: Yale University.

Descriptions of many North American Indian tribes arranged in a standardized ethnographic format.

* 28. Hunter, John E., compiler. *Inventory of Ethnological Collections in Museums of the United States and Canada.* Second Edition, enlarged and revised, Milwaukee, Wis.: Milwaukee Public Museum for The Committee on Anthropological Research in Museums of the American Anthropological Association and the Wenner-Gren Foundation for Anthropological Research, 1967.

Essential reading for the serious student of Indian affairs.

29. Jaquith, James R. "Bibliography of Anthropological Bibliographies of the Americas." *America Indigena* 30 (April 1970): 419–469.

Items 126, 282, 284, 307, 310 are of some interest, but this includes many items mentioned elsewhere.

30. Jorgensen, Joseph G. *American Reservation Indian.* Partially annotated bibliography. 1970–71. Mimeo.

31. Klein, B. & Icolari, D., editors. *Reference Encyclopedia of American Indian.* New York: B. Klein, 1967.

Unreliable potpourri of miscellanea, but it does contain some useful information on B.I.A. offices, museums, local associations, tribal councils, etc.

32. La Barre, Weston. "Twenty Years of Peyote Studies." *Current Anthropology* 1 (1960): 45–60.

Essential reading.

33. La Barre, Weston. "Materials for a History of Studies of Crisis Cults: A Bibliographic Essay." *Current Anthropology* 12 (February 1971): 3–44.

Vital.

34. Martinez, Cecilia J., & Heathman, J. E., computers. *American Indian Education: A Selected Bibliography.* Educational Resources Information Center/Center for Research and Social Systems. University Park: New Mexico State University, 1969.

* 35. Murdock, G. P. *Ethnographic Bibliography of North America.* 3rd edition. New Haven: Human Relations Area Files, 1960.

The most complete ethnographic bibliography of the North American Indian through 1960. Books, monographs, and articles are listed according to tribe, and areal maps are included. Some contemporary items are included.

36. Merriam, Alan P. "An Annotated Bibliography of Theses and Dissertations in Ethnomusicology and Folk Music Accepted at American Universities." *Ethnomusicology* 4 (January 1960): 21–39.

37. Merriam, Alan P. & Gillis, Frank. *Ethnomusicology and Folk Music: An International Bibliography of Dissertations and Theses.* Middletown, Conn.: Wesleyan University Press for the Society for Ethnomusicology, Special Series in Ethnomusicology no. 1, 1966.

38. Nader, Laura, Kock, K. F., & Cox, Bruce "North America" in "The Ethnography of Law: A Bibliographical Survey." *Current Anthropology* 7 (June 1966): 284-287.

39. National Anthropological Archives. *Catalog to Manuscripts at the National Anthropological Archives. National Museum of Natural History. Smithsonian Institution.* Boston: G. K. Hall & Co., 1975.

    Most of the material dates from the fifty years after the Bureau of American Ethnology was founded in 1879. Some 40,000 individual manuscript items are described under about 5,000 main entries. Much of the material has never appeared in print.

40. Newberry Library, Chicago. *Dictionary Catalog of the Edward E. Ayar Collection of Americana and American Indians.* 16 vols. Boston: G. K. Hall & Co., 1961.

    A well-indexed guide to one of the world's foremost collections of publications, maps, and manuscripts dealing with the American Indian. The Library is located in the Near North Side of Chicago.

41. Nissen, Karen M, Castillo, E. D., & Heizer, Robert F. *A Bibliography of California Indian History.* Berkeley: Dept. of Anthropology, University of California, n.d.

    A much larger version will soon be available. This form, however, is extremely useful. Entries listed on pp. 30-46 are listed in this bibliography. This section is entitled: "III E: PERIOD OF ANGLO CONQUEST (1846-1873): SOCIAL CONDITIONS."
    "Indian-White relations in the first twenty years of American rule are discussed in Cook (1943), the best survey of what happened during this period. A collection of newspaper reports dating from 1851-1866 (Heizer 1973) can be read as historical documentation. Conditions on reservations (Browne 1944) or in Southern California (Caughey 1952) or on one of the Mexican land grants awarded to Americans (Currie 1957) all sound pretty much the same. Cook (1943) traces the course of changing marriage-family patterns after 1850. Here again we lack any thorough treatment of what life as an Indian was like from the eighteen-fifties on." p. 30.

42. Oswalt, Wendell H. "The Kuskokwim River Drainage, Alaska: An Annotated Bibliography." *Anthropology Papers of the University of Alaska* 13 (1965): entire issue.

43. Peabody Museum of Archaeology and Ethnology, Harvard University.

Author and Subject Catalogues of the Library. 54 vols. Boston: G. K. Hall & Co., 1963.

A reproduction of the Peabody Museum card catalog including articles as well as books.

44. Pilling, Arnold. *Library Services and Guidelines For Evaluation of Books About North American Indians.* Lansing: Michigan Department of Education State Library Services, 1971. Mimeo.

45. Price, John A. *A List of Indian Publications.* Mimeo.

46. Price, John A. *Resources for the Study of Contemporary Indians and Eskimos of Canada.* February, 1971. Ditto.

47. Price, John A. *Resources for the Study of the Contemporary Indians, Metis, and Inuit of Canada.* 1972. Ditto.

48. Price, John A. *U.S. and Canadian Indian Periodicals Program in the Anthropology of Complex Societies.* Downsville, Ontario: York University, June, 1971. Mimeo.

49. Price, John A. "U.S. and Canadian Indian Urban Ethnic Institutions." Paper given at the American Anthropological Association meetings, November, 1973. Mimeo.

50. Rivet, P. *et. al.,* editors. "Bibliographies Americanists." *Journal de la Société des Americanistes de Paris.* Nouvelle Série 11. Paris, 1919–

Useful continuing bibliography on American Indians containing many European sources often overlooked by American scholars.

51. Ross, Norman A., compiler. *The Index to the Expert Testimony Before the Indian Claims Commission: The Written Reports.* New York: Clearwater Publishing Co., Inc., 1973.

52. Sabatini, Joseph O. American Indian Law: *A Bibliography of Books, Law Review Articles and Indian Periodicals.* Albuquerque: American Indian Law Center, School of Law, University of New Mexico, 1973.

53. San Jacinto Unified School District. *An Annotated Bibliography of Recommended Resource Materials—Elementary Grades.* San Jacinto, California, 1971. Mimeo.

54. Schusky, Ernest L. "A Center of Primary Sources for Plains Indian History." *Plains Anthropologist* 15, no. 48 (1970): 104–109.

55. Smithsonian Institution. "List of Publications of the Bureau of American Ethnology." *B.A.E. Bulletin 200.* Washington, D.C.: Smithsonian Institution Press, 1971.

Handy reference to all B.A.E. publications including Annual Reports, Bulletins, Publications of the Institute of Social Anthropology, Contributions to North American Ethnology, Introductions, and Miscellaneous Publications.

* 56. Snodgrass, Jeanne O. *American Indian Painters: A Biographical Directory with 1187 Indian Painters.* New York: Museum of the American Indian, Broadway at 155th Street., 1968.

57. Snodgrass, Marjorie P., compiler. *Economic Development of American Indians and Eskimos. 1930 through 1967.* U.S. Department of the Interior, July, 1968.

58. Stanley, Sam & Sturtevant, W. C. *Bibliography-Selected References on Present-Day Conditions Among U.S. Indians.* Washington, D.C.: Smithsonian Institution, n.d. Mimeo.

59. Stensland, Anna Lee. *Literature by and about the American Indian. An Annotated Bibliography for Junior and Senior High School Students.* Urbana: National Council of Teachers of English, 1973.

60. Swanton, J.R. "The Indian Tribes of North America," *B.A.E. Bulletin 145.* Washington, D.C.: Smithsonian Institution, 1953.

Includes a state by state compilation of North American Indian tribes and "tribelets" with useful information on derivation of tribal name, connections with other tribes, location, history, population, and connection in which the tribe became noted. An extensive bibliography is included.

61. Sylvestre, Guy. *Indian-Inuit Authors: An Annotated Bibliography.* Ottawa: Information Canada, 1974.

103 pages of items concerning adult and children's work, poetry and songs, anthologies, articles, addresses, conferences, linguistic materials and periodicals. Indexed.

62. UNESCO. *International Bibliography of the Social Sciences—Anthropology.* Annual publication.

Useful for post-1960.

* 63. U.S. Department of Health, Education and Welfare. *ERIC (Educational Resources Information Center).* Washington, D.C.

From the pamphlet "How to Use Eric," 1971: "ERIC is a national information system designed and supported by the U.S. Office of Education for providing ready access to results of exemplary programs, research and development efforts, and related information that can be used in more effective education programs. Through a network of specialized centers or clearinghouses, each of which is responsible for a particular educational area, current significant information relevant to education is monitored, acquired, evaluated, abstracted, and listed in ERIC reference products." Many studies concerning American Indian education are included throughout the eighteen ERIC "clearinghouses."

64. Weinman, Paul L. "Contemporary Movements." A Bibliography of the Iroquoian Literature, partially annotated. *Bulletin Number 411*. Albany: New York State Museum and Science Service, University of the State of New York, State Education Department, 1969, pp. 85–89.

65. Whiteside, Don. *Aboriginal People: A Selected Bibliography*. Ottawa: Strategic Planning, Citizenship Branch, Dept. of the Secretary of State, January, 1973. Mimeo.

Indexed and organized by topics. Concerns the U.S. and Canada.

66. Woods, Richard G., & Harkins, Arthur M. *A Review of Recent Research of Minneapolis Indians: 1968-1969*. Minneapolis: Training Center for Community Programs, U. of Minnesota, Dec. 1969.

II. Anthropologists and Indians

67. Basso, Keith H. Introduction to *Letters from the Field: The Ethnographic Correspondence of Granville Goodwin*. Tucson: U. of Arizona Press, 1973.

68. Basso, Keith H. "Southwestern Ethnology: A Critical Review." In *Annual Review of Anthropology*, vol. 2, pp. 221–252. Palo Alto: Annual Reviews, Inc., 1974.

69. Baxter, Sylvester. "An Aboriginal Pilgrimage." *Century Illustrated Monthly Magazine* 24 (1882): 526–536.

F. H. Cushing and some Zuni priests go to Boston in 1882.

70. Bodine, John J. "A Field Experience: Taos and Taos Pueblo." Paper given at American Anthropological Association meetings, Nov., 1969. Ditto.

71. Bruner, Edward M. *Ethnological Field Training Program*. Chicago: U. of Illinois Urban Indian Study, summer, 1966.

72. Bynum, Diana. "Discredited Research." (Harkins & Woods) *The Indian Historian* 4 (Spring 1971): 58–59.

73. Casagrande, Joseph B. "John Mink, Ojibwa Informant." In *The Company of Man* ed. by J. B. Casagrande. New York: Harper Torchbooks, 1960, pp. 467–488.

Mink lived at Lac Court Oreilles reservation in northwestern Wisconsin and died in 1943. A valuable and sensitive portrait.

74. Clifton, James A. "Chicago Was Theirs." 1970. Typescript.

A discussion of the history of the Prairie Potawatomi plus an account of the author's contacts with them.

75. Clinton, Lawrence, Chadwick, B. A., & Bahr, H. M. "Vocational Training for Indian Migrants: Correlates of 'Success' in a Federal Program." *Human Organization* 32 (Spring 1973): 17-28.

Much emphasis on methodology.

76. Collier, John. "The United States Indian Administration as a Laboratory of Ethnic Relations." *Social Research* 12 (1945): 265-383.

77. Collier, John, Jr. "Report of a Photographic Research Project." *Visual Anthropology: Photography as a Research Method.* New York: Holt, Rinehart & Winston, 1967, pp. 81-104.

An account of the photographic study made of twenty-two Indian households as a part of a research project on American Indian Urban Integration directed by Dr. James Hirabayashi, San Francisco State College. Pomo, Eskimo, Hualapai, Navajo, Kiowa, Choctaw, Sioux, and Seminole people are considered.

78. Crapanzano, Vincent. *The Fifth World of Forster Bennett. Portrait of a Navaho.* New York: Viking Press, 1972.

The subjective reactions of a newly minted anthropologist doing field work with the Navajo.

79. Dornstreich, Mark D. "Re criticisms made by students regarding an-thropologists vis-a-vis American Indians." *Fellow Newsletter,* American Anthropological Association 14, no. 6 (1973): 2ff.

80. Dozier, Edward P. "The Pueblo Indians of the Southwest. A Survey of the Anthropological Literature and A Review of Theory, Method, and Results." *Current Anthropology* 5 (April 1964): 79-97.

An examination of a representative selection and a survey of the main contributions of Pueblo studies to the development of anthropology. Archaeology, linguistics, ethnology and social anthropology—social organization, culture and personality, culture change and the present—are considered.

81. Edgerton, Robert B. "Some Dimensions of Disillusionment in Culture Contact." *Southwestern Journal of Anthropology* 21 (Autumn, 1965): 231-243.

Discusses, in part, fieldwork with the Menominee in 1959.

82. Efrat, Barbara, & Mitchell, Marjorie. "The Indian and the Social Scientist: Contemporary Contractual Arrangements on the Pacific Northwest Coast." *Human Organization* 33 (Winter 1974): 405–407.

"In British Columbia, native Indian groups are becoming increasingly concerned with the protection and preservation of their own culture as well as of natural resources on their land. Native groups are moving to demand that exploitation of their linguistic, archeological and ethnographic resources by social scientists be replaced by a relationship defined in native terms, according to native specifications and regulations." p. 406.

83. Einhohn, Arthur & Liddell, E. R. "Discussion. A Reply to Greenway." *The Indian Historian* 4 (Summer 1971): 45–48.

84. Fenton, William N. "Return to the Longhouse." *Crossing Cultural Boundaries. The Anthropological Experience.* San Francisco: Chandler Publishing Co., 1972, pp. 102–118.

A visit to Seneca friends of Coldspring Longhouse on the Allegany Reservation near Salamanca, N.Y.

85. Fox, Robin. *Encounter with Anthropology.* New York: Harcourt, Brace & Javanovich, Inc., 1973.

Some interesting remarks as to why Fox was concerned with problems associated with pueblo ethnography.

86. Freilich, Morris. "Scientific Possibilities in Iroquoian Studies." *Anthropologica,* n.s. 5, no. 2 (1963): 171–186.

87. Gearing, Frederick O. "Why Indians?" *Social Education* 32 (February 1968): 128–131; 146.

88. Goggin, John M. "The Mexican Kickapoo Indians." *Southwestern Journal of Anthropology* 7 (1951): 314–327.

A brief note for other North American anthropologists on the Kickapoo's present status and culture and on the outlook for intensive study. Goggin visited these people in 1949.

89. Hackenberg, R. A. *et al.* "Modernization Research on the Papago Indians." *Human Organization* 31 (summer 1972): whole issue.

90. Harkins, A. M. & Woods, R. W. "The Minneapolis Controversy: Response to a Negative Review." *The Indian Historian* 4 (spring 1971): 60–63.

91. Harris, Ramon I., editor. *Oyate Iyechinka Woglakapi. An Oral History Collection.* Vols. I, II, III. Vermillion: American Indian Research Project, University of South Dakota, 1970–71.

A useful series of manuscripts.

92. Harvard University—Radcliffe. *American Indian Project.* Announcement, 1967-68. Mimeo.

93. Hay, Thomas H. "A Technique of Formalizing and Testing Models of Behavior: Two Models of Ojibwa Restraint." *American Anthropologist* 75 (June, 1973): 708-730.

94. Hippler, Arthur E. "The Anthropologist and the American Indian—Continued." *Fellow Newsletter.* American Anthropological Association 14, no. 7, 1973. pp. 2ff.

95. Howard, James. "Report on Field Work Among the Oklahoma Seneca-Cayuga." *1960 Year Book.* American Philosophical Society, pp. 342-343.

96. Howard, James. "Future Needs of Ethnological Research in the Great Plains." *Great Plains Journal* 1 (Spring 1962): 27-31.

97. Indian Historian Press. *Anthropology and the American Indian. A Symposium.* San Francisco: American Indian Educational Publishers, 1973.

98. Kehoe, Alice B. "The Dakotas in Saskatchewan." In *The Modern Sioux* edited by Ethel Nurge. Lincoln: University of Nebraska Press, 1970, pp. 148-172.

Suggests and delineates some of the insights that could be gained from directed field studies comparing the Dakotas in Saskatchewan with those in the United States.

99. Kelly, William H. "Applied Anthropology in the Southwest." *American Anthropologist* 56 (August 1954): 709-719.

100. Kemnitzer, Luis. "Adjustment and Value Conflict in Urbanizing Dakota Indians Measured by Q-Sort Technique." *American Anthropologist* 75 (June 1973): 687-707.

101. Ledbetter, Elizabeth K. "Non-Directiveness: An Orientation to Life at Taos Pueblo." Paper given at the American Anthropological Association meeting, Nov. 1968.

102. Liberty, Margot. Interview Schedule. Urban Omaha Indian Study. Typed, n.d.

103. Lurie, Nancy O. "The Voice of the American Indian: Report on the American Indian Chicago Conference." *Current Anthropology* 2, no. 5 (1961): 478-500.

104. Lurie, Nancy O. "American Indian People and Action Anthropology." Paper given at the American Anthropological Association meetings, San Diego, 1970. Ditto.

105. Lurie, Nancy O. "Two Dollars." In *Crossing Cultural Boundaries. The Anthropological Experience,* pp. 151–163. Edited by Solon T. Kimball and James B. Watson. San Francisco: Chandler Publishing Co., 1972.

Fieldwork with Wisconsin Winnebagos.

106. McFeat, Tom F. S. "Museum Ethnology and the Algonkian Project." *Anthropology Papers No. 2.* Ottawa: National Museum of Canada, 1962.

An important work.

107. McNickle, D'Arcy. "The American Indian Today." *The Missouri Archaeologist* 5 (Sept. 1939): 1–10.

108. McNickle, D'Arcy. "Private Intervention." *Human Organization* 20 (Winter 1961-62): 208–215.

A preliminary examination of the role played by private organizations in Indian affairs.

109. Maddock, Kenneth. "Action Anthropology or Applied Anarchism?" *Anarchy 8* (October 1961): 232–236.

110. Manners, Robert A. "The Land Claims Cases: Anthropologists in Conflict." *Ethnohistory* 3, no. 1 (1956): 72–81.

111. Marriott, Alice. *Greener Fields.* New York: Greenwood Press, 1968.

An ethnographer's contact with Indians including her reflections and conclusions about anthropologists and Indians. An important book.

112. Maynard, Eileen. "The Growing Negative Image of the Anthropologist Among American Indians." *Human Organization* (Winter 1974): 402–404.

Why some Indians don't like anthropologists and what anthropologists can do about it.

113. Merriam, Alan P. Review of *Blackfeet and Buffalo* by James Willard Schultz. *Journal of American Folklore* 77 (April-June 1964): 166.

114. Nason, James D. "American Indian Heritage and Museums: An Inquiry Into Relationships." Paper given at the American Anthropological Association meetings, November, 1971.

115. Opler, Morris E., editor. *Grenville Goodwin Among the Western Apache. Letters from the Field.* Tucson: University of Arizona Press, 1973.

116. Pandey, Triloki Nath. "Anthropologists at Zuni." *Proceedings of the American Philosophical Society* 116, no. 4 (1972): 321–337.

Excellent. Of use to ethnographers and those interested in the history of anthropological thought.

117. Pandey, Triloki Nath. " 'India Man' Among American Indians." In *Encounter and Experience: Some Personal Accounts of Fieldwork.* Edited by A. Beteille and T. N. Madan. Delhi: Vikas, 1974 and Honolulu: U. of Hawaii Press, 1975.

118. Peterson, John H., Jr. "The Anthropologist as Advocate." *Human Organization* 33 (Fall 1974): 311–318.

   A discussion of some of the implications of his work as an employee of the Mississippi Choctaws.

119. Price, John A. "Holism Through Team-Ethnography." University of Wisconsin-Milwaukee Urban Conference, May, 1970. Mimeo.

120. Roberts, John M. *Three Navajo Households.* PMP 40:3. Cambridge: Papers of the Peabody Museum of American Archaeology and Ethnology, Harvard University, 1951.

   An interesting exercise in methodology.

121. Savishinsky, Joel S. "Coping with Feuding: The Missionary, the Fur Trader, and the Ethnographer." *Human Organization* 31 (Fall 1972): 281–290.

122. Schlesier, Karl H. "American Indian Action. Action Anthropology and the Southern Cheyenne." *Current Anthropology* 15 (Sept. 1974); 277–283.

   How one anthropologist helped traditional Cheyenne people get what they wanted.

123. Skinner, Alanson. "Recollections of An Ethnologist Among the Menomini Indians." *Wisconsin Archeologist* 20 (1921): 41–74.

124. Smith, M. Estellie. "The Observer." Revised version of a paper originally presented as a part of the Field Work Symposium, Southern Anthropological Society Meetings, New Orleans, 1969. Mimeo.

125. Smith, M. Estellie. "The Outsider." (Reflections re work with Rio Grande Pueblos.) Paper given at American Anthropological Association Meetings, Nov., 1969.

126. Spindler, George, & Goldschmidt, Walter. "Experimental Design in the Study of Culture Change." *Southwestern Journal of Anthropology* 8 (Spring, 1952): 68–83.

127. Stewart, O. C. "Kroeber and the Indian Claims Commission Cases." *Kroeber Anthropological Society Papers* 25 (1961): 181–191.

128. Stewart, Omer C. "Background of American Indian Conference." *Delphian Quarterly* 44 (1961): 22–31.

129. Stewart, Omer C. "Anthropologists as Expert Witnesses for Indians: Claims and Peyote Cases." Paper given at American Anthropological Association meetings, Nov., 1970.

130. Titiev, Mischa. *The Hopi Indians of Old Oraibi. Change and Continuity.* Ann Arbor: University of Michigan Press, 1972.

Consists largely of diary entries made between August, 1933, and March, 1934. A chapter, "Some Rites, Dances and Other Activities" is included plus some discussion and conclusions concerning fieldwork, culture change, and other topics.

131. Uchendu, Victor C. Part 3. "A Navajo Community" in Part III. "The Field Work Process." In *A Handbook of Method in Cultural Anthropology,* pp. 230-236. Edited by R. Naroll and R. Cohen. New York: Columbia University Press, 1973.

132. VanStone, James W. Part 4. "Arctic and Subarctic North America." In Part III. "The Field Work Process." In *A Handbook of Method in Cultural Anthropology,* pp. 237-245. New York: Columbia University Press, 1973.

133. Wahrhaftig, Albert. "Community and the Caretakers." *New University Thought,* vol. r, no. 4 (Winter 1966-67).

Tells of his experiences with some Office of Economic Opportunity administrators when he discussed the needs of the Cherokee people of Eastern Oklahoma. Essential reading.

134. Wax, Rosalie H. *Doing Fieldwork. Warnings and Advice.* Chicago: University of Chicago Press, 1971.

Adventures with the Sioux in South Dakota.

135. White, Leslie A. "The Anthropologist and the American Indian." *Fellow Newsletter.* American Anthropological Association 14, no. 6, pt. 2 (1973).

Anthropologists aren't as bad as some Indians want to make us feel.

136. White, Robert A. "Value Themes of the Native American Tribalistic Movement Among the South Dakota Sioux." *Current Anthropology* 15 (Sept. 1974): 284-303.

Includes comments by others and a rejoinder by White and Schlesier.

137. Young, Victoria A. S. "Anthros and Indians.": A Course in Conflict. Paper given at American Anthropological Association meetings, Nov., 1974.

A course taught on an experimental basis which poses questions of teaching models and classroom structure, particularly pertaining to discussing anthropology with Indian students.

III. History—Overview

138. Akweks, Aren (Ray Fadden). *History of the Oneida Nation.* Hogansburg, N.Y.: Akwesasne Counselor Organization, St. Regis Reservation, n.d.

    A loosely organized account. Interesting data on current events and people are included.

139. American Friends Service Committee. *Indians of California: Past and Present.* San Francisco: American Friends Service Committee, n.d.

    A useful survey.

140. "The American Indian." *Event* 11, no. 6 (1971).

* 141. Bahr, H. M., Chadwick, B. A., & Day, R. C. editors. *Native Americans Today: Sociological Perspectives.* New York: Harper & Row, 1972.

    An instructive anthology of papers. An unsuccessful effort is made to coordinate the various articles.

142. Beale, Calvin L. "An Overview of the Phenomenon of Mixed Racial Isolates in the United States." *American Anthropologist* 74 (June 1972): 704–710.

    Population groups of real or alleged tri-racial origin—Indian, White and Negro. A general summary of their histories is provided plus a suggested list of research needs.

143. Berkhofer, Robert F. Jr. Review of *The Indian and the White Man,* by W. E. Washburn. *Ethnohistory* 11 (Spring 1964): 183–184.

144. Berry, Brewton. *Almost White. A Study of Certain Racial Hybrids in the Eastern United States.* New York: The Macmillan Co., 1963.

    Some data on "part Indians."

145. Cahn, Edgar, editor. *Our Brother's Keeper: The Indian in White America.* New York: Community Press Book, World Publishing Co., 1969.

    An uncritical, widely quoted account.

146. Campbell, Sheila. "Forgotten Americans." *Commonlife Bulletin* 2, no. 4 (1970).

    Brief, general. A Methodist publication.

* 147. Canada. Yearbook Division, Statistics Canada. *Canada 1974.* The Annual Handbook of present conditions and recent progress. Published under the authority of the Minister of Industry, Trade and Commerce.

148. Canadian Association in Support of the Native Peoples. *Indian Hall of Fame,* n.d. Brochure.

149. Cash, Joseph H., & Hoover, H. T. *To Be An Indian. An Oral History.* New York: Holt, Rinehart & Winston, Inc., 1971.

150. Crowe, Keith J. *A History of the Original Peoples of Northern Canada.* Montreal: Arctic Institute of North America, McGill-Queen's University Press, 1974.

    Useful summary of the cultures of native people *vis-a-vis* non-native contact. Appendixes provide a list of associations serving northern native people and a bibliography.

151. *Crow Reservation, Montana.* Mimeo, n.d.

    Descriptive material available at the Crow Agency, Montana.

152. *The Eastern Cherokees. How They Live Today. Their History.* Knoxville, Tenn.: J. L. Caton, 1937.

* 153. Ferris, Robert G., editor. "Soldier and Brave. Historic Places Associated with Indian Affairs and the Indian Wars in the Trans-Mississippi West." *The National Survey of Historic Sites and Buildings* 12. Washington, D.C.: National Park Service, U.S. Department of the Interior, 1971.

    A good summary treatment. Excellent maps and photographs.

154. Fey, Harold, & McNickle, D'Arcy. *Indians and Other Americans. Two Ways of Life Meet.* Revised Edition. New York: Perennial Library, Harper and Row, 1970.

    A useful summary.

155. Golden, Gertrude M. *American Indians Now and Then.* San Antonio: Naylor Co., 1957.

156. Gooderhalm,Kent. *Nestrum Asa. The Way it Was in the Beginning.* Toronto: Griffin House, 1970.

    Excellent pictures with brief captions concerning Canadian natives.

157. Harkins, Lee F., editor. *The American Indian, 1926–1931.* 2 vols. New York: Liveright Publishing Corp., 1970.

158. *Hudson's Bay Company.* Winnipeg: Hudson's Bay House, n.d.

    A brief history of the Hudson's Bay Company.

159. Indian Historian Press. *Indian Voices. The First Convocation of American Indian Scholars.* San Francisco: American Indian Educational Publishers, 1970.

* 160. Josephy, Alvin M., Jr. *The Indian Heritage of America.* New York: A. A. Knopf, 1968; reprint edition, New York: Bantam Books, Inc., 1969.

Includes North, Central and South America. Some discussion of contemporary Indians.

161. Lagasse, Jean H. "Indians of Canada." *America Indigena* 26 (Oct. 1966): 387–394.

162. Leacock, E. B. & Lurie, Nancy, editors. *North American Indians in Historical Perspective.* New York: Random House, 1971.

One of the best textbooks on American Indians now available.

* 163. Lurie, Nancy O. "Historical Background." In *The American Indian Today,* pp 49–81. Edited by Levine and Lurie. Baltimore: Penguin Books Inc., 1970.

Good general summary of Indian-white relations.

164. McNickle, R. K. "Problems of the American Indian." *Editorial Research Reports* 1 (April 1949): 253-269.

165. McNickle, D'Arcy. "Indian and European: Indian-White Relations From Discovery to 1887." *The Annals of The American Academy of Political and Social Science* 311 (May 1957): 1-11.

* 166. McNickle, D'Arcy. *The Indian Tribes of the United States. Ethnic and Cultural Survival.* London: Institute of Race Relations, Oxford University Press, 1962.

167. McNickle, D'Arcy *et al.* "V. Indians in Contemporary Life. Indian, North American," pp. 75-79. *Encyclopedia Britannica,* 1969.

168. Marquis, Arnold. *A Guide to America's Indians: Ceremonies, Reservations, and Museums.* Norman: University of Oklahoma Press, 1974.

169. Mitchell F., & Skelton, J. W. "Church-state Conflict in Early Indian Education." *History of Education Quarterly* 6 (Spring 1966): 41-51.

170. Momaday, Scott. "The American Indian: A Contemporary Acknowledgement." *Intellectual Digest* 2 (Sept. 1971): 12-14.

171. National American Indian Planning Project. *Resources Directory.* Mimeo, n.d.

172. "The Navajos." *Life* 24 (1948): 75-83.

* 173. Oswalt, Wendell H. *This Land Was Theirs. A Study of the North American Indian.* Second edition. New York: John Wiley & Sons, 1973.

Some materials on the contemporary situation.

174. Owen, Roger, Deetz, James, & Fisher, Anthony, editors. *The North American Indians. A Sourcebook.* New York: Macmillan Co., 1967.

Some of the items are useful, but the whole is uncoordinated.

175. Patterson, E. Palmer II. *The Canadian Indian: A History Since 1500.* Collier-Macmillan Canada, Ltd.: 1972.

176. Proctor, Lisa. "Moccasins should be as beautiful as the flowers they walk among." *Exclusively Yours* 23 (31 July 1970): 13-21.

177. Richman, Robin. "Rediscovery of the Redman." *Life,* December 1, 1967, pp. 52-72.

178. Schusky, Ernest L. *The Right to be Indian.* Vermillion: Institute of Indian Studies, 1965.

A thoughtful consideration of a broad range of topics concerning contemporary American Indians.

179. Seiberling, Dorothy *et al.* "A Life Special: Our Indian Heritage." *Life,* July 2, 1971.

180. Shorris, Earl. *The Death of the Great Spirit. An Elegy for the American Indian.* New York: Signet Book, New American Library, 1971.

A dreary exercise in distortion.

181. Spencer, Robert F. "Western Arctic Cultures," pp. 789-792. *Encyclopedia Britannica,* 15th edition, 1974.

Excellent summary.

182. Spicer, Edward H. *A Short History of the Indians of the United States.* New York: D. Van Nostrand Co., 1969.

A brief but systematic presentation suggesting a number of interesting questions.

183. Steiner, Stan. *The New Indians.* New York: Harper & Row, 1968.

Some useful data, but very poorly organized.

184. Tyrrell, J. W. *Across the Sub-Arctics of Canada. A Journey of 3,200 Miles By Canoe and Snow-Shoe Through the Barren Lands.* London: T. Fisher Unwin, 1898; reprint edition, Toronto: Coles Publishing Co., 1973.

Some Eskimo and Indian ethnography.

* 185. Udall, Stewart *et al. Look to the Mountain Top.* San Jose, California: Gousha Publications, 1972.

Brief but useful papers with excellent illustrations.

186. Vogel, Virgil J. *This Country Was Ours. A Documentary History of the American Indian.* New York: Harper Torchbooks, 1974.

A small but valuable collection of information on native Americans from the time of initial European contact to the present; e.g., the political party platform planks relating to Indians from 1872 to the present; examples of modern Indian poetry. Appendixes include: selected audio-visual aids; selected museums with significant collections relating to American Indians; government agencies concerned with Indians in the U.S. and Canada; bibliographies.

* 187. Waddell, Jack O., & Watson, O. M. *The American Indian in Urban Society.* Boston: Little Brown & Co., 1971.

* 188. Walker, Deward E. Jr. *The Emergent Native American. A Reader in Culture Contact.* Boston: Little, Brown & Co., 1972.

189. Washburn, Wilcomb E. *The Indian and the White Man.* New York: Doubleday & Co., 1964.

190. Wax, Murray L. *Indian Americans. Unity and Diversity.* Englewood, N.J.: Prentice Hall, 1971.

191. Wingell, Bill. "We Just Live Here 'Cause We Have To." *Face-To-Face,* March, 1969, pp. 13-21.

192. Woodson, Carter. "Relations of Negroes and Indians in Massachusetts." *Journal of Negro History* 6 (Jan. 1921): 1053.

193. Young, Delbert A. *The Mounties.* Toronto: Hodder and Stoughton Ltd., 1968; reprint edition, Don Mills, Ontario: Paperjacks General Publishing Co. Ltd., 1973.

Some comment on contact with Indians.

194. Zentner, Henry. "Cultural Assimilation Between Indians and Non-Indians in Southern Alberta." *Alberta Journal of Educational Research* 9 (June, 1963): 79-86.

195. Zimmerman, William, Jr. "The Role of the Bureau of Indian Affairs Since 1933." *The Annals of the American Academy of Political and Social Science* 311 (May 1957): 31-40.

196. Zolla, Elemire. *The Writer and the Shaman.* New York: Harcourt, Brace & Jovanovich, 1973.

"The chief culprit and actual agent in the slaughter of Indians and their culture, brought about by the European settlement of America, was the idea of progress, which by its very nature demands the elimination of everything that it decrees old, obsolete, and nostalgic while it represses the love so congenial to man of that delicate wise patina that time deposits on the things of this world."

IV. Contemporary American Indian Images—Professional Indians of Various Kinds

197. Baerreis, David A., editor. *The Indian in Modern America. A Symposium Held at the State Historical Society of Madison.* Madison: The State Historical Society of Wisconsin, 1956.

A useful collection of brief papers, but reflecting the prejudices and misconceptions of the time.

198. Bancroft, H. H. "Anthropology and Ethnology," pp. 628-641. *The Book of the Fair. An Historical & Descriptive Presentation of the World's Science, Art and Industry As Viewed Through the Colombian Exposition at Chicago in 1893. Designed to Set Forth the Display Made by the Congress of Nations of Human Achievement in Material Form as the More Effectively to Illustrate the Progress of Mankind in all the Departments of Civilized Life.* Chicago & San Francisco: The Bancroft Publishers, 1895.

Indian villages built with Indians and Eskimos living in them. Penobscot, Navajo, Iroquois, etc. represented.

199. Brinkerhoff, Zula C. *The Spirit of Geronimo Returns.* By the author, 1973.

A random collection of flotsam held together only by the fact that they have something to do with American Indians. "The author is determined to educate white people to understand candidly how many Indians regard them."

200. Brown, Anthony, & Beatty, John. "The Media Indian Is the American Indian." Paper given at American Anthropological Association meetings, Nov., 1974.

The effects of the stereotype "Indian ideal" created by the mass media upon many Indian peoples who seem to be attempting to conform to this ideal.

201. Causey, Don. "Honest Injun." *Saturday Review of the Society* 1 (February 1973): 16-17.

Good data regarding a professional Indian living in Cherokee, North Carolina.

202. "Dan George. The Noble Non-Savage." *Time*, February 15, 1971, pp. 76-79.

* 203. Ewers, John C. "The Emergence of the Plains Indians As the Symbol of the North American Indian." *Smithsonian Report for 1964* (Publication 4636). Washington, D.C.: Smithsonian Institution, 1965, pp. 531-544.

204. Ewers, John C. "When Red and White Men Met." *Western Historical Quarterly* 2 (April 1971): 133-150.

Speech suggesting that both Indians and Whites are human beings capable of both virtue and error now and throughout the history of their contact.

* 205. Fiedler, Leslie A. *The Return of the Vanishing American.* New York: Stein & Day, 1968.

"Ostensibly about the Western novel, the fiction that dealt with the 'winning' of the West. But it is actually about all American fiction and the uniquely American experience it reflects." (Back jacket cover)

206. Forbes, Jack D. "Who Speaks for the Indian?" *Humanist* (Sept./Dec. 1967): 174-176.

207. Foreman, Carolyn Thomas. *Indians Abroad 1493-1938.* Norman: University of Oklahoma Press, 1943.

An account of Indians who were taken or traveled to Europe. A general discussion with specific remarks concerning Catlin's Indians and those employed by Buffalo Bill.

208. Fry, Alan. *Come a Long Journey.* New York: Manor Books Inc., 1971.

Delightful novel set along the Yukon River.

209. Gohl, E. H. "The Effect of Wild Westing." *American Indian Magazine: A journal of race progress* 2 (July-Sept. 1914): 226-228.

Gohl was a white "adopted" by the Onondaga. "A determined stand should be taken by all true friends of our American Indians to discourage and prevent whenever possible Indians making engagements with wild-west shows, theatrical troups, circuses, and most of the motion-picture firms. The Indian gains nothing of real value from the associations and environments he meets . . ." p. 226.

210. Greenway, John. "Will the Indians Get Whitey?" *National Review* 21 (March 1969): 223 ff.

Strange.

211. Gridley, Marion E. *Indians of Today.* 4th edition. Chicago: I.C.F.P. Inc., 1971.

Criteria for selection are not evident.

212. Gridley, Marion E. *Contemporary American Indian Leaders.* New York: Dodd, Mead & Co., 1972.

213. Gridley, Marion E. *American Indian Women.* New York: Hawthorn Books Inc., 1974.

Considerable overlap with her *Indians of Today,* 4th edition. Both are uncritical presentations of a few Indians apt to be known to the white public.

214. Hirschfelder, Arlene B., compiler. *American Indian Authors.* New York: American Association of Indian Affairs, 1970.

215. Hungry Wolf, Adolf. *The Good Medicine Book.* New York: Warner Paperback Library, 1973.

Written by a transculturated white to show other whites how to assume a strange kind of Indian identity.

216. Leonard, L. O. "Buffalo Bill's First Wild West Rehearsal." *The Union Pacific Magazine,* August, 1922, pp. 26–27.

Problems with staging a show.

* 217. Lurie, Nancy O. "Forked Tongue in Cheek or Life Among the Noble Civilages." Summer, 1973, mimeo.

218. McNamara, Brooks, "The Indian Medicine Show." *Educational Theatre Journal* 23 (December 1971): 431–449.

A fascinating dimension of the professional Indian experience.

219. Pearce, Roy H. *The Savages of America: A Study of the Indian and the Idea of Civilization.* Baltimore: Johns Hopkins University Press, 1953.

Excellent study concerning the Indian image in the non-Indian public mind.

220. Price, John A. "The Stereotyping of North American Indians in Motion Pictures." *Ethnohistory* 20 (Spring 1973): 153–171.

Chronological analysis as to perception of American Indians in commercial movies.

221. Ralph, Julian. "Behind the 'Wild West' Scenes." *Harper's Weekly* 38 (1965): 775ff.; originally printed August 18, 1894.

The Indians were enjoying themselves in Brooklyn off and on stage because "with three good meals a day, a bad Indian becomes a good one."

222. Roosevelt, Theodore. "Across the Navajo Desert." *The Outlook,* Oct. 11, 1913, pp. 309–317.

223. Russell, Don. *The Lives and Legends of Buffalo Bill.* Norman: University of Oklahoma Press, 1960.

Indians and their activities in the Wild West Show.

224. Russell, Don. *The Wild West. A History of the Wild West Shows.* Fort Worth: Amon Carter Museum, 1970.

225. Schreiber, Norman. "Buffy St. Marie—Public and Private." *Strobe* 1 (Sept. 1969): 24 ff.

An excellent entertainer and an interesting kind of professional Indian.

226. " '71 Futures with a Past: Apache Vacationland." *Friends.* January, 1971. Chevrolet Publication.

227. Shapiro, Samuel. "Tashtego—The White Man's Victim." *The American Indian* 8 (Winter 1958-59): 40-43.

Tashtego was a Nantucket Indian. Concerns the Indian image.

228. "Snakes Found Her Charming." *View, The Post-Crescent Magazine.* Appleton, Wis., August 8, 1971, pp. 1-4.

Concerns a Menomini woman who used to work as a snake charmer in a carnival side show.

229. "Strangers on a Continent. An American Indian's View of America." *Washington University Magazine* 42 (Summer 1972): 30-33.

230. Thanet, Octave. "The Trans-Mississippi Exposition." *The Cosmopolitan* 25 (October 1898):598-614.

Pp. 612-613 discuss the "Indian Congress." "There are Sioux, Omahas, Winnebagoes, Sacs and Foxes, Crows, Blackfeet, Cheyennes, Piutes, Apaches, Zunis, Navajos, Moquis, Cherokees, Creeks, Seminoles, Diggers, Umatillas, Comanches, Poncas, Delawares, in camp at present or shortly to be there." p. 612.

231. Turner, Katharine C. *Red Men Calling on the Great White Father.* Norman: University of Oklahoma Press, 1951.

Interesting, but must be used with great caution in conjunction with many other sources.

232. U.S. Congress. House. Executive Documents No. 1, Pt. 5. *The Indian Exhibit at the Columbian Exposition.* 53rd Cong., 2nd sess., 1893-94, pp. 392-395. Washington, D.C.: Govt. Printing Office, 1895.

233. Walker, James W. St. G. "The Indian in Canadian Historical Writing." *Historical Papers 1971.* The Canadian Historical Association, pp. 21-51.

234. Wax, Murray L. "The White Man's Burdensome 'Business.' " A Review Essay on the Change and Constancy of Literature on the American Indians." *Social Problems* 16 (Summer 1968): 106-113.

235. Yellow Robe, Chauncey. "The Menace of the Wild West Show." *American Indian Magazine; A journal of race progress* 2 (July-Sept., 1914): 224-228.

A Sioux wishes "to call your attention to the evil and degrading influence of commercializing the Indian before the world." Speech given at the Fourth Annual Conference of the Society of American Indians held at Madison, Wisconsin, Oct. 6-11, 1914.

236. YMCA Indian Guides Newsletter. "Tee Pee Times" Jan-Feb., 1973, Mimeo.

V. Material Culture-Food Getting-Food Habits-Arts & Crafts- Artists

237. "American Indian Expo." *Holiday Inn International Magazine.* July/August, 1973, pp. 28-29.

238. Bahti, Tom. *Southwestern Indian Arts & Crafts.* Flagstaff: KC Publications, 1966.

Brief, well-illustrated with suggested additional readings.

239. Balikci, Asen. "Chapter 8. The Netsilik Eskimos: Adaptive Processes." In *Man The Hunter,* pp. 78-82. Edited by R. B. Lee and Irven Devore. Chicago: Aldine Publishing Co., 1968.

Data concerning the period 1910-1930.

240. Bedinger, Margery. *Indian Silver. Navajo and Pueblo Jewelers.* Albuquerque: University of New Mexico Press, 1973.

Useful but leans heavily on other works.

241. Bond, Eugene W. "How to Build a Birchbark Canoe. At 82, Dan of the Montagnais tribe of Canada practices an almost vanished art." *Natural History* 64 (May 1955): 240-246.

242. Bradfield, Maitland. "The Changing Pattern of Hopi Agriculture." London: *Royal Anthropological Institute Occasional Paper No. 30,* 1971.

Fieldwork was done in 1966, 1967, and 1969.

243. Brody, J. J. *Indian Painters & White Patrons.* Albuquerque: University of New Mexico Press, 1971.

A revised doctoral dissertation organized around the following topics: American Indian painting prior to the twentieth century; Indian-White relationships; the beginnings of modern Indian painting; the self-taught painters; the early institutional painters; the later institutional painters; the transition to the mainstream. Far more should have been said about Indian-White relationships and the kind of painting which they produce.

244. Buckstaff, Karen. "Socio-Cultural Aspects of Basketry With Respect to Winnebago Culture." December, 1973, typescript.

245. Cain, H. Thomas. *Pima Indian Basketry.* Phoenix: Heard Museum of Anthropology and Primitive Art, 1962.

Includes historical background; types-periods-identification; materials; techniques; symbolism and design; modern basketry.

246. Cook, S. F. "The Mechanism and Extent of Dietary Adaptation Among Certain Groups of California and Nevada Indians." *Ibero-Americans* 18 (1941).

Records persistence of old dietary preferences.

247. Danker, Kathleen M. *Winnebago Clothing Styles.* Macy, Nebraska: Nebraska Indian Press, 1973.

Useful, with some attention given to modern powwow clothing.

248. Deitch, Lewis. "The Impact of Tourism Upon the Arts and Crafts of the Indians of the American Southwest." Paper given at the American Anthropological Association meetings, Nov., 1974.

This paper examines the contemporary impact of tourism upon the arts and crafts of the Southwestern Indians.

249. Dempsey, Hugh A. "Tailfeathers. Indian Artist." *Art Series No. 2.* Calgary: Glenbow-Alberta Institute, 1970.

Excellent pictures plus brief but useful commentary.

250. Denver Art Museum. "Metal Jewelry of the Peyote Cult." *Material Culture Notes No. 17.* Denver: Dept. of Indian Art, 1942.

251. Dunn, Dorothy. *American Indian Painting.* Albuquerque: University of New Mexico Press, 1968.

Good reproductions plus useful commentary regarding various artists.

252. Ewing, Robert A. "This is Gorman. An Indian and His Art." *New Mexico Magazine,* March/April, 1971, pp. 4–7.

253. Feder, Norman. "Plains Indian Metalworking with emphasis on hairplates." *American Indian Tradition* 8, no. 2 (1962): 55–76.

Eastern trade silver; survival of hairplates in eastern areas; flowering of metalwork 1865-1880; survival of hairplates on the Plains; other Plains silver items; bibliography.

254. Feder, Norman. "Plains Indian Metalworking, Part II." *American Indian Tradition* 8, no. 3 (1962): 93–112.

Trade German silver; present-day silversmiths; metalworking technique; making of a pair of peyote earrings; economics of the craft; conclusions. Extremely well done.

255. Fontana, Bernard L. *et al. Papago Indian Pottery.* (The American Ethnological Society, V. E. Garfield, editor). Seattle: University of Washington Press, 1962.

Chapter 2 on modern pottery making is of special interest but should be viewed in terms of the balance of the book.

256. Forbes, Anne. "A Survey of Current Pueblo Indian Paintings." *El Palacio* 57 (August 1950): 235-252.

257. Goldfrank, Esther S. "Irrigation Agriculture and Navaho Community Leadership: Case Material on Environment and Culture." *American Anthropologist* 47, n.s. (1945): 262-277.

Looks at several areas of the reservation.

258. Graburn, Nelson H. H. "Eskimo Soapstone Carving: Innovation and Acculturation." Paper given at the American Anthropological Association meetings, Nov. 1966. Ditto.

259. "Indian Craft Enterprise in the Northwest." *Human Organization* 20 (Winter 1961-62): 216-218.

Modern Indian craft enterprise is poorly developed in the Northwest.

260. Harlow, Francis H., & Young, John V. *Contemporary Pueblo Indian Pottery.* Albuquerque: University of New Mexico Press, 1974.

Brief but helpful to the novice.

261. Harrington, Richard. "Walrus Hunt.: *Natural History* 65 (January 1956): 29 ff.

Modern Iglulik hunting.

262. Harvey, Byron III. "The Fred Harvey Collection 1899-1963." *Plateau* 36 (Fall 1963): 33-53.

Useful background material in the study of Sou'hwest ethnography.

263. Harvey, Byron III. "A Sidelight on Navajo Blankets." *Masterkey* 39 (January-March 1965): 36-38.

264. Hawley, Florence, *et al.* "An Enquiry into Food Economy and Body Economy in Zia Pueblo." *American Anthropologist* 45 (1943): 547-556.

265. Helm, June, & Lurie, Nancy O. *The Subsistence Economy of the Dogrib*

Indians of Lac La Martre in the Mackenzie District of the Northwest Territories. Ottawa: Northern Coordination and Research Centre, Department of Northern Affairs and National Resources, Canada, 1961.

266. Hodge, William H. "Navaho Urban Silversmiths." *Anthropological Quarterly* 40 (October 1967): 185–200.

Why certain Navahos become silversmiths in an urban situation.

267. "Hopi Kachina Artist. Alvin James Maykya." *Arizona Highways* 49 (June 1973): 2 ff.

268. Howard, J. H. "An Omaha Dancing Ornament." *Museum News, University of South Dakota* 12 (November 1950): 1–2.

269. Howard, J. H. "Notes on Dakota Archery." *Museum News, University of South Dakota* 12 (December 1950): 1–3.

270. Howard, James. "The Northern Style Grass Dance Costume." *American Indian Hobbyist* 7 (Fall 1960): 18–27.

271. Hughes, Phyllis, compiler and editor. *Pueblo Indian Cookbook.* Albuquerque: University of New Mexico Press, 1974.

More than 70 recipes of dishes eaten by pueblo people.

272. *Indian City USA Pottery.* Anadarko, Oklahoma: n.d.

Advertising brochure.

273. Kenyon, Karl W. "Last of the Tlingit Sealers." *Natural History* 64 (June 1955): 294–298.

274. Kuh, Katharine. "The First Americans as Artists." *Saturday Review,* Sept. 4, 1971, pp. 44–45.

275. Kupferer, Harriet. "Material Changes in a Conservative Pueblo." *El Palacio* 69 (1962): 248–251.

Santo Domingo, New Mexico.

276. Menominee County Women's Club. *Indian Cook Book.* Mimeo, n.d.

277. Nurge, Ethel. "Dakota Diet: Traditional and Contemporary," pp 35–91. *The Modern Sioux.* Lincoln: University of Nebraska Press, 1970.

278. Peterson, Karen D. "Chippewa Mat-Weaving Techniques." *Bureau of American Ethnology Bulletin 186,* Anthropological Paper 67. Washington, D.C." Government Printing Office, 1963.

Minnesota Chippewa at Red Lake Reservation.

279. Ray, Dorothy Jean. *Artists of the Tundra and the Sea.* Seattle: University of Washington Press, 1961.

Alaskan Eskimos. Excellent photographs and text.

280. Rogers, Edward S. *The Material Culture of the Mistassini. Bulletin 218.* Ottawa: National Museum of Canada, 1967.

281. Rogers, Edward S. "Subsistence Areas of the Cree-Ojibwa of the Eastern Subarctic: A Preliminary Study." *Bulletin No. 204,* Anthropological Series No. 40 (Contributions to Ethnology V). Ottawa: National Museum of Canada, 1967.

282. Rogers, Edward S. *The Quest for Food and Furs, The Mistassini Cree, 1953-1954. Publications in Anthropology No. 5.* Ottawa: National Museum of Man, 1973.

283. Schneider, Richard C. *Crafts of the North American Indians. A Craftsman's Manual.* New York: Van Nostrand Reinhold Co., 1972.

The best book now available.

284. Slobodin, Richard. "Leadership and Participation in a Kutchin Trapping Party," pp. 56-89. In *Contributions to Anthropology: Band Societies. Bulletin 228, Anthropological Series No. 84.* Edited by David Damas. Ottawa: National Museum of Canada, 1969.

A first-hand account of a trapping party of Kutchin Indians in the upper drainage of the Peel River in February-March, 1947.

285. "Stalking the Wild Rice." *Northliner Magazine* 2 (Fall, 1971): 6-10.

286. Stanislawski, Michael B. "Hopi and Hopi-Tewa Ceramic Tradition Networks." Paper given at American Anthropological Association meetings, Nov., 1974.

Pottery making at First and Third Mesa villages examining traditional information flow.

287. Sturtevant, William C. "Seminole Men's Clothing," pp. 160-174. In *Essays on the Verbal and Visual Arts. Proceedings of the 1966 Annual Spring Meeting, American Ethnological Society.* Edited by June Helm. Seattle: University of Washington Press, 1967.

288. Swinton, George. *Eskimo Fantastic Art.* Calgary: U. of Manitoba, 1972.

Excellent photographs with a brief discussion.

289. Swinton, George. *Sanavik Cooperative Baker Lake Sculpture 1974.* Ottawa: Privately printed, 1974.

290. Tax, Sol *et al.* Addendum III. "The Tama Indian Crafts." Project Summary Statement. Ditto, n.d.

 To be read in conjunction with the *Documentary History of the Fox Project 1948-1959.* Edited by Gearing, Netting, and Peattie, 1960.

291. Tryk, Sheila. "Red is Chic." *New Mexico Magazine,* Nov., Dec., 1973, pp. 17-19.

 Indian-derived women's fashions.

292. Vanstone, James W. *Athapaskan Adaptations. Hunters and Fishermen of the Subarctic Forests.* Chicago: Aldine Publishing Co., 1974.

 An excellent introduction with some modern data.

293. Waugh, F. W. *Iroquois Foods and Food Preparation.* Memoir 86, No. 12, Anthropological Series. Ottawa: Dept. of Mines, Geological Survey, 1916.

 Classic.

294. "Where Indians Find Their Place in the Arts." *Friends.* General Motors-Chevrolet Advertisement, Feb. 1970.

 Santa Fe School.

295. Wright, Margaret. *Hopi Silver. The History and Hallmarks of Hopi Silversmithing.* Flagstaff: Northland Press, 1972.

 A well illustrated but brief treatment.

296. Wyman, Leland C. "Big Lefthanded, Pioneer Navajo Artist." *Plateau* 40 (Summer 1967): 1-13.

297. Young, Alice. "Navajo Land Keeps Alive Its Native Crafts." *Lapidary Journal,* June, 1967, pp. 402-408.

VI. Social Organization

298. Aberle, David F. "An Economic Approach to Modern Navajo Kinship." Unpublished paper given at the American Anthropological Association meetings, Dec., 1967. Mimeo.

299. American Ethnological Society. *Proceedings Supplement, 1971. Alliance in Eskimo Society.* Edited by Lee Guemple. Seattle: University of Washington Press, 1972.

 Papers on social forms and behavior; alliance and conflict; Central Eskimo Associations; kinship and alliance; divorce; conflicts of loyalties; North Alaskan whaling.

66 SOCIAL ORGANIZATION

300. Basehart, Harry W. "Historical Changes in the Kinship System of the Oneida Indians." Ph.D. dissertation, Harvard University, 1952.

Published historical data supplemented by observations on the Wisconsin Oneida community.

301. Basso, Keith H. Preface. *The Social Organization of the Western Apache* by Grenville Goodwin. Reprinted by the U. of Arizona Press, Tucson, 1969.

302. Boyer, Ruth M. "The Matrifocal Family among the Mescalero: Additional Data." *American Anthropologist* 66 (June 1964): 593–602.

Field work was done in 1959.

303. Brockman, C. Thomas. "The Social Classes at the Modern Flathead Indian Reservation." Tokyo: *8th Congress of Anthropological and Ethnolgical Sciences* (1968): 188–190.

304. Brockmann, C. Thomas. "Correlation of Social Class and Education on Flathead Indian Reservation, Montana." *Rocky Mountain Social Science Journal* 8 (October 1971): 11–17.

305. Brown, Donald N. "Social Structure as Reflected in Architectural Units at Picuris Pueblo, New Mexico." Paper read at the American Anthropological Association meetings, Nov., 1968. Ditto.

306. Clifton, James A. "The Southern Ute Tribe as a Fixed Membership Group." *Human Organization* 24 (Winter 1965): 310–327.

Social structure and cultural change of the Southern Utes.

307. Clifton, James A. "Factional Conflict and the Indian Community: The Prairie Potawatomi Case." In *The American Indian Today* edited by Levine and Lurie. Baltimore: Penguin Books, Inc., 1970. pp. 184–211.

Potawatomi near Mayetta, Kansas.

308. Cline, Michael S. "Community Factionalism and Teacher Survival in the Alaskan Bush." *Human Organization* 33 (Spring, 1974): 102–106.

309. Damas, David. "Igluligmiut Kinship and Local Groupings: A Structural Approach." *Bulletin No. 196, Anthropological Series No. 64.* Ottawa: National Museum of Canada, 1963.

Examines the important alignments of personnel in Igluligmiut society. Field research carried out in the Iglulik region of northern Canada between August 1960 and August 1961.

310. Damas, David. "Characteristics of Central Eskimo Band Structure," pp. 116–134. In *Contributions to Anthropology: Band Societies Bulletin 228.*

Anthropological Series No. 84. Edited by David Damas. Ottawa: National Museum of Canada, 1969.

Describes the group structure of the Copper Eskimo, the Netsilik Eskimo, and Iglulik Eskimo for the period that extended into the 1920's.

311. Dobyns, Henry F., & Euler, R. C. "Wauba Yuma's People: The Comparative Socio-Political Structure of the Pai Indians of Arizona." *Prescott College Studies in Anthropology No. 3.* Prescott: Prescott College Press, 1970.

312. Donald, Leland. "Leadership in a Navajo Community." *Anthropos 65* (1970): 867–880.

Based on field work from June to September, 1964. Discusses two "types" of leadership in a modern community.

313. Dozier, Edward P. "Factionalism at Santa Clara Pueblo." *Ethnology 5* (April 1966): 172-185.

Describes a schism at the pueblo which began in 1894 and finally ended in 1935 with the adoption of an elective form of government under the Indian Reorganization Act of 1934.

314. Dunning, R. W. "Rules of Residence and Ecology Among the Northern Ojibwa." *American Anthropologist* 61 (October 1959): 806-816.

Furthers the studies of Julian Steward and A. I. Hallowell. Data gathered at Pekangekum Lake, Ontario, during the period September, 1954 to August, 1955 and at various brief intervals.

315. Eggan, Fred. "Alliance and Descent in Western Pueblo Society," pp. 175-184. *Process and Pattern in Culture.* Edited by R. A. Manners. Chicago: Aldine Publishing Co., 1964.

316. Ellis, Florence Hawley. "An Outline of Laguna Pueblo History and Social Organization." *Southwestern Journal of Anthropology* 15 (Winter 1959): 325-347.

Essential reading for an understanding of the current situation.

317. Ellis, Florence H. "A Reconstruction of the Basic Jemez Pattern of Social Organization with Comparisons to Other Tanoan Social Structures." *University of New Mexico Publications in Anthropology No. 11.* Albuquerque: University of New Mexico Press, 1964.

318. Fenton, W. N. "Factionalism at Taos Pueblo, New Mexico," pp. 297-344. *Anthropological Paper No. 56, Bulletin 164,* Bureau of American Ethnology, Smithsonian Institution. Washington, D.C.: Govt. Printing Office, 1957.

Fenton attempted to study the native forms and understand the traditional ways of governing. He lived in Santa Fe and made nine visits to the pueblo in 1949 (?).

319. Fenton, William N. "The Iroquois Confederacy in the Twentieth Century: A Case Study of the Theory of Lewis H. Morgan in 'Ancient Society.' " *Ethnology* 4 (July 1965): 251-265.

320. Fogleman, Billye Y. S. "The Appropriation Hypothesis: Primary Group Interaction Among Urban Indians." Paper given at the American Anthropological Association meetings, 1971. Mimeo.

321. Fox, J. R. "Veterans and Factions in Pueblo Society." *Man,* nos. 200 & 201 (October 1961): 173-176.

War veterans in the pueblo have an "integrating influence" for the community as a whole.

322. French, David H. "Factionalism in Isleta Pueblo." *Monograph 14, American Ethnological Society.* New York: J. J. Augustin, 1948.

Looks at the secular aspects only of Isleta life.

323. Fryer, E. R. "Navajo Social Organization and Land Use Adjustment." *The Scientific Monthly* 55 (July-Dec., 1942): 408-422.

Useful general statement by a BIA reservation superintendent.

324. Goldsmith, Mary. "Women's Position and the Transition from Rank to Stratified Society: The Hopi." Paper given at the American Anthropological Association meetings, 1974. Mimeo.

325. Hackenberg, Robert A. "The Parameters of an Ethnic Group: A Method for Studying the Total Tribe." *American Anthropologist* 69 (October 1967): 478-492.

Papago.

326. Halseth, Odd S. "Report of Economic and Social Survey of the Keres Pueblo of Zia, New Mexico." *El Palacio* 16 (1924): 66-75.

327. Hawkes, Ernest William. *The "Inviting-In" Feast of the Alaskan Eskimo. Memoir 45, No. 3, Anthropological Series.* Ottawa: Dept. of Mines, Geological Survey, 1913.

328. Hawley, Florence and Senter, Donovan. "Group-Designed Behavior Patterns in Two Acculturating Groups." *Southwestern Journal of Anthropology* 2 (1946): 133-151.

A pueblo community vis-a-vis a Spanish settlement.

329. Helm, June. "Bilaterality in the Socio-Territorial Organization of the Arctic Drainage Dene." *Ethnology* 4 (October 1965): 361–385.

   Fieldwork done in the 1950–1961 period. Four bands of Hare, Slave, and Dogrib studied. Sound ethnography.

330. Helm, June, & Lurie, Nancy. *The Dogrib Hand Game. Bulletin 205*. Ottawa: National Museum of Canada, 1966.

331. Helm, June. "Chapter 22 d. The Statistics of Kin Marriage: A Non-Australian Example," pp. 216–217. In *Man the Hunter*. Edited by R. B. Lee and Irven DeVore. Chicago: Aldine Publishing Co., 1968.

   Hare data used, collected in 1957.

332. Honigmann, John J. "Social Networks in Great Whale River. Notes on an Eskimo, Montagnais-Naskapi, and Euro-Canadian Community." *Bulletin No. 178, Anthropological Series No. 54*. Ottawa: National Museum of Canada, 1962.

   Data gathered during 1949–1950.

333. Hoover, J. W. "Generic Descent of the Papago Villages." *American Anthropologist,* n.s. 37 (1935).

334. Hurt, Wesley R., & Brown, R. M. "Social Drinking Patterns of the Yankton Sioux." *Human Organization* 24 (Fall, 1965): 222–230.

335. Johnson, Nels. "The Legitimation of New Role-Content: A Kwakiult Cultural Broker." Paper given at Central States Anthropological Society meetings, May, 1969. Mimeo.

336. Lagasse, Jean H. *The People of Indian Ancestry in Manitoba. A Social and Economic Study*. Vols. I, II, III. Winnipeg: Feb., 1959.

   Second in importance only to the Hawthorne Report.

337. Lamphere, Louise. "Ceremonial co-operation and networks: a reanalysis of the Navajo outfit." *Man* 5 (March 1970): 39–59.

   Interesting enough for the community of Ramah, but the limits of generalization are narrow.

338. Lang, Gottfried O. & Kunstadter, Peter. "Survey Research on the Uintah and Ouray Ute Reservation." *American Anthropologist* 59 (June 1957): 527–532.

339. Lieberman, Leonard. "Atomism and Mobility Among Underclass Chippewas and Whites." *Human Organization* 32 (Winter 1973): 337–348.

340. Leubben, Ralph. "Navajo Status and Leadership in a Modern Mining Situation." *Plateau* 35 (Summer 1962): 1-14.

341. MacNeish, June Helm. "Kin Terms of the Arctic Drainage Dene: Hare, Slavey, Chipewyan." *American Anthropologist* 62 (April 1960): 279-295.

A thoughtful analysis.

342. McGee, Harold F. "Ethnic boundaries and strategies of ethnic interaction: a history of Micmac-White relations in Nova Scotia." Ph.D. dissertation, University of Southern Illinois-Carbondale, 1974.

343. McKennan, Robert A. "Athapaskan Groupings and Social Organization in Central Alaska," pp. 93-114. In *Contributions to Anthropology: Band Societies. Bulletin 228, Anthropological Series No. 84.* Edited by David Damas. Ottawa: National Museum of Canada, 1969.

Based on observations made intermittently between 1929-1962.

344. Malan, Vernon D. "The Social System of the Dakota Indians." *Extension Circular 606.* Brookings: Cooperative Extension Service, South Dakota State College, n.d.

345. Malan, Vernon D. "The Dakota Indian Family. Community Studies on the Pine Ridge Reservation." *Bulletin 470.* Brookings: Rural Sociology Dept., South Dakota State College, 1958.

"The sociological study of families undergoing cultural transition." p. 3.

346. Malan, Verson D., & Powers, Joseph F. "The Crow Creek Indian Family." *Bulletin 487.* Brookings: South Dakota State College, Agricultural Experiment Station, 1960.

The ultimate goal of this study is to provide data that can be used as a basis in formulating adequate programs designed to enable the families residing on the Crow Creek Indian Reservation to better their social and economic position.

347. Merriam, Alan P. "The Hand Game of the Flathead Indians." *Journal of American Folklore* 68 (July-Sept., 1955): 313-324.

348. Nicholas, Ralph W. "Factions: a Comparative Analysis. Political Systems and the Distribution of Power," pp. 21-61. *Association of Social Anthropologists Monographs 2.* General editor, M. Banton. London: Tavistock Publications, 1965.

349. Opland, David V. "Marriage and Divorce for the Devils Lake Indian Reservations." *North Dakota Law Review* (Winter 1971): 317-334.

350. Ortiz, Alfonso. "Dual Organization as an Operational Concept in the Pueblo Southwest." *Ethnology* 4 (October 1965): 389-406.

An analysis of one aspect of San Juan Pueblo organization done by a San Juan-born anthropologist who received his Ph.D. degree from the University of Chicago.

351. Pilling, Arnold R. "Genealogy, Anthropology and the American Indian Family History." *Family Trails* 2 (Fall 1969): 1–23. Michigan Department of Education, Bureau of Library Services.

352. Ridington, Robin. "Kin Categories Versus Kin Groups: A Two-Section System Without Sections." *Ethnology* 8 (October 1969): 460–467.

The kinship system of the Beaver can be seen as a two-section system without sections, i.e., a system with two ego-centric conceptual marriage categories that have not crystalized into a sociocentric moiety system because of ecological conditions that favor flexibility in marriage and group affiliation. Fieldwork has been done from 1964 to the present.

353. Robbins, Lynn Arnold. "Blackfeet families and households." Ph.D. dissertation. Eugene: University of Oregon, 1971.

354. Rogers, Edward S. "Band Organization Among the Indians of Eastern Subarctic Canada." *Contributions to Anthropology: Band Societies. Bulletin 228, Anthropological Series No. 84,* pp. 21–50. Edited by David Damas. Ottawa: National Museum of Canada, 1969.

A definitive study.

355. Schusky, Ernest L. *Politics and Planning in a Dakota Indian Community.* Vermillion: Monograph of the Institute on Indian Studies, 1959.

A description of Lower Brule social organization and the politics of settlement payment for land taken by the Fort Randall Dam.

356. Shepardson, Mary. "Factionalism in a Navajo Community." Unpublished Paper read at the Southwestern Anthropological Association meetings, Berkeley, California, 1961.

Shiprock, New Mexico.

357. Siegel, Bernard J. "Social Disorganization in Picuris Pueblo." *International Journal of Comparative Sociology* 6 (September 1965): Leiden, The Netherlands.

358. Smith, James G. E. "Proscription of Cross-Cousin Marriage Among the Southwestern Ojibwa." *American Ethnologist* 1 (November 1974): 751–762.

Important data on social structure. Rocky Cree and Caribou Eater Chipewyan material used for comparison. Fieldwork done between 1967 and 1970.

359. Spoehr, Alexander. *Camp, Clan, and Kin Among the Cow Creek Seminole of*

Florida. Anthropological Series Field Museum of Natural History 33 (1941): 2-27.

Around 175 people live either on Brighton Reservation or in scattered camps west of Fort Pierce on the east coast of the peninsula. This band has preserved aspects of social organization which have not survived among the Oklahoma Seminole and Creeks, but they have not remained static, untouched by contacts with whites. Work done in 1939.

360. Spoehr, Alexander. *Kinship System of the Seminole.* Anthropological Series, Field Museum of Natural History 33 (1942): 31-113.

Concerns Oklahoma Seminole with emphasis on the kinship system prior to 1903 allotment, and then compares this with the Florida form. Many conclusions are questionable. Field work done in 1938-39.

361. Spoehr, Alexander. *The Florida Seminole Camp.* Anthropological Series, Field Museum of Natural History 33 (1944): 121-150.

Special attention given to the nature and significance of the extended family.

362. Stearns, Marylee. "An analysis of the social organization of a modern Haida community." Ph.D. dissertation. Los Angeles, University of California, 1973.

363. Stevenson, David. "The social organization of the Clyde Inlet Eskimos," Ph.D. dissertation, University of British Columbia, 1972.

364. Suttles, Wayne. "The persistence of intervillage ties among the Coast Salish." *Ethnology* 2 (October 1963): 512-526.

365. Voget, Fred. "Kinship Changes at Caughnawaga." *American Anthropologist* 55 (August 1953): 385-394.

Fieldwork done in 1949 and 1950. Some data taken from Morgan.

366. Zurcher, Louis A. "The Leader and the Lost: A Case Study of Indigenous Leadership in a Poverty Program Community Action Committee." *Genetic Psychology Monographs 76,* first half (1967): 23-93.

The Kansas Potawatomis and their responses to various "improvement" programs.

VII. Population Dynamics

367. "Age and Sex Characteristics of Alaska's Population." *Alaska. Review of Businesss and Economic Conditions* 9 (March 1972): 1-52. University of Alaska, Institute of Social, Economic and Government Research.

Considerable 1970 census data are presented, making it possible to derive some conclusions about population change, migration, and population distribution *via* "race" and other variables.

368. "Alaska's Population and School Enrollments." *Alaska. Review of Business and Economic Conditions* 8 (December 1971): 1–48.

Based upon poorly qualified 1970 census returns. Some comparisons are possible using data for school enrollment by "race" of around a ten year period.

369. Bock, Philip K. "Patterns of Illegitimacy on a Canadian Indian Reserve: 1860-1960." *Journal of Marriage and the Family* 26 (May 1964): 142-148.

Micmac data. Accounts for fluctuations in the number of illegitimate births by relating them to variations in the degree of social and cultural integration.

370. Bodine, John J. "Population Structure of Taos Pueblo." *California Anthropologist*. State College of California at Los Angeles, 1971.

371. Basso, Keith H. Preface (with Morris E. Opler). In *Apachean Culture History and Ethnology*. Edited by Keith H. Basso & Morris Opler. Anthropological Papers of the University of Arizona, Tucson: University of Arizona Press, 1971.

372. California. Dept. of Industrial Relations, Division of Fair Employment Practices. *American Indians in California*. San Francisco, 1965.

Statistics on residence in urban and reservation areas, educational attainment, employment, income, family size 1959–1960.

373. California. Senate. *State Interim Committee on California Indian Affairs*. Sacramento, 1955.

Statistical report on land, education, etc.

374. Cook, Sherburne F. "Interracial Warfare and Population Decline Among the New England Indians." *Ethnohistory* 20 (Winter 1973): 1-24.

Vital for an understanding of New England native population today.

375. Downs, James F. *et al.* "American Indian Demographic Research in the Greater Los Angeles Area." Paper given at the Southwestern Anthropological Association meeting at UCLA, 1965. Mimeo.

Brief but useful descriptive material.

376. Ebihara, May M. & Kelly, Gail Margaret. "A Survey of the Indian Population of Portland Oregon in the Summer of 1955." Honors Paper, Reed College, Portland, Oregon, 1955.

Brief but useful.

* 377. Hadley, J. Nixon. "Demography of the American Indians." The *Annals of the American Academy of Political and Social Science* 311 (May 1957): 23–30.

* 378. Hillery, G. A., Jr. "Navajos and Eastern Kentuckians; A Comparative Study in the Cultural Consequences of the Demographic Transition." *American Anthropologist* 68 (February 1966): 52–70.

* 379. Hillery, George A. Jr., & Essene, Frank J. "Navajo Population: An Analysis of the 1960 Census." *Southwestern Journal of Anthropology* 19 (Autumn 1963): 297–313.

* 380. Hippler, Arthur E. "Some Observations on the Persistence of Alaskan Native Village Populations." *Alaska. Review of Business and Economic Conditions. Research Note No. A1* (September 1969): 1–20.

    Despite the growth of urban centers via migration from many smaller villages, these will not disappear or even decline in the foreseeable future.

381. Hobart, Charles W. "Socio-Economic Correlates of Mortality and Morbidity Among Inuit Infants." Seminar Paper, Department of Sociology, University of Alberta, Edmonton, 1974. Mimeo.

382. Hoffman, Frederick L. *The Navaho Population Problem.* Proceedings of the 23rd International Congress of Americanists, New York, September 17, 1922. New York (1930): 620–632.

383. Howard, James. "The Identity and Demography of the Plains-Ojibwa." *Plains Anthropologist* 6, no. 13 (1961): 171–178.

* 384. Johnston, Denis Foster. "An Analysis of Sources of Information on the Population of the Navaho. *Bulletin 197, Bureau of American Ethnology.* Washington D.C.: Smithsonian Institution, Government Printing Office, 1966.

    A valuable discussion concerning U.S. Census data.

385. Kroeber, A. L. "California Indian Population About 1910." *University of California Publications in American Archaeology and Ethnology* 47 (1957): 218–225.

    Concludes there were 20,000.

386. Kunitz, Stephen J. *et al.* "A Census of Flagstaff Navajos." *Plateau* 41 (Spring 1969): 156–163.

    Kunitz is an M.D.

* 387. Kunitz, Stephen J. "Demographic Change among the Hopi and Navajo Indians." *Lake Powell Research Bulletin No. 2.* Rochester: National Science Foundation, 1973.

* 388. Kunitz, Stephen J. "Factors Influencing Recent Navajo and Hopi Population Changes." *Human Organization* 33 (Spring 1974): 7–16.

389. Liberty, Margot P., & McGinty, I. N. "1970 Census of the Indian Community of Lincoln, Nebraska." Mimeo, n.d.

390. Paredes, J. Anthony, & Lenihan, Kaye. "Native American Population in the Southeastern States: 1960–70." *Florida Anthropologist* 26 (June 1973): 45–56.

   Heavy reliance on federal census data.

391. Price, John A. *A Census of Indians in Los Angeles,* revised edition. July, 1966, mimeo.

392. Schmid, Calvin F., & Nobbe, Charles E. "Socioeconomic Differentials Among Nonwhite Races." *American Sociological Review* 30 (December 1965): 909–922.

393. Schmid, Calvin, & Nobbe, C. E. "Socio-Economic Differentials Among Nonwhite Races in the State of Washington." *Demography* 2 (1965): 549 ff.

394. Stucki, Larry R. "The Case Against Population Control: The Probable Creation of the First American Indian State." *Human Organization* 30 (Winter 1971): 393–400.

   The key variable in explaining the great difference in power that now exists between the Navajo tribe and other Indian groups is population size and a number of other closely related factors.

VIII. Reservations/Rural Areas As Communities

395. Abel, Anna Heloise. "Indian Reservations in Kansas and the Extinguishment of Their Title." *Kansas Historical Society Transactions* 8 (1904): 72–109.

396. Ahenakew, Edward. *Voices of the Plains Cree.* Edited by Ruth M. Buck. Toronto: McClelland & Stewart Ltd., 1973.

   Most data provided by Chief Thunderchild. Concerns events prior to 1876, but makes observations on the beginning of the reserve period.

397. Bicknell, A. D. "The Tama County Indians. *Annals of Iowa* 4 (1899): 196–208.

   Observations regarding the "Musquakies" in 1897 and 1898. A biased account of living conditions.

398. Blu, Karen I. " 'We People': Understanding Lumbee Indian Identity in a Tri-racial Situation." Ph.D. dissertation, University of Chicago, 1972.

* 399. Bock, Philip K. "The Micmac Indians of Restigouche: History and Contemporary Description." *Bulletin No. 213, Anthropological Series No. 77.* Ottawa: National Museum of Canada, 1966.

Field work conducted in 1961. Describes the contemporary culture of a Micmac Reserve using the historical background to suggest significant continuities and discontinuities from aboriginal times to the present.

400. Bodine, John J. *Attitudes and Institutions of Taos, New Mexico: Variables for Value System Expression.* Ann Arbor: Published on demand by University Microfilms, 1967.

401. Bodine, John J. "A Tri-Ethnic Trap: The Spanish Americans in Taos." *Spanish-Speaking People in the United States. Proceedings, Annual Spring Meeting, American Ethnological Society.* Edited by June Helm. Seattle: University of Washington Press, 1968, pp. 145–153.

402. Bosch, James W. *Fort Defiance. A Navajo Community in Transition.* Window Rock: The Public Services Division, The Navajo Tribe, I, 1961, Mimeo.

Research done at Fort Defiance, 1959. An examination of the historical developments in Navajo housing.

403. Braroe, Niels Winther. "Reciprocal Exploitation in an Indian-White Community." *Southwestern Journal of Anthropology* 21 (Summer 1965): 166–178.

404. Braroe, Niels Winther. "Change and Identity: Patterns of Interaction in an Indian-White Community." Ph.D. dissertation, University of Illinois, 1972.

405. Breed, Jack. "Better Days For the Navajos." *National Geographic,* December, 1958, pp. 809–847.

406. Browne, J. R. *The Indians of California.* San Francisco: Colt Press, 1944.

Discusses how unpleasant Indian reservations in the area were.

407. Burnford, Sheila. *Without Reserve.* Boston: Little Brown & Co., 1969.

An account of the author's contacts with some Cree and Ojibwa in Ontario.

408. Burt, Jesse, & Ferguson, R. B. *Indians of the Southeast: Then and Now.* Nashville: Abingdon Press, 1973.

Useful appendices with some information concerning modern conditions.

409. California. State Advisory Committee on Indian Affairs. *Indians in Rural and Reservation Areas.* Sacremento: 1966.

410. California. Supreme Court of the State of California. *Byrne v. Alas.* 74 Cal. 628, 1888.

Rancherias on Mexican land grants.

411. Campbell. Maria. *Halfbreed.* New York: Saturday Review Press, 1973.

Concerns Metis in Saskatchewan.

412. Caughey, J. W. *The Indians of Southern California in 1952: The B. D. Wilson Report and a Selection of Contemporary Comment.* San Marino: Huntington Library, 1952.

413. Centennial Committee. *Arpin Centennial, 1873-1973.* Amherst: Helback Printing, Inc., 1973.

Vital for the understanding of the nature of nearby Indian settlements. Well illustrated.

414. Clifton, James A., & Isaac, Barry. "The Kansas Prairie Potawatomi: On the Nature of a Contemporary Indian Community." *Transactions of the Kansas Academy of Science* 67 (Spring 1964): 1-24.

The present reservation-based group does constitute a viable community in the technical sense of the term.

* 415. Collins, June McCormick. "Valley of the Spirits. The Upper Skagit Indians of Western Washington." *Monograph 56, American Ethnological Society.* Seattle: University of Washington Press, 1974.

One chapter is devoted to "recent times."

416. Colson, Elizabeth. "Indian reservations and the American Social Systems." Paper given at the American Anthropological Association meetings, 1968. Ditto.

* 417. Colson, Elizabeth. *The Makah Indians: a study of an Indian tribe in modern American society.* Minneapolis: University of Minnesota Press, 1953.

A classic study.

418. Commonwealth Club of California. *Indians in California.* Transactions of the Commonwealth Club 21, no. 3. San Francisco, 1926.

419. "Contemporary Perspectives: Wisconsin Indians." Conference held at the University of Wisconsin-River Falls, Sept. 27, 28, 1973.

420. Cook, S. F. "The Conflict Between the California Indian and White Civilization. III. The American Invasion, 1848-1870." *Ibero-Americana* 23 (1943).

Extensive data on general living conditions.

421. Correll, J. Lee *et al. Proposed Findings of Fact in Behalf of the Navajo Tribe of Indians in Area of the Overall Navajo Claim (Docket 229)*. Vols. 1–6. Window Rock, Arizona: The Navajo Tribe, 1967, Mimeo.

Vital for an understanding of the Navajo people. Archeology, ethnohistory, history and culture. 1200 + pages.

422. Cory, David M. *Within Two Worlds*. Chapters 4 & 5. New York: Friendship Press, 1955, pp. 43–65.

Concerns modern Canadian native people.

423. Crane, Leo. *Indians of the Enchanted Desert*. London: Leonard Parsons, Ltd., 1926.

A classic. Written by a former BIA "Indian agent" upon retirement from active service. Concerns his work with the Navajo and Hopi.

424. Crane, Leo. *Desert Drums. The Pueblo Indians of New Mexico 1540–1928*. Boston: Little, Brown & Co., 1928.

Another classic.

425. Currie, A. H. "Bidwell Rancheria." *California Historical Society Quarterly* 36 (1957): 313–325.

Concerns an Indian village controlled by a white who held Mexican land grants before 1846.

426. Cushman, Dan. *Stay Away, Joe*. Great Falls, Montana: Stay Away Joe Publishers, 1965.

Fascinating novel about Indians using and being used by reservation culture.

* 427. Dane, J. K., & Griessman, B. Eugene. "The Collective Identity of Marginal Peoples: The North Carolina Experience." *American Anthropologist* 74 (June 1972): 694–704.

The 6000 Indians in Haliwa and Sampson Counties.

428. Davids, Elmer L. "Our People—Past, Present and Future. The Stockbridge-Munsee Band of Mohican Indians." 1974, mimeo.

429. de Coccola, Raymond & King, Paul. *Ayorama*. Don Mills: PaperJacks, 1973.

Excellent account of the "Krangmalit" by a Catholic missionary based on twelve years observation.

430. Deer, Ada. "The Effects of Termination on the Menominee. Submitted to the Republican National Resolutions (Platform) Committee." August 14, 1972. Mimeo.

431. Delorme, David F. "A Socio-economic Study of the Turtle Mountain Band of Chippewa Indians and a Critical Evaluation of Proposals Designed to Terminate Their Federal Wardship Status." Ph.D. dissertation, University of Texas, 1955.

432. Dempsey, Hugh A. "A Blackfoot Winter Count." *Occasional Paper No. 1.* Calgary: Glenbow-Alberta Institute, 1965.

433. Densmore, Frances. "A Study of Some Michigan Indians." *Anthropological Papers No. 1.* Ann Arbor: Museum of Anthropology, University of Michigan, 1949.

Mentions Keweenaw Community and Beaver Island. Some material on the Upper Peninsula Reservations.

434. Dobyns, Henry F. *The Apache People (Coyotero).* Phoenix: Indian Tribal Series, 1971.

435. Dobyns, Henry F. *The Papago People.* Phoenix: Indian Tribal Series, 1972.

436. Dobyns, Henry F. *The Mescalero Apache People.* Phoenix: Indian Tribal Series, 1973.

437. Dobyns, Henry F., & Euler, Robert C. *The Havasupai People.* Phoenix: Indian Tribal Series, 1971.

* 438. Dobyns, Henry F., & Euler, Robert C. *The Navajo People.* Phoenix: Indian Tribal Series, 1972.

439. Dorn, Edward, & Lucas, LeRoy. *The Shoshoneans: the People of the Basin-Plateau.* New York: Wm. Morrow & Co., 1966.

Describes some aspects of contemporary existence for Northern Paiutes, Western Shoshones, and Fort Hall Shoshones.

* 440. Downs, James F. *The Two Worlds of the Washo. An Indian Tribe of California and Nevada.* New York: Holt, Rinehart & Winston, 1966.

Field work done "a few months in 1959 and several shorter trips in the area in subsequent years." p. 3. An instructive account.

441. Downs, James F. *The Navajo.* New York: Holt, Rinehart & Winston, 1972.

Good general description of the "Nez Ch'ii" or Pinon community in the 1960's.

* 442. Dozier, Edward P. "The Hopi-Tewa of Arizona." *University of California Publications in American Archaeology and Ethnology* 44, no. 3 (1954): 259-376.

". . . a study of the distinctive elements of their culture. It is concerned with the history of these people, and particularly with the social mechanism by which they have preserved their identity during three centuries of close association not only with the Hopi on First Mesa but also with the Spanish and the Anglo-Americans." p. 259. Field work done during 1949-1951. Dozier was born at Santa Clara Pueblo.

443. Dozier, Edward P. "The Pueblos of the South-Western United States." *Journal of the Royal Anthropological Institute* 90 (March 1960): 146-160.

Presents social structural data on the pueblos of the south-western United States and offers an ecological explanation for the cultural differences between the western and eastern pueblos.

444. Dozier, Edward P. *Hano. A Tewa Indian Community in Arizona.* New York: Holt, Rinehart & Winston, 1966.

A diluted version of his 1954 publication, "The Hopi-Tewa of Arizona."

445. Dozier, Edward P. *The Pueblo Indians of North America.* New York: Holt, Rinehart & Winston, Inc., 1970.

Essential reading for all those interested in pueblo ethnology.

446. Dube, Galibois & Associates. "Methodology of Estimating the Housing Requirements for the Indian Bands in Canada." Quebec: 1970, mimeo.

447. Dube, Galibois & Associates. Addendum to "Methodology of Estimating the Housing Requirement for the Indian Bank in Canada." Quebec: 1970, mimeo.

448. Dunning, R. W. "Some Problems of Reserve Indian Communities: A Case Study." *Anthropologica* N.S. 6, no. 1 (1964): 3-38.

Typological analysis of northern and southern reserve communities.

449. Dutton, Bertha P. *Let's Explore Indian Villages. Tour Guide for the Santa Fe Area.* Albuquerque: University of New Mexico Press, 1974.

Outline for four exploratory trips to Indian villages near Santa Fe. Notes on prehistory and current activites plus a map.

450. Dyk, Walter. *Son of Old Man Hat. A Navaho Autobiography.* New York: Harcourt, Brace & Co., 1938.

Concerns an elderly Navajo, Left Handed, living in the Lukachukai area of the reservation. The narrative begins with the story of his birth in the spring of 1868 and ends with his marriage about twenty years later. Essential for the understanding of Navajo life during this period.

451. Dyk, Walter. "A Navaho Autobiography." *Viking Fund Publications In Anthropology. No. 8.* New York: Viking Fund Inc., 1947.

The "life history" of Old Mexican, covering forty-eight years of his life from 1871 when he was five to 1919 when he was fifty-three. He was born south of Aneth, Utah. Little data are given about his early years. This work is vital to the understanding of Navajos.

452. Embry, Carlos B. *America's Concentration Camps; the facts about our Indian reservations today.* New York: D. McKay Co., 1956.

Loosely structured but important.

453. Emerick, Richard G. "Man of the Canyon: Excerpts from a Life in a Time-in a Place-in a Culture." *Readings in Introductory Anthropology,* Vol. 2, Berkeley: McCutchan Publishing Corp., 1970, pp. 267–292.

Life history of a seventy-one year old Havasupai man "Mark."

454. Erdman, Joyce M. *Handbook on Wisconsin Indians.* Madison: Governor's Commission on Human Rights, State of Wisconsin, 1966.

Contains the imperfections of the 1952 version and gives undue emphasis to the negative aspects of Indian life. There are many errors of fact.

455. Fay, George E., editor. *Journal of the Wisconsin Indians Research Institute* 1 (October 1965): whole issue. Oshkosh: Wisconsin State University.

Various papers concerning the Menominee situation between 1950 and 1965. Mimeo.

456. Fenton, William N., & Gulick, John, editors. "Symposium on Cherokee and Iroquois Culture." *Bureau of American Ethnology Bulletin 180.* Washington, D.C.: Smithsonian Institution, Government Printing Office, 1961.

Twenty-five papers with commentary. Eight of these are concerned with the contemporary situation.

* 457. Fewkes, J. Walter. "The Pueblo Settlements Near El Paso, Texas." *American Anthropologist* 4, n.s. (1902): 57–75.

Good ethnography.

458. Fischer, Ann. "History and Current Status of the Houma Indians." In *The American Indian Today,* pp. 212–235. Edited by Levine and Lurie. Baltimore: Penguin Books, Inc., 1970.

Useful account of a group in Louisiana.

459. Fischer, Gerhard, editor. "Stockbridge-Munsee Tribe and F.S.A. Lands." *Newsletter, Lutheran Human Relations Council of Wisconsin* 2 (August 1970): whole issue.

460. Fontana, Bernard L. "The Hopi-Navajo Colony on the Lower Colorado River: A Problem in Ethnohistorical Interpretation." *Ethnohistory* 10 (Spring 1963): 162-182.

A thoughtful analysis.

461. Fontana, Bernard L. with Weaver, Thomas, Sekaquaptewa, Emory, Krutz, Gordon, Lobo, Frank, and Bainton, Barry. *The Arizona Indian People and Their Relationship to the State's Total Structure.* Phoenix: Arizona Academy, 1971.

462. Fox, J. R. "Cochiti Indians of America." *New Society* no. 29 (April 1963): 15-17.

Brief but useful description.

463. Frisch, Jack A. "Tribalism Among the St. Regis Mohawks: A Search for Self-Identity." Paper given at the Central States Anthropological Society meeting, 1969.

* 464. Garbarino, Merwyn S. *Big Cypress. A Changing Seminole Community.* New York: Holt, Rinehart & Winston, 1972.

Sound ethnography. Garbarino did fieldwork in Florida between 1964 and 1968 for a total of eighteen months.

465. Gearing, Fred. "Today's Mesquakies." *The American Indian* 7 (Spring 1955): 24-37.

Good general description.

* 466. Gearing, Frederick O. *The Face of the Fox.* Chicago: Aldine Publishing Co., 1970.

"This book is about American Indians. It presents a selective description of one Indian community, the 600 Fox Indians who live just outside Tama, Iowa. Besides describing the community, the study claims to diagnose its acute discomfort and to name a cure." (From the dust jacket.)

467. Gearing, Fred, McC. Netting, Robert, & Peattie, L. R., editors. *Documentary History of the Fox Project, 1948-1959.* Chicago: Department of Anthropology, University of Chicago, 1960.

Chronicles the development of Action Anthropology as it has been worked out and thought out with respect to a living Indian community, that of the Meskwaki or Fox Indians near Tama, Iowa.

468. Gibson, John. *A Small and Charming World.* Toronto: Collins, 1972.

The author lived for three years along the coast of northern British Columbia. An informal but informative account.

469. Gilbert, William H., Jr. "Memorandum Concerning the Characteristics of the Larger Mixed-Blood Racial Islands of the Eastern United States." *Social Forces* 24, no. 4 (1946): 438–447.

470. Gilbert, William H., Jr. "Surviving Indian Groups of the Eastern United States." *Smithsonian Institution Annual Report for 1948.* Washington, D.C.: Government Printing Office, 1949, pp. 407–438.

Comments on Indians in Maine, New Hampshire, Vermont, Massachusetts, Rhode Island, Connecticut, New York, New Jersey, Pennsylvania, Delaware, Maryland, West Virginia, Virginia, North Carolina, South Carolina, Georgia, Florida, Alabama, Mississippi, Louisiana, Arkansas, Missouri, Texas, Tennessee, Ohio, Indiana, Illinois. Essential reading.

471. Gilbert, William H., Jr. "The Cherokees of North Carolina: Living Memorials of the Past." *Smithsonian Institution Annual Report for 1956.* Washington, D.C.: Govt. Printing Office, 1957, pp. 529–555.

Valuable data in spite of its title.

472. Goldfrank, Esther S., editor. "Isleta Paintings," with introduction and commentary by E. E. Parsons. *Bulletin 181. Bureau of American Ethnology, Smithsonian Institution.* Washington D.C.: Govt. Printing Office, 1962.

One hundred and forty paintings of Isleta life done by Joe Lente during the period 1936–1941. Lente stated, in part, to E. C. Parsons: "I have no way of making a living, no farm. . . . If I had some way to get help in this world I would have never done this." p. 1. Annotated Glossary of Isleta Terms by G. L. Trager.

473. Goldfrank, Esther S. "The Artist of 'Isleta Paintings' in Pueblo Society." *Smithsonain Contributions to Anthropology.* 5 Washington, D.C.: Smithsonian Press, 1967.

Valuable ethnography. Full texts of the letters to E. C. Parsons are reproduced and will repay a careful reading.

474. Governor's Commission on Human Rights. *Proceedings. Section on Indian Affairs.* Madison: University of Wisconsin, 1951.

475. Governor's Commission on Human Rights. *Handbook on Wisconsin Indians.* Madison: The State of Wisconsin, 1952.

Not well received by Indian residents of the state and by today's standards remarkably racist in character.

476. Green, Charles R. *Early Days in Kansas in Keokuk's Time on the Kansas Reservation.* Olathe, Kansas: privately printed, 1912.

477. Green, S. H. "A Statement Concerning the Effect of Social Conditions on the School Presented to the Social Development Policy Committee of the Ontario Cabinet by the Red Lake Board of Education." Red Lake: 1974, mimeo.

The school system cannot cope with the social problems of deprived people, especially Indians.

478. Griffin, John W., editor. *The Florida Indian and His Neighbors.* Winter Park, Florida: Inter-American Center, Rollins College, 1949.

479. Griffith, James S. "The Catholic Religious Architecture of the Papago Reservation, Arizona." Ph.D. dissertation, University of Arizona, 1973.

480. Gubatayao, Max. "Hill 57 Makes Indian Medicine." *The American Indian* 8 (Winter 1958-59): 2-5.

A hill near Great Falls, Montana. About 400 Indians live here.

481. Hagen, E. E., & Shaw, L.C. *The Sioux on the Reservations: The American Colonial Problem.* Preliminary Edition. Cambridge: M.I.T. Center for International Studies, 1960.

482. Harmsworth, Harry C. "Family Structure on the Fort Hall Indian Reservation." *The Family Life Coordinator* (January 1965): 7-9.

Shoshone-Bannock.

483. Hassinger, Edward W. "A Study of a Minority Group's Social Contacts: The Lower Sioux Community of Morton, Minnesota." M. A. Thesis, University of Minneapolis, Minneapolis, Minnesota, 1951.

* 484. Hawthorn, H. G. "The Survival of Small Societies." In *Pilot Not Commander, Anthropologica n.s. Vol. 13, Nos. 1-2. Essays in Memory of Diamond Jenness.* Edited by Pat and Jim Lotz. Ottawa: St. Paul University, 1971, pp. 63-84.

485. Helm, June. "The Lynx Point People: The Dynamics of a Northern Athapaskan Band." *National Museum of Canada. Bulletin No. 176.* Ottawa: 1961.

486. Helm, June. "Chapter 13. The Nature of Dogrib Socioterritorial Groups." In *Man the Hunter,* pp. 118-125. Edited by R. B. Lee and Irven DeVore. Chicago: Aldine Publishing Co., 1968.

487. Helm, June. "Chapter 2. The Dogrib Indians." In *Hunters and Gatherers*

Today, pp. 51–89. Edited by M. G. Bicchieri. New York: Holt, Rinehart & Winston, 1972.

A useful summary of a variety of specific studies.

488. Helm, June and Damas, David. "The Contact-Traditional All-Native Community of the Canadian North: The Upper Mackenzie Bush: Athapaskans and the Igluligmiut." *Anthropologica* n.s. 5, no. 1 (1963): 9–22.

489. H. H. "The Present Condition of the Mission Indians in Southern California." *The Century Magazine* (August 1883): 511–529.

490. Hickerson, Harold. "Some Implications of the Theory of the Particularity or 'Atomism' of Northern Algonkians." *Current Anthropology* 8 (1967): 313–343.

491. Hillerman, Tony. *The Blessing Way.* New York: Harper and Row, 1970.

A suspense novel with a Navajo Reservation setting and a Navajo detective. Excellent atmosphere material.

492. Hillerman, Tony. *Dance Hall of the Dead.* New York: Harper and Row, 1973.

A well written novel with a Navajo detective as hero at Zuni and the Ramah Navajo community.

* 493. Hippler, Arthur E. *Barrow and Kotzebue: An Exploratory Comparison of Acculturation and Education in Two Large Northwestern Alaska Villages.* University of Minnesota: Training Center for Community Programs, December, 1969.

494. Hippler, Arthur E. *The Big Villages in Northwest Alaska. A Dimension in the Acculturation of Alaskan Eskimos.* Manuscript, 1969.

495. Hoffman, W. J. "Hugo Ried's Account of the Indians of Los Angeles County, California." *Bulletin of the Essex Institute* 17 (1885): 1–3.

496. Holmes, W. H. *Anthropological Studies in California.* Report of the U.S. National Museum for 1900, pp. 155–188. 1902.

Observations on living conditions of California Indians at the turn of the century.

497. Honigmann, John J., editor. "Ethnographic Survey of Churchill." *Working Paper No. 3. Urbanization in the Arctic and Subarctic,* 1968.

498. Hopkins, Sarah Winnemucca. "Life Among the Piutes: Their Wrongs and Claims. 1883. Reprinted in *Old West* 2 (Fall 1965): 49–96.

A classic.

499. Houghton, Ruth E. M. "The Fort McDermitt Indian reservation: social structure and the distribution of political and economic power." M. A. Thesis, University of Oregon, 1968.

500. Houghton, Ruth E. "Adaptive strategies in an American Indian reservation community: the war on poverty." Ph.D. dissertation, University of Oregon, 1973.

501. Howard, James H. "The Turtle Mountain 'Chippewa'." *North Dakota Quarterly* 26 (Spring 1958): 37-46.

502. Howard, James. "The Yamasee: A Supposedly Extinct Southeastern Tribe Rediscovered." *American Anthropologist* 62 (August 1960): 681-682.

503. Howard, James. "The St. Ann's Day Celebration of the Micmac Indians, 1962." *Museum News. South Dakota Museum* 26 (March-April 1965): 5-13.

504. Howard, James H. "The Canadian Dakota Experience." Paper given at the American Anthropological Association meetings, Nov., 1973.

505. Howard, James, & Gluckman, Stephen J. "Micmac Indians of Nova Scotia: A Photo Feature." *Museum News, South Dakota Museum* 26 (March-April 1965): 14-20.

506. Huden, John C., compiler. "Indian Place Names of New England." *Contributions of the Museum of the American Indian, Heye Foundation* 18 (1962).

507. Hudson, Charles M. Jr. "The Catawba Nation." *University of Georgia Monographs, No. 18.* Athens: University of Georgia Press, 1970.

508. Hudson, Charles Melvin, Jr. *The Southeastern Indians.* University of Tennessee Press, in press, 1974.

509. Hume, William. Articles on modern conditions in various New Mexico Pueblos. In the *Albuquerque Journal,* 1970.

    Sandia, 8/9; Isleta, 8/23; Nambe, 8/30; Jemez, 9/14; Tesque, 9/20; San Ildefonso, 11/29; Santa Clara, 10/4; Zia, 10/25; Taos, 11/15; San Juan, 11/22.

510. Iliff, Flora Gregg. *People of the Blue Water. My Adventures Among the Walapai and Havasupai Indians.* New York: Harper and Brothers, 1954.

    Written by a biased white school teacher around the beginning of the century. Useful.

511. Inglis, G. B. "An Approach to the Analysis of Reserve Populations as Partial Societies." Paper given at American Anthropological Association meetings, Nov., 1968.

512. Inglis, Gordan Bahan. "The Canadian Indian Reserve: community, population and social system." Ph.D. dissertation, University of British Columbia, Vancouver, 1970.

513. Issac, Barry L. "The Prairie Potawatomi Community." *Search* 4 (Spring 1964): 60-61. Lawrence: University of Kansas.

514. Johnson, Frederick. "The Indians of New Hampshire." *Appalachia* 6 (1940): 3-15.

515. Johnston, B. E. *California's Gabrielino Indians.* Southwest Museum, Hodge Anniversary Publication Fund 8 (1962).

Pp. 128-189 covers Gabrielino history during the mission, Mexican and American periods.

516. Jones, G. O., & McVean, N.S. "The Indians." Chapter II in *History of Wood County, Wisconsin.* Minneapolis & Winona, Minnesota: H. C. Cooper Jr. & Co., 1923.

517. Kasch, C. "The Yokayo Rancheria." *California Historical Society Quarterly* 26 (1947): 209-216.

A historical sketch.

* 518. Katzer, B. "The Caughnawaga Mohawks: Occupations, Residence, and the Maintenance of Community Membership." Ph.D. dissertation, Columbia University. University Microfilms, 1972.

519. Keech, Roy A. "Two Days and Nights in a Pueblo." *El Palacio* 35, no. 21-22 (1933): 185-195.

Jemez.

520. Keesing, Felix. The *Menomini Indians of Wisconsin.* New York: Johnson Reprint Corporation, 1971.

The Menominees from initial white contact to 1940.

521. Kelsey, C. E. *Census of Non-Reservation California Indians, 1905-1906.* Berkeley: University of California Archaeological Research Facility, 1971.

Detailed census giving names of persons and location of landless Indians, mainly in northern California.

522. Kluckhohn, Clyde. "The Ramah Navaho." *Anthropological Paper No. 79, Bureau of American Ethnology Bulletin 196,* Smithsonian Institution. Washington, D.C.: Government Printing Office, 1966.

523. Kluckhohn, Richard, editor. *Culture and Behavior. Collected Essays of Clyde Kluckhohn.* New York: The Free Press of Glencoe, 1962.

Several important papers on the Navajo are included.

524. Kroeber, Theodora, & Heizer, Robert F. *Almost Ancestors. The First Californians.* San Francisco: Sierra Club, 1968.

Excellent pictures and commentary. Necessary reading for those interested in the California native people.

525. Kupferer, Harriet J. "Impotency and Power: A Cross-Cultural Comparison of the Effect of Alien Rule." In *Political Anthropology,* pp. 61-71. Edited by M. Swartz, V. W. Turner & Arthur Taden. Chicago: Aldine Press, 1966.

The Cree at Rupert's House.

526. Kupferer, Harriet. "The 'Principal People,' 1960: A Study of Cultural and Social Groups of the Eastern Cherokee." *Anthropological Paper No. 78. Bureau of American Ethnology Bulletin 196,* Smithsonian Institution, pp. 215-325. Washington, D.C.: Government Printing Office, 1966.

527. Kupferer, Harriet. "The Isolated Eastern Cherokee." In *The American Indian Today,* pp. 143-159. Edited by Levine and Lurie. Baltimore: Penguin Books, Inc., 1970.

528. Lancaster, Hal. "Restless Reservation Problems of the Navajo Reflect the Dilemma of American Indians." *Wall Street Journal,* October 13, 1971.

529. Lange, Charles H. *Cochiti.* Austin: University of Texas Press, 1959.

The best study ever made of a pueblo group.

530. Larson, Anna V. "The Lutheran Church and the Indian in the Timberland Country of Northern Minnesota." Northern Minnesota Committee for Intercultural Outreach in Cooperation with the Department of Intercultural Outreach, Division of American Missions. Chicago: National Lutheran Council, 1958. Mimeo.

531. Leacock, Eleanor Burke. "The Seabird Community." In *Indians of the Urban Northwest.* Edited by Marian W. Smith. New York: Columbia University Press, 1949.

532. Leacock, Eleanor. "The Montagnis-Naskapi Band." In *Contributions to Anthropology: Band Societies. Bulletin 228, Anthropological Series No. 84,* pp. 1-17. Edited by David Damas. Ottawa: National Museum of Canada, 1969.

A broad historical perspective integrated with modern conditions.

533. League of Women Voters. "A Study of the Oneida Indians of Wisconsin." Appleton, Wisconsin: 1956. Mimeo, 15 pp.

534. Levitan, Sara, & Hetrick, Barbara. *Big Brother's Indian Programs—With Reservations.* New York: McGraw-Hill, 1971.

Very general. Trite.

535. Levy, Jerrold E. "Kiowa and Comanche: A Report from the Field." *Anthropology Tomorrow* 6 (1958): 30-44.

536. Levy, Jerrold E. *South Tuba. A Western Navajo Wage Work Community.* Tuba City, Arizona: United States Public Health Service Indian Hospital, Nov., 1962.

537. Levy, Jerrold E. with Henderson, E. R. "A Survey of Navajo Community Studies, 1936-1974." *Lake Powell Research Project Bulletin No. 6,* in press, 1974.

538. Liberty, Margot. "Background and Culture of the Omaha Indians: Preliminary Sketch." Lincoln, Nebraska, June, 1971, ditto.

* 539. Liberty, Margot P. "The Urban Reservation." Ph.D. dissertation. University of Minnesota, 1973.

Investigates the persistence of Omaha culture with assessment of the relative influences of assimilation and pluralism in shaping its present contours.

540. Livingston, Marilyn Gerber. "Klamath Indians in Two Non-Indian Communities: Klamath Falls and Eugene-Springfield." M. A. Thesis. University of Oregon, June, 1959.

541. Loomer, C. W. "Land Tenure Problems in the Bad River Indian Reservation of Wisconsin." *Research Bulletin 188.* Madison: Agricultural Experiment Station, University of Wisconsin, Dec., 1955.

542. Lukens, Janet. "Michigan Chippewa Field Notes." 1970.

The Chippewas near Mt. Pleasant, Michigan.

543. Lummis, C. "Exiles of Cupa." *Out West* 16 (1902): 25-30.

544. Lummis, C. *Condition of the Mission Indians in 1905.* Sequoya League Bulletin II, 1905.

545. Lurie, Nancy O., & Miller, Helen M. *Historical Background of the Winnebago People.* Privately prepared and printed for the Wisconsin Winnebago Business Committee, 1964. Revised, 1965.

546. Lurie, Nancy O. *Winnebago.* Draft to be used in the *New Handbook—North American Indians.* Smithsonian Institution, 1974. Manuscript.

547. MacGregor, Gordon. *Warriors Without Weapons.* Chicago: University of Chicago Press, 1946.

Dakota Sioux. A classic.

* 548. MacGregor, Gordon. "Changing Society: The Teton Dakotas." In *The Modern Sioux,* pp. 92–106. Edited by Ethel Nurge. Lincoln: University of Nebraska Press, 1970.

An analysis of a Teton Dakota tribe and the Indian agency as two separate entities or social systems in interaction.

549. McDonald, Peter. *Report on the Navajo Nation to the Navajo Tribal Council, Fall Session.* Window Rock, Arizona: Oct. 31, 1972.

* 550. McFee, Malcolm. *Modern Blackfeet. Montanans on a Reservation.* New York: Holt, Rinehart & Winston, 1972.

Field work done in 1959 and at intervals since that time. Some useful descriptive material.

551. McPartland, Thomas. S. "A Preliminary Socio-Economic Study of the Sisseton-Wahpeton Sioux." Vermillion: Institute of Indian Studies, University of South Dakota, Dec., 1955.

552. Malan, Vernon D., & Schusky, Ernest L. "The Dakota Indian Community. An Analysis of the Non-Ranching Population of the Pine Ridge Reservation." *Bulletin 505.* Brookings: Rural Sociology Dept., Agricultural Experiment Station, South Dakota State College, n.d.

Good ethnography.

553. Martin, John F. "A Reconsideration of Havasupai Land Tenure." *Ethnology* 7 (October 1968): 450–460.

554. Merriam, Alan P. "Letter to the Editor (concerning the Flathead Indians)." *Society for Ethnomusicology Newsletter* 8 (Sept.-Oct., 1974): 2.

555. Montell, Lynwood. "The Coe Ridge Colony: A Racial Island Disappears." *American Anthropologist* 74 (June 1972): 710–719.

The ninety year history of a racially isolated community—whites, blacks, Indians—in the Kentucky-Tennessee border area is examined.

556. Nurge, Ethel, editor. *The Modern Sioux, Social Systems and Reservation Culture.* Lincoln: University of Nebraska Press, 1970.

* 557. Opler, Morris. "The Creek 'Town' and the Problem of Creek Indian Political Reorganization." In *Human Problems in Technological Change: A Casebook,* pp. 165–180. Edited by Edward H. Spicer. New York: Russell Sage Foundation, 1952.

* 558. Opler, Morris E. "The Creek Indian Towns of Oklahoma in 1937." *Papers in Anthropology 13* (Spring 1972). Norman, Department of Anthropology and Anthropology Club, University of Oklahoma.

559. Ortiz, Alfonso, editor. *New Perspectives on the Pueblos.* Albuquerque: University of New Mexico Press, 1972.

An excellent collection of papers concerning prehistory, ethnohistory, and ethnology. An impressive contribution to the literature.

* 560. Oswalt, Wendell H. *Napaskiak: An Alaskan Eskimo Community.* Tucson: University of Arizona Press, 1963.

561. Oswalt, Wendell H. *Alaskan Eskimos.* San Francisco: Chandler Publishing Co., 1967.

A well organized and valuable statement.

562. Oswalt, Wendell H. "The Eskimos (Yuk) of Western Alaska." In *Modern Alaskan Native Material Culture,* pp. 73–95. College: University of Alaska Museum, 1972.

563. Paredes, J. Anthony. "The Emergence of Contemporary Eastern Creek Indian Identity." Reprinted from "Social and Cultural Identity." *Southern Anthropological Society Proceedings No. 8,* pp. 63–80. Edited by T. K. Fitzgerald. Athens: The University of Georgia Press, 1974.

Data from a small, nonreservation, rural community in Alabama are presented. They demonstrate the importance of particular events in shaping the development of one example of contemporary Indian identity.

564. Pennington, Campbell. *The Tarahumar of Mexico.* Salt Lake City: University of Utah Press, 1963.

565. Pennington, Campbell W. *The Tepehuan of Chihuahua. Their Material Culture.* Salt Lake City: University of Utah Press, 1969.

566. Peterson, Fredrick A., & Ritzenthaler, Robert. "The Kickapoos are Still Kicking." *Natural History* 64 (April 1955): 200 ff.

Concerns Kickapoos in northern Mexico.

* 567. Peterson, John Holbrook, Jr. "The Mississippi band of Choctaw Indians: their recent history and current social relations." Ph.D. dissertation, University of Georgia, 1970.

* 568. Peterson, John H., Jr. "Socio-Economic Characteristics of the Mississippi Choctaw Indians." *Report 34. Education Series 9.* Research Coordinating Unit for Vocational-Technical Education, Social Science Research Center, Mississippi State University, June, 1970. Mimeo.

569. Pollitzer, William S. "The Physical Anthropology and Genetics of Marginal People of the Southeastern United States." *American Anthropologist* 74 (June 1972): 719–734.

Concerned with distinctive gene pools developed by blacks-whites-Indians in the southeastern United States.

570. Price, John, editor. "The Luiseno Indians in 1965." UCLA Field School, xerox.

571. Rachlin, Carol K. "Tight Shoe Night: Oklahoma Indians Today." In *The American Indian Today,* pp. 160–183. Edited by Levine and Lurie, Baltimore: Penguin Books Inc., 1970.

Indians in central and western Oklahoma.

572. Raymer, Patricia. "Wisconsin's Menominees: Indians on a Seesaw." *National Geographic,* August, 1974, pp. 228–251.

573. Ridgeway, James. "The Lost Indians." *The New Republic,* December 4, 1965, pp. 17–20.

574. Ridgeway, James. "More Lost Indians." *The New Republic,* December 11, 1965, pp. 19–22.

575. Ritzenthaler, Robert. *The Oneida Indians of Wisconsin.* Bulletin of the Milwaukee Public Museum 19, no. 1, November, 1950.

576. Ritzenthaler, Robert. *The Potawatomi Indians of Wisconsin.* Bulletin of the Milwaukee Public Museum 19, no. 3, January, 1953.

577. Ritzenthaler, Robert, & Peterson, Frederick. *The Mexican Kickapoo Indians.* Publications in Anthropology 2, Milwaukee Public Museum, 1956.

Excellent but based on a very brief encounter.

578. Roberts, John M., & Schneider, David. *Zuni Daily Life.* Behavior Science Reprint, Human Relations Area Files Press, 1965.

579. Roberts, John M, & Schneider, David. *Zuni Kin Terms.* Behavior Science Reprint. Human Relations Area Files Press, 1965.

580. Robertson, Heather. *Reservations Are For Indians.* Toronto: James, Lewis, & Samuel, 1970.

A stark description of the bad life on some reserves in Canada.

581. Roessel, Robert A., Jr. *Indian Communities in Action.* Edited by Broderick H. Johnson. Tempe: Arizona State University, 1967.

* 582. Rogers, Edward S. "The Round Lake Ojibwa." *Occasional Paper 5.* Toronto: Art and Archaeology Division, Royal Ontario Museum, University of Toronto, 1962.

A substantial ethnography. Fieldwork done at Weagamow Lake continuously from July, 1958, until 1959.

* 583. Rohner, Ronald P. "The People of Gilford: A Contemporary Kwakiult Village." *Bulletin 225.* Ottawa: National Museum of Canada, 1967.

584. Rohrl, Vivian. "The People of Mille Lac." Ph.D. dissertation. University of Minnesota, 1967.

585. Roufs, Timothy G. "Wicket: A Successful Indian Community." Unpublished Paper given at the Central States Anthropological Society Meetings, 1967.

* 586. Rountree, Helen C. "Powhatan's Descendants in the Modern World: Community Studies of the Two Virginia Indian Reservations with Notes on Five Non-Reservation Enclaves." *The Chesopiean 10* (June 1972): 61–98. Norfolk, Virginia: the Chesopiean Archaeological Association.

* 587. Sasaki, Tom T. *Fruitland, New Mexico. A Navaho Community in Transition.* Ithaca: Cornell University Press, 1960.

588. Service, Elman. "Recent Observations on Havasupai Land Tenure." *Southwestern Journal of Anthropology 3* (1947): 360–366.

589. Shames, Deborah, editor. *Freedom with Reservation. The Menominee Struggle to Save Their Land and People.* Madison: National Committee to Save the Menominee People and Forests, 1972.

* 590. Shepardson, Mary, & Hammond, Blodwen. *The Navajo Mountain Community. Social Organization and Kinship Terminology.* Berkeley: University of California Press, 1970.

591. Simons, Suzanne L. "Sandia Pueblo: Persistence and Change in a New Mexican Indian Community." Ph.D. dissertation, University of New Mexico, 1970.

592. Slobodin, Richard. *Metis of the Mackenzie District.* Centre Canadien de Recherches en Anthropologie. Ottawa: Université Saint-Paul, 1966.

593. Smith, Ann. *Ethnography of the Northern Utes.* Albuquerque: University of New Mexico Press, 1975.

Considers various groups of Utes in Colorado and Utah. Data collected during the 1930's.

594. Smith, M. Estellie. "Three Tiwa Communities and Their Response to Stress for Change." Mimeo, n.d.

Compares Ysleta del Sur, Isleta, and Taos.

595. Smith, Valene L. "Kotzebue: a modern Alaskan Eskimo Community." Ph.D. dissertation, University of Utah, 1966.

596. Spaulding, Philip T. "The Metis of Ile-à-la-Crosse." Ph.D. dissertation, University of Washington, Seattle, 1970.

597. Speck, Frank. "A Social Reconnaissance of the Creole Houma Indian Trappers of the Louisiana Bayous." *America Indigena* 3 (April, July 1943): 135-146 and 211-220.

598. Speck, Frank G. "Notes on Social and Economic Conditions Among the Creek Indians of Alabama in 1941." *America Indigena* 7 (July 1947).

* 599. Spicer, Edward. *Pascua. A Yaqui Village in Arizona.* Chicago: University of Chicago Press, 1940.

600. Spindler, George, & Spindler, Louise. *Dreamers Without Power. The Menomini Indians.* New York: Holt, Rinehart & Winston, 1971.

Some useful descriptive material. The title is unfortunate and misleading.

601. Spingarn, Lawrence P. "Children of Uncas—The New England Indian Today." *The American Indian* 8 (Winter 1958-59): 36-39.

602. Standing Rock Tribal Library. *Hou Kola!!! Directory of Services on the Standing Rock Sioux Reservation.* 1974.

* 603. Stern, Theodore. "Chickahominy: The Changing Culture of a Virginia Indian Community." *Proceedings of the American Philosophical Society* 96 (April 1952): 157-230.

* 604. Stern, Theodore. "The Klamath Tribe. A People and Their Reservation." *American Ethnological Society Monograph 41.* Edited by June Helm. Seattle: University of Washington Press, 1965.

Definitive or very close to it.

605. Taylor, John M. "Decadence Amidst the Mesas." *World* 2, no. 8 (1973): 21-23.

The strange town of Santa Fe, New Mexico.

606. Thomas, R. M. *The Mission Indians: A Study of Leadership and Cultural Change.* Unpublished Ph.D. dissertation, UCLA, 1964.

607. Thompson, Edgar T. "The Little Races." *American Anthropologist* 74 (October 1972): 1295–1306.

Thoughtful and general analysis of mixed groups.

608. Trager, George L. "The Tanoan Settlement of the Rio Grande Area: A Possible Chronology." *Studies in Southwestern Ethnolinguistics.* The Hague: Mouton & Co., 335–350.

609. Trager, George L., & Smith, Estellie. "A Note on the Tigua Indians (Ysleta Del Sur) of Ysleta, El Paso, Texas." *The Florida Anthropologist* 22 (March-December 1969): 30–33.

610. *Upper Mississippi Project. Final Report.* March, 1968. (Selected pages.).

* 611. VanStone, James W. *Point Hope. An Eskimo Village in Transition.* The American Ethnological Society. Edited by V. E. Garfield. Seattle: University of Washington Press, 1962.

Concerned with the functioning of a modern Eskimo community of western Alaska. Historical data used for background, but study is largely functional and acculturational. Fieldwork done in 1955–56.

612. Vogt, E. Z., & Albert, E. M., editors. *People of Rimrock. A Study of Values in Five Cultures.* Cambridge: Harvard University Press, 1966.

613. Wahrhaftig, Albert L., & Thomas, R. K. "Renaissance and Repression: The Oklahoma Cherokee." *Trans-Action* (February 1969): 42–48.

* 614. Walker, Deward E., Jr., editor. "An Exploration of the Reservation System in North America. A Special Issue." *Northwest Anthropological Research Notes* 5 (Spring 1971).

615. Wallis, Wilson D. "The Canadian Dakota." *Anthropological Papers of the American Museum of Natural History* 41, no. 1. New York: 1947.

Field work was done during four months in 1914 at the Dakota reservation near Portage La Prairie, Manitoba. Some data were also gathered near Brandon. Data concerning a wide variety of aspects of early 20th century life are presented.

616. Ward, Duren H. "Meskwakia." *Iowa Journal of History* 4 (1906).

617. Waters, Frank. "Sky City: Venerable and Venerated, Acoma Faces the Future." *New Mexico Magazine,* July-August, 1970, pp. 4–11.

618. Waters, Frank. "The Middle Place Between Old and New Zuni Pueblo." *New Mexico Magazine,* November-December, 1971, pp. 11–12.

619. Weaver, Thomas. *Indians in Rural and Reservation Areas: Report for the California State Advisory Commission on Indian Affairs.* Sacramento: State of California Printing Office, 1966.

620. Weaver, Thomas, editor. *The Arizona Indian People and Their Relationship to the State's Total Structure.* Phoenix: Arizona Academy, 1971.

621. Weaver, Thomas, editor. *Indians of Arizona. A Contemporary Perspective.* Tucson: University of Arizona Press, 1974.

622. Weidemann, Wayne H., & Fuguitt, Glenn V. "Menominee: Wisconsin's 72nd County." *Population Note No. 3.* Madison: Department of Rural Sociology, College of Agriculture, University of Wisconsin, 1963. Mimeo. 33 pp.

623. Weist, K. M. "The Northern Cheyennes: Diversity in A Loosely Structured Society." Ph.D. dissertation, University of California, 1970. Ann Arbor: University Microfilms, xerox copy.

624. Welch, James. *Winter in the Blood.* New York: Harper & Row, 1974.

An excellent novel, written by an Indian, about Blackfoot in Montana. The time is the present. Life is grim on a small cattle ranch.

625. Welch, Joseph. "Brothers of Passamaquodia." *Ramparts* 5 (March 1967): 40-45. Menlo Park, California.

626. "Where the Tribes Gather." *The Herald Focus.* Wausau Daily Record-Herald. April 19, 1974, pp. 1-3.

627. White, Leslie A. "The Pueblo of Sia, New Mexico." *Bulletin 184, Bureau of American Ethnology, Smithsonian Institution.* Washington, D.C: Government Printing Office, 1962.

628. Wilson, Edmund. *Apologies to the Iroquois.* New York: Vintage Books, Random House, 1966.

* 629. Winnebago Wittenberg Community. *Grant Proposal Describing Some Community Activites.* Typed, n.d.

630. Wisconsin Legislative Council. *Report of Menominee Indian Study Committee.* Submitted to the Governor and the 1969 Legislature, January, 1970.

631. Wisconsin Peace Action Committee. *Wisconsin Enquirer—A Short History of Menominee Troubles.* 1971.

632. Wissler, Clark. *Red Man Reservations.* New York: Collier Books, 1971. Originally published as *Indian Cavalcade or Life on the Old-Time Indian Reservations.* New York: Sheridan House, 1938.

Indian reservations at the turn of the century in the Plains area. Essential reading.

633. Wolf, Bernard. *Tinker and the Medicine Men. The Story of a Navajo Boy of Monument Valley.* New York: Random House, 1973.

Excellent pictures and commentary.

634. Wright, Muriel H. *A Guide to the Indian Tribes of Oklahoma.* 4th printing, 1951.

Substantial but now dated. A new edition should be issued.

635. Young, Robert W. *The Navajo Yearbook. Report No. 8, 1951–1961. A Decade of Progress.* Window Rock: Navajo Agency, 1961.

636. The Zuni People. *The Zunis. Self-Portrayals.* Alvina Quam, translator. Albuquerque, University of New Mexico Press, 1972.

IX. Linguistics—Languages

637. Basso, Keith H. "The Western Apache Classificatory Verb System: A Formal Analysis." *Southwestern Journal of Anthropology* 24, no. 3 (1968): 252–266.

638. Basso, Keith H. "Ice and Travel Among the Fort Norman Slave: Folk Taxonomies and Cultural Rules." *Language in Society* 1, no. 1 (1972): 31–49.

639. Basso, Keith H. with Anderson, Ned. "A Western Apache Writing System: the Symbols of Silas John." *Science* 180 (1973): 1013–1022.

640. Black, Robert A. "Hopi Rabbit-Hunt Chants: A Ritualized Language." *Essays on the Verbal and Visual Arts. Proceedings of the Annual Spring Meeting, American Ethnological Society.* Edited by June Helm. Seattle: University of Washington Press, 1966.

641. Bodine, John J. "Taos Names: A Clue to Linguistic Acculturation." *Anthropological Linguistics.* (May 1968): 23–27.

* 642. Chafe, Wallace L. "Estimates Regarding the Present Speakers of North American Indian Languages." *International Journal of American Linguistics.* 28 (1962): 162–171.

* 643. Chafe, Wallace L. "Corrected Estimates Regarding Speakers of Indian Languages." *International Journal of American Linguistics* 31 (1965): 345–346.

644. Dempsey, Hugh A. "Indian Names for Alberta Communities." *Occasional Paper No. 4.* Calgary: Glenbow-Alberta Institute, 1969.

645. Dozier, Edward P. "Kinship and Linguistic Change among the Arizona Tewa." *International Journal of American Linguistics* 21 (July 1955): 242–257.

646. Fox, Robin. "Multilingualism in Two Communities." *Man* 3 (Sept., 1968): 456–464.

Compares Cochiti with Tory Island off the coast of Donegal. Fox attempts to determine if there are any meaningful patterns in the differential use of the various languages within the communities. He concludes that language is more than just a mirror of reality but is an effective part of the reality of social change.

647. Mickelson, Norma I., & Calloway, C. G. "Cumulative Language Deficit Among Indian Children." *Exceptional Children* 36 (November 1969): 187–190.

648. Spencer, Robert F. "The Phonemes of Keresan." *International Journal of American Linguistics.* 12 (1946): 229–236.

649. Spencer, Robert F. "Spanish Loanwords in Keresan." *Southwestern Journal of Anthropology* 3 (1947): 130–146.

650. Walker, Willard. "The Design of Writing Systems for Native Literacy Programs." Prepared for the Symposium on American Indian Languages II. American Anthropological Association meeting, November, 1968.

651. White, Harriet. "Some Observations of Culture and Language Maintenance in a New Mexico Indian Pueblo." Xerox copy of manuscript August, 1971. 32 pp.

Concerns Jemez.

652. White, John K. "On the Revival of Printing in the Cherokee Language." *Current Anthropology* 3 (December 1962): 511–514.

X. Stability and Change in Culture

653. Adair, John, & Vogt, Evon. "Navaho and Zuni Veterans: A Study of Contrasting Modes of Culture Change." *American Anthropologist* 51 (October-December 1949): 547–561.

654. Adair, John. "A Pueblo G.I." In *The Company of Man,* pp. 489–503. Edited by J. B. Casagrande. New York: Harper Torchbooks, 1960.

Useful descriptive data plus a discussion of the problems associated with doing research in a pueblo.

655. "After 100 Years, the Navajo." *The Arizona Republic* 7 (January 1968).

656. Ames, David W., & Fisher, Burton R. "The Menominee Termination Crisis: Barriers in the Way of a Rapid Cultural Transition." *Human Organization* 18 (Fall 1959): 101–111.

657. Armsby, E. R., & Rockwell, J. G. "New Directions Among Northern California Indians." *The American Indian* 4, no. 3 (1948): 12–23.

658. Artichoker, John, Jr. reviser. *Indians of South Dakota. Bulletin No. 67A.* Pierre: South Dakota Department of Public Instruction in cooperation with the South Dakota Indian Commission, 1956.

   Useful general information. Somewhat biased.

* 659. Atamian, Sarkis. "The Anaktuvuk Mask and Cultural Innovation." *Science* 151 (March 18, 1966): 1337–1345.

   Excellent study of the creation and acceptance of Caribou hide masks by some Eskimos in western Alaska.

660. Bahti, Tom. *Southwestern Indian Tribes.* Flagstaff: KC Publications, 1968.

   A brief discussion of 38 tribes/communities in the contemporary Southwest. Excellent illustrations and photographs.

661. Bailey, Garrick A. "Changes in Osage Social Organization: 1673–1969." Ph.D. dissertation, University of Oregon, 1969.

662. Basso, Keith H. "Semantic Aspects of Linguistic Acculturation." *American Anthropologist 69,* no. 5 (1967): 471–477.

663. Basso, Keith H. *The Cibecue Apache.* New York: Holt, Rinehart & Winston, 1970.

   Considerable material on the contemporary situation.

664. Basso, Keith H. "Western Apache Ecology: From Horticulture to Agriculture." With P. Bion Griffin and Mark P. Leone. In *Apachean Culture History and Ethnology.* Edited by Keith H. Basso and Morris E. Opler. *Anthropological Papers of the University of Arizona,* No. 21. Tuscon: University of Arizona Press, 1971.

665. Basso, Keith H. Review of *The Jicarilla Apaches* by Gertrude Van Roekel. The Naylor Press. In *American Anthropologist* 75 (1973): 422–423.

666. Bean, L. "Cultural Change in Cahuilla Religious and Political Leadership Patterns." In *Culture Change and Stability,* pp. 1–10. Edited by R. Beale, Los Angeles: University of California Press, 1964.

667. Bean, Lowell John. "Cahuilla Indian Cultural Ecology." Ph.D. dissertation, University of California, Los Angeles, 1970.

668. Bee, Robert L. "Changes in Yuma Social Organization." *Ethnology* 2 (April 1963): 207–227.

669. Bee, Robert L. "Sociocultural Change and Persistence in the Yuma Indian Reservation Community." Ph.D. dissertation, University of Kansas, 1967.

    Fieldwork done in 1961 and 1966.

* 670. Bennett, John W. *Northern Plainsmen. Adaptive Strategy and Agrarian Life.* Chicago: Aldine Publishing Co., 1969.

    A studying of the varying modes of adaptation of four distinct cultural groups on the plains of Saskatchewan: Indians, ranchers, farmers, and Hutterites. Research was done in the early 1960's. Ecological analysis at its best.

671. Bennett, Kay. *Kaibah: Recollection of a Navajo Girlhood.* Great West and Indian Series 27. Los Angeles: Westernlore Press, 1964.

    "The story of an average Navajo girl during the period from 1928 to 1935." Useful data concerning how one Navajo family lived during seven critical years.

672. Berreman, Gerald D. "Aleut Reference Group Alienation, Mobility and Acculturation." *American Anthropologist* 66 (April 1964): 231–250.

    Essential.

673. Bigart, Robert J. "Patterns of Cultural Change in a Salish Flathead Community." *Human Organization* 30 (Fall 1971): 229–237.

* 674. Bishop, Charles A. *The Northern Ojibwa and the Fur Trade: An Historical and Ecological Study.* Toronto: Holt, Rinehart & Winston of Canada, Ltd., 1974.

    Archival materials and field observations are used. Argues that Northern Ojibwa social organization has switched from a clan-totem system at contact to a flexible bilateral one today.

675. Blackman, Margaret. "Ethnohistoric Changes in the Haida Potlatch Complex." Paper given at the American Anthropological Association meetings, Nov., 1974.

    Changes in Haida potlatch brought about by acculturation.

676. Bodine, John J. "Symbiosis at Taos: The Impact of Tourism on the Pueblo." Paper given at Central State Anthropological Society meetings, 1964.

677. Bodine, John J. "Cultural Stability vs. Instability of Taos Pueblo Indians." *American Philosophical Society Year Book* (1964): 456–459.

678. Bodine, John J. "Acculturation Processes and Population Dynamics." In *New Perspectives on the Pueblos.* Edited by Alfonso Ortiz. Albuquerque: University of New Mexico Press, School of American Research, 1972.

679. Bodine, John J. "Tourism and Culture Change in the Eastern Pueblos of New Mexico." Paper given at the American Anthropological Association meetings, Nov., 1974.

    The different effect of the tourist on the eighteen Eastern Pueblos.

680. Boggs, Stephen T. "Culture Change and the Personality of Ojibwa Children." *American Anthropologist* 60 (February 1958): 47–58.

    Field work done in 1951–52 in Wisconsin and Manitoba.

681. Boissevain, Ethel. "The Detribalization of the Narragansett Indians: A Case Study." *Ethnohistory* 3 (1956): 225–245.

    Indians of Rhode Island in 1880.

682. Boissevain, Ethel. "Narragansett Survival: A Study of Group Persistence Through Adapted Traits." *Ethnohistory* 6 (Fall, 1959): 347–359.

    Considers the means now used by this group to maintain their identity.

683. Brown, Donald N. "Structural Change at Picuris Pueblo, New Mexico." Ph.D. dissertation, University of Arizona, 1973.

684. Bullen, Adelaide K. "Chapter 24. Florida Indians of Past and Present." In *Florida from Indian Trail to Space Age 1.* Edited by Tebeau. Delray Beach: Southern Publishing Co., 1965.

    Brief comments, photographs concerning Seminole.

685. California Indian Legal Services, Inc. *An Explanation of Termination.* Berkeley: California Indian Legal Services, 1968.

* 686. Campisi, Jack. "Ethnic Identity and Boundary Maintenance in Three Oneida Communities." Ph.D. dissertation, State University of New York at Albany, 1974.

    Describes the social structure of three Oneida Indian communities so as to examine the mechanisms by which ethnic identity has been maintained in the face of extended contact with a dominant culture.

687. Capron, Louis. "Florida's Emerging Seminoles." *National Geographic,* November, 1969, pp. 717–734.

    Excellent pictures.

688. Castile, George P. "Federal Indian Policy and the Sustained Enclave: An Anthropological Perspective." *Human Organization* 33 (Fall, 1974): 219–228.

Some possible changes associated with recent shifts in federal policy.

689. Chance, Norman A. "Culture Change and Integration: An Eskimo Example." *American Anthropologist* 62 (December 1960): 1028–1044.

Concerns North Alaskan Eskimo, village of Kaktovik. Data collected in the summer of 1958. These Eskimos have been able to adjust to acculturation without the disintegration of their community.

690. Chance, Norman A. "Acculturation, Self-Identification and Personality Adjustment." *American Anthropologist* 67 (April 1965): 372–393.

Concerns North Alaskan Eskimos-Kaktovik village, Barter Island, 400 miles northeast of Fairbanks. The village men are in a better position to make a successful psychological adaptation to the process of acculturation than the women. Fieldwork done in the 1950's.

691. Chance, Norman A., editor. "Conflict in Culture: Problems of Developmental Change Among the Cree." In *Document 2: Working Papers of the Cree Developmental Change Project.* Ottawa: Canadian Research Centre for Anthropology, St. Paul University, 1968.

Fieldwork done in the 1960's with Waswanipi-Mistassini Cree. The Cree Project is a long-term study of socio-economic change and political development. The nature and quality of development schemes, the factors influencing Cree Indian involvement in them, and the social and psychological impact of this involvement on Indian life are three major points of reference.

692. Christian, Jane M. "The Navajo. A People in Transition, Part I." *Southwestern Studies* 2 (Fall 1964): 3–35.

A summary of several published sources concerning the development of Navajo tribal government.

693. Christian, Jane M. "The Navajo. A People in Transition, Part II." *Southwestern Studies* 2 (Winter 1965): 39–69.

A continuation of Part I.

694. Clemmer, Richard. "The Fed-up Hopi: Resistence of the American Indian and the Silence of the Good Anthropologists." *Journal of the Steward Anthropological Society* 1 (Fall 1969): 18–40.

Describes the Hopi resistence to acculturation. Some attention is given to theoretical implications.

695. Clemmer, Richard O. "Directed resistence to acculturation: a comparative study of the effects of non-Indian jurisdiction of Hopi and western Shoshone communities." Ph.D. dissertation, University of Illinois, 1972.

696. Clifton, James A. "Sociocultural Dynamics of the Prairie Potawatomi Drum Cult." *Plains Anthropologist* 14 (May 1969): 85-93.

   Discusses the contemporary Potawatomi Drum Cult in terms of both internal and external processes of change, examines and attempts to account for a major re-direction of the Cult's manifest goals, and discusses the functions of its ritual activities in the contemporary reservation community.

697. Collier, John. "Comments on the Essay of Robert A. Manners, 'Pluralism and the American Indian.' " *America Indigena* 22 (1962): 205-208.

   A total misunderstanding and rejection of Manners' argument.

698. Collier, John. "Final Reply of John Collier." *America Indigena* 23 (1963): 76-77.

   "The issue raised in Dr. Manners' original essay is a wider, profounder issue than perhaps he himself, as yet, knows." p. 77.

699. Collins, Daniel. "The Racially-Mixed People of the Ramapos: Undoing the Jackson White Legends." *American Anthropologist* 74 (October 1972): 1276-1285.

   A racially mixed group in the Ramapo Valley near Suffern, New York.

700. Colson, Elizabeth. "Assimilation of an American Indian Group." In *Beyond the Frontier. Social Process and Cultural Change,* pp. 209-226. Edited by Bohannan and Plog. New York: American Museum Sourcebooks in Anthropology, The Natural History Press, 1967.

701. Cook, S. F. "Racial Fusion Among the California and Nevada Indians." *Human Biology* 15 (1943): 153-167.

702. Cook, S. F. "The Conflict Between the California Indian and White Civilization: IV. Trends in Marriage and Divorce Since 1850." *Ibero-Americana* 24 (1943).

703. Corrigan, Samuel W. "The Plains Indian Powwow: Cultural Integration in Manitoba and Saskatchewan." *Anthropologica* N.S. 12 (1970): 253-277.

   Interesting data on Pan-Indianism.

704. Cowan, Clara B. "Assimilation of the Cherokees (As Revealed in a Hundred Urban Families)." M.A. Thesis, University of Missouri, 1941.

705. Dempsey, Hugh A. "Jerry Potts, Plainsman." *Occasional Paper No. 2*, Calgary: Glenbow-Alberta Institute, 1966.

706. Diamond, Stanley, Sturtevant, William C., Fenton, William H. "Memorandum Submitted to Subcommittees on Indian Affairs of the Senate and House of Representatives." *American Anthropologist* 66 (June 1964): 631–633.

> Concerns the Allegany Seneca. "Our intention is to help clarify the cultural component in the question of Indian rights, and suggest a basis for just compensation in the event of the whole or partial abrogation of these rights."

707. Dixon, Joseph K. *The Vanishing Race. The Last Great Indian Council. A Record in Picture and Story of the Last Great Indian Council, Participated in by Eminent Indian Chiefs From Nearly Every Indian Reservation in the United States, Together With the Story of Their Lives as Told by Themselves—Their Speeches and Folklore Tales—Their Solemn Farewell and the Indians' Story of the Custer Fight.* Rodman Wanamaker, 1913. Reprint edition, New York: Popular Library, 1972.

> Held in 1909 at the Little Big Horn, Montana. Not as overwhelming as the title suggests, but worth a careful reading against a background of reality.

* 708. Downs, James F. "The Cowboy and the Lady: Models as a determinant of the rate of acculturation among the Pinon Navajo." *Kroeber Anthropological Society Papers* No. 29 (Fall 1963). Reprint.

> Sexual determinants in acculturation and the imperfections of current models for the study of acculturation.

709. Downs, James F. "The Consequences of a Dry Well." *American Anthropologist* 67, no. 6, part 1 (1965): 1387–1416.

> Concerns Pinon Navajo. Detailed description of a Navajo extended family when confronted with a diminishing water supply.

* 710. Dozier, E. P., Simpson, G. E., and Yinger, M. J. "The Integration of Americans of Indian Descent." *The Annals of the American Academy of Political and Social Science* 311 (May 1957): 158–165.

> An influential statement.

711. Dunning, R. W. "Some Implications of Economic Change in Northern Ojibwa Social Structure." *Canadian Journal of Economics and Political Science* 24, no. 4 (1958).

712. Dunning, R. W. "Ethnic Relations and the Marginal Man in Canada." *Human Organization* 18 (Fall 1959): 117–122.

713. Dunning, R. W. *Social and Economic Change among the Northern Ojibwa.*
Toronto: University of Toronto Press, 1959.

Excellent scholarship.

714. Einhorn, Arthur. "Cycles of Reciprocity: The History, Impressions and
Problems of Cultural Continuity as Seen in a Comparison of Reservation and
Urban Indians." Central States Anthropological Society meetings, May,
1969.

Iroquois data.

715. Euler, Robert C. "Environmental Adaptation at Sia Pueblo." *Human
Organization* 12 (Winter 1954): 27–30.

Reports a recent Indian Service attempt to establish a land improvement
program at Sia, and demonstrates the role of Sia culture-history in the
acceptance or rejection of this project. Fieldwork done in the spring of
1952.

716. Fenton, William. N. "From Longhouse to Ranch-type House. The Second
Revolution of the Seneca Nation." In *Iroquois Culture, History, and
Prehistory, Proceedings of the 1965 Congress on Iroquois Research,* pp. 7–
22. Edited by E. Tooker. Albany: New York State Museum and Science
Service, 1967.

Concerns new housing built for families moved because of the building of
the Kinzua Dam. Seneca of the Allegany and Cattaragus reservations are
involved. The political, social and ceremonial dimensions are discussed.

717. Fontana, Bernard L. "The Melting Pot That Wouldn't. Ethnic Groups in the
American Southwest Since 1846." *American Indian Culture and Research
Journal* 1, no. 2 (1974): 18–24. Los Angeles: University of California.

718. Freilich, Morris. "Cultural Persistence Among the Modern Iroquois."
Anthropos 53 (1958): 473–483.

719. Friedl, Ernestine. "Persistence in Chippewa Culture and Personality."
American Anthropologist 58 (October 1956): 814–825.

Why Chippewa culture and personality have persisted.

720. Garbarino, Merwyn S. "Decision-Making Process and the Study of Culture
Change." *Ethnology* 6 (October 1967): 465–470.

"In a study of changing economic and political conditions at the Big
Cypress Indian Reservation I found that, although the form of voting was
accepted with enthusiasm by the residents, it was accepted without the
function and meaning it has in the non-reservation society of the United

States. Although 'leaders' are now elected, decisions are still made on the basis of unanimity, the traditional way for making community decisions." p. 465.

721. Gillen, John, and Raimy, B. "Acculturation and Personality." *American Sociological Review* 5 (1940): 351-380.

722. Gillen, John. "Acquired Drives in Culture Contact." *American Anthropologist* 44 (1942): 545-554.

723. Goldfrank, Esther S. "Changing Configurations in the Social Organization of a Blackfoot Tribe During the Reserve Period (The Blood of Alberta, Canada)." *Monographs of the American Ethnological Society* 8. Edited by A. I. Hallowell. Seattle: University of Washington Press, 1945.

Based on nine weeks of fieldwork in the summer of 1939. She concludes that the quick divorce of a money economy from a horse economy by those who begin to farm in 1910 is due to the fact that they had the smallest stake in the benefits offered by their society. The programs of the Canadian government have not succeeded in resolving the social conflicts in the community.

724. Gould, R. A., Fowler, D. D., and Fowler, C. S. "Diggers and Doggers: Parallel Failures in Economic Acculturation." *Southwestern Journal of Anthropology* 28 (Autumn 1972): 265-281.

Both the Western Desert Aborigines of Australia and the Numic-speaking Indians of the Great Basin of North America have followed a pattern of economic acculturation characterized by increased dependence on European food and goods rather than by the establishment of a viable relationship to the world economy.

* 725. Graburn, Nelson H. H. *Eskimos Without Igloos. Social and Economic Development in Sugluk.* Boston: Little, Brown and Co., 1969.

Concerns the history and sequence of changes among Eskimos along the south coast of the Hudson Strait, the Takamiut, "people of the shadow." Fieldwork done in 1959, 1964, and 1968.

726. Graves, T. D. "Psychological Acculturation in a Tri-Ethnic Community." *Publication No. 102. IBS.* Boulder: University of Colorado, n.d.

727. Graves, T. D., & Van Arsdale, M. "Values, Expectations and Relocation: The Navaho Migrant to Denver." *Publication 92. IBS.* Boulder: University of Colorado, n.d. Mimeo.

728. Graves, Theodore D. "Psychological Acculturation in a Tri-Ethnic Community." *Southwestern Journal of Anthropology* 23 (Winter 1967): 337-350.

729. Griffith, Charles R. "Navaho Intercultural Marriage: A Study of

Acculturation in a Small Group." Ph.D. dissertation, Harvard University, 1960.

Navaho-black relations. An excellent study.

730. Gulick, John. *Cherokees at the Crossroads.* Chapel Hill: University of North Carolina Press, 1960.

A very general analysis.

731. Hallowell, A. Irving. "The Impact of the American Indian on American Culture." *American Anthropologist* 59 (December, 1963). 519-531.

732. Hallowell, A. I. "American Indians, White and Black: The Phenomenon of Transculturalization." *Current Anthropology* 4 (April 1957): 201-217.

Required reading for all those interested in North American ethnology.

733. Hawley, Florence. "An Examination of Problems Basic to Acculturation in the Rio Grande Pueblos." *American Anthropologist* 50 (1948): 612-624.

734. Hawley, Florence. *Some Factors in the Indian Problem in New Mexico.* Albuquerque: University of New Mexico Press, 1948.

735. Hedgepeth, William *et al.* "America's Indians. Reawakening of a Conquered People." *Look,* June 2, 1970, pp. 23 ff.

736. Heizer, R. F., & Almquist, A. J. *The Other Californians.* Berkeley: University of California Press, 1971.

Deals briefly with the first two decades of Indian-American relations; treats with the Indian indenture act of 1850.

737. Heizer, Robert F., editor. "They Were Only Diggers. A Collection of Articles from California Newspapers, 1851-1866, on Indian and White Relations." *Publications in Archaeology, Ethnology and History No. 1.* Ramona, California: Ballena Press, 1974.

A collection of 188 newspaper articles on California Indian-White relations.

738. Helm, June, Rogers, E. S., and Smith, J. G. E. "Intercultural Relations and Cultural Change in the Subarctic Shield and Mackenzie Lowlands." Chapter in forthcoming *Volume VI. The Subarctic. Handbook of North American Indians.* Edited by June Helm. Washington, D.C.: Smithsonian Institution. Draft, n.d.

739. Henriksen, Georg. "Hunters in the Barrens. The Naskapi on the Edge of the White's Man's World." *Newfoundland Social and Economic Studies No. 12.* St. John's: Institute of Social and Economic Research, Memorial University of Newfoundland, 1973.

Fieldwork done between 1966 and 1968. "The Naskapi live in two different worlds: in the winter, they roam the interior of Labrador, hunting caribou; in the summer, they live in or around the village of Davis Inlet on the coast of Labrador." One of the themes explored in the book is the contrast in the social life between these two worlds.

740. Hicks, George L. "Catawba Acculturation and the Ideology of Race." In *Symposium on New Approaches to the Study of Religion,* pp. 116–124. Edited by June Helm. Proceedings of the Annual Spring Meeting, American Ethnological Society. Seattle: University of Washington Press, 1964.

741. Hill, W. W. "Comments. Intercultural Relations in the Greater Southwest." *American Anthropologist* 56, no. 4, part 1 (1954): 657–658.

742. Hinlaw, Gil. "Santo Domingo Irked by California Charity." *Albuquerque Journal,* April 4, 1963.

An interesting reaction of a New Mexico Pueblo community.

743. Hinton, Thomas B. "A Survey of Indian Assimilation in Eastern Sonora." *Anthropological Papers of the University No. 4.* Tucson: University of Arizona Press, 1959.

A survey to determine what, if anything, remains of the aboriginal groups of the area. The three groups considered (Opata, Jova, Lower Pima) are no longer tribal Indians, but instead represent varying degrees of assimilation into modern Mexico. Fieldwork done in 1955–1956.

744. Hippler, Arthur E. "Some Unplanned Consequences of Planned Culture Changes." Manuscript, January, 1969.

Alaska.

745. Hippler, Arthur E. "The Game of Black and White at Hunters Point." *Trans-action* (1970): 56–63.

746. Hoffman, James. "A Comeback for the Vanishing American?" *Exclusively Yours* 22 (October 14, 1969): 11–20.

747. Holden, David E. W. "Modernization Among Town and Bush Cree in Quebec." *Canadian Review of Sociology and Anthropology* 6, no. 4 (1969): 237–248.

* 748. Howard, James H. "Pan-Indian Culture of Oklahoma." *Scientific Monthly* 81 (November 1955): 215–220.

749. Howard, James, and Gluckman, Stephen J. "The Micmac Bowl Game." *American Indian Tradition* 8, no. 5 (1962): 206–209.

750. Howard, James H. "Environment and Culture: The Case of the Oklahoma

Seneca-Cayuga." *Oklahoma Anthropological Society Newsletter* 19, no. 6 (1970): 1-13.

751. Howard, James. "The Ponca Shinny Game." *The Indian Historian* 4 (Fall 1971): 10-15.

752. Howard, James. *Pan-Indianism.* Personal Communication, 1972.

753. Hudson, Charles M., editor. "Red, White, and Black. Symposium on Indians in the Old South." *Southern Anthropological Society. Proceedings, No. 5.* Athens: University of Georgia Press, 1971.

* 754. Hughes, Charles C. "Under Four Flags: Recent Culture Change Among the Eskimos." *Current Anthropology* 6 (February 1965): 3-73.

An excellent account. Necessary reading.

755. "Indian Agent H. N. Rust—Conflict of Interest." *San Francisco Chronicle,* August 24, 1892.

Account of a venal Mission Indian agent's activities; reprinted in *Reprints of Various Papers on California Archaeology, Ethnology and Indian History.* Edited by R. F. Heizer. Berkeley: Archaeological Research Facility, 1973.

* 756. Jackson, Helen Hunt. "A Century of Dishonor." In *The Early Crusade for Indian Reform.* Edited by A. F. Rolle. New York: Harper Torchbooks, Harper & Row, 1965. Original edition, Harper & Brothers, 1881.

Discusses Delawares, Cheyennes, Nez Perces, Sioux, Poncas, Winnebagos, Cherokees. Essential reading.

757. Jacobs, Wilbur R. *Dispossessing the American Indian.* New York: Charles Scribner's & Sons, 1972.

"A chronicle of dispossession and an historical explanation of the process of acculturation by which a new culture was formed on the American frontier . . . the first effort of a historian to apply the concept of cultural ecology to a contact situation." (From the dust cover). Appendix 2 is titled: "Chronological Highlights of Early Native-White Contacts in Australia and Papua-New Guinea." Very useful maps.

758. James, Bernard J. "Social-Psychological Dimensions of Ojibwa Acculturation." *American Anthropologist* 63, no. 4 (1961): 721-746.

Important.

* 759. James, Bernard. "Continuity and Emergence in Indian Poverty Culture." *Current Anthropology,* 11 (October-December 1970): 435-452.

An important statement.

760. Keesing, Felix M. "Culture Change. An Analysis and Bibliography of Anthropological Sources to 1952." *Stanford Anthropological Series No. 1.* Stanford: Stanford University Press, 1953.

A limited number of selections considered, but nevertheless useful.

761. Kehoe, Alice B. *The Roads of Life: Dakota and Cree Adaptations to Twentieth-Century Saskatchewan.* Toronto: Holt, Rinehart and Winston of Canada Ltd., in press.

762. Kennard, Edward A. "Post-War Economic Changes Among the Hopi." *Essays in Economic Anthropology.* Proceedings of the annual spring meetings, American Ethnological Society, pp 25–32. Seattle: University of Washington Press, 1965.

763. Koch, Walton B. "The Native Alaskan Social Movement." Ph.D. dissertation, Washington State University, 1971.

764. Kupferer, Harriet J. "Cherokee Change: A Departure from Lineal Models of Acculturation." *Anthropologica* N.S. 5, no. 2 (1963): 187–198.

North Carolina Cherokee.

765. Kurtz, Ronald J. "Role Change and Cultural Change: The Canyoncito Navaho Case." Ph.D. dissertation, University of New Mexico, 1963.

766. La Farge, Oliver, editor. *The Changing Indian.* Norman: University of Oklahoma Press, 1942.

Useful collection of papers written by Kennard, Linton, J. H. Provinse, Beatty, MacGregor, etc.

767. La Farge, Oliver. "Termination of Federal Supervision: Disintegration and the American Indians." *The Annals of the American Academy of Political and Social Science* 311 (May 1957): 41–46.

768. La Farge, Oliver. "The Enduring Indian." *Scientific American,* February, 1960, pp. 37–45.

769. Landy, David. "Tuscarora Tribalism and National Identity." *Ethnohistory* 5 (1958): 250–284.

770. Lang, Gottgtied O. "A Study in Culture Contact and Culture Change: the Whiterocks Utes in Transition." *Anthropological Papers of the University of Utah, No. 14.* Salt Lake City, University of Utah, 1953.

771. LaViolette, Forest E. *The Struggle for Survival. Indian Cultures and the Protestant Ethnic in British Columbia.* Toronto: University of Toronto Press, 1973.

Some Indians' response to white society with emphasis given to potlatch law, the land question and the rise of groups of an economic or 'protestant' nature.

772. Laxson, Joan Dorothy. "Aspects of Acculturation Among American Indians. Emphasis on Contemporary Pan-Indianism." Ph.D. dissertation, University of California, Berkeley, 1972.

773. Leacock, Eleanor B. Review of *Menomini Women and Culture Change* by Louis Spindler. *American Anthropologist* 65, no. 4 (1963); 940-942.

774. Leacock, Eleanor. Review of *Cultural Stability and Change Among the Montagnais Indians of the Lake Melville Region of Labrador* by John McGee. In *American Anthropologist* 65, no. 4 (1963): 942-943.

775. Leacock, Eleanor. Review of "Ecological Factors and Social Change Among the Mistanini Cree,: by Rolf Knight. In *American Anthropologist* 71, No. 3 (1969): 512-514.

776. Lesser, Alexander. "Education and the Future of Tribalism in the United States: The Case of the American Indian." *Social Service Review* 35 (June 1961): 1-9.

Essential.

777. Levine, Stuart. "The Survival of Indian Identity." In *The American Indian Today,* pp. 9-45. Edited by Levine and Lurie. Baltimore: Penguin Books Inc., 1970.

A general and sometimes vague exploration of white misconceptions concerning Indians.

778. Levy, Jerrold E. "After Custer: A Study of Changing Kiowa Political and Social Organization from the Reservation Period to the Present." Ph.D. dissertation, University of Chicago, 1959.

779. Lewis, Claudia. *Indian Families of the Northwest Coast. The Impact of Change.* Chicago: University of Chicago Press, 1970.

Salish living on the east coast of Vancouver Island.

780. Lewis, Nathan B. "The Last of the Narragansetts." *Bulletin No. 1, Worcester Historical Society.* Worcester, Massachusetts: 1897.

781. Lurie, Nancy O. "Comments on Bernard J. James's Analysis of Ojibwa Acculturation." *American Anthropologist* 64, no. 4 (1962): 826-833.

782. Lurie, Nancy O. "The Enduring Indian." *Natural History* 75 (November 1966): 10-22.

783. Lurie, Nancy O. "Menominee Termination." *The Indian Historian* (Winter 1971): 31-45. Reprint.

784. Lurie, Nancy O. "Menominee Termination: From Reservation to Colony." *Human Organization* 31 (Fall 1972): 257-270.

785. McFee, Malcolm. "The 150% Man, a Product of Blackfeet Acculturation." *American Anthropologist* 70 (December 1968): 1096-1108.

Uses a questionable theoretical framework.

786. MacGregor, G. "The Social and Economic Adjustment of the Indians of the Sacramento Jurisdiction of California." *Proceedings of the [Fifth] Pacific Science Congress* 6, no. 4 (1939): 53-58.

787. MacNeish, June Helm. "Problems of Acculturation and Livelihood in a Northern Indian Band." *Contributions à l'étude des sciences de l'homme* 3 (1956): 169-181.

788. McNickle, D'Arcy. "The Indian Tests the Mainstream." *The Nation,* September 26, 1966, pp. 275-279.

789. McNickle, D'Arcy. *Native American Tribalism. Indian Survivals and Renewals.* (Revised and expanded version of *The Indian Tribes of the United States*). New York: Institute of Race Relations, Oxford University Press, 1973.

790. Madigan, La Verne. "Indian Survival in the Great Plains." *Indian Affairs* 22 (September 1957).

791. Makofsky, Abraham. "Tradition and Change in the Lumbee Community of Baltimore." Ph.D. dissertation, Catholic University, Washington, D.C., 1971.

792. Malan, Vernon D. *To Change a Culture.* Brookings: Agricultural Experiment Station, South Dakota University, n.d.

The difficulties of the Pine Ridge Sioux successfully adjusting to the non-Indian world.

793. Malan, Vernon D. "Theories of Culture Change Relevant to the Study of the Dakota Indians." *Plains Anthropologist* 6 (February 1961).

794. Manners, Robert A. "Pluralism and the American Indian." *America Indigena* 22 (1962): 25-38.

"In order that most American Indian groups may grow or live at all, it may be necessary that they abandon their Indian 'way of life,' whatever that may be. If sheer survival demands the loss of their 'identity' as a group it is too bad, but others have had to pay this price before. It may well be the price most American Indians will have to pay for their continued existence as individuals." p. 38.

795. Manners, Robert A. "Robert A. Manners Answers John Collier's Comments on His Article." *America Indigena* 23 (1963): 71-75.

A carefully measured statement to the effect that Collier is being irrational.

796. Mason, Leonard. "The Swampy Cree: A Study of Acculturation." *Anthropological Papers No. 13.* Ottawa: National Museum of Canada, 1967.

797. Mead, Margaret. "The Changing Culture of an Indian Tribe." *Columbia Contributions to Anthropology. Volume 15.* New York: Columbia University Press, 1932. Reprint edition, New York: Capricorn Books, 1966 (with a new introduction).

The Omaha are referred to as the "Antlers." Fieldwork was done in 1930. Mead is concerned largely with the study of tribal women as they reacted to white contact.

798. Meriam, Lewis *et al. The Problem of Indian Administration.* Baltimore: Institute for Government Research, Studies in Administration, Johns Hopkins Press, 1928.

Necessary reading for all those concerned with American Indians.

799. Miller, J. J. "The Anthropology of Keres Identity." Ph.D. dissertation, Rutgers University, 1972. Ann Arbor: University Microfilms, on demand.

Loud echoes of Levi-Strauss. To be read in conjunction with the works of F. Eggan, Robin Fox, and Charles Lange. Stimulating.

800. *Mississippi Band of Choctaw Indians. An Era of Change.* Philadelphia, Mississippi: 1972.

801. Moore, Harvey C. "Culture Change in a Navaho Community." In *American Historical Anthropology. Essays in Honor of Leslie Spier,* pp. 123-136. Edited by C. L. Riley & W. W. Taylor. Carbondale: University of Southern Illinois Press, 1967.

802. Morgan, Lael. *And the Land Provides. Alaskan Natives in a Year of Transition.* Garden City, New York: Doubleday and Company, 1974.

Personal account of life in six Alaskan villages facing modernization through huge oil company investments and U.S. land claim awards. Sixty photographs.

* 803. Nagata, Shuichi. *Modern Transformations of Moenkopi Pueblo.* Champaign-Urbana: *Illinois Studies in Anthropology No. 6,* 1970.

One of the finest studies ever made of the Hopi. Essential reading.

804. National Lutheran Council. *The Lutheran Church and the Indian in the Timberland Country of Northern Minnesota.* Mimeo, 1950. (Northern Minnesota Committee for Intercultural Outreach in cooperation with Department of Intercultural Outreach, Division of American Missions.)

805. Nelson, Richard K. "The Western Kuchin: A Study in Human Adaptation." Ph.D. dissertation, University of California-Santa Barbara, 1971.

806. Newcomb, W. W., Jr. "A Note on Cherokee-Delaware Pan-Indianism." *American Anthropologist* 57 (October 1955): 1041–1045.

807. Ortiz, Alfonso. "A Processual Analysis of a Social Movement in the Rio Grande Pueblos." M.A. thesis, University of Chicago, 1963.

808. Oswalt, Wendell H. "Guiding Culture Change Among Alaskan Eskimos." *American Indigena* 21, no. 1 (1960): 65–83, and 21, no. 2 (1960): 152–170.

809. Oswalt, Wendell H. "Caribou Eskimos Without Caribou." *The Beaver Outfit* 291 (1961): 12–17.

810. Oswalt, Wendell H. *Mission of Change in Alaska.* San Marino: The Huntington Library, 1963.

811. Oswalt, Wendell H., & VanStone, James. "Partially Acculturated Communities: Canadian Athapaskans and West Alaskan Eskimos." *Anthropologica* n.s. 5, no. 1 (1963): 23–31.

812. Owen, Roger C. *Marobavi: A Study of an Assimilated Group in Northern Sonora.* Tucson: Anthropological Papers of the University of Arizona, No. 3, 1959.

* 813. Paine, Robert, editor. "Patrons and Brokers in the East Arctic." *Newfoundland Social and Economic Papers No. 2.* St. John's: Institute of Social and Economic Research, Memorial University of Newfoundland, 1971.

An excellent study of native-white relations.

814. Paredes, J. Anthony *et al.* "On James's 'Continuity and Emergence in Indian Poverty Culture.' " *Current Anthropology* 14 (February-April 1973): 158–167.

815. Parry, Keith William John. "To Raise These People Up: An Examination of

a Mormon Mission to an Indian Community as an Agent of Social Change."
Ph.D. dissertation, University of Rochester, New York, 1972.

816. Perry, Richard J. "The Apache Continuum: An Examination of the Survival
of San Carlos Apache Society." Ph.D. dissertation, Syracuse University,
1971.

817. Polgar, Steven. "Biculturation of Mesquakie Teenage Boys." *American
Anthropologist* 62 (April 1960): 217-235.

818. Porter, Kenneth W. "Relations Between the Negro and Indian Within the
Present Limits of the United States." *The Journal of Negro History* 17 (July
1932): 287-367.

    Excellent.

819. Porter, Kenneth W. "Notes Supplementary to Relations Between the Negro
and Indian Within the Present Limits of the United States." *The Journal of
Negro History* 18 (July 1933): 282-321.

820. Prucha, Francis P., editor. *Americanizing the American Indians. Writings by
the "Friends of the Indian" 1880-1900.* Cambridge: Harvard University
Press, 1973.

821. Radin, Paul. "The Influence of the Whites on Winnebago Culture." *State of
Wisconsin Historical Society Proceedings* 61 (1913): 137-145.

822. Randle, Martha Champion. "Iroquois Women, Then and Now." *Bureau of
American Ethnology Bulletin 149, Anthropological Papers No. 8,* pp. 167-
180. Smithsonian Institution. Washington, D.C.: Government Printing
Office, 1951.

823. Rarihokwats (Jerry Gambill). Review of *Dispossessing the American Indian:
Indians and Whites on the Colonial Frontier.* By Wilbur R. Jacobs. New
York: Scribners, 1972. In *The Saturday Review,* July 8, 1972, p. 70.

824. Roth, George. "Ethnic Incorporation: American Indians versus Africa."
Paper given at the American Anthropological Association meetings, Nov.,
1974.

    Theoretical study of the incorporation of American Indians into national
    society using theories of incorporation developed for new African nations.

825. Roufs, Tim. "Myth in Method: More on Ojibwa Culture." *Current
Anthropology* 15 (September 1974): 307-310.

    A continuation of the discussion of B. James vs. Paredes, Pelto, and Roufs
    in *Current Anthropology* 14, pp. 158-167.

826. Roundtree, Helen C. "Change Came Slowly: The Virginia Powhatan Case." Paper given at the American Anthropological Association meetings, Nov., 1974.

Examination of changes in Powhatan culture despite the lack of government sponsored agencies, missionaries or boarding schools.

827. Rowley, Graham. "The Canadian Eskimo Today." *The Polar Record* 16, no. 101 (1972): 201-205.

828. Roy, Prodipto and Walker, Della M. "Assimilation of the Spokane Indians." *Bulletin 628.* Institute of Agricultural Sciences. Pullman: Washington State University Magazine, 1961.

829. Sanchez, Thomas. *Rabbit Boss.* New York: Ballantine Books, 1974.

Interesting novel concerning the Washo-white confrontation.

830. Sanford, Margaret. "Pan-Indianism, Acculturation, and the American Ideal." *Plains Anthropologist* 16-53 (1971): 222-227.

831. Sasaki, Tom T. "Situational Changes and the Fruitland Navaho." *Journal of Social Issues* 14, no. 4 (1958): 17-24.

832. Satterlee, James L., & Malan, Vernon D. "History and Acculturation. The Dakota Indians." *Pamphlet No. 119.* Brookings: Agricultural Experiment Station, South Dakota State College of Agriculture, 1956.

An extremely general and brief summary. Some useful data are provided.

833. Savishinsky, Joel S., & Frimmer, S. B. "The Middle Ground: Social Change in an Arctic Community, 1967-1971." *Ethnology Division Paper No. 7, Mercury Series.* Ottawa: National Museum of Man, 1973.

* 834. Savishinsky, Joel S. *The Trail of the Hare: Life and Stress in an Arctic Community.* New York: Gordon and Breach, 1974.

Examines the relationship between ecological stress and human adaptability.

835. Schusky, Ernest. "Pan-Indianism in the Eastern United States." *Anthropology Tomorrow* (December 1957): 116-123.

836. Schusky, Ernest L. *Dakota Indians in Today's World.* New York: Board of National Missions, United Presbyterian Church, 1962.

Mimeo.

* 837. Schusky, Ernest L. "Culture Change and Continuity in the Lower Brule Community." *The Modern Sioux,* pp. 107-122. Edited by Ethel Nurge. Lincoln: University of Nebraska Press, 1970.

838. Schusky, Ernest L. *The Forgotten Sioux.* Chicago: Nelson Hall Co., 1975.

A history of the Lower Brule beginning with the Upper Missouri Indian Agency and extending through 1960. The book is meant to illustrate how federal policy affected one particular reservation and how it was most often people with the best of intentions who worked the worst effects on Indians.

839. Shaffer, Helen B. "Changing Status of American Indians." In *Editorial Research Reports,* pp. 381-398. May 26, 1954.

840. Shepardson, Mary, & Hammond, Blodwen. "Change and Persistence in an Isolated Navajo Community." *American Anthropologist* 66 (October 1964): 1029-1050.

Concerns the Rainbow Plateau, Navajo Mountain area in the northwest part of the reservation.

* 841. Shimony, Annemarie Anrod. "Conservatism Among the Iroquois at the Six Nations Reserve." *Yale University Papers in Anthropology 65,* 1961.

One of the best studies ever done of an aspect of Iroquois life.

* 842. Siegel, Bernard J. "Acculturation." *Critical Abstracts, North America. Stanford Anthropological Series No. 2.* Stanford: Stanford University Press, 1955.

843. Siegel, Bernard J. "Some Structure Implications for Change in Pueblo and Spanish New Mexico." In *Intermediate Societies, Social Mobility, and Communication. Proceedings of the Annual Spring Meeting of the American Ethnological Society,* pp. 37-44. Edited by V. F. Ray. Seattle: University of Washington Press, 1959.

844. Simmons, F. F. "Changes in Indian Life in the Clear Lake Area, Along the Northern Fringe of Mexican Influence in Early California." *American Indigena* 13, no. 2 (1953): 103-108.

An historical survey.

845. Smith, D. "Ethnic Unity and Disharmony in a Changing Northern Community." Paper given at the Central States Anthropological Society meetings, May, 1969. Mimeo.

846. Smith, Derek G. "The Implications of Pluralism for Social Change Programmes in a Canadian Arctic Community." A paper presented at the Society for Applied Anthropology meetings, April, 1969. Mimeo.

847. Smith, Derek G. "Natives and Outsiders: Pluralism in the MacKenzie River Delta, Northwest Territory, Canada." Ph.D. dissertation, Harvard University, 1972.

848. Smith, June E. "Anomie and Acculturation: A Case Study Among the Ojibway." M.A. Thesis, McMaster University, 1962.

849. Smith, Robert J., editor. "Culture Change and the Small Community." *The Journal of Social Issues* 14 (1958).

850. Smith, Valene L. "Eskimo Perceptions of Tourists in Four Alaskan Communities." Paper given at the American Anthropological Association meetings, 1974.

    Problems of tourism in Kotzebue, Nome, Point Hope, and Gambell.

851. Smitheram, Henry. "Cultural Conflict—General and Specific." *Exploration* 10 (November 1969): 33–36.

852. Sparks, Joseph P. "The Indian Stronghold and the Spread of Urban America." *Arizona Law Review* 10 (Winter 1968): 706-724.

* 853. Spaudling, Philip. "The Social Integration of a Northern Community: White Mythology and Metis Reality." In *A Northern Dilemma: Reference Papers,* pp. 90–111. Edited by Arthur K. Davis *et al.* Vol. 1. Bellingham, Washington: Western Washington State College, 1967.

* 854. Speck, Frank G. "Cultural Problems in Northeastern North America." *Proceedings of the American Philosophical Society* 65 (1926): 272-311.

855. Speck, F. G. "Negroes and the Creek Nation." *Southern Workman,* 37, pp. 106–110.

856. Speck, Frank G. "Reflections Upon the Past and Present of the Massachusetts Indians." *Bulletin, Massachusetts Archaeological Society* 4 (April 1943): 33–38.

* 857. Spicer, Edward H. "Worlds Apart. Cultural Differences in the Modern Southwest." *Arizona Quarterly* 13, no. 3 (1957): 197-230.

858. Spicer, Edward H., editor. *Perspectives in American Indian Culture Change.* Chicago: University of Chicago Press, 1961.

    Good theoretical discussion plus papers on Mandan, Kwakiutl, Yaqui, Rio Grande Pueblos, Navaho, Wasco-Wishram by other anthropologists.

859. Spicer, Edward H. *Cycles of Conquest. The Impact of Spain, Mexico and the United States on the Indians of the Southwest. 1533-1960.* Tucson: University of Arizona Press, 1962.

    Essential reading.

860. Spicer, Edward H. "Persistent Cultural Systems. A Comparative Study of Identity Systems That Can Adapt to Contrasting Environments." *Science* 174 (November 19, 1971): 795–800.

An interesting way of looking at modern Indian behavior.

861. Spindler, George D. "Socio-Cultural and Psychological Processes in Menomini Acculturation." *University of California Publications in Culture and Society.* Berkeley: University of California Press, 1955.

862. Spindler, Louise S. "Women and Cultural Change: A Case Study of the Menomini Indians." Ph.D. dissertation, Stanford University, 1956.

863. Spindler, Louise, & Spindler, George. "Male and Female Adaptations in Culture Change." *American Anthropologist* 60 (April 1958): 217–233.

864. Spindler, Louise. "Menomini Women and Culture Change." *Memoir 91. American Anthropological Association* 64, part 2. February, 1962.

865. Steen, Sheila C. "The Psychological Consequences of Acculturation among the Cape Breton Micmac." 1951.

866. Steinbring, Jack. "Recent Studies among the Northern Ojibwa." *Manitoba Archaeological Newsletter* 1 (Winter 1964): 9–12.

867. Steward, Julian H. "The Changing American Indian." In *The Science of Man in the World Crisis,* pp. 282–305. Edited by Ralph Linton. New York: Columbia University Press, 1945.

Valuable. Considers the more than 15,000,000 people in the Western Hemisphere who are classed as Indians. U.S. Indians are considered as a part of the larger whole.

868. Stewart, Omer C. "Ute Indians before and after White Contact." *Utah Historical Quarterly* 34 (1966): 38–61.

869. Stewart, W. D., & Schweitzer, Doug. "The Definition and Evaluation of Values and Goals in a Cross-Cultural Region." *The Musk Ox* 7 (1970): 32–52.

870. Suttles, Wayne. "Persistence of Intervillage Ties Among the Coast Salish." *Ethnology* 2 (October 1963): 512–525.

871. Suttles, Wayne. "Affinal Ties, Subsistence, and Prestige Among the Coast Salish." *American Anthropologist* 62 (April 1960): 296–305.

872. Tamarin, Alfred. *We Have Not Vanished. Eastern Indians of the United States.* Chicago: Follett Publishing Co., 1974.

Brief and very general. Attempts only to state that Indians are still living in the eastern part of the United States.

873. Tantaquidgeon, Gladys. "New England Indian Council Fires Still Burn." *Indians At Work* 2 (February 1935): 20–24.

874. Taylor, Herbert C., Jr. "The Parameters of a Northern Dilemma." In *A Northern Dilemma: Reference Papers,* Vol. 1, pp. 1–7. Edited by Arthur K. Davis, *et. al.* Bellingham, Washington: Western Washington State College, 1967.

875. Theodoratus, Dorothea. "Identity Crises: Changes in Life Style of the Manchester Band of Pomo Indians." Ph.D. dissertation, Syracuse University, 1971.

876. Thomas, Robert K. "Pan-Indianism." In *The American Indian Today,* pp. 128–140. Edited by Levine and Lurie. Baltimore: Penguin Books Inc., 1970.

877. Tiedke, Kenneth E. "A Study of the Hannahville Indian Community, Menominee County, Michigan." *Special Bulletin 369.* East Lansing: Michigan State College, Agricultural Experiment Station, April, 1951.

878. Torok, C. H. "Tyendinaga Acculturation." In *Iroquois Culture, History, and Prehistory. Proceedings of the 1965 Congress on Iroquois Research,* pp. 31–33. Edited by E. Tocker. Albany: New York State Museum and Science Service, 1967.

879. Useem, Ruth Hill. "The Aftermath of Defeat. A Study of Acculturation Among the Rosebud Sioux of South Dakota." Unpublished Ph.D. dissertation, University of Wisconsin-Madison, 1947.

880. Usher, Jean. "The Long Slumbering Offspring of Adam: The Evangelical Approach to the Tsimshian." *Anthropologica,* n.s. 13 (1971): 37–61.

881. Usher, Peter J. "The Canadian Western Arctic. A Century of Change." *Anthropologica,* n.s. 13 (1971): 169–183.

882. Valentine, Victor F., & Young, R. G. "The Situation of the Metis of Northern Saskatchewan in Relation to His Physical and Social Environment." *North,* January-February 1967, pp. 21–27.

883. Vallee, Frank G. *Kabloona and Eskimo in the Central Keewatin: Trends and Comparisons.* Ottawa: Department of Northern Affairs and National Resources, May, 1962. (Also published by the Canadian Research Centre for Anthropology, St. Paul University, 1967).

884. Vallee, Frank G. "Differentiation Among the Eskimo in Some Canadian

Arctic Settlements." *Sociological Research in the Arctic*. Ottawa: Northern Coordination and Research Centre Department of Northern Affairs and National Resources, 1962; reprint edition, in *Canada: A Sociological Profile*, 2nd ed., pp. 277-286. Edited by W. E. Mann. Canada: Copp Clark Publishing Co., 1971.

885. Voget, Fred. "The Reservation Community as an International System." Mimeo, n.d.

886. Voget, Fred. "A Shoshone Innovator." *American Anthropologist* 52 (January-March 1950): 53-63.

887. Voget, Fred. "Acculturation at Caughnawaga." *American Anthropologist* 53 (1951): 220-231.

888. Voget, Fred W. "The American Indian in Transition." *American Anthropologist* 58 (April 1956): 249-264.

889. Voget, Fred. "The American Indian in Transition: Reformation and Status Innovations." *American Journal of Sociology* 52 (January 1957): 369-378.

890. Vogt, Evon Z. "Navajo Veterans. A Study of Changing Values." *Reports of the Rimrock Project Values Series, No. 1*. Cambridge: Papers of the Peabody Museum of American Archaeology and Ethnology, Harvard University 41, no. 1, 1951.

891. Vogt, Evon Z. "The Acculturation of American Indians." *The Annals of the American Academy of Political and Social Science* 311 (May 1957): 137-146.

892. Wahrhaftig, A. L. *Social and Economic Characteristics of the Cherokee Population of Eastern Oklahoma*. Ann Arbor: University Microfilms, 1970.

893. Walker, Deward E., Jr. "The Nez Perce Sweat Bath Complex: An Acculturational Analysis." *Southwestern Journal of Anthropology* 22 (Summer 1966): 133-171.

894. Walker, Deward E., Jr. "Acculturative Stages in the Plateau Culture Area." Paper given at the American Anthropological Association meetings, 1967. Mimeo.

895. Walker, Deward E., Jr. "Measures of Nez Perce Outbreeding and the Analysis of Cultural Change." *Southwestern Journal of Anthropology* 23 (Summer 1967): 141-158.

896. Wallace, Ben J. "Oklahoma Kickapoo Cultural Change." *Plains Anthropolgist,* Part I (1969): 14-44.

897. Watkins, Arthur V. "Termination of Federal Supervision: The Removal of Restrictions Over Indian Property and Person." *The Annals of the American Academy of Political and Social Science* 311 (May 1957): 47–55.

898. Wax, Murray L. "Cultural Pluralism, Political Power, and Ethnic Studies." In *Learning and Culture. Proceedings of the 1972 Annual Spring Meeting, American Ethnological Society,* pp. 163–174. Edited by Kimball and Burnett. Seattle: University of Washington Press, 1973.

899. Weaver, Sally M. "Proposed Changes in the Legal Status of Canadian Indian Women: The Collision of Two Social Movements." Unpublished paper given at the American Anthropological Association meetings, Nov., 1973. Mimeo.

900. Weppner, Robert S. "Socioeconomic Barriers to Assimilation of Navajo Migrant Workers." *Human Organization* 31 (Fall 1972): 303–314.

901. White, Robert, S. J. "American Indian Crisis." *Social Order* 11 (May 1961): 201–211.

902. Willhelm, Sidney M. "Red Man, Black Man and White America: The Constitutional Approach to Genocide." *Catalyst,* no. 4 (Spring 1969).

903. Wissler, Clark. "Chapter VII. European and American Indian Cultures in Contact." In *Race and Culture Contacts,* pp. 112–123. Edited by Edward B. Reuter. New York: McGraw-Hill, 1934.

A valuable paper, if viewed from the perspective of the period in which it was written. Contains many useful generalizations and a large number of wrong conclusions.

904. Witt, Shirley Hill. "Native Women Today." *Civil Rights Digest* 6 (Spring 1974): 29–35.

XI. Migration Patterns

905. Armstrong, O. K., & Armstrong, Marjorie. "The Indians Are Going to Town." *Readers' Digest,* January, 1955, pp. 39–43.

Monumental distortion of reality. Included only to show how wildly inaccurate some journalists can be.

906. Bigony, Beatrice. "Migrants to the cities: a study of the socio-economic status of Native Americans in Detroit and Michigan." Ph.D. dissertation, University of Michigan, 1974.

* 907. Blumenfeld, Ruth. "Mohawks: Round Trip to the High Steel." *Trans-Action* 3 (November-December 1965): 19-21.

908. Brinker, Paul A., & Taylor, Benjamin J. "Southern Plains Indian Relocation Returnees." *Human Organization* 33 (Summer 1974): 139-146.

A shallow examination of the urban relocation of 323 Southern Plains Indians from western Oklahoma from 1968 to 1972.

909. Carter, Russell E. "Rapid City, South Dakota." *The American Indian* 64 (Summer 1958): 29-38.

Apt description.

910. Chadwick, Bruce A., & White, L. C. "Correlates of Length of Urban Residence among the Spokane Indians." *Human Organization* 32 (Spring 1973): 9-16.

Non-economic factors, particularly Indian ancestry and Indian self-identification, explain Spokane Indian people's migration to and continued residence in an urban setting.

911. Cook, S. F. "Migration and Urbanization of the Indians of California." *Human Biology* 15 (1943): 33-45.

Movement from rural to urban settings.

912. Dobyns, Henry F. "Papagos in the Cotton Fields." M.A. Thesis, University of Arizona, 1950.

913. Fontana, Bernard L. "The Off Reservation Papagos." *Program and Proceedings of the Arizona Commission of Indian Affairs.* Held in Sells, Arizona, Dec. 7, 1957. Tucson: mimeo, 1958, pp. 6 ff.

Modern Papago life.

914. Frantz, Charles. "The Urban Migration and Adjustment of American Indians Since 1940." M.S. Thesis, Haverford College, 1951.

Dakota Sioux.

* 915. Gillespie, Beryl C. "Yellowknives; *Quo Iverunt?*" In *Migration and Anthropology. Proceedings, Annual Spring Meeting, American Ethnological Society,* pp. 61-71. Edited by Robert F. Spencer. Seattle: University of Washington Press, 1970.

916. Graves, Theodore D. "Alternative Models for the Study of Urban Migration." *Institute of Behavioral Science, Publication 91.* Boulder: University of Colorado, n.d.

917. Graves, T. D., & Van Arsdale, Minor. "Perceived Opportunities, Expectations, and the Decision to Remain on Relocation: The Case of the Navajo Indian Migrant to Denver, Colorado." 1965, mimeo.

918. Hansen, Niles M. "Reservation Development Versus Migration: A Study of the Locational Preferences of Indian High School Seniors in the Southwest." *Discussion Paper 16.* Austin: Center for Economic Development, The University of Texas, 1971. Mimeo.

* 919. Hanson, Marshall Roy. "Plains Indians and Urbanization." Ph.D. dissertation, Stanford University, 1962.

Urban-reservation migration of the Crow and Cheyenne.

920. Harmer, Ruth Mulvey. "Uprooting the Indians." *Atlantic Monthly,* March, 1956, pp. 54-57.

Relocation is bad.

* 921. Hodge, William. "The Albuquerque Navahos." *Anthropological Papers No. 11.* Tucson: University of Arizona Press, 1969.

A study of migration patterns and the specific forces associated with urban-reservation movement.

922. Hurt, Wesley R., Jr. "The Urbanization of the Yankton Indians." *Human Organization* 20 (Winter 1961-62): 226-231.

923. Knodel, Walter J. Personal correspondence in the files of W. H. Hodge concerning Indian urban migration from the Chief, Branch of Employment Assistance, Bureau of Indian Affairs, Washington, D.C., 1966.

924. Liberty, Margot. "Family Structure of Omaha Indian 'Commuters.' " Ditto, n.d.

925. Madigan, La Verne. *The American Indian Relocation Program.* New York: Association on American Indian Affairs, Inc., 1956.

The best single statement of the federal government's relocation program and its implications.

926. Metzler, William. "Relocation of the Displaced Worker." *Human Organization* 22 (Summer 1963): 142-145.

927. Nasatir, David. "Relocation and the American Indian." Mimeo, 1958.

928. Ortiz, Alfonso. "Tewa Commuters. A Study in Industrial Effects." Manuscript, n.d.

Essential reading.

* 929. Oswalt, Wendell H. "Historical Populations in Western Alaska and Migration Theory." *Anthropology Papers of the University of Alaska* 11, no. 1 (1962): 1–14.

930. Padfield, Harland, & Martin, W. E. *Farmers, Workers, and Machines.* Tucson: University of Arizona Press, 1965.

Scattered data concerning Indians.

931. Padfield, Harland, & Van Willigen, John. "Work and Income Patterns in a Transitional Population: The Papago of Arizona." *Human Organization* 28 (Fall 1969): 208–216.

932. Paredes, J. Anthony. "Toward a Reconceptualization of American Indian Urbanization: A Chippewa Case." *Anthropological Quarterly* 44 (October 1971): 256–271.

933. Peck, John Gregory. "Urban Station: Migration Patterns of the Lumbee Indians." Ph.D. dissertation, University of North Carolina, 1972.

934. Peterson, John H., Jr. "Assimilation, Separation, and Out-Migration in an American Indian Group." *American Anthropologist* 74 (October 1972): 1286–1295.

Concerns Mississippi Choctaw.

935. Roark, Sue. "Ethnicity and Identity in North-Eastern Oklahoma." Paper given at American Anthropological Association meetings, Nov., 1974.

Analysis of inter-group relations among non-reservation Indians of north-eastern Oklahoma.

* 936. Savishinsky, Joel S. "Stress and Mobility in an Arctic Community: the Hare Indians of Colville Lake, Northwest Territories." Ph.D. dissertation, Cornell University, 1970.

* 937. Schusky, E. L. "Contemporary Migration and Culture Change on Two Dakota Reservations." *Plains Anthropologist* 7, no. 17 (1962): 178–183.

938. Smith, Valene L. "In-migration and Factionalism: An Eskimo Example." Paper given at the American Anthropological Association meetings, Nov., 1969.

* 939. Uchendu, Victor C. "Navaho Harvest Hands: An Ethnographic Report." Stanford: Food Research Institute, Stanford University, February, 1966. Ditto.

Data gathered about 1965, "in two different settings: the migrant's home-base on the reservation and off-reservation work communities. The eastern

Navaho area, the Crownpoint sub-agency was selected for the homebase. Five work camps, in two States—three in New Mexico and two in Arizona—constituted the off-reservation base. 344 households, randomly selected from these two settings, made up the sample. This yielded a total household population of 1,558 of which 595 were migrant workers—304 males and 291 females." p. 40.

"Navaho general migration pattern is northward to Colorado, Utah, and Idaho in spring, eastern New Mexico and Colorado in fall, and southwestern Arizona in winter." p. 41.

One of the most valuable studies ever made of Navaho behavior.

940. Vandemark, Dorothy. "Raid on the Reservation." *Harpers,* March 4, 1956, pp. 48–53.

941. Wilson, Carmen. "Intraurban Mobility of American Indians. Study of Milwaukee." Milwaukee: Department of Anthropology, University of Wisconsin-Milwaukee, 1970. Ditto.

Graduate student project.

942. Witt, Shirley Hill. "Migration into San Juan Indian Pueblo, 1726-1968." Ph.D. dissertation, University of New Mexico, 1970.

XII. City Living

943. Ablon, Joan. "Relocated American Indians in the San Francisco Bay Area. Concepts of Acculturation Success and Identity in the City." Ph.D. dissertation, University of Chicago, 1963.

The descriptive data are useful, but are presented in disorganized form.

944. Ablon, Joan. "Relocated American Indians in the San Francisco Bay Area: Social Interaction and Indian Identity." *Human Organization* (1963): 296-304.

Contains some useful description data, but her conclusions are unfounded.

945. Ablon, Joan. "American Indian Relocation: Problems of Dependency and Management in the City." *Phylon* 26, no. 4 (1965): 362-371.

A useful but very general programatic paper.

946. "An Urban Indian Says: We Want to Speak for Ourselves." *Together,* January, 1970, pp. 8–11. (Methodist Publication).

947. Barger, W. K. "Integration to Town Life and Adjustment in the Canadian

North." Paper given at the American Anthropological Association meetings, Nov., 1974.

Evaluation of social and psychological adjustment for both Eskimos and Indians in a newly developed town in Northern Canada.

948. Burley, Sally *et al.* "Some Factors Affecting the Adjustment of Relocated American Indians With Special Reference to the San Francisco-Oakland Area. An Exploratory Survey." Master of Social Work Thesis, University of California, 1958.

949. California. Department of Industrial Relations. *American Indians of California.* San Francisco, November, 1965.

950. Conaway, Mary Ellen. "Essay on Social Networks." M.A. Thesis, University of Wisconsin-Milwaukee, 1970.

Concerns some Milwaukee Indian residents. Data collected during 1968–1969.

951. Conly, Robert L. "The Mohawks Scrape the Sky." *National Geographic,* July, 1952, pp. 133–142.

Interesting pictures of some Mohawks who are part-time residents in New York City. Vague, misleading commentary.

* 952. Cook, James. "An Indian is as an Indian Does." *Chicago Tribune Magazine,* August 2, 1970, p. 44.

A well written general statement about contemporary Indians in Chicago.

953. Cottier, Belva D. "Summary and Background. San Francisco Area Indians." San Francisco: Urban Indian Health Board Inc., 1974. Mimeo.

A general but useful summary of a broad spectrum of conditions.

954. Craig, Gregory W., Harkins, A. M., & Woods, Richard G. "Indian Housing in Minneapolis and Saint Paul." Training Center for Community Programs, University of Minnesota, July, 1969.

955. Cudney, Jo. "Gallup's Indian Community Center." *New Mexico Magazine,* March, 1961, pp. 29 ff.

Superficial, public relations article.

956. Davis, Arthur K. "Urban Indians in Western Canada: Implications for Social Theory and Social Policy." *Transactions of the Royal Society of Canada* 6, series 4 (June 1968): 217–228.

957. Dosman, Edgar J. *Indians: The Urban Dilemma.* Toronto: McClelland & Stewart Ltd., 1972.

Cree Indians in Saskatoon, Saskatchewan.

958. Drilling, Laverne, Harkins, A., & Woods, W. "The Indian Relief Recipient in Minneapolis: An Exploratory Study." University of Minnesota, August, 1969. Mimeo.

959. Fish, Lewis J. "Model Training Center for American Indians." *Training in Business and Industry.* (September 1973): 54–55.

960. Fiske, Shirley. "Ethnicity and Address in Urban Environment." Paper given at American Anthropological Association meetings, Nov., 1974.

How migration from reservation to urban areas forces Navajos to adapt their traditional address system.

961. Fogleman, Billye Y. S. "Adaptive mechanisms of the North American Indian to an Urban Setting." Ph.D. dissertation, Southern Methodist University, 1972.

962. Frantz, Charles. "Urban Residence and American Indian Acculturation. A Case Analysis." Paper given at the Central States Anthropological Society meetings, 1953.

963. Garbarino, Merwyn S. "A Multicultural Indian in Reservation Society." Paper given at the American Anthropological Association meetings, 1967. Mimeo.

Concerns a Seminole girl from Big Cypress living in Miami and working in a bank.

964. Garbarino, Merwyn S. "Seminole Girl." *Trans-Action* 7, no. 4 (1970): 40–46.

965. Gayler, Lucy Boutwell. "A Case Study in Social Adjustment of One Hundred Osage Families." Master of Social Work Thesis, University of Oklahoma, 1936.

The study was made to gain some estimate of the present status of the fast-disappearing full bloods of the Osage tribe. She looked at Osages living in Pawhuska.

966. Gebhardt, Elizabeth. "Acculturation in an Urban Native American Setting—Pressures from Within." Paper given at the American Anthropological Association meetings, Nov., 1974. Mimeo.

Forces and attitudes within a residentially dispersed and multitribal Indian community.

967. Getty, Harry T. "Papagos in Tucson, Arizona: A Case Study." Paper given at the American Association for the Advancement of Science meetings, 1966. Ditto.

968. Goodner, James. *Indian Americans in Dallas: Migrations, Missions, and Styles of Adaptation.* Minneapolis: Training Center for Community Programs, University of Minnesota, 1969. Mimeo.

969. Graczyk, Randolph. "The Three Indian Organizations of Milwaukee. A Comparative Study." Milwaukee: University of Wisconsin, 1970.

   A graduate student paper.

970. Graves, Theodore D., & Lave, C. A. "Determinants of Urban Migrant Indian Wages." *Human Organization* 31 (Spring 1972): 47-62.

971. Graves, Theodore D. "The Navajo Urban Migrant and his Psychological Situation." *Ethos* (Fall 1973): 321-324.

972. Guillemin, Jeanne. *The Urban Indian as Migrant: A Research Perspective.* Spring, 1970, mimeo.

973. Guillemin, Jeanne. "Micmac Indians in Boston: Research in Progress." Paper given at the American Anthropological Association meetings, 1970. Ditto.

974. Haggarty, Patrick. "The Indian Community in Milwaukee. Preliminary Report of an In-Progress Study." 1966.

   A term paper done by a graduate student at the University of Wisconsin-Milwaukee.

975. Harkins, Arthur, & Woods, R. G. "Attitudes of Minneapolis Agency Personnel Toward Urban Indians." University of Minnesota, December, 1968. Mimeo.

976. Harkins, Arthur M., & Woods, R. G. "Attitudes and Characteristics of Selected Wisconsin Indians." Minneapolis: Training Center for Community Programs, University of Minnesota, July, 1969.

977. Harkins, Arthur M. "Proposal for a Reservation-Urban American Indian Affairs Center at the University of Minnesota, Minneapolis." October 25, 1969. Mimeo.

978. Harkins, Arthur M, Woods, R. G., & Sherarts, I. K. "Indian Education in Minneapolis: An Interim Report." Minneapolis: Training Center for Community Programs, University of Minnesota, December, 1969.

979. Harkins, A. M., & Woods, R. G. "The Social Programs and Political Styles

of Minneapolis Indians: An Interim Report." Minneapolis: Training Center for Community Programs, University of Minnesota, December, 1969. Mimeo.

980. Harkins, A. M., & Woods, R. G. "American Indians in St. Paul: An Interim Report." Minneapolis: Training Center for Community Programs, University of Minnesota, February, 1970.

981. Harkins, Arthur M., & Woods, R. G. "Indian Americans in Duluth. A Summary and Analysis of Recent Research." Minneapolis: Training Center for Community Programs, University of Minnesota, May, 1970.

982. Hartman, David W. "The Ethno-History of Three American Ethnic Groups." Research proposal, 1971. Ditto.

983. Hartman, David. "Adaptation to Urban Poverty: A Study of Behavioral and Attitudinal Adaptations in a Multi-ethnic Community." Research proposal, 1972.

Detroit area.

984. Hartman, David. "A Diachronic-Ecological Analysis of an Inner-City Community." Research proposal, 1972. Ditto.

Detroit area.

* 985. Hirabayashi, James, et al. "Chapter 7. Pan-Indianism in the Urban Setting." In The Anthropology of Urban Environments. Monograph Number 11, pp. 77–88. Edited by T. Weaver and D. White. The Society for Applied Anthropology Monograph Series, 1972.

* 986. Honigmann, John J., & Honigmann, Irma. Eskimo Townsmen. Ottawa; Canadian Research Centre for Anthropology, University of Ottawa, 1965.

Frobisher Bay and environs. Data collected March-August, 1963.

987. Honigmann, John J. "Adaptation of Indians, Eskimo, and Persons of Partial Indigenous Background in a Canadian Northern Town." American Anthropological Association meetings. Prepared for the 38th International Congress of Americanists, meeting in Stuttgart-Munchen, 1968, Mimeo.

988. Honigmann, J. J., & Honigmann, Irma. "Family Background and School Behavior in an Arctic Town." Paper given at American Anthropological Association meetings, 1968.

989. Honigmann, John J. "Five Canadian Arctic and Subarctic Towns: Their Native Populations." 1968.

990. Honigmann, John J. "Housing for New Arctic Towns." Paper given at American Anthropological Association meetings, 1970.

991. "The Indian as Seen in Suburbs." *Minneapolis Tribune.* July 3, 1970.

992. "Indians 1968. Challenging the City. Some Make It. More Don't." *Chatelaine.* November, 1968.

993. Kelly, Roger E., & Cramer, J. O. "A Survey of Urbanization in Northern Arizona." Paper given at the Pecos Conference, Trinidad, Colorado, 1965.

994. Kelly, Roger, & Cramer, John. *American Indians in Small Cities. Rehabilitation Monographs No. 1.* Flagstaff: Northern Arizona University, 1966.

995. Kemnitzer, Luis S. "Reservation and City As Parts of A Single System: The Pine Ridge Sioux." Unpublished paper given at the Southwestern Anthropological Association meetings, 1969.

996. Klein, Laura F. "Tlingit Women and Town Politics." Paper given at the American Anthropological Association meetings, Nov., 1974.

997. Krutz, Gordon. "Compartmentalization as a Factor in Urban Adjustment: The Kiowa Case." Paper given at the Conference of the Southwest Anthropological Society, 1969. Ditto.

998. Kunitz, Stephen J., Levy, J. E., & Odoroff, C. L. "A One Year Follow-Up of Navajo Migrants to Flagstaff, Arizona." *Plateau* 42 (Winter 1970): 92–106.

999. League of Women Voters of Minneapolis. *Indians in Minneapolis.* April, 1968, mimeo.

1000. Lovrich, Frank. "The Assimilation of the Indian in Rapid City." M.A. Thesis, University of South Dakota, 1952.

1001. Luebben, Ralph A. "A Study of Some Off-Reservation Navaho Miners." Ph.D. dissertation, Cornell University, 1955.

Rico, Colorado.

1002. Luebben, Ralph A. "Prejudice and Discrimination Against Navahos in a Mining Community." *Kiva* 30 (October 1964): 1–18.

1003. Lurie, Nancy O. "The Indian Moves to an Urban Setting." Address to *Resolving Conflicts—A Cross-Cultural Approach,* pp. 72–86. Kenora, Ontario, March 20, 1967.

1004. McCaskill, Donald N. "Migration Adjustment and Integration of the Indian Into the Urban Environment." M.A. Thesis, Carleton University, Ottawa, 1970.

1005. McEwen, Ernest R. "An Action Research Project on the Problem of

Migrating Native People." Toronto: Indian-Eskimo Association of Canada, n.d.

1006. McGreevy, Susan. "The Urban Indian and Ethnic Identity." Paper given at the American Anthropological Association meetings, 1974.

The importance of an Urban Indian Center as a mediator between the individual and his alien environment and as a reinforcer of Indian identity.

1007. Manitowabi, Edna. "An Ojibwa Girl in the City." *This Magazine Is About Schools* 4 (1970): 8-24. Ontario, Canada.

1008. Manzolillo, Lola R. "The American Indian in an Urban Situation: Minneapolis, Minnesota. A Study in Applied Anthropology." M.A. Thesis, University of Minnesota, 1955.

1009. Marcuse, B. "Report to the Community Chest and Councils of the Greater Vancouver Area Committee on the Canadian Indian in an Urban Community (Vancouver)." Unpublished paper available from Library, University of British Columbia. 1961.

1010. Martin, Harry W. "Correlates of Adjustment Among American Indians in an Urban Environment." *Human Organization* 23 (Winter 1964): 290–295.

1011. Melling, John. Chapters 8, 9, 11, 12, 13, and 14 from *Right to a Future, The Native Peoples of Canada.* Anglican Church of Canada and The United Church of Canada, 1967.

1012. "Minnesota's Urban Indians." *CURA Reporter* 1 (October 1970). University of Minnesota, Center for Regional and Urban Affairs.

1013. Molohon, Kathryn T. "The American Indian and Urban Adjustment: Trilevelled Identity and the Catalysis of Organization." Berkeley: Department of Anthropology, University of California, August, 1967. Mimeo.

1014. Mudgett, Carol. "Tribal Affiliation As Related to Occupational Mobility Among Milwaukee Indians." University of Wisconsin-Milwaukee, Department of Anthropology. Mimeo.

Ms. Mudgett was a graduate student at the University of Wisconsin-Milwaukee.

1015. Nagler, Mark. *Indians in the City.* Ottawa: Canadian Research Centre for Anthropology, St. Paul University, 1970.

1016. *The Navaho Urban Relocation Research Project: A Symposium Presented at the Annual Meeting of the American Anthropological Association.* November, 1965.

A collection of papers done by graduate students from the University of Colorado, Boulder.

1017. Neog, Prafulla, Woods, R. G., & Harkins, A. M. "Chicago Indians: The Effects of Urban Migration." Minneapolis: Training Center for Community Programs, University of Minnesota, 1970. Mimeo.

1018. Northrop, Gordon D. "Pan-Indianism in the Metropolis: A Case Study of An Emergent Ethno-Syncretic Revitalization Movement." Ph.D. dissertation, Michigan State University, 1970. Xerox Copy: Ann Arbor, University Microfilms.

1019. Paredes, J. Anthony. "Chippewa Townsmen: Some Social and Cultural Characteristics." Unpublished paper, n.d.

1020. Paredes, J. Anthony. "Chippewa Townsmen: A Study in Small-Scale Urban Adaptation." Ph.D. dissertation, University of New Mexico, 1970.

1021. Paredes, J. Anthony. "Interaction and Adaptation Among Small City Chippewa." Unpublished paper given at the American Anthropological Association meetings, 1971. Mimeo.

1022. Parker, Seymour. "Navaho Adjustment to Town Life: A Preliminary Report of the Navahos Residing in Farmington." Cornell Southwest Project, 1954.

1023. Powell, Peter, editor. *1965 Annual Report*. Chicago: St. Augustine's Center for American Indians. Mimeo.

An organization which has among its interests alcohol and drug abuse.

1024. Price, John A. "American Indians in Los Angeles: A Study of Adaptation to a City." 1966 UCLA Ethnographic Field School. (incomplete)

1025. Price, John A. "American Indians In Los Angeles: A Study of Adaptation to a City." (Revised edition, 1967). Mimeo.

1026. Price, John A., & McCaskill, Don N. "The Urban Integration of Canadian Indians." June, 1971, ditto.

1027. Ritzenthaler, Robert, & Sellers, Mary. "Indians in an Urban Situation." *Wisconsin Archeologist* 36 (December 1955): 147-161.

The conclusions are based on what data one class of graduate student social workers were able to obtain in one night.

1028. Robinson, W. W. *The Indians of Los Angeles: A Story of the Liquidation of a People*. Los Angeles: G. Dawson, 1952.

1029. Rumley, Ella R. "A Look At Tucson's Indians." Mimeo, n.d.

1030. Smith, J. G. E. "The Emergence of Micro-Urban Villages Among the Northern Athapaskans or the Decline and Fall of the Contact-Traditional Community in the North Canadian 'Bush'." Manuscript, n.d.

1031. Sparks, Joe P. "The Indian Stronghold and the Spread of Urban America." *Arizona Law Review* 10 (Winter 1968): 706–724.

A consideration of what happens when the Indian comes to the city and the city comes to the Indian.

1032. Steele, C. Hoy. "Urban Indians and Colonization." Ditto, n.d.

1033. Steiner, Stan. *The Lost Tribe of City Indians.* New York: Crowell-Collier Press, 1972.

* 1034. Trillin, Calvin. "U.S. Journal: Los Angeles. New Group in Town." *The New Yorker,* April 18, 1970, pp. 92-104.

Navajos and other Indians.

* 1035. Trillin, Calvin. "U.S. Journal: Gallup, New Mexico." *New Yorker,* September 25, 1971, pp. 108–114.

1036. Trillin, Calvin & Koren, Edward. "A Reporter at Large (The Gallup Intertribal Indian Ceremonial)." *The New Yorker,* August 5, 1972.

1037. Uhlmann, Julie M. Z. "The Impact of Urbanization on the Fertility Behavior of Papago Indian Women." Abstract, Ph.D. dissertation, University of Colorado, 1973.

1038. Uhlmann, Julie M. "The Contemporary Urban Indian Woman." Paper prepared for the 33rd annual meeting of the Society for Applied Anthropology, March, 1974. Ditto.

1039. Uhlmann, Julie M. "Boundary Maintenance in the Urban Environment: The Papago Case." Paper given at the American Anthropological Association meetings, Nov., 1974.

Examination of some of the boundary maintaining mechanisms used in Tucson, Arizona, by the Papago.

* 1040. Waddell, Jack O. "Papago Indians at Work." *Anthropological Papers of the University of Arizona, No. 12.* Tucson: University of Arizona Press, 1969.

1041. Waddell, Jack O. "Resurgent Patronage and Lagging Bureaucracy in a Papago Off-Reservation Community." *Human Organization* 29 (Spring 1970): 37-42.

Examines a particular case where Papago Indians, accustomed to a patron/client pattern, are being asked to acquire behavior patterns more appropriate to a bureaucratic institution in "Copper Town," Arizona.

1042. Waddell, J. O. & Watson, O. M., editors. "American Indian Urbanization." *Institute Monograph Series No. 4. Institute for the Study of Social Change.* Lafayette: Purdue University, Department of Sociology and Anthropology, 1973.

1043. Wells, Robin F. "Patterns of Urban Adaptation by Relocated Indians in California." Mimeo, n.d.

1044. Weltfish, Gene. "When the Indian Comes to the City." *The American Indian* 1 (1944): 6-11.

1045. West, Ralph L. "The Adjustment of the American Indian in Detroit: A Descriptive Study." Unpublished M.A. Thesis, Wayne University, 1950.

West is a Cheyenne-Arapaho.

1046. White, John. "The American Indian in Chicago: The Hidden People." Manuscript, n.d.

1047. White, Robert A., S.J. "The Urban Adjustment of the Dakota Indians in Rapid City, South Dakota. A Progress Report." Mimeo, 1963. 28 pp.

1048. Willard, William. "The Development of an Urban Enclave on An Integrative Mechanism: The Navajo Case." Unpublished paper, Southwestern Anthropological Association meetings, 1969.

1049. Willard, William, editor. *Urban Tribes: American Indians in the City.* Tucson: University of Arizona Press, in process.

1050. Wipperman, Betty. "Projected Study of Degree of Acculturation of Relocated American Indians in Milwaukee as Related to Certain Selected, Sociological Factors." Mimeo, n.d.

1051. Woods, Richard G., & Harkins, Arthur M. "Indian Employment in Minneapolis." Minneapolis: Training Center for Community Programs, University of Minnesota, 1968.

1052. Woods, Richard G., & Harkins, A.M. "Indian Americans in Chicago." Minneapolis: Training Center for Community Programs, University of Minnesota, November, 1968. mimeo.

XIII. Economics

* 1053. Adams, John W. *The Gitksan Potlatch: Population Flux, Resource Ownership and Reciprocity.* Toronto: Holt, Rinehart & Winston of Canada, 1973.

   Thirteen months were spent in the field, July, 1965—May, 1967, working largely in seven villages. Population flux, resource ownership and reciprocity are examined via the potlatch. A well written account intended for the general reader.

* 1054. Adams, William Y. "Shonto: A Study of the Role of the Trader in a Modern Navaho Community." *Bulletin 188, Bureau of American Ethnology, Smithsonian Institution.* Washington, D.C.: Government Printing Office, 1963.

   Field investigation carried out between 1954 and 1956. Valuable descriptive materials presented within an anemic theoretical framework.

1055. "Alaska's Economy in 1968." *Alaska* 6, no. 3 (1969): 1-12.

   The economic increases in the state had little, if any, effect on the average Alaskan.

1056. *The American Indian National Bank, Profile.* Washington, D.C., n.d.

1057. "Anchorage Costs of Living, 1960-1970." *Alaska* 7, no. 4 (1970): 1-8.

   Low income residents/natives suffer the most from the high cost of living in Anchorage.

1058. Angulo, J. de. "Indians in Overalls." *Hudson Review* 3 (1950): 327-377.

1059. Blau, Harold "Notes on the Onondaga Bowl Game." In *Iroquois Culture, History, and Prehistory. Proceedings of the 1965 Congress on Iroquois Research,* pp. 35-49. Edited by E. Tooker. Albany: New York State Museum and Science Service, 1967.

   One of the few reliable references concerning the role of a traditional game in contemporary ritual life.

* 1060. Brockmann, C. Thomas. "Reciprocity and Market Exchange on the Flathead Reservation." *Northwest Anthropological Research Notes* 5, No. 1 (Reprint): 77-96.

1061. Canada. Northern Science Research Group. Department of Indian Affairs and Northern Development. *The Bankslanders: Economy and Ecology of a Frontier Trapping Community.* Ottawa: 1970-1971.

   Valuable.

1062. Chapman, H. H. "The Menominee Indian Timber Case History. Proposals for Settlement." 1957, mimeo.

A history of the Federal management of the timberlands belonging to the Menominee Tribe of Wisconsin, the relations between the U.S. Department of Agriculture and Interior, the LaFollette Act of 1908 for sustained yield management and its administration and abuse, the Jurisdictional Act enabling the Tribe to sue for damages, the Hearings before the U.S. Court of Claims, the Award and its findings, and proposed future policy for the reservation.

1063. Downs, James F. "Animal Husbandry in Navajo Society and Culture." *University of California Publications in Anthropology Vol. 1.* Berkeley: University of California Press, 1964.

"Field data were gathered in three trips to Pinon, Arizona, totaling seven months, during which my wife, my son and I lived on a Navajo homestead and participated, as we were able, in the economic, social and ceremonial life of our hosts." p. 1.

1064. Hall, Tom Aldis. "Socio-Economic Status of the Cherokee Indians." M.A. thesis, University of Oklahoma, 1934.

1065. Helm, June. "Patterns of Allocation Among the Arctic Drainage Dene." In *Essays in Economic Anthropology. Proceedings of the Annual Spring Meeting of the American Ethnological Society,* pp. 33-45. Seattle: University of Washington Press, 1965.

1066. Hendry, Charles E. *Beyond Traplines.* Toronto: Ryerson Press, 1969.

1067. Jamieson, Stuart. "Native Indians and the Trade Union Movement in British Columbia." *Human Organization* 20 (Winter 1961-62): 219-225.

Most Indians have had only casual or intermittent contact and involvement with trade unions because the majority are casual, seasonal workers in fields which offer variable and seasonal employment such as logging and sawmilling, fishing and canning, and, to a much lesser extent, longshoring, construction, etc.

1068. Kelly, William H. "The Economic Basis of Indian Life." *The Annals of the American Academy of Political and Social Science* 311 (May 1957): 71-79.

1069. Kelly, William H. "United States." *Indianist Yearbook* 22, pp. 115-124. Mexico: Inter-American Indian Institute, 1962.

Socio-economic conditions of Indians.

1070. Kelly, William H. "Indian Adjustment and the History of Indian Affairs." *Arizona Law Review* 10 (Winter 1968): 559-578.

The dominant pattern of Indian-white relations has been one of Indian exploitation and discrimination by the dominant white society.

* 1071. LaFontaine, Frank. "The Native American Credit Problem." *American Indian Law Review* 2 (Summer 1974): 29–40.

    Explores the credit problems of Indians living on or near Indian reservations.

1072. McNitt, Frank. *The Indian Traders.* Norman: University of Oklahoma Press, 1962.

    Excellent. Concerns white traders working in Navajo country for the most part.

* 1073. Malan, Vernon. "The Dakota Indian Economy. Factors Associated with Success in Ranching." *Bulletin 509.* Brookings: South Dakota State College, Agricultural Experiment Station, 1963.

    Ranching and non-ranching Sioux compared. Field work was done in the spring and summer of 1960.

1074. Meaders, Margaret. *The Indian Situation in New Mexico. New Mexico Business Reprint.* January, March, July, and August, 1963.

* 1075. Mekeel, H. Scudder. "The Economy of a Modern Teton Dakota Community." *Yale University Publications in Anthropology No. 6.* 1936.

    Classic.

1076. Mooney, Kathleen. "Urban and Reserve Indian Economics and Domestic Organization." Ph.D. dissertation, University of Michigan, 1974.

1077. Munsell, Marvin. "Land and Labor at Salt River." Ph.D. dissertation, University of Oregon, 1967.

    Economic determinants of household composition.

1078. Nowak, Michael. "Income and Subsistence Patterns in Eskimo Communities." Paper given at the American Anthropological Association meetings, Nov., 1974.

    Exploration of the theory that the poorest Eskimo families in southwestern Alaska are the most acculturated since a specific cash income is required to participate in traditional subsistence activities.

1079. Nybroten, Norman, editor. "Economy and Conditions of the Fort Hall Indian Reservation." *Idaho Bureau of Business and Economic Research, Report No. 9.* July, 1964.

1080. "Personal Income Patterns in Alaska." *Alaska* 6, no. 1 (1969): 1–10.

In Alaska almost all victims of poverty, in both urban and rural areas, are non-white—chiefly Eskimo, Indian, or Aleut.

1081. "Red Bread!" *McCall's,* May, 1972, p. 63.

1082. Sasaki, Tom. T., & Basehart, Harry W. "Sources of Income Among Many Farms—Rough Rock Navajo and Jicarilla Apache: Some Comparisons and Comments." *Human Organization* 20 (Winter 1961–62): 187–190.

Compares the current economic adjustment of two relatively isolated Indian communities in the American Southwest. Brief.

1083. Simpson, James R. "Uses of Cultural Anthropology in Economic Analysis: A Papago Indian Case." *Human Organization* 29 (Fall 1970): 162–168.

1084. Useem, Ruth H., and Eicher, Carl K. "Rosebud Reservation Economy." In *The Modern Sioux,* pp. 3–34. Edited by Ethel Nurge. Lincoln: University of Nebraska Press, 1970.

Data taken largely from two studies twenty years apart.

1085. Wolf, Roger C. "Needed: A System of Income Maintenance for Indians." *Arizona Law Review* 10 (Winter 1968): 597–616.

The Indians' problems under current welfare programs demonstrate the need for a system of income maintenance (e.g. negative income tax) to supplant the existing structure.

XIV. Anthropology of Development

1086. Aberle, David F. "Navajo Relocation? A Pending Problem." *Fellow Newsletter, American Anthropological Association* 14, no. 5 (1973): 2.

1087. Aberle, S. D. "The Pueblo Indians of New Mexico: Their Land, Economy, and Civil Organization." *Memoir No. 70. American Anthropological Association.* 1948.

1088. Abrahamson, John D. *Westward Alaska. The Native Economy and Its Resource Base.* Federal Field Committee for Development Planning in Alaska, 1968.

A careful compilation of data taken from 125 individual sources. Basic conclusions and policy recommendations are provided.

1089. Acres Research and Planning Ltd. *The Sarnia Reserve Industrial Survey.* Niagara Falls. 1965: Mimeo.

Chippewas of Sarnia Band Council.

1090. Alaska. Community Action Program. Arctic Native Brotherhood. "Employment Development Conference." Nome: Nov. 30-Dec. 1, 1967. Mimeo.

Causes of unemployment.

1091. "The Alaska Marine Highway System." *Alaska* 7, no. 5 (1970): 1-16.

A discussion of some of the implications of public and private transportation needs. Current main road, rail and marine transportation routes are included. Useful data for studying Native migration processes.

1092. "Alaska's Economy in 1967." *Alaska* 5, no. 2 (1968): 1-16.

The poorest people living in Alaska are natives.

1093. "Alaska's Petroleum Leasing Policy." *Alaska* 7, no. 3 (1970): 1-12.

Provides useful insights into some of the issues involved in the Native Land Claims controversy. Who will benefit from the oil?

1094. American Indian National Bank. *Profile.* Washington, D.C., n.d.

A description of a major financial adventure of American Indians aided by white consultants.

1095. Austin, Charles M. "Gene Crawford: Helping Lutherans Help Indians." *The Lutheran* 10 (October 1972): 20-23.

1096. Bad River Overall Economic Development Committee. *Overall Economic Development Plan for the Chippewa Bad River Band, Bad River Reservation, Odanah, Wisconsin.* Prepared by Arle Dewall in cooperation with the Bad River Overall Economic Development Committee. 1973, mimeo.

* 1097. Balikci, Asen. "Development of Basic Socio-Economic Units in Two Eskimo Communities." *Bulletin No. 202, Anthropological Series No. 69.* Ottawa: National Museum of Canada, 1964.

Considers Pelly Bay, 1960, and Povungnituk, 1958. Excellent.

* 1098. Bee, Robert L. "Self-Help at Fort Yuma: A Critique." *Human Organization* 29 (Fall 1970): 155-161.

One of the best studies of its kind.

* 1099. Bennett, Robert L. "Building Indian Economies with Land Settlement Funds." *Human Organization* 20 (Winter 1961-62); 159-163.

What the Utes are doing and should be doing with monies from land claims.

1100. Bennett, Robert L. "Problem and Prospects in Developing Indian Communities." *Arizona Law Review* 10 (Winter 1968): 649–660.

1101. Berger, Edward B. "Indian Mineral Interest—A Potential for Economic Advancement." *Arizona Law Review* 10 (Winter 1968): 675–689.

Current leasing procedures have not worked in the Indians' best interests.

1102. Biggart, Robert James. "Indian Culture and Industrialization." *American Anthropologist* 74, no. 5 (1972): 1180–1188.

Over-generalized.

1103. Block, William E. Jr. "Alaskan Native Claims." *Natural Resources Law* (April 1971): 223–250.

1104. Boyce, George A. *When Navajos Had Too Many Sheep: the 1940's.* San Francisco: The Indian Historian Press, 1974.

Some useful data, but overlaps with many other sources.

1105. Chance, Norman A. "Economic Opportunity and Cultural Viability Among the Canadian Cree: A Strategy for Developmental Change." Paper given at the American Anthropological Association meetings, 1968. Ditto.

1106. Collings, Thomas W. "The Northern Ute Economic Development Program: Social and Cultural Dimensions." Ph.D. dissertation, University of Colorado, 1971.

1107. Dobyns, Henry F. "Experiment in Conservation: Erosion Control and Forage Production on the Papago Indian Reservations in Arizona." In *Human Problems in Technological Change,* pp. 209–223. Edited by E. H. Spicer. New York: Russell Sage Foundation, 1952.

1108. Dobyns, Henry F. "Thirsty Indians." *Human Organization* 11 (Winter 1952): 33–36.

1109. Dobyns, Henry F. "The Plight of the Papagos." *Frontier* (March 1952): 13–14.

1110. Dobyns, Henry F. "Reformation in the Cotton Fields." *Chicago Jewish Forum* 12 (Winter 1953): 95–101.

* 1111. Duran, Elizabeth C., & Duran, J. A., Jr. "The Cape Croker Indian Reserve Furniture Factory Project." *Human Organization* 32 (Fall 1973): 231–242.

This reserve is located on Bruce Peninsula in Ontario. The paper is an examination of the reasons for the failure of the enterprise.

1112. Edwards, Newton. "Economic Development of Indian Reserves." *Human Organization* 20 (Winter 1961–62): 197–202.

A biased account of economic development of North Carolina Cherokees, Seminoles in Florida, White Mountain Apaches, and Alaskan Natives.

1113. Eicher, Carl K. "Constraints on Economic Progress on the Rosebud Sioux Indian Reservation." Ph.D. dissertation, Harvard University, 1961.

1114. Eicher, Carl K. "An Approach to Income Improvement on the Rosebud Sioux Indian Reservation." *Human Organization* 20 (Winter 1961–62): 191–196.

Analyzes constraints on economic progress operative in the Rosebud reservation economy from 1950–1960 and suggests an approach to income improvement for the 1960–1970 period.

1115. Esber, George S., & Albanese, Charles. "Advocacy Planning with American Indians." Paper given at the American Anthropological Association meetings, Nov., 1974.

A lawyer, an architect and an anthropologist are collaborating with a band of Western Apaches to plan a new village site in Payson, Arizona. This paper analyzes some of the operative processes in advocacy planning and discusses the findings to date.

1116. Fuchs, Estelle. "The Navajos Build a College" *Saturday Review,* March 4, 1972, pp. 58–62.

Naive account of a faction-ridden institution.

1117. Geller, Al. "White Man's Business, Indian Style." *Lion,* 1972, pp. 14–17.

* 1118. Getty, Harry T. "San Carlos Apache Cattle Industry." *Human Organization* 20 (Winter 1961–62): 181–186.

Describes how the San Carlos Apache first entered the cattle industry, the type of organization they developed, and their difficulties in adjusting to the functional requirements of this market enterprise.

1119. Getty, Harry T. "The San Carlos Indian Cattle Industry." *Anthropological Papers of the University of Arizona, No. 7.* Tucson: University of Arizona Press, 1963.

1120. Gilbreath, Kent. *Red Capitalism. An Analysis of the Navajo Economy.* Norman: University of Oklahoma Press, 1973.

"Deals with the development of the reservation's tertiary, or small business, sector. Given the limitations of the reservation's capital and entrepreneurial resources, the development of Navajo small businesses offers an opportunity for immediate economic benefits." p. 6. Fails to take into account crucial political and social factors.

1121. Gordon, Suzanne. *Black Mesa. The Angel of Death.* New York: The John Day Co., 1973.

Strip mining of coal and the Hopis.

1122. Heiser, M. F., & Harvey, Gina C. "A Conceptual Development Model for Amerindian Community Schools." Paper given at the American Anthropological Association meetings, Nov., 1974.

First year progress report on NIE-funded study in ten schools in different cultural and linguistic areas.

1123. Hlady, Walter M. *A Community Development Project Amongst the Churchill Band at Churchill, Manitoba.* University of Saskatchewan: Mimeograph Center for Community Studies, 1960. 4th printing, 1970.

1124. Hough, Henry W. *Development of Indian Resources.* Denver: World Press, Inc., 1967.

Very general. Ignores a number of critical social and political problems involved in economic development.

1125. Lagasse, Jean H. "Community Development in Manitoba." *Human Organization* 20 (Winter 1961-62): 232-237.

Describes the Community Development program of the Department of Welfare of the Province of Manitoba.

1126. Lang, Gottfried O. "Economic Development and Self-Determination: The Northern Ute Case." *Human Organization* 20 (Winter 1961-62): 164-171.

Explores via role analysis how the Utes used their capital resources, what processes were involved in the creation of a program, and what sociopolitical forms emerged as a consequence of these events.

1127. Larson, Adlowe L. "Statement of—re. Retail Food Prices at Trading Posts, Navajo Reservation." 1972, mimeo.

Larson is on the staff at the University of Wisconsin-Madison.

1128. Lear, John. "Northwest Passage to What?" *Saturday Review,* November 1, 1969, pp. 55-64.

Concerns the possibilities of moving Alaskan oil to refineries via tanker.

1129. McFeeley, Mark B. "Note. Need for a Federal Policy in Indian Economic Development." *New Mexico Law Review* 2 (January 1972): 71-80.

1130. Macgregor, Gordon. "Community Development and Social Adaptation." *Human Organization* 20 (Winter 1961-62): 238-242.

Concerns the present situation of those Indian peoples who have lost their aboriginal economy and seek to re-establish productive Indian communities and to rediscover a meaning to life.

* 1131. Manuel, George, & Posluns, Michael. *The Fourth World. An Indian Reality.* New York: The Free Press, 1974.

An important book. Manuel is a Shuswap. Posluns is a white free lance writer. The "Fourth World" is a desired but as yet nonexistent condition where the use of white technology and its life-enhancing potential occur within the framework of the values of the peoples of the "Aboriginal World." Manuel is presently the President of the National Indian Brotherhood. The bulk of his remarks center around the Canadian situation.

* 1132. Martin, John F. "The Organization of Land and Labor in a Marginal Economy." *Human Organization* 32 (Summer 1973): 153–162.

Havasupai and why they don't produce more of their own food.

1133. Miller, Helen Miner, & Lurie, Nancy O. "Report on Wisconsin Winnebago Project Contribution of Community Development to the Prevention of Dependency." 1963, mimeo.

1134. Mochon, Marion. "The Non-Productive Reservation Community: An Acculturative Model." Paper given at the Central States Anthropological Society meetings, 1968.

1135. *The Navajo Yearbook of Planning in Action.* Window Rock: Navajo Agency, 1955.

This and other numbers are essential reading.

1136. *The Navajo Yearbook 1957.* Window Rock: Navajo Agency, 1957.

1137. *The Navajo Yearbook 1958.* Window Rock: Navajo Agency, 1958.

1138. *The Navajo Yearbook 1951–1961. A Decade of Progress.* Window Rock: Navajo Agency, 1961.

1139. Olson, Thomas W. "Comments. State Jurisdiction Over Real Estate Developments on Tribal Lands." *New Mexico Law Review* 2 (January 1972): 81–90.

1140. Peotter, Patti Sue. "Alaskan Native Land Claims and the Trans-Alaskan Pipeline System." Typed manuscript, December, 1972.

The term paper of an undergraduate student.

1141. Randall, Arthur G. "Forest Resources of the Indian Township, Passamaquoddy Reservation." Maine: Department of Indian Affairs, 1968. Mimeo.

1142. Reifel, Ben. "Relocation on the Fort Berthold Indian Reservation, North Dakota." Doctor of Public Administration dissertation, Harvard University, 1952.

More commentary is needed to support the large number of excellent photographs.

1143. Ritzenthaler, Robert. "The Impact of War on an Indian Community." Brief Communications: *American Anthropologist* 45 (1943): 325–326.

The Chippewa working for Simpson Electric.

1144. Ritzenthaler, Robert E. "The Menominee Indian Sawmill: A Successful Community Project." *Wisconsin Archeologist* n.s. 32, no. 2 (1951): 39–44.

"Success" is used here in a very relative sense.

1145. Sorkin, Alan L. "American Indians and Federal Aid." Brookings Studies in Social Economics. Washington, D.C.: Brookings Institution, 1971.

1146. Streib, Gordon F. "An Attempt to Unionize a Semi-Literate Navaho Group." *Human Organization* 11, no. 1 (1952): 23–31.

The attempt was not successful.

1147. Stucki, Larry R. "The Entropy Theory of Human Behavior: Indian Miners in Search of the Ultrastable State During a Prolonged Copper Strike." Ph.D. dissertation, University of Colorado, 1970.

1148. Taylor, Benjamin J. "Indian Manpower Resources: The Experiences of Five Southwestern Reservations." *The Arizona Law Review* 10 (Winter 1968): 579–596.

Attempts to analyze the current state of Indian manpower, age sixteen and over, on the Fort Apache, San Carlos, Acoma, Laguna, and Papago reservations. Concludes that "the congressional desire to raise the Indians' standard of living has not yet been realized."

1149. Thorson, Douglas. "Report on the Labor Force and the Employment Conditions of the Oneida Indians." Madison, Wisconsin: October, 1958, xerox copy. (Obtained from the Human Rights Commission).

1150. Tuttle, Roger L. "Economic Development of Indian Lands." *University of Richmond Law Review* 5 (Spring 1971): 319–329.

1151. U.S. Department of the Interior. Bureau of Reclamation. *Livestock Industry in Alaska. Kenai Peninsula, Kodiak and Adjoining Islands.* January, 1967.

1152. Useem, John, Macgregor, G., & Useem, Ruth. "Wartime Employment and Cultural Adjustments of the Rosebud Sioux." *Human Organization* (January-March 1943): 1-9.

1153. Usher, Peter J. "Geographers and Northern Development: Some Social and Political Considerations." Unpublished paper presented to the Canadian Association of Geographers, Toronto, 1974. Mimeo.

1154. Van Willigen, John. "The role of the Community Level Worker in Papago Indian Development." Ph.D. dissertation, University of Arizona, 1971.

1155. Van Willigen, John. "Concrete Means and Abstract Goals: Papago Experiences in the Application of Development Resources." *Human Organization* 32 (Spring 1973): 1-8.

The resources available to Papago communities are inconsistent with the abstract goals of community development.

1156. Voget, Fred, editor. "American Indians and Their Economic Development." Special Issue. *Human Organization* 20 (Winter 1961-62).

The papers are listed by author elsewhere in this section.

1157. Ward, Delbert B. *et al. Zuni Pueblo 1985.* Salt Lake City: Fourth Year Planning Project, Department of Architecture, University of Utah, 1967.

An intriguing scheme developed by students and faculty for the future architectural development of the pueblo based upon its current physical condition. A series of valuable maps are provided plus statistics on current population, land use, etc. Required reading for those with a serious interest in the peoples of the Southwest.

1158. Weaver, Thomas, editor. *Political Organization and Business Management in the Gila River Indian Community.* Tucson: Bureau of Ethnic Research, University of Arizona, 1971.

1159. Weaver, Thomas, editor. *Tribal Management Procedures Study of Seven Reservations (Ak Chin, Camp Verde, Cocopah, Fort McDowell, Havasupai, Hualapai, and Payson).* Tucson: Bureau of Ethnic Research, University of Arizona, 1974.

1160. Wisconsin. Office of Minority Business Enterprise. *Directory of Minority Businesses in Wisconsin. Non-Retail Firms.* Madison: 1974.

1161. Wolff, Anthony. "Showdown at Four Corners." *Saturday Review,* June 3, 1972, pp. 29-41.

Strip mining of coal.

* 1162. Wolforth, John. *The Evolution and Economy of the Delta Community.* Ottawa: Mackenzie Delta Research Project, Northern Science Research Group, Department of Indian Affairs and Northern Development, 1971.

    Concerns both natives and whites.

XV. Personality and Culture (Including Folklore)

1163. Aamodt, Agnes M. "Enculturation Process and the Papago Child: An Inquiry into the Acquisition of Perspectives on Health and Healing." Ph.D. dissertation, University of Washington, Seattle, 1971.

* 1164. Aberle, David F. "The Psychosocial Analysis of a Hopi Life History." *Comparative Psychology Monographs 21,* no. 1, serial No. 107, December, 1951.

    The work is of some interest with regard to methodology, but one can learn more about Hopi life by reading the material this analysis considers; cf., L. W. Simmons (editor), *Sun Chief. The Autobiography of a Hopi Indian.* New Haven: Yale University Press, 1942.

1165. Barnouw, Victor. "The Phantasy World of a Chippewa Woman." *Psychiatry* 12 (February 1949): 67–76.

* 1166. Barnouw, Victor. "Acculturation and Personality Among the Wisconsin Chippewa." *Memoir No. 72. American Anthropologist* 52, no. 4, part 2. (October 1950). American Anthropological Association.

    A classic study.

* 1167. Barnouw, Victor. "Reminiscences of a Chippewa Mide Priest." *Wisconsin Archeologist* 35, no. 4 (1954): 83–112.

    Wisconsin Chippewa.

* 1168. Barnouw, Victor. *Culture and Personality,* Revised Edition. Homewood: The Dorsey Press, 1973.

    Some Indian data provided.

1169. Basso, Keith H. "The Gift of Changing Woman." *Anthropological Paper No. 76, Bulletin 196, Bureau of American Ethnology. Smithsonian Institution.* Washington, D.C.: Government Printing Office, 1966. pp. 113–173.

    Concerns description and analysis of Western Apache girl's puberty rite at Cibecue on the Fort Apache Reservation, Arizona.

* 1170. Basso, Keith H. "Western Apache Witchcraft." *Anthropological Papers of the University of Arizona No. 15.* Tucson: University of Arizona Press, 1969.

A classic study.

1171. Basso, Keith H. "Western Apache Witchcraft." In *Systems of North American Witchcraft and Sorcery.* Edited by Deward E. Walker, Jr. Moscow: Anthropological Monographs of the University of Idaho, No. 1, 1970.

1172. Basso, Keith H. " 'To Give up on Words': Silence in Western Apache Culture." *Southwestern Journal of Anthropology* 26 (Autumn 1970): 213–230.

1173. Basso, Keith H. "Wise Words of the Western Apache: Metaphor and Semantic Theory." To appear in *Meaning in Anthropology: Current Approaches to the Analysis of Cultural Symbols.* Edited by Keith H. Basso and Henry A. Selby. Albuquerque: University of New Mexico Press, 1974.

1174. Betzinez, Jason, & Nye, W. S. *I Fought with Geronimo.* New York: Bonanza Books, 1959.

Interesting data on his experiences at Carlisle and afterward.

* 1175. Bibeau, Don, Gawboy, Carl, & Lyons, Naomi. *Everything You Ever Wanted to Ask About Indians But Were Afraid to Find Out.* St. Cloud, Minnesota: North Star Press, 1971.

Written by Chippewas. Regarded by other Indians as a classic.

1176. Boatman, John F. "Drinking Among Indian Teenagers." M.A. thesis, University of Wisconsin-Milwaukee, 1968.

Some useful descriptive material.

1177. Borland, Hal. *When the Legends Die.* New York: J. B. Lippincott Co., 1963. Reprint edition: New York: Bantam, 1964.

A novel concerning Utes.

1178. Boyer, L. Bryce. "Folk Psychiatry of the Apaches of the Mescalero Indian Reservation." *Magic, Faith, and Healing,* pp. 384–419. Edited by Ari Kiev. New York: Free Press, MacMillan Co., 1964.

"Apache psychiatry coincides with faith healing," p. 414. Fieldwork was done between 1958–1961.

1179. Boyer, Bryce. "A Psychoanalytic View of Some Aspects of Symbolism in Apache Mythology." Paper given at the American Anthropological Association meetings, Nov., 1974.

Apache folklore concerning the acquisition of supernatural power.

1180. Brandon, William. "American Indians: the Alien Americans." *The Progressive* 33, no. 12 (1969): 13–17.

1181. Brandon, William. "American Indians: the Un-Americans." *The Progressive* 34, no. 1 (1970): 35–39.

1182. Bushnell, John N. "From American Indian to Indian American: The Changing Identify of the Hupa." *American Anthropologist* 70 (December 1968): 1108–1116.

1183. Chavarria, Michael. "Day of the Dance." (Poem) *New Mexico Magazine,* November-December, 1970, p. 60.

 Written by a Tewa.

1184. Cochise, Ciye "Nino" as told to Griffith, A. K. *The First Hundred Years of Nino Cochise.* New York: Pyramid Communications, Inc, 1972.

 An informal life history beginning about 1872 through 1970.

1185. Corle, Edwin. *Fig Tree John.* New York: Liveright Publishing Co., 1935. Reprint edition, New York: Pocket Books, 1972.

 A novel about an Apache who tries to withdraw from modern society.

* 1186. Cox, Bruce A. "What is Hopi Gossip About? Information Management and Hopi Factions." *Man* 5 (March 1970): 88–98.

1187. Crumrine, N. Ross. "The House Cross of the Mayo Indians of Sonora, Mexico. A Symbol in Ethnic Identity." *Anthropological Papers of the University of Arizona No. 8.* Tucson: University of Arizona Press, 1964.

1188. Deer, Ada with Simon, R. E., Jr. *Speaking Out.* Chicago: Children's Press, 1970.

 Ms. Deer is a prominent member of the Menominee community.

1189. Deloria, Ella. *Speaking of Indians.* New York: Friendship Press, Inc., 1944.

 Contains some material pertaining to the Dakota of this century, but with an obvious bias or even distortion. The author has a degree from Teachers' College, Columbia University. Her father was the Rev. Philip Deloria, an Episcopal clergyman. She is a senior relative of Vine Deloria, Jr.

* 1190. Devereux, George. "Mohave Ethnopsychiatry and Suicide: The Psychiatric Knowledge and the Psychic Disturbances of an Indian Tribe." *Bulletin 175, Bureau of American Ethnology, Smithsonian Institution.* Washington, D.C.: Government Printing Office, 1961.

 Data gathered during the period 1932–1950 in the Parker, Arizona, area for the most part. Devereux successfully attempts to make a contribution to anthropology, the history of psychiatry, and theoretical and clinical psychiatry.

* 1191. Devereux, George. *Reality and Dream. Psychotherapy of a Plains Indian.* New York: Doubleday Anchor Books, 1969.

A unique classic. One of the few verbatim accounts of an entire psychotherapy ever published.

1192. Dundes, Alan. "African Tales Among the North American Indians." *Southern Folklore Quarterly* 29 (September 1965): 207–219.

A brief survey and commentary concerning the interaction between Negro and Indian folklore with emphasis on southeastern data.

1193. Dundes, Alan. "North American Indian Folklore Studies." *Journal de la Société des Americanistes* 56 (1967): 53–79.

Vital for the understanding of the topic.

1194. Eastman, Charles A. *Indian Boyhood.* New York: McClure, Phillips & Co., 1902. Reprint edition, New York: Dover Publications, Inc., 1971.

"The imperfect record of my boyish impressions and experiences up to the age of fifteen years." p. iv. Contains certain obvious biases; e.g. "the Indian no longer exists as a natural and free man. Those remnants which now dwell upon the reservations present only a sort of tableau—a fictitious copy of the past." p. iv.

1195. Eastman, Charles A. *The Soul of the Indian. An Interpretation.* Boston: Houghton Mifflin Co., 1911.

An interesting apologia, arguing that the Indian "ancient religion" and Christianity are essentially the same. Should be read in conjunction with his other works.

1196. Eastman, Charles A. *Indian Scout Craft and Lore.* Boston: Little, Brown & Co., 1914. Reprint edition, New York: Dover Publications Inc., 1974.

Brief remarks intended for the Boy Scouts and the Camp Fire Girls. However, it contains some useful data on his early years.

1197. Eastman, Charles A. *From the Deep Woods to Civilization. Chapters in the Autobiography of an Indian.* Boston, Little, Brown & Co., 1929.

Important data concerning a Sioux cultural broker and his activities during the latter part of the 19th century. Should be read in conjunction with his *Indian Boyhood.*

* 1198. Ellis, Florence H. "Patterns of Aggression and the War Cult in Southwestern Pueblos." *Southwestern Journal of Anthropology* 7 (Summer 1951): 177–201.

1199. Enemikeese. *The Indian Chief: An Account of the Labours, Losses, Sufferings, and Oppression of KE-ZIG-KO-E-NE-NE (David Sawyer). A Chief of the Ojibbeway Indians in Canada West.* London: Sold at 66, Paternoster Row, 1867; reprint edition, Toronto: Coles Publishing Co., 1974.

1200. Evaneshko, Veronica. "Tonawanda Seneca Ethnic Identity: Functional and Processual Analyses." Ph.D. dissertation, University of Arizona, 1974.

1201. Farrer, Claire R. "Politeness-Mescalero Apache Style." Paper given at the American Anthropological Association meetings, Nov., 1974.

The Apaches' ways of waiting to see a specialist, seeking a chance to gain the floor for talk and gesturing are discussed with respect to their value system.

1202. Fink, Marianne A. "Personality Differences of Acculturation in Navaho Adolescent Girls as Revealed by the Rorschach Test." M.A. thesis, University of New Mexico, 1950.

Written by the widow of Edward Dozier.

* 1203. Foulks, Edward F. "The Arctic Hysterias of the North Alaskan Eskimos." *Anthropological Studies No. 10.* American Anthropological Association, 1972.

Biological-psychological-cultural analysis. Essential reading.

1204. Fox, J. R. "Pueblo Baseball: A New Use for Old Witchcraft." *Journal of American Folklore* 74, no. 291 (1961): 9–16.

"The baseball teams, based on voluntary recruitment and stressing competition, allow for the acting out of aggressive and competitive tendencies." p. 15.

1205. Freeman, Robert. *For Indians Only.* Escondido, California: Brinck Lithographing Co., n.d.

A joke book written by a Sioux-Mission Indian. "The first known joke book done entirely by an American Indian."

1206. French, David. "When is an Indian?" Paper read at the American Anthropological Association meetings, 1962.

1207. Frisbie, Charlotte Johnson. *Kinaalda. A Study of the Navaho Girl's Puberty Ceremony.* Middletown: Wesleyan University Press, 1967.

Fieldwork done during the summers of 1963 and 1964 at Chinle and Lukachukai, Arizona. Excellent ethnography.

1208. Fry, Alan. *How A People Die.* New York: Tower Publications, Inc., 1970.

A novel concerning alienation and the Canadian Indian.

1209. Fry, Alan. *The Revenge of Annie Charlie.* Garden City, New York: Doubleday & Co., 1973.

A novel about Canadian Indians. Very enjoyable reading.

1210. Fuchs, Estelle, and Havighurst, R. J. *To Live on This Earth: American Indian Education.* Garden City, New York: Doubleday Anchor Books, 1973.

General but useful. The data are presented with an unusual kind of honesty.

1211. Gold, Dolores. "Psychological Changes Associated with Acculturation of Saskatchewan Indians." *Journal of Social Psychology* 71 (1967): 177–184.

1212. Goldfrank, Esther S. "Isleta Variants: A Study of Flexibility." *Journal of American Folk Lore* 39 (1926): 70–78.

Fieldwork in the fall of 1924. Concerned with how her folklore data compares with that of E. C. Parsons when both used the same informant one year apart. They were interested in how thematic material may be handled by the same man, and in how far the individual's personal taste and conscious play is responsible for variations in theme and plot complex.

1213. Gooderham, Kent, editor. *I Am An Indian.* Toronto: J. M. Dent & Sons Ltd., 1969.

Excellent collection of materials written by Canadian native peoples.

1214. Gossen, Gary H. "A Version of the Potawatomi Coon-Wolf Cycle: A Traditional Projection Screen for Acculturative Stress." *Search* 4 (Spring 1964): 8–14.

The Potawatomis in Mayetta, Kansas, 1963.

1215. Graves, T. D. "The Personal Adjustment of Navajo Indian Migrants to Denver, Colorado." *Research Report No. 19. Institute of Behavioral Science.* Boulder: University of Colorado, n.d. Mimeo.

1216. Hallowell, A. I. "Chapter 18. Background for a Study of Acculturation and the Personality of the Ojibwa." *Culture and Experience,* pp. 333–344. New York: Schocken Books, 1967.

* 1217. Hallowell, A. I. "Chapter 19. Acculturation and the Personality of the Ojibwa." *Culture and Experience,* pp. 345–357. New York: Schocken Books, 1967.

1218. Hallowell, A. I. "Chapter 20. Values, Acculturation, and Mental Health." *Culture and Experience,* pp. 358–366. New York: Schocken Books, 1967.

1219. Helm, June, DeVos, G. A., and Carterette, Teresa. "Variations in Personality and Ego Identification in a Slave Indian Kin-Community." *National*

Museum of Canada Bulletin 180, Part II, Paper No. 5, pp. 94–138. Ottawa: National Museum of Canada, 1962.

1220. Hertzberg, Hazel W. *The Search for an American Indian Identity.* Syracuse: Syracuse University Press, 1971.

1221. Hicks, George L, & Kertzer, D. I. "Making a Middle Way: Problems of Monhegan Identity." *Southwestern Journal of Anthropology* 28 (Spring 1972): 1–24.

1222. Hieb, Louis Albert. "The Hopi Ritual Clown: Life as It Should Not Be." Ph.D. dissertation, Princeton University, 1972.

1223. Hill, Carol. "Indian Island, Maine." In *Subsistence, U.S.A.,* pp. 89–107. New York: Subsistence Press Book, Holt, Rinehart, and Winston, 1973.

A brief, journalistic presentation of the thoughts of a Penobscot woman married to a white lawyer and absorbed with the task of being "Indian."

* 1224. Hippler, Arthur E. "The Athapascans of Interior Alaska: A Culture and Personality Perspective." *American Anthropologist* 75 (October 1973): 1529–1541.

* 1225. Hippler, Arthur E. "The North Alaska Eskimos: A Culture and Personality Perspective." *American Ethnologist* 1 (August 1974): 449–469.

1226. Honigmann, John J., & Honigmann, Irma. "Alcohol in a Canadian Northern Town." *Working Paper No. 1.* 1968, mimeo.

1227. Howard, James H. "The Dakota Heyoka Cult." *The Scientific Monthly* 10 (Spring 1954): 69–74.

1228. Howard, James. "Altamaha Cherokee Folklore and Customs." *Journal of American Folklore* 72 (April-June 1959): 134–138.

1229. Howard, James. "Peyote Jokes." *Journal of American Folklore* 75 (January-March 1962): 10–14.

1230. Huffaker, Clair. *Nobody Loves a Drunken Indian.* New York: Paperback Library, 1969.

A novel about Indians on the outskirts of a large Southwestern city.

1231. Hughes, Charles C. "Reference Group Concepts in the Study of a Changing Eskimo Culture. In *Cultural Stability and Cultural Change, Proceedings of the Annual Spring Meeting of the American Ethnological Society,* pp. 7–14. Edited by V. F. Ray. Seattle: University of Washington Press, 1957.

1232. Johnson, E. Pauline. *Flint and Feather. The Complete Poems of E. Pauline Johnson* (Tekahionwake). Don Mills, Ontario: Paperjacks, 1972.

A Mohawk and a remarkable woman. The poems were originally published in 1917.

1233. Johnson, Guy B. "Personality in a White-Indian-Negro Community." *American Sociological Review* 4 (1939): 516-523.

Southeastern United States.

1234. Jordan, Jan. *Give Me the Wind*. Englewood Cliffs, New Jersey: Prentice-Hall, Inc., 1973.

Novel

1235. Josephy, Alvin M., Jr. "Indians in History. The Whiteman's Books Speak With Forked Tongue." *The Atlantic Monthly,* June, 1970, pp. 67-72.

* 1236. Kaplan, Bert & Johnson, Dale. "The Social Meaning of Navaho Psychopathology and Psychotherapy." In *Magic, Faith and Healing,* pp. 174-200. Edited by Ari Kiev. New York: Free Press-MacMillan Co., 1964.

"Where some conception of the etiology of psychopathology exists, therapeutic process will be organized on the basis of this conception and aimed at removing the causes, or remedying the conditions from which the patient is understood to be suffering. The illnesses themselves will be oriented to and shaped by these conceptions." p. 203.

1237. Kostash, Myrna. "An Interview with a Cree Indian." *Miss Chatelaine* 9 (February 8, 1972): 56-92.

1238. Kraus, Robert F. "Changing Patterns of Suicidal Behavior in North Alaskan Eskimos." Paper read at the 2nd International Symposium on Circumpolar Health, Nordic Council for Arctic Medical Research. Oulu, Finland, June 21-24. 1971 Xerox.

Kraus is a psychiatrist.

1239. Kraus, Robert F. "Emergency Evaluation of Suicide Attempters." *Pennsylvania Medicine* 75 (1972): 60-62.

* 1240. Kraus, Robert F. "A Psychoanalytic Interpretation of Shamanism." *The Psychoanalytic Review* 59 (1972): 19-32.

1241. Kraus, Robert F. "Eskimo Suicide." Paper to be read at the American Psychiatric Association Convention, 1973. Xerox.

1242. Kraus, Robert F. "Suicidal Behavior in Alaskan Natives." Xerox, n.d.

1243. Kraus, Robert F. "Suicidal Behavior in Four Native American Cultures." Research Precis, xerox, n.d.

* 1244. Kroeber, Theodora. *Ishi in Two Worlds.* Berkeley: University of California Press, 1961.

The definitive study of this interesting person.

1245. Krutz, Gordon V. "The Native's Point of View as an Important Factor in Understanding the Dynamics of the Oraibi Split." *Ethnohistory* 20 (Winter 1973): 79–89.

Shows how the inclusion of the native's interpretation of history offers a broader view into the dynamics of human behavior.

1246. Kupferer, Hariet J. "Stress Points in a Conservative Pueblo." Unpublished paper given at the American Anthropological Association meetings, 1968.

Santo Domingo, New Mexico.

1247. LaBarre, Weston. *The Autobiography of a Kiowa Indian.* Microcard Publication of Primary Records in Culture and Personality 2:14. Madison: Microcard Foundation, 1957.

* 1248. Ladd, John. *The Structure of a Moral Code. A Philosophical Analysis of Ethical Discourse Applied to the Ethics of the Navaho Indians.* Cambridge: Harvard University Press, 1957.

Valuable and possibly unique.

1249. Lang, Samuel V., Jr. "Children of the Flathead: A Study of Culture-and-Personality in a Changing Society." M.A. thesis, University of Montana, 1966.

1250. Lantis, Margaret. "Alaskan Eskimo Cultural Values." *Polar Notes* 1 (1959): 35–48.

* 1251. Lantis, Margaret. *Eskimo Childhood and Interpersonal Relationships. Nunivak Biographies and Genealogies.* Seattle: University of Washington Press, 1960.

1252. LaPointe, Frank. *The Sioux Today.* New York: Crowell-Collier Press, 1972.

Brief descriptions of various Sioux adolescents. Useful.

1253. Leacock, Eleanor, Burke, and Shriver, Joanne. "Harrison Indian Childhood." In *Indians of the Urban Northwest.* Edited by Marian W. Smith. New York: Columbia University Press, 1949.

1254. Leforge, Thomas H. as told to Marquis, T. B. *Memoirs of a White Crow Indian.* Lincoln: Bison Books, University of Nebraska Press, 1974.

A "squaw man" living with the Crow at the end of the 19th century.

1255. Leighton, A. L., & Hughes, C. C. "Notes on Eskimo Patterns of Suicide." *Southwestern Journal of Anthropology* 11 (Winter 1955): 327–338.

1256. Leighton, Alexander H. "The Mental Health of the American Indian—Introduction." *American Journal of Psychiatry* 125 (August 1968): 113 ff.

Also contains brief notes by McNickle, "The Sociocultural Setting of Indian Life"; and Saslow, "Research on Psychosocial Adjustment of Indian Youth."

* 1257. Leon, Robert L. "Maladaptive Interaction Between Bureau of Indian Affairs Staff and Indian Clients." *American Journal of Orthopsychiatry* 35 (July 1957): 723–728.

1258. Levy, Jerrold E. "The Fate of Navajo Twins." *American Anthropologist* 66 (August 1964): 883–887.

1259. Levy, Jerrold E. "Navajo Suicide." *Human Organization* 24 (Winter 1957): 308–318.

1260. Levy, Sydelle Brooks. "Insiders or Outsiders: The Symbols of Ethnic Identity." Unpublished paper given at the American Anthropological Association meetings, 1973.

* 1261. Lewis, Thomas H. "The *Heyoka* Cult in Historical and Contemporary Oglala Sioux Society." *Anthropos* 69 (1974): 17–32.

Useful data on the involved question of ceremonial clowns and related matters. Lewis is a psychiatrist.

1262. Loh, Jules. "The Soul of the Navajo." *Esquire.* November, 1970, pp. 162–184.

* 1263. MacAndrew, Craig, and Edgerton, R. B. "Chapter 7. Indians Can't Hold Their Liquor." In *Drunken Comportment. A Social Explanation.* Chicago: Aldine Publishing Co., 1969.

Good summary of the literature.

1264. McCone, R. Clyde. "Death and the Persistence of Basic Personality Structure Among the Lakota." *Plains Anthropologist* 13, no. 42, pt. 1, (1968): 305–309.

1265. McElroy, Ann P. "The Effects of Urbanization on Eskimo Child Life and Personality. Working Paper No. 2. Urbanization and the Arctic and Sub Arctic." Paper given at the Canadian Sociology and Anthropology Association meetings, 1968. Ditto.

1266. MacNeish, June Helm. "Contemporary Folk Beliefs of a Slave Indian Band." *Journal of American Folklore* 67 (1954): 185–198.

* 1267. McNickle, D'Arcy. *The Surrounded.* New York: Dodd, Mead & Co., 1936.

An excellent novel concerning the differences and similarities between Indian and non-Indian life in the United States and their implications for one young Indian man. This work should be read by more people.

1268. Marriott, Alice, & Rachlin, Carol. "Indians: 1966. Four Case Histories." *Southwest Review* (Spring 1966): 149–160.

1269. Martin, Harry W., Sutker, Leon, & Hales. "Mental Health of Eastern Oklahoma Indians: An Exploration." *Human Organization* 27 (Winter 1968): 308–315.

* 1270. Metayer, Maurice, editor. *I, Nuligak.* Pocket Book Edition. Richmond Hill: Simon and Schuster of Canada, Ltd., 1971.

A Kitigariukmeut. He was probably born around 1895. Essential reading.

1271. Miller, Frank C., & Caulkins, D. Douglas. "Chippewa Adolescents: A Changing Generation." *Human Organization* 23 (Summer 1964): 150–159.

1272. Miller, Frank. "Humor in a Chippewa Tribal Council." *Ethnology* 6 (July 1967): 263–271.

1273. Mitchell, Emerson, & Allen, T. D. *Miracle Hill. The Story of a Navaho Boy.* Norman: University of Oklahoma Press, 1967.

From the eastern portion of the reservation.

1274. Momaday, N. Scott. *House Made of Dawn.* New York: Signet, 1968.

Concerns Jemez Pueblo and environs.

1275. Momaday, N. Scott. *The Way to Rainy Mountain.* Albuquerque: University of New Mexico Press, 1969.

The Kiowa.

1276. Neely, Sharlotte. "Intraethnic Differences Among the Eastern Cherokee Indians." Paper given at the American Anthropological Association meetings, Nov., 1974.

1277. Neihardt, John G. *When the Tree Flowered. An Authentic Tale of The Old Sioux World.* New York: The Macmillan Co., 1951; reprint edition, New York: Pocket Book, Simon and Schuster Inc., 1973.

Contributes to an understanding of Sioux life.

1278. Newcomb, Franc Johnson. *Hosteen Klah. Navaho Medicine Man and Sand Painter.* Norman: University of Oklahoma Press, 1964.

* 1279. Oestreich, Nancy (Lurie, Nancy O.). "Trends of Change in Patterns of Child Care and Training Among the Wisconsin Winnebago." *Wisconsin Archeologist* n.s. 29, no. 3–4 (1948): whole issue.

* 1280. Opler, Morris. "Some Points of Comparison and Contrast between the Treatment of Functional Disorders by Apache Shamans and Modern Psychiatric Practice." *American Journal of Psychiatry* 92, no. 6 (1936): 1371–1387.

1281. Opler, Morris. "Humor and Wisdom of Some American Indian Tribes." *New Mexico Anthropologist* 3, no. 1 (1938): 3–10.

1282. Opler, Morris. "The Sacred Clowns of the Chiricahua and Mescalero Indians." *El Palacio* 44, nos. 10–12 (1938): 75–79.

1283. Opler, Morris E. *Apache Odyssey. A Journey Between Two Worlds.* New York: Holt, Rinehart & Winston, 1969.

Concerns the Mescalero Apache "Chris." Data gathered in the 1930's.

* 1284. Ortiz, Alfonso. *The Tewa World. Space, Time, Being and Becoming in a Pueblo Society.* Chicago: University of Chicago Press, 1969.

Useful. An analysis of the cosmological and ritual systems of the Tewa.

1285. Osterreich, Helgi, & John, Vera P. "Learning Styles Among Indian Children." Paper given at the American Anthropological Association meetings, Nov., 1974.

Verbal and visual learning styles among Pueblo Indian children are explored.

1286. Parker, Chief Everett & Okedoska. *The Secret of No Face.* Healdsburg, California; Native American Publishers, North American Publishing Co., 1972.

Written primarily for Indians.

1287. Parker, Seymour. "Ethnic Identity and Acculturation in Two Eskimo Villages." *American Anthropologist* 66 (April 1964): 325–340.

An interesting exercise in methodology.

1288. Pelletier, Wilfred. *Two Articles*. Toronto: Newin Publishing Co., n.d.

"Childhood in an Indian Village" and "Some Thoughts About Organization and Leadership." Pelletier is an Odawa Indian.

1289. Pelletier, Wilfred and Poole, Ted. *No Foreign Land: The Biography of a North American Indian*. New York: Random House, Pantheon Books, 1973.

1290. Pelto, Gretel. "Life on the Upper Mississippi: Social and Psychological Adaptations in a Marginal Rural Area." Ph.D. dissertation University of Minnesota, 1970.

1291. Pelto, P. "The Upper Mississippi Research Project." Manuscript, February, 1972.

1292. Red Fox, Chief. *The Memoirs of Chief Red Fox*. Greenwich: Fawcett Crest, 1972.

A nearly successful act of plagarism. A significant portion of the contents was taken from J. H. McGregor's *The Wounded Knee Massacre: From the Viewpoint of the Sioux*. Nearly 100,000 copies of the Red Fox "version" were sold.

1293. Robbins, R. H. "Alcohol and the Identity Struggle; Some Effects of Economic Change on Interpersonal Relations." *American Anthropologist* 75 (February 1973): 99–122.

1294. Rogers, John. *Red World and White: Memories of a Chippewa Boyhood*. Norman: University of Oklahoma Press, 1974.

1295. Rosen, Kenneth, editor. *The Man to Send Rain Clouds. Contemporary Stories by American Indians*. New York: Viking Press, 1974.

Excellent.

1296. Rosenthal, Bernard G. "Development of Self-Identification in Relation to Attitudes Towards the Self in the Chippewa Indians." *Genetic Psychology Monographs* 90 (1974): 43–141.

Study of the relation between development of identification of the self, self-evaluation, and correct perceptual differentiation of the Chippewa and white ethnic groups among Chippewa Indian children of Lac du Flambeau, Wisconsin.

1297. Rountree, Helen C. "Being an Indian in Virginia: Four Hundred Years in Limbo." Paper given at the American Anthropological Association meetings, 1971.

1298. Saslow, Harry L., & Harrover, M. J. "Research on Psychological Adjustment of Indian Youth." *American Journal of Psychiatry* 125, no. 2 (1968): 224–231.

1299. Scott, Lalla. *Karnee. A Paiute Narrative.* Greenwich: Fawcett Publications, 1973.

> "Related by a half-breed woman who was born nearly a hundred years ago. Deserted by her rancher father, Annie Lowry rejected her white heritage to live with her Paiute mother in the Indian colony near Lovelock, Nevada." (From the back cover.)

1300. Sealey, D. Bruce, & Kirkness, V. J., editors. *Indians Without Tipis. A Resource Book by Indians and Metis.* Winnipeg: William Clare Ltd., 1973.

> An interesting example of the genre.

1301. Searcy, Ann. "The Value of Ethnohistorical Reconstructions of American Indian Typical Personality: The Case of the Potawatomi." Reprinted from *Transactions of the Kansas Academy of Science* 68, no. 2 (1965).

* 1302. Simmons, Leo W. *Sun Chief. The Autobiogralhy of a Hopi Indian.* New Haven: Yale University Press, 1942.

> Probably the most thoroughly studied (or imposed upon) human being on the face of the earth. Essential reading.

1303. Slobodin, Richard. "Some Social Functions of Kutchin Anxiety." *American Anthropologist* 62 (February 1960): 122–133.

* 1304. Snake, Reuben A., Jr. *Being Indian Is. . . .* Macy, Nebraska: Nebraska Indian Press, 1972.

> Observations on Indian ethnicity. This publication has met the approval of many Indians.

1305. Spencer, Robert F. "Exhortation and the Klamath Ethos." *Proceedings American Philosophical Society* 100 (1953): 77–86.

1306. Spindler, George. "Sociocultural and Psychological Processes in Menomini Acculturation." *Publications in Culture and Society, No. 5.* Berkeley: University of California Press, 1955.

1307. Stage, Thomas B., & Keast, T. J. "A Psychiatric Service for Plains Indians." Paper given at the 121st Annual Meeting of the American Psychiatric Association, 1965.

1308. Standing Bear, Luther. *My People the Sioux.* London: Williams and Norgate Ltd., 1928; reprint edition, Lincoln: Bison Books, University of Nebraska Press, 1974.

> Standing Bear was in the first class at Carlisle, saw the Ghost Dance uprising from the Pine Ridge Reservation, toured Europe with Buffalo Bill's Wild West Show, and spent his later years working in the Indian rights movement of the 1920's.

1309. Standing Bear, Chief (Luther). *Land of the Spotted Eagle.* Boston: Houghton Mifflin Co., 1933.

The last three chapters of the book are of special interest: Chapter 7, "Indian Wisdom;" Chapter 8, "Later Days"; and Chapter 9 "What the Indian Means to America."

1310. Stark, Matthew, & Pelto, P. J. "Economic and Social Deprivation Among Minnesota Indians." Unpublished paper, n.d.

1311. Stull, Donald D. "Modernization and Symptoms of Stress: Attitudes, Accidents and Alcohol Use Among Urban Papago Indians." Ph.D. dissertation, University of Colorado, 1973.

1312. Tefft, Stanton K. "Intergenerational Value Differentials and Family Structure Among the Wind River Shoshone." Brief Communications. *American Anthropologist* 70 (April 1968): 330–333.

* 1313. Teicher, Morton I. "Windigo Psychosis. A Study of a Relationship between Belief and Behavior Among the Indians of Northeastern Canada." *Proceedings, Annual Spring Meeting, American Ethnological Society.* Seattle: University of Washington, 1960.

A careful analysis of largely historical material. More data are needed on the current situation.

1314. Thompson, Bobby, & Peterson, J. H., Jr. "Mississippi Choctaw Identity: Genesis and Change." Paper presented at the annual meeting of the American Ethnological Society, 1973.

1315. Trager, George L. "A Status Symbol and Personality at Taos Pueblo." *Southwestern Journal of Anthropology* 4 (Autumn 1948): 299–304.

1316. Trimble, Charles *et al. Shove It, Buster. We'd Rather Have Our Land!* Denver: American Indian Press Association, 1971.

A joke book written by and for Indians.

1317. Valory, D. *Yurok Doctors and Devils: A Study in Identity, Anxiety, and Deviance.* Ann Arbor: University Microfilm, published on demand.

Based on six summer field sessions, (1964–1969) in Del Norte and Humboldt Counties, California. Heavy reliance also placed on the published and unpublished work of others, e.g. Kroeber, E. H. Erikson, E. W. Count, Robert Spott, and Sylvia Beyer.

1318. Van Steen, Marcus. *Pauline Johnson. Her Life and Work.* Toronto: Hodder and Stoughton, 1965.

The Mohawk poet.

1319. Vizenor, Gerald. *The Everlasting Sky. New Voices from the People Named the Chippewa.* New York: Crowell-Collier Press, 1972.

Vizenor is a Chippewa enrolled at White Earth Reservation in Minnesota.

* 1320. Wallace, A. F. C. "The Modal Personality Structure of the Tuscarora Indians." *Bulletin 150, Bureau of American Ethnology, Smithsonian Institution.* Washington, D.C.: Government Printing Office, 1952.

1321. Waubageshig, editor. *The Only Good Indian. Essays by Canadian Indians.* Toronto: New Press, 1972.

A thoughtful collection of essays.

1322. Wax, Rosalie H., & Thomas, R. K. "American Indians and White People." *Phylon* 22 (Winter 1961): 305–317.

An introduction to Indian etiquette for whites.

1323. Weltfish, Gene. "The Question of Ethnic Identity. An Ethnohistorical Approach." *Ethnohistory* 6 (Fall 1959): 321–347.

1324. Willard, William with Webb, J. "Suicide Among Six Indian Groups: A Study in Variation." In *Suicide in Different Cultures.* Edited by Norman Farberow. In process.

* 1325. Wilson, Alan, & Dennison, Gene. *Laughter: The Navajo Way. Humorous Stories of the People. Volume One.* Gallup Branch: University of New Mexico, July, 1970.

XVI. Formal Education

1326. Antoine, Fr. Michel J. "Towards a Working Philosophy for an Applied Ethnic Studies Program." University of Montana term paper, n.d.

1327. Basso, Keith H. Review of *Formal Education and Culture Change.* By Edward Parmee. New York: McGraw-Hill. In the *American Anthropologist* 71, no. 1 (1969): 197–198.

1328. Belding, Nanceye, Woods, R. G., and Harkins, A. M. "Evaluation Report: 1968–1969. University of Minnesota Cultural Education Specialist and Associate Program." Minneapolis: Training Center for Community Programs, University of Minnesota, June, 1969. Mimeo.

1329. Bergman, Robert. "Problems of Cross-Cultural Educational Research and Evaluation: The Rough Rock Demonstration School." Minneapolis: Training Center for Community Programs, University of Minnesota, December, 1969. Mimeo.

1330. Bonner, Myrtle. "Educational and Other Influences in the Cultural Assimilation of the Cherokee Indians of the Qualla Reservation in North Carolina." M.A. thesis, Alabama Polytechnic Institute, 1950.

* 1331. Bryde, John F., S.J. "The Sioux Indian Student: A Study of Scholastic Failure and Personality Conflict." Pine Ridge, South Dakota: Holy Rosary Mission, 1966. Offset.

1332. California. Ad Hoc Committee on California Indian Education. *California Indian Education: Report on the First All-Indian Statewide Conference on California Indian Education.* Modesto: 1967.

1333. *Catalog. Native American Studies Division.* Berkeley: University of California, 1973–74.

1334. Dickeman, Mildred. "The Integrity of the Cherokee Student." In *The Culture of Poverty: A Critique,* pp. 140–179. Edited by E. B. Leacock. New York: Simon & Schuster, 1971.

Concerns the relations between Cherokee students and their teachers with emphasis on the destructive role played by interpersonal relations within schools. Considers Cherokees in northeastern Oklahoma.

1335. Eastman, Elaine Goodale. *Pratt. The Red Man's Moses.* Norman: University of Oklahoma Press, 1935.

Some useful data on Carlisle Indian School and the "Outing System." Biased.

1336. Fannin, Paul J. "Indian Education. A Test for Democracy." *Arizona Law Review* 10 (Winter 1968): 661–673.

A useful summary of some aspects of the question.

1337. "Frontier College: Media On An Indian Reserve." *Newsletter. Challenge for Change. National Film Board of Canada.* No. 4 (Spring-Summer 1969).

1338. "Give It Back to the Indians: Education on the Reservation and Off." *Carnegie Quarterly* 17 (Spring 1969).

1339. Granzberg, Gary R. "The Impact of Television on Cree Child Development." Paper given at the American Anthropological Association meetings, Nov., 1974.

How TV watching disrupts and "westernizes" the traditional patterns of Cree child development.

1340. *Handbook. C. Warren Jones Indian Training and Bible School.* Albuquerque, New Mexico, 1958-1959. Mimeo.

1341. Harkins, Arthur M., Sherarts, I. K. & Woods, R. G. "Public Education of the Prairie Island Sioux. An Interim Report." Minneapolis: Training Center for Community Programs, University of Minnesota, December, 1969.

1342. Havighurst, Robert J. "The Dilemma of the American Indian: Can Education Serve Two Contrasting Cultures?" Reprint from *Educare Journal,* n.d.

1343. Havighurst, Robert J. "Education Among American Indians: Institutional Aspects." *The Annals of the American Academy of Political and Social Science* 311 (May 1957): 105-115.

1344. "Headstart in the Grand Canyon." *Saturday Review,* July 22, 1972, pp. 34-37.

1345. Henninger, Daniel, and Esposito, Nancy. "Regimented Non-Education Indian Schools." *New Republic* 160 (February 15, 1969): 18-21.

1346. Hertzberg, Hazel W., editor. "Teaching About American Indians." *Social Education* 36 (May 1972).

1347. Hood, John *et al. The Student's Handbook.* Albuquerque Indian School, 1956-57. Mimeo.

   A very pointed discussion of how Indian students should and should not behave.

* 1348. Humphrey, Theodore. "Self-concept and Academic Achievement Among Plains Indians." Ph.D. dissertation, University of Colorado, 1971.

1349. "Indian Teacher Training Under Tribal Control. Mississippi State University." Summary of paper given at the annual meeting of the National Indian Education Association, 1973.

1350. "Institute for Teachers of Chippewa Indian Children." Wisconsin State University, Eau Claire, August 27-30, 1967. Mimeo.

* 1351. Jackson, Curtis E. "Identification of Unique Features in Education at American Indian Schools." Ph.D. dissertation, University of Utah, 1965.

1352. Kelly, William H. *A Study of Southern Arizona School-Age Indian Children 1966-1967.* Tucson: Bureau of Ethnic Research, University of Arizona, 1967.

1353. Kickingbird, Kirke, editor-in-chief. "The ABD's of Indian Bilingual Education." *Education Journal* 2, no. 2 (1973). Washington, D.C." Institute for the Development of Indian Law.

* 1354. King, A. Richard. *The School at Mopass. A Problem of Identity.* New York: Holt, Rinehart & Winston, 1967.

The educational process in a residential school for Indian children in the Yukon Territory of Northwest Canada. This is a case study of how children learn the subculture of the school and how, in this process, the intended aims of education, as advanced by teachers and school administrators, are defeated.

1355. Kleinfeld, J. S. "Characteristics of Successful Boarding Home Parents of Eskimo and Athapascan Indian Students." *Human Organization* 32 (Summer 1973): 191-204.

1356. Krush, T. P. *et al.* "Some Thoughts on the Formation of Personality Disorder: Study of an Indian Boarding School Population." *American Journal of Psychiatry* 122 (February 1966): 868-876.

1357. La Flesche, Francis. *The Middle Five. Indian Schoolboys of the Omaha Tribe.* Madison: University of Wisconsin Press, 1963.

Important.

1358. Leon, Robert L. *et al.* "An Emotional and Educational Experience for Urban Migrants." Austin: Department of Psychiatry, University of Texas, n.d.

Leon is a psychiatrist.

1359. Mckinley, Francis. "What Are New Horizons? *Journal of American Indian Education* 5, no. 1 (1965): 25-33.

1360. Medicine, Bea. "Self-Direction in Sioux Education." Paper given at the American Anthropological Association meetings, Nov., 1974.

Special focus upon native views of learning in new community colleges among the Lakota Sioux in South Dakota.

1361. Michener, Byran P. "The Development, Validation and Applications of a Test for Need-Achievement Motivation Among American Indian High School Students." Ph.D. dissertation, University of Colorado, 1971.

1362. Miles, Janet. "How To Get Along with American Indians in the Classroom." November, 1972, manuscript (term paper).

Ms. Miles is a Chippewa. She did her undergraduate work at the University of Wisconsin-Oshkosh.

1363. Minnesota. State Department of Education. "The Ojibwa: A History Resource Unit." *Focus: Indian Education* 4 (March-April 1973): whole issue.

1364. "The Native American at the University of Wisconsin-Madison." n.d.

1365. Navajo Division of Education. *Eleven Programs for Strengthening Navajo Education.* Window Rock: The Navajo Tribe, 1973.

1366. Oswalt, Wendell H. "The School at Eskimo Point." *North* 7, no. 6 (1960): 14–16.

* 1367. Parmee, Edward A. *Formal Education and Culture Change. A Modern Apache Indian Community and Government Education Programs.* Tucson: University of Arizona Press, 1968.

San Carlos Reservation, Arizona.

1368. Pilling, Patricia L., & Pilling, A. R. "The Weitchpec P.T.A.: the Yurok and the School." Paper given at the Central States Anthropological Society meetings, 1969.

1369. Powell, J. W. "Proper Training and the Future of the Indians." *The Forum* (1894–1895): 622–629.

Some surprising and reactionary ideas by the Chief of the Bureau of American Ethnology.

1370. Powers, Joseph F. *Brotherhood Through Education. A Guide for Teachers of American Indians.* Fayette: Upper Iowa University, 1965.

Brief, intended for those having little or no prior experience with Indians.

1371. Pratt, Richard Henry. *Battlefield and Classroom. Four Decades with the American Indian. 1867–1904.* Edited by R. M. Utley. New Haven: Yale University Press, 1964.

Useful description of the early days at Carlisle.

1372. Reboussin, Roland, & Goldstein, J. W. "Achievement Motivation in Navaho and White Students." *American Anthropologist* 68 (June 1966): 740–744.

1373. Roessel, Robert A., Jr. *Education for the Adult Indian Community.* Tempe: Indian Education Center, College of Education, Arizona State University, 1964.

1374. Sockey, Clennon E. "Development in Indian Education." *BIA Education Research Bulletin* 3 (September 1974): 1–8.

Sockey is the Director of Indian Education Programs for the Bureau of Indian Affairs, Washington, D.C.

1375. Steere, Caryl *et al. Indian Teacher Aide Handbook.* Tempe: Arizona State University, 1965.

1376. Thompson, Hildegard. "Education Among American Indians: Institutional Aspects." *The Annals of the American Academy of Political and Social Science* 311 (May 1957): 95–104.

1377. Wax, Murray. "American Indian Education as a Cultural Transaction." *Teachers College Record* 64, no. 8 (1963): 693–704.

* 1378. Wax, Murray *et al.* "Formal Education in an American Indian Community." Supplement to *Social Problems* 11 (Spring 1964).

   "Isolation—lack of communication, social distance—is the cardinal factor in the problem of Indian education on the Pine Ridge Reservation." p. 102.

1379. Wax, Rosalie H. & Wax, Murray. "Dropout of American Indians at the Secondary Level." 1964, mimeo.

* 1380. Wax, Rosalie, and Wax, Murray. "Indian Education for What?" In *The American Indian Today,* pp. 257–267. Edited by Levine and Lurie. Baltimore: Penguin Books, Inc., 1970.

   A thoughtful essay.

1381. Wax, Murray and Wax, Rosalie. "Cultural Deprivation as an Educational Ideology." In *The Culture of Poverty: A Critique,* pp. 127–139. Edited by E. B. Leacock. New York: Simon and Schuster, 1971.

1382. Wax, Rosalie H. "The Warrior Dropouts." *Transaction* 4, no. 6 (1967): 40–46.

* 1383. Wolcott, Harry F. *A Kwakiutl Village and School.* New York: Holt, Rinehart & Winston, 1967.

   Observations made between 1962 and 1965 on a small island near the coast of British Columbia. Sound ethnography.

1384. Woods, Richard G., & Harkins, Arthur M. "Education-Related Preferences and Characteristics of College-Aspiring Urban Indian Teen-Agers: A Preliminary Report." May, 1969, mimeo.

XVII. Political Organization and Politicians. Indian- Government Relations

* 1385. Abler, Thomas. "Factional Dispute and Party Conflict in the Political System of the Seneca Nation (1845-1895): an Ethnohistorical Analysis." Ph.D. dissertation, University of Toronto, 1969.

1386. Akwesasne Notes. *BIA I'm Not Your Indian Any More. Trail of Broken Treaties. Mohawk Nation via Rooseveltown, New York.* 1973.

   One account of events before and after the brief occupation by Indians of the Bureau of Indian Affairs office building in Washington, D.C. in November, 1972.

1387. Alberta. Indian Association of Alberta. "Report to the Department of Indian Affairs." *Treaty and Aboriginal Rights Research.* Edmonton: 1974. Mimeo.

1388. Alberta. Indian Chiefs of Alberta. *Citizens Plus.* A Presentation by the Indian Chiefs of Alberta to Right Honourable P. E. Trudeau, Prime Minister and the Government of Canada, June, 1970.

1389. Arizona. *Annual Report of the Arizona Commission of Indian Affairs,* 1966–1967. Mimeo.

Includes state budget, population figures by reservation, and brief descriptions of various state financed programs concerning health, economic development, law enforcement, etc.

1390. Arizona. *Annual Report of the Arizona Commission of Indian Affairs,* 1967–1968. Mimeo.

Contents topically similar to 1966-1967.

1391. Arizona. *Annual Report of the Arizona Commission of Indian Affairs, 1968–1969.* Mimeo.

Contents topically similar to the 1966-1967 report.

1392. Arizona. *Annual Report of the Arizona Commission of Indian Affairs, 1969–1970.* Mimeo.

Contents topically similar to the 1966-1967 report.

1393. Arizona. *Annual Report of the Arizona Commission of Indian Affairs, 1970–1971.* Mimeo.

Contents topically similar to the 1966-1967 report.

1394. Arizona. *Annual Report of the Arizona Commission of Indian Affairs,* 1971–1972. Mimeo.

Contents topically similar to the 1966-1967 report.

1395. Arizona. *Annual Report of the Arizona Commission of Indian Affairs, 1972–1973.* Mimeo.

Contents topically similar to the 1966-1967 report plus a special section on the Cocopah.

1396. Arizona. *Annual Report of the Arizona Commission of Indian Affairs, 1973–1974.* Mimeo.

Contents topically similar to the 1966-1967 report plus a special section on the Camp Verde Yavapai.

1397. Arizona. *Tribal Directory-1967.* Arizona Commission of Indian Affairs, Mimeo.

Population of reservations; map of Arizona; names, addresses and telephone numbers of various tribal officials; partial listing of federal and state employees working with reservation communities.

1398. Arizona. *Tribal Directory-1968.* Arizona Commission of Indian Affairs. Mimeo.

Contents topically similar to 1967 Directory.

1399. Arizona. *Tribal Directory-1969.* Arizona Commission of Indian Affairs. Mimeo.

Contents topically similar to 1967 Directory.

1400. Arizona. *Tribal Directory-1970.* Arizona Commission of Indian Affairs. Mimeo.

Contents topically similar to 1967 Directory.

1401. Arizona. *Tribal Directory-1971.* Arizona Commission of Indian Affairs. Mimeo.

Contents topically similar to 1967 Directory.

1402. Arizona. *Tribal Directory-1973.* Arizona Commission of Indian Affairs. Mimeo.

Contents topically similar to 1967 Directory.

1403. Association of American Indian Affairs, Inc. "Alaska: Deadline for Justice." *Indian Affairs* 75 (July-September 1969): 1-4.

1404. Association on American Indian Affairs, Inc. "The 26th Annual Convention of the National Congress of American Indians." *Noticiero Indigenista* 29 (December 1969): 349-364.

1405. Bailey, Garrick. "Indian Tribal Government in the United States." Paper given at the American Anthropological Association meetings, Nov., 1974. ·

Operation of the tribal governments of the Osage, Creek and Choctaw including lack of sufferage for the majority of tribal members and the relationship of tribal governments to the BIA.

* 1406. Baldassin, William R., & McDermott, John T. "Jurisdiction Over Non-Indians: An Opinion of the 'Opinion,' " *American Indian Law Journal* 1 (Winter 1973): 13-22.

The inherent powers of Indian tribes are far more extensive than have been recognized and exercised in the past. The time has come to recognize the full power and authority of tribal governments to regulate all conduct within the boundaries of the reservation.

*1407. Beatty, Donald R. *History of the Legal Status of the American Indian with Particular Reference to California.* San Francisco: R and E Research Associates, 1974.

> History 1492–1848. Legal status during American control 1848–1865. Post Civil War 1865–1900. Treaty arrangements, wardship, Reorganization Act of 1934. With Bibliography.

* 1408. Bee, Robert L. "Tribal Leadership in the War on Poverty: A Case Study." *Social Science Quarterly* (December 1969): 676–686.

> Should be read in conjunction with his 1970 paper.

1409. Bell, Joseph N. "America's Oldest Debt: Justice for the Indians." *Good Housekeeping,* January, 1971, pp. 78 ff.

1410. Berman, Allen B. "Association of Leadership Roles and Economic Development: Fort Mojave Indians." Paper read at the Central States Anthropological Society meeting, May, 1969. Mimeo.

> Examines the changes occurring in the Fort Mojave Indian leadership roles in response to an increasing involvement with the American cash economy.

1411. Blakeslee, Donald J. "Development of the Nebraska Governor's Commission on Indian Affairs." 1970, typescript.

> A chronological outline of the development of the commission within which the various factional disputes are stressed.

* 1412. Bodine, John J. "Blue Lake: A Struggle for Indian Rights." *American Indian Law Review* 1 (Winter 1973): 23–32.

> A history of the legal struggle by the Taos Pueblo community to regain possession of a geographical area sacred to them.

1413. Branam, James T. "Property Rights: Intertribal Mineral Rights in the Arkansas Riverbed." *American Indian Law Review* 2 (Summer 1974): 125–135.

> Concerns dispute between the Cherokee and Choctaw-Chickasaw over mineral rights.

1414. Brandon, William. "American Indians: The Real Revolution." *The Progressive* 34, no. 2 (1970): 26–30.

1415. Brophy, William A., & Aberle, S. D. *The Indian: America's Unfinished Business: Report of the Commission on the Rights, Liberties, and Responsibilities of the American Indian.* Norman: University of Oklahoma Press, 1966.

* 1416. Bunker, Robert. *Other Men's Skies.* Bloomington: Indiana University Press, 1956; reprint edition, New York: Kraus Reprint Co., 1972.

An account of one Bureau of Indian Affairs official's encounters with the pueblo and Navajo people of New Mexico before and after World War II.

1417. Burnett, Donald L. "Indian Hunting, Fishing and Trapping Rights: The Record and the Controversy." *Idaho Law Review* 7 (1970): 49–75.

Tension between Indian treaty rights and the state power to regulate hunting, fishing and trapping has not been resolved in more than one hundred years. It will not be resolved soon. Indians must develop more potent political organizations to protect their interests since the federal government cannot do so.

* 1418. Burnette, Robert. *The Tortured Americans.* Englewood Cliffs: Prentice Hall, 1971.

One Sioux politician's version of Indian politics.

* 1419. Burnette, Robert, & Koster, John. *The Road to Wounded Knee.* New York: Bantam Books, 1974.

Summary of events associated with Wounded Knee II.

1420. Caldwell, George *et al.* "The Emerging Indian Crisis." *Canadian Welfare* (July-August 1967): 12–32. A reprint.

1421. California. Senate. *Progress Report to the Legislature.* Senate Interim Committee on California Indian Affairs. Sacramento, 1957.

1422. California. Senate. *Progress Report to the Legislature.* Senate Interim Committee on California Indian Affairs. Sacramento, 1959.

1423. California. State Advisory Commission on Indian Affairs. *Progress Report to the Governor and the Legislature on Indians in Rural and Reservation Areas.* February, 1966.

1424. California. State Advisory Committee on Indian Affairs. *Final Report to the Governor and Legislature.* Sacramento, 1969.

1425. California. Supreme Court of the State of California. *Anderson v. Mathews.* 174 Cal. 537, 163 Pac. 902, 1917.

Citizenship of non-reservation Indians.

1426. Canada. Indian-Eskimo Association of Canada. *Report of Executive Director to the Ninth Annual Meeting of Members.* Submitted by E. R. McEwen. Toronto, 1968. Mimeo.

A profile of the present situation, touching on the problems and issues. Provides a background against which activities can be evaluated.

1427. Canada. Indian-Eskimo Association of Canada. *Native Rights in Canada.* Toronto: 1970.

* 1428. Canada. *Indian Treaties and Surrenders. From 1680 to 1890.—In Two Volumes. Volume I.* Ottawa: Printed by Brown Chamberlin, Printer to the Queen's Most Excellent Majesty, 1891; reprint edition, Toronto: Coles Publishing Co., 1971.

   Treaty Numbers 1–138. Maps.

* 1429. Canada. *Indian Treaties and Surrenders. From 1680 to 1890.—In Two Volumes. Volume II.* Ottawa: Printed by Brown Chamberlin, Printer to the Queen's Most Excellent Majesty, 1891; reprint edition, Toronto: Coles Publishing Co., 1971.

   Treaty Numbers 140–280. Maps.

* 1430. Canada. *Indian Treaties and Surrenders From No. 281 to No. 483. Volume III.* Ottawa: Printed by C. H. Parmelee, Printer to the King's Most Excellent Majesty, 1912; reprint edition, Toronto: Coles Publishing Company, 1971.

   Maps.

1431. Cardinal, Harold. *The Unjust Society. The Tragedy of Canada's Indians.* Edmonton: M. G. Hurtig Ltd., 1969.

   Cardinal is a Cree politician.

1432. Cohen, Felix S. "Americanizing the White Man." *American Scholar* 21 (April 1952): 177–191.

* 1433. Cohen, Felix S. "The Erosion of Indian Rights, 1950–1953: A Case Study in Bureaucracy." *Yale Law Journal* 62, no. 348 (1953): 348–390.

   A classic statement which will richly repay a careful reading.

1434. Cohen, Felix S. "Indian Wardship. The Twilight of a Myth." *The American Indian* 11 (Summer 1953): 8–14.

   Indians are not second-class citizens since they are not wards nor are they under guardianship. They are entitled to the enjoyment of all the rights of other citizens, not eventually, but now.

* 1435. Cohen, W. H., & Mause, Philip J. "The Indian: The Forgotten American." *Harvard Law Review* 81 (June 1968): 1818–1858.

   Essential reading for the serious student of contemporary Indian affairs. Begins with a brief look at demographic, administrative and legal patterns in Indian life. Then discusses tribal courts, goals and strategy for the development of reservations, and concludes with a thoughtful section on "focuses" for community development.

1436. Collier, Peter. "The Red Man's Burden." *Ramparts* 8 (February 1970): 26–38.

The Indian occupation of Alcatraz, beginning in November, 1969; commentary concerning the troubles of a Shoshone-Bannock girl; the Navajo Reservation and its problems.

1437. Collier, Peter. "The Theft of a Nation: Apologies to the Cherokees." *Ramparts* 9 (September 1970): 36–45.

Ungracious remarks concerning W. W. Keeler and his "leadership" of the Oklahoma Cherokees.

1438. Commission on the Rights, Liberties, and Responsibilities of the American Indian. *A Program for Indian Citizens. A Summary Report.* Albuquerque, January, 1961.

1439. Cork, Ella. *The Worst of the Bargain.* San Jacinto: Foundation for Social Research, 1962.

Concerns the Iroquois of Six Nations Reserve in southern Ontario and the injustices which the white power structure has done.

1440. Corry, John. "A Man Called Perry Horse." *Harpers Magazine,* October, 1970, pp. 81–84.

A young Indian militant and some of his ideas.

1441. Crary, Margaret. *Susette La Flesche, Voice of the Omaha Indians.* New York: Hawthorn Books, Inc., 1973.

A late 19th, early 20th century Indian woman politician.

1442. Cumming, Peter A., and Mickenberg, N.H., editors. *Native Rights in Canada,* 2nd edition. Toronto: The Indian-Eskimo Association of Canada in association with General Publishing Co., Ltd., 1972.

An expanded and revised form of the first edition. Attempts to make natives and their white allies aware of the implications of treaties, and to apprise the Canadian public of the legal theory and history of aboriginal rights.

1443. Dale, Edward Everett. *The Indians of the Southwest. A Century of Development Under the United States.* Norman: University of Oklahoma Press, 1949.

Traces the relations of the Indians of New Mexico, Arizona, Utah, Nevada, and California with the federal government since 1848.

1444. Dellwo, Robert D. "Indian Water Rights—The Winters Doctrine Updated." *Gonzaga Law Review* 6 (Spring 1971): 215–240.

1445. Deloria, Vine, Jr. *Custer Died for Your Sins.* New York: Macmillan Co., 1969.

A well written political tract.

1446. Deloria, Vine, Jr. *We Talk, You Listen. New Tribes, New Turf.* New York: The Macmillan Co., 1970.

Whites can achieve a secular kind of salvation. "Tribalism" is the answer.

1447. Deloria, Vine, Jr., editor. *Of Utmost Good Faith.* San Francisco: Straight Arrow Books, 1971; reprint edition, New York: Bantam Books, 1972.

A useful collection of treaties, speeches, judicial rulings, congressional bills, and hearings from 1830 to the present.

1448. Deloria, Vine, Jr. *God Is Red.* New York: Grosset & Dunlap, 1973.

Institutionalized Christianity has failed whites in this country and should be reworked along "new" guidelines.

1449. Deloria, Vine, Jr. *Behind the Trail of Broken Treaties. An Indian Declaration of Independence.* New York: Dell Publishing Co., Inc., 1974.

1450. Deloria, Vine, Jr. *The Indian Affair.* New York: Friendship Press, 1974.

1451. Dixon, Michael R. "Chief of the Cherokees." *Cimarron Review* 9 (March 1969): 46–55.

The simple adoration of W. W. Keeler by an employee.

1452. Dobyns, Henry F. "The Indian Reorganization Act and Federal Withdrawal." *Applied Anthropology* 7 (Spring 1948): 35–44.

1453. Dobyns, Henry F. "Papago Pilgrims on the Town." *The Kiva* 16 (September-October 1950): 27–32.

1454. Dobyns, Henry F. "Therapeutic Experience of Responsible Democracy." *Midcontinent American Studies Journal* 6 (Fall 1965): 171–186.

Concerns Indian-federal government relations. Vital to the understanding of the contemporary American Indian experience.

1455. Dollar, Clyde. "The Second Tragedy at Wounded Knee. A 1970's Confrontation and Its Historical Roots." *The American West* 10 (September 1973): 4 ff.

* 1456. Drucker, Philip. "The Native Brotherhoods: Modern Intertribal Organizations on the Northwest Coast." *Bulletin 168, Bureau of American Ethnology, Smithsonian Institution.* Washington, D.C.: Government Printing Office, 1958.

Data gathered 1952–1954. Concerns the Alaska Native Brotherhood and Native Brotherhood of British Columbia. Classic.

1457. Dunn, Marty. *Red on White. The Biography of Duke Redbird.* Toronto: New Press, 1971.

Redbird is a Canadian Indian militant.

1458. Dunning, R. W. "Some Aspects of Governmental Indian Policy and Administration." *Anthropologica,* n.s. 4, no. 2 (1962).

1459. Ellis, Hal William. "Federal Taxation: Exclusion of Earnings on Allotted Indian Land From Federal Income Taxation." *American Indian Law Review* 2 (Summer 1974): 119-124.

1460. Ellis, Richard N. *General Pope and U.S. Indian Policy.* Albuquerque: University of New Mexico Press, 1970.

Federal policy toward Indians west of the Mississippi from 1862-1886.

1461. Ericson, Robert, & Snow, D. Rebecca. "The Indian Battle for Self-Determination." *California Law Review* 58, no. 2 (1970): 445-490.

1462. Ervin, Alexander M. "Civic Capacity and Transculturation: The Rise and Role of the Alaska Federation of Natives." Ph.D. dissertation, University of Illinois at Urbana-Champaign, 1974.

Reconstructs recent political history which has been affecting the culture and society of native Alaskans, and from this reconstruction it infers or analyses processes.

1463. Euler, Robert C. "Aspects of Political Organization Among the Puertocito Navajo." *El Palacio* 68 (Summer 1961): 118-120.

The community is also known as "Alamo."

1464. Euler, Robert C., & Dobyns, Henry F. "Ethnic Group Land Rights in the Modern State: Three Case Studies." *Human Organization* 20 (Winter 1961-62): 203-207.

Summarizes pertinent evidence from hydroelectric projects undertaken by the state power authorities within the reservations of the Tuscarora, Hualapai, and Navajo Indians.

1465. Faulhaber, Dwight L. "Power of a State to Impose An Income Tax on Reservation Indians." *Willamette Law Journal* 6 (December 1970): 515-524.

1466. Fernadez, F. F. "Except a California Indian: A Study in Legal Discrimination." *Southern California Quarterly* 50 (1968): 161-176.

1467. Fischbacher, Theodore. "A Study of the Role of the Federal Government in the Education of the American Indian." Ph.D. dissertation, Arizona State University, 1967.

1468. Forbes, Jack D. "A Comprehensive Program for Tribal Development in the United States." *Human Organization* 24 (Summer 1965): 159–161.

1469. French, Stewart. "Alaska Native Claims Settlement Act." Ottawa: The Arctic Institute of North America, 1972.

1470. Friedman, Howard M. "Interest in Indian Claims: Judicial Protection of the FISC." *Valpariso University Law Review* 5 (Fall 1970): 26–47.

* 1471. Gallagher, H. G. *Etok: A Story of Eskimo Power.* New York: G. P. Putnam's Sons, 1974.

    Concerns "Charles Edwardsen, Jr., a young Eskimo radical with a strange authority." Dust jacket.

1472. Gambill, Jerry. "Indians, White Men and I." *Humanist,* September/December, 1967, pp. 180–182.

1473. Gamino, John. "Bureau of Indian Affairs: Should Indians Be Preferentially Employed?" *American Indian Law Review* 2 (Summer 1974): 111–118.

    Gamino believes that they should.

1474. Ghobashy, Omar Z. *The Caughnawaga Indians and the St. Lawrence Seaway.* New York: Devin-Adair Co., 1961.

    Examines the question of the expropriation of Caughnawaga land for the St. Lawrence Seaway Authority.

* 1475. Goodrich, C. S. "The Legal Status of the California Indian." *California Law Review* 14 (1926): 83–100, 157–187.

    The best available study of California Indians and the law. Certain important state laws and Court decisions affecting Indians are cited.

1476. Green, L. C. "Canada's Indians: Federal policy, international and constitutional law." *Ottawa Law Review* 4 (Summer 1970): 101–131.

1477. Green, L. C. "The Canadian Bill of Rights, Indian Rights, and the United Nations." *Chitty's Law Journal* 22 (January 1974), 22–28.

1478. Harper, Allan G. "Canada's Indian Administration: The 'Indian Act.'" *America Indigena* 6 (October 1946): 297–314.

* 1479. Hass, Theodore H. "The Legal Aspects of Indian Affairs from 1887 to 1957." *The Annals of the American Academy of Political and Social Science* 311 (May 1957): 12–22.

1480. Haynes, C. Derek. *Law and the Eskimo in Canada Today.* Toronto: Indian-Eskimo Association of Canada, 1960.

1481. Helm, June. "Deloria on Wounded Knee." *Fellow Newsletter, American Anthropological Society* 14, no. 6 (1973): 13–14.

1482. Henning, Marilyn J. "The Ethnography of an American Indian Protest System: A Symbolic Interaction View." Ph.D. dissertation, University of Kansas, 1972.

1483. Huck, Susan L. M. "Renegades. The Second Battle of Wounded Knee." *American Opinion. An Informal Review,* May, 1973.

1484. Indians of All Tribes. *Alcatraz Is Not An Island.* Edited by Peter Blue Cloud. Berkeley: Wingbow Press, 1972.

1485. Indian Rights Association. *The Case of the Mission Indians in Southern California and the Action of the Indian Rights Association in Supporting the Defense of Their Legal Rights.* Philadelphia: Indian Rights Association, 1886.

1486. Institute for the Development of Indian Law. *Legislative Review.* Washington, D.C. Indian Legal Information Development Service 2, nos. 7 & 8, 1974.

1487. Institute of Social, Economic, and Government Research. "Native Land Claims." *Alaska, Review of Business and Economic Conditions* 4, no. 6 (1970): 1–12.

1488. Jenness, Diamond. "Eskimo Administration: I. Alaska." *Technical Paper No. 10.* Washington, D.C.: Arctic Institute of North America, 1962.

   1867–1960. Discussion proceeds by major events and categories.

1489. Jenness, Diamond. "Eskimo Administration: III. Labrador." *Technical Paper No. 16.* Washington, D.C.: Arctic Institute of North America, 1965.

   1771–1962. Discussion proceeds by major events and categories.

* 1490. Jenness, Diamond. "Eskimo Administration: V. Analysis and Reflections." *Technical Paper No. 21.* Washington, D.C.: Arctic Institute of North America, 1968.

   Essential.

1491. Johnson, C. C. "A Study of Modern Southwestern Indian Leadership." Ph.D. dissertation, University of Colorado, 1960.

1492. Johnson, David C. "State Taxation of Indians: Impact of the 1973 Supreme Court Decisions." *American Indian Law Review* 2 (Summer 1974): 1–27.

Discusses four Supreme Court cases of 1973 involving the issue of a state's power to tax Indians. Indians probably can gain immunity from state taxation within prescribed limits.

1493. Johnson, K. M. *K344, or The Indians of California vs. the United States.* Los Angeles: Dawson Book Shop, 1966.

1494. Jones, Gary T. "Enforcement Strategies for Indian Landlords." *American Indian Law Review* 2 (Summer 1974): 41–60.

Indians today are not gaining benefits comparable to white land owners. Some possibilities for improving the situation are discussed.

1495. Jones, Thomas. "Recent Developments in the American Indian Movement." Undergraduate term paper, 1973. 17 pp.

1496. Jorgensen, J. G., & Lee, R. G., editors. "The New Native Resistance: Indigenous Peoples' Struggles and the Responsibilities of Scholars." *Module 6.* New York: An MSS Modular Publication, Inc. 1973.

1497. Josephy, Alvin M., Jr. *Red Power. The American Indians' Fight for Freedom.* New York: American Heritage Press, 1971.

A useful collection of papers.

* 1498. Kappler, Charles. J. *Indian Treaties 1778–1883.* New York: Interland Publishing Inc., 1972. Originally published as *Indian Affairs: Laws and Treaties, Volume 2 (Treaties).* Washington, D.C.: Government Printing Office, 1904.

Vital for the serious student of Indian-federal relations.

1499. Kelly, J. M. "Extent of the 'Fair and Honorable Dealings' Section of the Indian Claims Commission Act." *St. Louis University Law Journal* 15 (Spring 1970): 491–507.

1500. Kelly, Lawrence C. *The Navajo Indians and Federal Indian Policy, 1900–1935.* Tucson: University of Arizona Press, 1968.

A valuable and well written account.

1501. Kenny, R. W. *History and Proposed Settlement, Claims of California Indians.* Sacramento: California State Library, Documents Section, California State Printing Office, 1944.

Re K344.

1502. Kerr, James R. "Constitutional Rights, Tribal Justice, and the American Indian." *Journal of Public Law* 18, no. 2 (1969): 311–338.

1503. Kerr, John A. "The Indian Treaties of 1876." *The Dalhousie Review* 8 (1938): 187–195.

* 1504. Kickingbird, Kirke, & Ducheneaux, Karen. *One Hundred Million Acres.* New York: Macmillan & Co., 1973.

A somewhat biased account of the Indian land claims situation.

1505. Kleinfelder, Bob. "Alternative to Paternalism." *Lion,* October, 1972, pp. 10–13.

1506. La Course, Richard. "Indian Politics in Changing Times." Reprint from *Race Relations Reporter* 4 (June 25, 1973).

1507. Lange, Charles H. "Education and Leadership in Rio Grande Pueblo Culture Change." *The American Indian* 8 (Winter 1958–59): 27–35.

1508. League of Women Voters of the United States. *Indian—And Proud of It!* Washington, D.C.: League of Women Voters Fund Publication, 1971. Mimeo.

1509. Lee, Edith. "Forked Tongues and Wounded Knees." A First Hand Account of the Federal Government Aiding and Abetting a Reign of Terror by Known Criminals. Privately Printed, n.d.

1510. Leigh, L. H. "The Indian Act: The Supremacy of Parliament, and the Equal Protection of the Laws." *McGill Law Journal* 16 (June 1970): 389–398.

1511. Leupp, Francis E. "Outlines of an Indian Policy." *Outlook,* April 15, 1905, pp. 946–950.

* 1512. Leupp, Francis E. *The Indian and His Problem.* New York: Charles Scribner's Sons, 1910; reprint edition, Johnson Reprint, 1970.

The head waters of paternalism. Written by a Commissioner of Indian Affairs.

1513. Leupp, Francis E. *In Red Man's Land.* Chicago: Fleming H. Revell, 1914.

1514. Levy, Jerrold E. with Kunitz, S. J. "Navajo Voting Patterns." *Plateau* 43 (1970): 1–8.

1515. Lindquist, G. E. E. "Indian Treaty Making." *Chronicles of Oklahoma.* 26 (1948–49): 416–448.

1516. Long, Joseph K. "An Anthropological Analysis of the Midwest Indian Association, Inc." 1967. Mimeo, 20 pp.

1517. Lummis, Charles F. *Bullying the Moqui.* Edited with introduction by R. Easton and M. Brown. Prescott: Prescott College Press, 1968.

1518. Lurie, Nancy O. "Anthropology and Indian Claims Litigation: Problems, Opportunities, and Recommendations." *Ethnohistory* 2 (1955): 357–375.

1519. Lurie, Nancy O. "A Reply to 'The Land Claims Cases.' Anthropologists in Conflict." *Ethnohistory* 3 (1956): 256–279.

1520. Lurie, Nancy O. "The Indian Claims Commission Act." *The Annals of the American Academy of Political and Social Science* 311 (May 1957): 56–70.

1521. Lurie, Nancy O. "Open Letter to Carl Olien and Robert Smith etc. re Winnebago Office of Economic Opportunity Relationships." March 27, 1967, mimeo.

1522. Lurie, Nancy O. "Data Re Winnebago Claims Case." June, 1969, mimeo.

1523. Lurie, Nancy O. "Wisconsin: A Natural Laboratory for North American Indian Studies." 1969, mimeo.

1524. Lurie, Nancy O. "Anthropologists in the U.S. and the Indian Claims Commission." Paper given at the American Ethnological Society-Northeastern Anthropological Society meetings, 1970. Ditto.

1525. Lynch, Robert. "Politics in a Northern Paiute Community." Ph.D. dissertation, University of Minnesota, 1971.

* 1526. Lysck, K. M. "Indian Hunting Rights: Constitutional Considerations and the Role of Indian Treaties in British Columbia." *University of British Columbia Law Review* 2 (March 1966): 401–421.

1527. McLoone, John L. "Indian Hunting and Fishing Rights." *Arizona Law Review* 10 (Winter 1968): 725–739.

* 1528. MacNeish, June Helm. "Leadership Among the Northeastern Athabascans." *Anthropologica* n.s. 2, no. 2 (1956): 131–163.

1529. Magnuson, Ed. & Johnson, Keith. "The Angry American Indian: Starting Down the Protest Trail." *Time,* February 9, 1970, pp. 14–20.

1530. Major, Robert. Project: *Homeless Native People in Kenora.* Prepared for Grand Council Treaty #3. Kenora, 1974. Mimeo.

     Major is an Ojibway Indian.

1531. Manitoba Indian Brotherhood. *Annual Report Submitted to the Indian*

Chiefs of Manitoʌa at the Annual Meeting, February 21-22-23, 1973. Winnipeg.

Essential.

1532. Manitoba Metis Federation Inc. "Statutory Land Rights. Volume I. A Study of the Statutory and Aboriginal Rights of Metis People in Manitoba." Winnipeg: 1973. Mimeo.

A report intended for use in various legal actions.

1533. Melling, J. "Recent Developments in Official Policy towards Canadian Indians and Eskimos." *Race* 7 (April 1966): 379-399.

1534. Mickenberg, Neil H. "Aboriginal Rights in Canada and the United States." *Osgoode Hall Law Journal* 9, no. 1 (1971): 119-156.

1535. *Midwest Directory 1967. Organizations, Agencies and Institutions Relating to Indian Affairs.* Vermillion: Institute of Indian Studies, University of South Dakota, 1967.

* 1536. Miller, Frank. "Problems of Succession in a Chippewa Council." In *Political Anthropology,* pp. 173-185. Edited by M. Swartz. Chicago: Aldine Publishing Co., 1966.

1537. Mirrieless, Edith R. "The Cloud of Mistrust." *Atlantic Monthly,* 199, no. 1 (1957): 55-59.

1538. Mission Indian Federation, Inc. *California Indians Charge Violation of Indian Claims Act of 1946.* 1966, 40 pp.

Reproduces many documents, letters, and newspaper articles.

1539. Mission Indian Federation, Inc. *Posterity Demands the Truth.* 1967.

40 pages dealing with land claims cases.

1540. Morris, Alexander. *The Treaties of Canada with the Indians of Manitoba and the North-West Territories Including the Negotiations on Which They Were Based, and Other Information Relating Thereto.* Toronto: P. R. Randall, 1862; reprint edition, Toronto: Coles Publishing Co., 1971.

1541. Morris, Terry. "LaDonna Harris: A Woman Who Gives a Damn." *Redbook*, February, 1970, pp, 75ff.

1542. Myer, Dillon S. "Indian Administration: Problems and Goals." *Social Service Review* 27 (March 1953): 193-200.

1543. NAACP Legal Defense and Educational Fund, Inc., with the cooperation of

The Center for Law and Education, Harvard University. *An Even Chance.* New York: 1971.

An analysis of the Johnson-O'Malley Act of 1934 and its influence on educational programs for Indians.

1544. "Native America Fights for Survival!" *Tempo* 2 (March 1970). New York: National Council of Churches.

1545. Oakes, Richard. "Alcatraz is not an Island." *Ramparts* 11 (December 1972): 36-41.

* 1546. Ortiz, Alfonso. Review of Vine Deloria's *Custer Died for Your Sins.* In *American Anthropologist* 73 (August 1971): 953-955.

A valuable analysis of Deloria's work.

1547. Osborne, Ralph, editor. *Who Is the Chairman of This Meeting? A Collection of Essays.* Toronto: Neewin Publishing Co., 1972.

* 1548. Pandey, Triloki Nath. "Tribal Council Elections in a Southwestern Pueblo." *Ethnology* 7 (January 1968): 71-85.

1549. Parker, Alan, and Trudell, R., project coordinators. *The Indian Civil Rights Act, Five Years Later. A Report of and Evaluation by Indian Lawyer, Tribal Council Representatives, and Indian Court Judges.* 1973. Mimeo.

125 pages plus appendices.

1550. Pease, Gregory. "Constitutional Revision—Indians in the New Mexico Constitution." *Natural Resources Journal* 9 (July 1969): 466-470.

1551. Pelletier, Emile. *Aboriginal Rights. Volume Two of A Study of the Statutory and Aboriginal Rights of Metis People in Manitoba.* Winnipeg: Manitoba Metis Federation Press, 1973.

* 1552. Peterson, Helen L. "American Indian Political Participation." *The Annals of the American Academy of Political and Social Science* 311 (May 1957): 116-126.

1553. Pierre, George. *American Indian Crisis.* San Antonio, Texas: The Naylor Company, 1971.

Pierre is an Indian politician.

1554. Piser, Bob. "Box Canyon for the Navajo." Series of articles on tribal government reprinted from *The Arizona Republic,* 1961.

The federal government and the incumbent tribal administration do not have the best interests of the Navajo people at heart.

1555. Price, Monroe E. "Lawyers on the Reservation: Some Implications for the Legal Profession." *Law and Social Order Arizona State Law Journal* 2 (1969): 161–206.

* 1556. Price, Monroe E. *Law and the American Indian. Readings, Notes and Cases.* Indianapolis: Bobbs-Merrill Co., Inc., 1973.

1557. Prucha, F. P. "New Approaches to the Study of the Administration of Indian Policy." *Journal of the National Archives* (Spring 1971): 15–19.

1558. Purser, Joyce. "The Administration of Indian Affairs in Louisiana, 1903–1920." *Journal of the Louisiana Historical Association* 5 (1964): 401–421.

1559. Regina v. George. "The Unilateral Abrogation of Indian and Eskimo Treaty Rights." Supreme Court of Canada. Cartwright, Fauteux, Abbott, Martland, Judson, Ritchie and Hall JJ., in *Criminal Reports* 47 (1966): 395–400. Edited by C. A. G. Palmer. Toronto: The Carswell Co., Ltd.

Indians and Eskimos must follow the same game laws as non-natives.

* 1560. Reiblich, G. Kenneth. "Indian Rights Under the Civil Rights Act of 1968." *Arizona Law Review* 10 (Winter 1968): 617–648.

Considers the Act in relation to legislative history; previous federal Indian policy; and the accomplishment of the desirable purpose of integrating the American Indian into our system of government without breaking faith with the historical semi-sovereign power of internal government assured to many Indian tribes by treaties and other dealings with them. Concludes that federal law cannot insure protection of Indian civil rights.

1561. "Resolving Conflicts—A Cross-Cultural Approach." Kenora, Ontario: University of Manitoba, 1967.

Indians in Kenora.

1562. Rice, W. G., Jr. "The Position of the American Indian in the Law of the United States." *Journal of Comparative Legislation and International Law* 16, 3rd series (1934): 307–308.

1563. Riddell, R. G. "A Study in the Land Policy of the Colonial Office, 1763–1855." *The Canadian Historical Review* 18 (December 1937): 385–405.

1564. Robinson, W. W. *Land in California.* Berkeley: University of California Press, 1948.

Pages 19–20 give claims cases.

* 1565. Ross, John Alan. "Political Conflict on the Colville Reservation." *Northwest Anthropological Research Notes* 2 (1968): 29–91.

1566. Sanders, D. E. "The Bill of Rights and Indian Status." *University of British Columbia Law Review,* 7, no. 1 (1972): 81–105.

1567. Schell, Herbert E. *History of South Dakota.* Third edition, revised. Lincoln: University of Nebraska Press, 1974.

Some consideration of the "new Indian militancy."

* 1568. Schifter, Richard. "Trends in Federal Indian Administration." *South Dakota Law Review* 15 (Winter 1970): 1–21.

1569. Schmeckebier, Lawrence F. *The Office of Indian Affairs.* Baltimore: Johns Hopkins Press, 1927; reprint edition, Brookings Institution: Institute of Government Research, Service *Monograph 48.*

1570. Schusky, Ernest L. "Mission and Government Policy in Dakota Indian Communities." *Practical Anthropology* 10 (May-June 1963): 109–114.

1571. Schusky, Ernest L. "American Indians and the 1968 Civil Rights Act." *America Indigena* 29 (April 1969): 369–376.

Schusky concluded that in spite of this Act "much change is still necessary before Indians will have the same rights as other citizens."

* 1572. Schusky, Ernest L. "An Indian Dilemma." *International Journal of Comparative Sociology* 11 (March 1970): 58–66.

The dilemma facing Indians in the United States today is to choose between their rights as tribal members and their civil liberties as U.S. citizens.

1573. Schusky, Ernest L. "Political and Religious Systems in Dakota Culture." *The Modern Sioux,* pp. 140–147. Edited by Ethel Nurge. Lincoln: University of Nebraska Press, 1970.

It is the structure of the relationship between dominant white systems and Dakota communities that limits Indian action or the development of effective indigenous systems.

1574. Scott, Duncan C. "Indian Affairs, 1840-1867." In *Canada and Its Provinces. A History of the Canadian People and Their Institutions,* pp. 331–364. Edited by A. Shortt and A. G. Doughty. Toronto: Publishers' Association of Canada Ltd., 1913.

1575. Sheehan, Bernard W. *Seeds of Extinction. Jeffersonian Philanthropy and the American Indian.* Chapel Hill: The University of North Carolina Press, 1973.

Explores the paradoxical story of how the Jeffersonian generation, with the best of goodwill, tore the Indians' culture apart. Many of the living roots of modern federal policy can be found here.

1576. Shepardson, Mary. "Navajo Ways in Government. A Study in Political Process." *Memoir 96, American Anthropological Association* 65:3, Part 2. June, 1963.

1577. Shepardson, Mary. "Problems of the Navajo Tribal Courts in Transition," *Human Organization* 24 (Fall 1965): 250-253.

* 1578. Shortt and Doughty. "The Royal Proclamation, 1763 by George III." In *Documents Relating to the Constitutional History of Canada 1759-1791.* Ottawa: 1907. Revised December, 1972.

Important document for consideration of today's treaty problems.

* 1579. Smith, J. G. E. "Leadership among the Southwestern Ojibwa." *Publications in Ethnology, No. 7.* Ottawa: National Museum of Man, 1973.

1580. Smith, M. Estellie. "A Comparative Analysis of Tiwa Government and Law." May, 1968, mimeo.

Factionalism and its implications at Isleta.

1581. Smith, M. Estellie. "Governing Systems and Cultural Change Among the Southern Tiwa." Paper given at American Anthropological Association meetings, 1968.

* 1582. Smith, M. Estellie. "Governing at Taos Pueblo." *Eastern New Mexico University Contributions in Anthropology* 2, no. 1 (1969).

"Taos socioculture can be seen to be a blend of conservation retentions and even anachronisms, and adaptive innovations in response to changing needs." p. 39.

1583. Smith, M. Estellie. "Political Entrepreneurship." Paper given at the American Anthropological Association meetings, 1971.

Concerns Isleta largely in the 1950's-1960's era.

1584. Southwest Research Associates. *Report of the Oklahoma Indian Council, Inc. 1962-1965.* Mimeo, 1965.

* 1585. Spencer, Robert F. "Sketch of Laguna Land Ways." *El Palacio* 47 (1940): 214-227.

1586. Stern, Theodore. "Livelihood and Tribal Government on the Klamath Indian Reservation." *Human Organization* 20 (Winter 1961-62): 172-180.

Examines the relationship of economic interests to tribal government as it existed until recently upon the Klamath Indian Reservation in south-central Oregon.

1587. Stevens, Carl. "Reapportionment: One Man, One Vote, As Applied to Tribal Government." *American Indian Law Review* 2 (Summer 1974): 137–146.

A general, brief survey with specific examples.

1588. Stewart, Omer C. "Chippewa Indian Claims." *The Delphian Quarterly* 42, no. 4 (1959): 35–40.

1589. Svensson, Frances. *The Ethnics in American Politics: American Indians.* Minneapolis: Burgess Publishing Co., 1973.

A disappointing work.

1590. Talbert, Carol. "Experiences at Wounded Knee.' *Human Organization* 33 (Summer 1974): 215–217.

1591. Thomas, Robert K. "Powerless Politics." *New University Thought* 4 (Winter 1966-67): 44–53.

1592. Thomas, Robert K. "Colonialism: Classic and Internal." *New University Thought* 4 (Winter 1966-67): 37–44.

1593. Tobias, H. J., & Woodhouse, Charles E. *Minorities and Politics.* Albuquerque: University of New Mexico Press, 1969.

1594. Udall, Stewart L. "The State of the Indian Nation—An Introduction." *Arizona Law Review* 10 (Winter 1968): 553–558.

A statement to the effect that the federal government has not done an effective job in maintaining and promoting Indian affairs.

1595. Vance, John T. "The Congressional Mandate and the Indian Claims Commission." *North Dakota Law Review* 45 (Spring 1969): 325–336.

1596. Washburn, Wilcomb E. "Philanthropy and the American Indian: The Need for a Model." *Ethnohistory* 15 (Winter 1968): 43–56.

1597. Washburn, Wilcomb E. *Red Man's Land. White Man's Law.* New York: Scribners, 1971.

A collection of papers.

1598. Wax, Murray, & Wax, Rosalie. "Federal Programs and Indian Target Populations." In *Majority and Minority. The Dynamics of Racial and Ethnic Relations,* pp. 491–502. Edited by N. R. Yetman and C. Hoy Steele. Boston: Allyn and Bacon, Inc., 1971.

1599. Whitaker, Gretel H. "Indian Politics in James Lake." Paper given at the Central States Anthropological Society Meetings, 1967.

1600. White, Jay Vincent. "Taxing Those They Found Here. An Examination of the Tax Exempt Status of the American Indian Institute for the Development of Indian Law." Washington, D.C., 1974.

1601. Williams, Aubrey W., Jr. "Navajo Political Process," *Smithsonian Contributions to Anthropology 9.* Washington, D.C.: Smithsonian Institution Press, 1970.

Describes the function of various political structures and their incorporation into the Navajo way of life. Data collected between January 1961 and December 1963.

1602. Willis, William S. "Divide and Rule: Red, White and Black in the Southeast." *Journal of Negro History* 48 (July 1963): 157-176.

* 1603. Wilson, Dorothy Clarke. *Bright Eyes. The Story of Susette La Flesche, an Omaha Indian.* New York: McGraw-Hill Book Co., 1974.

Sister of Francis La Flesche. Wife of Henry Tibbles. The well-written story of a successful Indian woman and politician amid the currents of late 19th century America.

1604. Wilson, H. Clyde. "Jicarilla Apache Political and Economic Structures." *University of California Papers in American Archeology and Ethnology* 48, no. 4 (1964): 297-360.

1605. Witt, Shirley Hill. "Nationalistic Trends Among American Indians." In *The American Indian Today,* pp. 93-127. Edited by Levine and Lurie. Baltimore: Penguin Books Inc., 1970.

1606. Witte, Edwin E. "Claim of the La Point Band of the Chippewa Indians of the Bad River Indian Reservation Against the State of Wisconsin." Madison: Wisconsin Legislative Reference Library, 1927. Mimeo.

1607. Workshop on American Indian Affairs, 1956. *Federal Indian Legislation and Politics. A Study Packet.* Chicago: Privately printed, 1957.

An interesting analysis of federal-Indian relations organized around: general policy; reservation resources; community services; reservation development and relocation; tribal claims and Indian Claims Commission.

1608. Wounded Knee Communiques. Dittoed material regarding Wounded Knee Affair distributed on the University of Wisconsin Campus at Madison, 1973.

1609. *Why Wounded Knee?* Coordination and Information Committee, 1974.

Report.

XVIII. Social Control

1610. Ackerman, Lillian A. "Marital Instability and Juvenile Delinquency Among the Nez Perces." *American Anthropologist* 73, no. 3 (1971): 595–603.

Data collected during the summer of 1965. No information supplied concerning number of informants, or other aspects of the field situation. Marital instability, loss of aboriginal communal discipline, the various dimensions of social disorganization contribute to deviation.

* 1611. American Friends Service Committee. *Uncommon Controversy. Fishing Rights of the Muckleshoot, Puyallup, and Nisqually Indians.* Seattle: University of Washington Press, 1970.

1612. American Indian Law Review Inc. *American Indian Law Review* 1 (Winter 1973). College of Law, University of Oklahoma, Norman.

By far the most useful publication of its kind.

1613. Basso, Keith H. "Introduction and Notes." In *Western Apache Raiding and Warfare.* Edited by Keith H. Basso. Tucson: University of Arizona Press, 1971.

* 1614. Black, Robert A. "Hopi Grievance Chants: A Mechanism of Social Control." *Studies in Southwestern Ethnolinguistics,* pp. 54–67. The Hague: Mouton & Co., 1967.

1615. Blanchard, Kendall. "Team Sports and Conflict Resolution Among the Mississippi Choctaw." Paper given at the American Anthropological Association meetings, 1974.

Function of modern team sports in minimizing disruptive aggression in Choctaw society. Changing patterns of Choctaw athletic behavior are analyzed.

1616. Brown, Donald N. "Ceremonial Competition in a Non-Competitive Culture." Paper given at the American Anthropological Association meetings, 1974.

Competition at Picuris Pueblo in ceremonial foot racing and political activities is seen as essential for the maintenance of the community.

* 1617. Burnett, Donald L., Jr. "An Historical Analysis of the 1968 'Indian Civil Rights' Act." *Harvard Journal on Legislation* 9 (May 1972): 557–626.

1618. California. *People v. Bray.* 105 Cal. 344, 1894. See also California Penal Code, Sec. 397, amended Statutes of 1893, p. 98.

Selling liquor to Indians.

1619. California. Statues of California, 1850, Ch. 38. *Act to Regulate Elections.*

Voters limited to "white male citizens of the U.S. and white male citizens of Mexico who shall have elected to become a citizen of the U.S." under the Treaty of Guadalupe Hidalgo, 1848. California Indians entitled to vote in California Constitution of 1879, Art. II, Pt. 1.

1620. California. Statutes of California, 1850, Ch. 133; amended April 18, 1860 in Statutes of California, Ch. 231. *Act for the Government and Protection of Indians, April 22, 1850.*

Act legalizing what can only be called Indian slavery in California. Act and amendments reprinted in Heizer and Almquist 1971: 212–217. Examples of Indian indenturing discussed in Heizer and Almquist 1971: 40–58.

1621. California. Statutes of California, 1854, Ch. 12. *Act Prohibiting Transfer of Arms or Ammunition to Indians of Either Sex.*

Repealed in California Statutes, 1913, Ch. 56, p. 57.

1622. California. California Statutes, 1864, Ch. 209, Sec. 68, p. 213; California Statutes, 1866, Ch. 342, Secs. 56–58, p. 398; California Statutes, 1869-1870, Ch. 556; Amended Statutes, 1873-1874, Sec. 26; Amended Statutes, 1880, pp. 38, 47; California Statutes 1902, Ch. 77; California Statutes 1909, Ch. 594, Sec. 3. *Right of Indians to Attend Public Schools.*

In 1921 the State Legislature revised Sec. 1662 of the Political Code and permitted Indians to attend public schools.

1623. California. Supreme Court of the State of California. *Thompson v. Doaksum.* 68 Cal. 593; 10 Pac. 199, 1886.

Land title.

1624. Cohen, Fay. "Notes on American Indian Movement." Minneapolis, Minnesota, 1968. Typescript.

1625. Cohen, Fay G. "The Indian Patrol: Social Control and Social Change in an Urban Context." Ph.D. dissertation, University of Minnesota, 1973.

Concerns the Minneapolis-St. Paul area.

1626. "Criminal Procedure: Habeas Corpus As an Enforcement Procedure Under the Indian Civil Rights Act of 1968. 25 United States Code, 1971.

1627. Davis, Laurence. "Court Reform in the Navajo Nation." *Journal of the American Judicature Society* (to Promote the Administration of Justice) 43 (August 1959): 53-55.

1628. Deane, Captain Burton. *Mounted Police Life in Canada. A Record of Thirty-One Years' Service, 1883-1914.* London: Cassell and Co., Ltd., 1916; reprint edition, Toronto: Coles Publishing Co., 1973.

Some remarks concerning Indians.

1629. DuMars, Charles T. "Indictment Under the 'Major Crimes Act'—An Exercise in Unfairness and Unconstitutionality." *Arizona Law Review* 10 (Winter 1968): 691-705.

The handling of Indian criminal affairs is replete with instances of inequality of treatment between Indians and non-Indians.

* 1630. Ellis, Florence H. "Authoritative Control and the Society System in Jemez Pueblo." *Southwestern Journal of Anthropology* 9 (Winter 1953): 385-394.

* 1631. Farber, W.O., Odeen, P. A., & Tschetter, R. A. "Indians, Law Enforcement and Local Government. A Study of the Impact of the Off-Reservation Indian Problem on South Dakota Local Government with Special Reference to Law Enforcement." *Report No. 37.* Vermillion: Government Research Bureau in cooperation with the Institute of Indian Studies, State University of South Dakota, 1957.

A thoughtful, comprehensive statement.

1632. Folsom, R. D. "American Indians Imprisoned in the Oklahoma Penitentiary: 'A Punishment More Primitive Than Torture.' " *American Indian Law Review* 2 (Summer 1974): 85-109.

1633. Foreman, Grant. "The Indian and the Law." *Oklahoma Bar Association Journal* 17 (1946): 82-91.

1634. Freeman, Ethel Cutler. "Lawlessness in an Indian Tribe as a Microcosm of World Trends." Tokyo: *Eighth Congress of Anthropological and Ethnological Sciences,* pp. 191-193. 1968.

Seminole Indians in Big Cypress Swamp, Florida.

1635. Gabourie, Fred W. "Justice and the Urban American Indian." *Journal of the State Bar of California.* (January-February 1971): 36-49.

Justice is in short supply for Indian urban residents.

* 1636. Hughes, Charles Campbell. "From Contest to Council: Social Control Among the St. Lawrence Island Eskimos." In *Political Antrhopology,* pp. 255-263. Edited by M. Swartz. Chicago: Aldine Publishing Co., 1966.

1637. Institute of Indian Studies. *1st Annual Conference for Indian Tribal Judges. Program and Proceedings.* Vermillion: State University of South Dakota, 1959.

1638. Institute of Indian Studies. *2nd Annual Conference on Indian Affairs. Program and Proceedings.* "Indian Education, Goals and Means." Vermillion: State University of South Dakota, 1956.

1639. Institute of Indian Studies. *3rd Annual Conference on Indian Affairs. Program and Proceedings.* "Indian Problems of Law and Order." Vermillion: State University of South Dakota, 1957.

1640. Institute of Indian Studies. *4th Annual Conference on Indian Affairs. Program and Proceedings.* "Employment." Vermillion: State University of South Dakota, 1958.

1641. Institute of Indian Studies. *5th Annual Conference on Indian Affairs. Program and Proceedings.* "Tribal Rehabilitation Programs." Vermillion: State University of South Dakota, 1959.

1642. Institute of Indian Studies. *6th Annual Conference on Indian Affairs. Program and Proceedings.* "The Indian and State Government." Vermillion: State University of South Dakota, 1960.

1643. Institute of Indian Studies. *8th Annual Conference on Indian Affairs. Program and Proceedings.* "Indian Art in a Changing Society." Vermillion: State University of South Dakota, 1962.

1644. Kelley, Thomas P. *Run Indian Run. The Story of Simon Gun-an-noot.* Don Mills, Ontario: Paperjacks, General Publishing Co. Ltd., 1972.

An account of "justice" for an Indian in the early part of this century.

1645. Lawton, H. *Willie Boy: A Desert Manhunt.* Balboa Island, California: Paisano Press, 1960.

The chase and killing of a Chemehuevi, "Willie Boy," in 1909. Excellent.

* 1646. Levy, J. E., Kuntiz, S. J., & Everett, M. "Navajo Criminal Homicide." *Southwestern Journal of Anthropology* 25 (Summer 1969): 124–152.

1647. Luebben, Ralph A. "The Navajo Dilemma—A Question of Necessity." *The American Indian* 8 (Winter 1958-59): 6–16.

1648. Luebben, Ralph. "Anglo Law and Navaho Behavior." *Kiva* 29 (February 1964): 60–75.

Navahos in Rico, Colorado.

1649. Merrill, M. H. "Introduction to the Function of a Journal of Indian Law." *American Indian Law Review* 1 (Winter 1973): 5–12.

A thoughtful discussion of the term "Indian law," and its implications.

1650. *Navaho Tribal Code. Volume I.* Orford, New Hampshire: Equity Publishing Corp., 1962.

1651. *Navaho Tribal Code. Volume 2.* Orford, New Hampshire: Equity Publishing Corp., 1962.

1652. "Pueblo Shooting Brings Charges." *The Albuquerque Tribune,* April 13, 1961.

1653. "Remember Wounded Knee." St. Paul: Wounded Knee Defense/Offense Committee, 1973.

1654. Reynolds, Ray, Lamphere, L., & Cook, C. E., Jr. "Time, Resources and Authority in a Navaho Community." *American Anthropologist* 69 (April 1967): 188–199.

1655. Smith, M. Estellie. "A Tri-cultural Analysis of Violence." Revised version of a paper presented at the American Anthropological Association meetings, 1972. Mimeo.

Compares Taos Pueblo in the 17th century, the Spanish-Americans of Taos Valley during the 18th and 19th centuries, and a number of Hippie communes scattered throughout the valley in the mid-20th century.

1656. Spiker, LaRue. "Under the Indian Sign. A Blanket Over Homicide." *The Nation*, April 26, 1965, pp. 483–486.

1657. Stewart, Omer. "Questions Regarding American Indian Criminality." *Human Organization* 23 (Spring 1964): 61–66.

1658. Strickland, Rennard. "American Indian Law and the Spirit World." *American Indian Law Review* 1 (Winter 1973): 33–53.

An examination of the traditional legal system of the Cherokees.

1659. Woods, Richard G., & Harkins, A. M. "Rural and City Indians in Minnesota Prisons." Minneapolis: Training Center for Community Programs, University of Minnesota, January, 1970.

1660. Woods, Richard G., & Harkins, A. M. "Indians and other Americans In Minnesota Correctional Institutions." Minneapolis: Training Center for Community Programs, University of Minnesota, March, 1970. Mimeo.

XIX. Music—Dance

* 1661. Basso, Keith H. Review of *American Indian Ceremonial Dances*. By John Collier. *Ethnohistory* 19 (1973): 295–296.

1662. Beede, Aaron McGaffey. "The Dakota Indian Victory-Dance." *North Dakota Historical Quarterly* 9 (April 1942): 167–178.

Held November 30, 1918, to celebrate the end of World War I. Beede was an Episcopal missionary.

* 1663. Densmore, Frances. "Music of Acoma, Isleta, Cochiti and Zuni Pueblos." *Bulletin 165, Bureau of American Ethnology, Smithsonian Institution.* Washington, D.C.: Government Printing Office, 1957.

Music recorded in 1928, 1930, 1940 by Isleta, Cochiti and Zuni members of the "Stand Rock" Indian Ceremonial at Wisconsin Dells, Wisconsin. The Edward Hunt family supplied the Acoma material.

* 1664. Fenton, W. N. "The Iroquois Eagle Dance. An Offshoot of the Calumet Dance." *Bulletin 156, Bureau of American Ethnology, Smithsonian Institution.* Washington, D.C.: Government Printing Office, 1953.

Fieldwork done 1933–1936 in western New York. "The theme of this investigation is that the diversity of individual expression in cultural situations reflects the personal history of the individual within the culture of his group." p. 1.

1665. Haima, Paula. "The Powwow at Oshkosh." April 9, 1974, typescript.

Excellent description written by an undergraduate of a powwow held as part of the spring "Indian Week" activities at the University of Wisconsin-Oshkosh campus.

1666. Howard, James H. "The Dakota Indian Victory Dance. World War II." *North Dakota History* 18 (1951): 31–40.

1667. Howard, James H. "Notes on the Dakota Grass Dance." *Southwestern Journal of Anthropology* 7 (1951): 82–85.

* 1668. Howard, James & Kurath, Gertrude P. "Ponca Dances, Ceremonies, and Music." *Ethnomusiocology* 3 (January 1959): 1–14.

* 1669. Howard, James. "The Compleat Stomp Dancer." *Museum News, South Dakota Museum* 26 (May-June 1965): 1–23.

1670. Howard, James H. "The Plains Gourd Dance as a Revitalization Movement." Paper given at the American Anthropological Association meetings, 1974.

Recent use of the "Gourd Dance" among many groups whose ancestors never performed it—now secular and intertribal in nature.

* 1671. Kurath, Gertrude P. "The Tutelo Harvest Rites: A Musical and Choreographic Analysis." *Scientific Monthly* 76, no. 3 (1953): 153-162.

1672. Kurath, Gertrude P. "Modern Ottawa Dancers." *Midwest Folklore* 5, no. 1 (1955): 15-22.

1673. Kurath, Gertrude P. "Pan-Indianism in Great Lakes Tribal Festivals." *American Journal of Folklore* 70 (1957): 179-182.

* 1674. Kurath, Gertrude P. "Iroquois Music and Dance: Ceremonial Arts of Two Seneca Longhouses." *Bulletin 187, Bureau of American Ethnology, Smithsonian Institution.* Washington, D.C.: Government Printing Office, 1964.

New York State and Six Nations Reserve, Ontario.

* 1675. Kurath, Gertrude P. "Dance and Song Rituals of Six Nations Reserve, Ontario." *Bulletin 220.* Ottawa: National Museum of Canada, 1968.

Observations made from 1948-1964.

1676. Kurath, Gertrude P. *Michigan Indian Festivals.* Ann Arbor Publishers, 1968.

* 1677. Kurath, Gertrude P. with Garcia, Antonio. "Music and Dance of the Tewa Pueblos." *Number 8. Museum of New Mexico Research Records.* Santa Fe: Museum of New Mexico Press, 1970.

Without parallel.

1678. Kurath, Gertrude P. "Powwow!" *Wisconsin Trails* 13 (Summer 1972): 11-16.

1679. Lange, Charles H. "King's Day Ceremonies at a Rio Grande Pueblo, January 6, 1940." *El Palacio* 58 (1951): 398-406.

1680. Lange, Charles H. "The Feast Day Dance at Zia Pueblo, New Mexico, August 15, 1951." *The Texas Journal of Science* 1 (March 30, 1952): 19-26.

1681. Lange, Charles H. "*Tablita* or Corn, Dances of the Rio Grande Pueblo Indians." *The Texas Journal of Science* 11(March 1957): 59-74.

1682. Merriam, Alan P. *Flathead Indian Music.* Missoula: Montana State University Music Foundation, 1950. (With Barbara W. Merriam)

1683. Merriam, Alan P. "Notes on Cheyenne Songs." *Journal of the American Musicological Society* 3 (Fall 1950): 289–290.

1684. Merriam, Alan P. "Flathead Indian Instruments and Their Music." *Musical Quarterly* 37 (July 1951): 368–375.

1685. Merriam, Alan P. *Songs and Dances of the Flathead Indians.* New York: Ethnic Folkways Library, 12" LP P445, Nov., 1953. Album notes, 8 pp. illus.

1686. Merriam, Alan P. "The Selection of Recording Equipment for Field Use." *Kroeber Anthropological Society Papers* 10 (Spring 1954): 5–9.

1687. Merriam, Alan P. "The Use of Music in the Study of a Problem of Acculturation." *American Anthropologist* 57 (February 1955): 28–34.

1688. Merriam, Alan P. *The Ethnography of Flathead Indian Music.* Missoula, Montana: Western States Branch, American Anthropological Association, Western Anthropology, No. 2, 1955. (Wtih Barbara W. Merriam)

1689. Merriam, Alan P. Review of *Enemy Way Music* by David P. McAllester. In *American Anthropologist* 58 (February 1956): 219–220.

1690. Merriam, Alan P. "Music of the Flathead Indian." *Tomorrow* 4 (Spring 1956): 103–107.

1691. Merriam, Alan P. "Washo Peyote Songs." *American Anthropologist* 59 (August 1957): 615–641. (With Warren L. D'Azevedo).

1692. Merriam, Alan P. Review of *Songs and Dances of Great Lakes Indians* by Gertrude Kurath and *Indian Music of the Southwest* by Laura Boulton. In *Journal of the International Folk Music Council* 10 (1958): 108–109.

1693. Merriam, Alan P. "The Northwestern University Laboratory of Comparative Musicology." *The Folklore and Folk Music Archivist* 1 (December 1958): 1, 4.

1694. Merriam, Alan P. with Spier, Robert. "Chukchansi Yokuts Songs," In *Actas del XXXIII Congreso Internacional de Americanistas, Vol. II.* pp. 6611–638. San Jose, Costa Rica: Lehmann, 1959.

1695. Merriam, Alan P. *The Anthropology of Music.* Evanston: Northwestern University Press, 1964.

1696. Merriam, Alan P. "The Importance of Song in the Flathead Indian Vision Quest." *Ethnomusicology* 9 (May 1965): 91–99.

1697. Merriam, Alan P. Review of *Folk and Traditional Music of the Western*

Continents by Bruno Nettl. In *American Anthropologist* 68 (August 1966): 1061–1063.

* 1698. Merriam, Alan P. *Ethnomusicology of the Flathead Indians.* Chicago: Aldine Publishing Co., 1967.

1699. Merriam, Alan P. "Music and the Origin of the Flathead Indians: A Problem in Culture History." In *Music in the Americas,* pp. 129–138. Edited by George List and Juan Orrego-Salas. Bloomington, Indiana: Indiana University Research Center in Anthropology, Folklore, and Linguistics, Inter-American Music Monograph Series, Vol. 1, 1967.

1700. Merriam, Alan P. "Washo Peyote Songs." In *Washo-Peyote Songs: Songs of the American Indian Native Church—Peyotist.* By Warren L. d'Azevedo and Alan P. Merriam. New York: Ethnic Folkways Library, Notes for 12" LP album FE 4384, 1972.

1701. Merriam, Alan P. Review of *Nez Perce Songs of Historical Significance* by Loran Olsen. In *Ethnomusicology* 17 (January 1973): 152–153.

1702. Merriam, Alan P. Review of "People and Their Music. Paul Collaer, *Music of the Americas.*" In *Natural History* 82 (April 1973): 78–83.

1703. Merriam, Alan P. "Style: Eskimo and American Indian Song." In *Silver Burdett Music,* pp. 106–109. Edited by Elizabeth Crook, Bennett Reimer, and David S. Walker. Morristown, New Jersey: General Learning Corp., 1973.

1704. Merriam, Alan P. "Keynote Address: Anthropology and the Dance." In *New Dimensions in Dance Research: Anthropology and Dance—The American Indian,* pp. 9–27. Edited by Tamara Comstock. New York: Committee on Research in Dance, 1974.

* 1705. Nettl, Bruno. "North American Indian Musical Styles." *American Folklore Society.* Philadelphia: 1954.

1706. Nettl, Bruno. "Studies in Blackfoot Indian Musical Culture, Part 1. Traditional Uses and Functions." *Journal of the Society for Ethnomusicology* 9 (May 1967): 141–160.

1707. Powers, William K. "Contemporary Expressive Culture Music and Dance." Paper given at the American Anthropological Association meetings, 1974.

Examples from the Pine Ridge Sioux Indian Reservation give an indication of how overt cultural expressions such as music and dance can serve as indices of culture stability and change.

1708. Ridington, Robin. "Beaver Indian Dreaming and Singing." *Anthropologica* n. s. 13 (1971): 115–128.

1709. Rynkiewich, Michael A. "Elaboration of Chippewa Powwows." Paper read at the Central States Anthropological Society meetings, 1967.

An important paper.

1710. Slotkin, J. S. "An Intertribal Dancing Contest." *Journal of American Folklore* 68 (1955): 224–228.

The Menomini and other western Great Lakes peoples.

* 1711. Society of American Indian Tradition. "American Indian Music." Parts 1-7. In *American Indian Hobbyist/Tradition,* Volumes 7-8 by William Powers. Alton, Illinois: 1961–1962.

Articles on modern Indain music and dancing. A wide variety of other subjects having to do with contemporary American Indian life are covered in these and other issues. Unfortunately, this journal is defunct.

1712. Stewart, Tyrone H., & Smith, Jerry. *The Oklahoma Feather Dancer.* Tulsa: American Indian Crafts and Culture, 1973.

Excellent text, photographs and line drawings.

1713. Thompson, Gilbert. "An Indian Dance at Jemez, New Mexico." *American Anthropologist* 2 o.s. (October 1889): 351–355.

* 1714. Ware, Naomi. "Survival and Change in Pima Indian Music." *Ethnomusicology* 14 (January 1970): 100–113.

* 1715. Wilder, Carleton Stafford. "The Yaqui Deer Dance: A Study in Cultural Change." pp. 145-210. *Bulletin 186, Anthropological Paper 66, Bureau of American Ethnology, Smithsonian Institution.* Washington, D.C.: Government Printing Office, 1963.

XX. Religion

1716. Aberle, David F., & Stewart, O. C. "Navaho and Ute Peyotism: A Chronological and Distributional Study." *University of Colorado Studies. Series in Anthropology No. 6.* Boulder: University of Colorado Press, 1957.

* 1717. Aberle, David F. "The Peyote Religion Among the Navaho." *Viking Fund Publications in Anthropology No. 42.* New York: Wenner-Gren Foundation, 1966.

* 1718. Abrams, George. "Moving of the Fire. A Case of Iroquois Ritual Innovation." In *Iroquois Culture, History, and Prehistory. Proceedings of the 1965 Congress on Iroquois Research,* pp. 23-24. Edited by E. Tooker. Albany: New York State Museum and Science Service, 1967.

Description of ritual associated with the moving of the fire of the Cold-spring Longhouse, June 12, 1965.

1719. Albers, Patricia. "Contemporary Ceremonialism: Economics and Interaction." Paper given at the American Anthropological Association meetings, 1974.

Function of contemporary powwows among the Dakota.

1720. Amoss, Pamela T. "The Persistence of Aboriginal Religious Beliefs and Practices Among the Nooksack Coast Salish." Ph.D. dissertation, University of Washington, 1971.

1721. Bahti, Tom. *Southwestern Indian Ceremonials.* Flagstaff: KC Publications, 1970.

Brief, but well-illustrated with an apt supporting narrative, concerning some ceremonial events that are often open to the public.

* 1722. Berkhofer, Robert F., Jr. *Salvation and the Savage. An Analysis of Protestant Missions and American Indian Response, 1787-1862.* Lexington: University of Kentucky Press, 1965; reprint edition, New York: Atheneum, 1972.

1723. Bodine, John J. "The Sacred Blue Lake of the Taos Indians." *Persimmon Hill.* Oklahoma City: National Cowboy Hall of Fame, 1974.

* 1724. Brunton, Bill B. "Ceremo..ial Integration in the Plateau of Northwestern North America." *Northwest Anthropological Research Notes* 2 (1968): 1-28.

Examines the ceremonial nature of Plateau inter-group relations, demonstrates the role played by ceremonialism in binding Plateau groups into larger ceremonial entries. Shows that this ceremonial integration persists (1966) tying reservations to one another.

* 1725. Capron, Louis. "The Medicine Bundles of the Florida Seminole and the Green Corn Dance." *Bulletin 151, Anthropological Paper No. 35, Bureau of American Ethnology, Smithsonian Institution,* pp 155-210. Washington, D.C.: Government Printing Office, 1953.

Clear, honest ethnography.

1726. Casagrande, Joseph. "Ojibwa Bear Ceremonialism: The Persistence of a Ritual Attitude." *Acculturation in the Americas. Proceedings and Selected Papers of the 29th International Congress of Americanists,* pp. 113-117. Edited by Sol Tax. Chicago: University of Chicago Press, 1952.

* 1727. Chafe, Wallace L. "Seneca Thanksgiving Rituals." *Bulletin 183, Bureau of American Ethnology, Smithsonian Institution.* Washington, D.C.: Government Printing Office, 1961.

Texts presented are based on tape recordings made in August, 1959, with Chief Corbett Sundown as speaker. Classic ethnography.

* 1728. Collins, John James. "Peyotism and Religious Membership at Taos Pueblo, New Mexico." *The Southwestern Social Science Quarterly* 48 (1967): 183–191.

* 1729. Collins, John James. "A Descriptive Introduction to the Taos Peyote Ceremony." *Ethnology* 7 (October 1968): 427–449.

* 1730. Colton, Harold S. *Hopi Kachina Dolls.* Revised edition, Albuquerque: University of New Mexico Press, 1959.

Basic to the analysis of the subject. Concerns the design, traditions and identification of 266 Hopi kachinas.

1731. Cousland, Harold. "First Lights of Christmas." *New Mexico Magazine,* November-December, 1970, pp. 11–12.

"Pueblo Indians" of Tortugas near Las Cruces, New Mexico.

1732. Coze, Paul. "Living Spirits of Kachinam." *Arizona Highways,* June, 1971, *passim.*

* 1733. Dangberg, Grace M., editor. "Letters to Jack Wilson, the Paiute Prophet Written Between 1908 and 1911." *Bulletin 164, Anthropological Paper 55, Bureau of American Ethnology, Smithsonian Institution,* pp. 279–296. Washington, D.C.: Government Printing Office, 1957.

Fascinating data. A brief introduction followed by twenty letters written by Indians to the Prophet.

1734. De Laguna, Frederica. "Mungo Martin 1879–1962." *American Anthropologist* 65 (August 1963): 894–896.

An eloquent obituary and interesting account of the funeral of a great and good man.

1735. Demsey, H. A. "Blackfoot Ghost Dance." *Occasional Paper No. 3.* Glenbow-Alberta Institute, 1968.

1736. Dobyns, Henry F., & Euler, Robert C. "The Ghost Dance of 1889 Among the Pai Indians of Northwestern Arizona." *Prescott College Studies in Anthropology No. 1.* Prescott: Prescott College Press, 1967.

1737. DuBois, C. *The 1870 Ghost Dance.* Berkeley: University of California Anthropological Records 3 (1), 1939.

1738. Emerick, Richard G. "Notes on Death, Burial and Shamanism Among the

Havasupai." In *Readings in Introductory Anthropology, Vol. 2*, pp. 173–177. Berkeley: McCutchan Publishing Corp., 1970.

Fieldwork was done between 1949 and 1954.

* 1739. Feraca, S. E. "Wakinyan: Contemporary Teton Dakota Religion Museum of the Plains Indian." *Studies in Plains Anthropology and History, Number 2*. Browning, Montana: Museum of the Plains Indian, 1963.

Discusses the Sun Dance, Vision Quest, Yuwipi Cult, Clowns, the Horse Dance, Peyotism and Herbalism. A classic ethnography.

* 1740. Fortune, R. F. "Omaha Secret Societies." *Columbia Contributions to Anthropology Vol. 14*. New York: Columbia University Press, 1932.

An engaging and valuable study. Fieldwork done in the 1920's. "I have set down how these people feel as well as what they think and do, or rather what they did; for in these days feeling and thinking are still curiously of the old quality, and action only has suffered a very considerable transmutation from the influence of White contact. They are very distinctly as dissociated personalities, in mind and in emotion moulded by one culture, in what their hands and feet are compelled to do to keep their bodies from hunger and privation not exactly moulded, but hewn and battered into some apology of shape by a radically differing culture." p. 3.

* 1741. Fox, Robin. "Therapeutic Rituals and Social Structure in Cochiti Pueblo." *Human Relations* 13 (1960): 291–303.

"The patient's neurosis was based on a disturbance of those motives and sentiments on which the matrilineal clan system itself depends for its continuance. The cure, resulting from one of those curious instances of unconscious cultural insight, consisted of reaffirming those sentiments and reordering those disturbed motives by making an adjustment at the level of social organization—by the patient into two new lineages." p. 301. Fox spent five months in all during the summers of 1958 and 1959 at Cochiti.

1742. Fox, Robin. "Witchcraft and Clanship in Cochiti Therapy." In *Magic, Faith, and Healing*, pp. 174–200. Edited by Ari Kiev. New York: Free Press-MacMillan Co., 1964.

"Cochiti culture provides the sources of its people's illnesses; it provides the media of expression for them; it mobilizes help for patients; it effects the cure, and it ensures reinforcement." p. 198.

1743. Funmaker, Walter W. "The Bear in Winnebago Culture: A Study in Cosmology and Society." M.A. thesis, University of Minnesota, 1974.

Funmaker is a Wisconsin Winnebago.

1744. Gayton, A. H. "The Ghost Dance of 1870 in South-central California."

Publications in American Archaeology and Ethnology 28, pp. 57–82. Berkeley: University of California, 1930.

Possible evidence of the Ghost Dance.

1745. Gilmour, J. H. "An Indian Prophet: a Banning Witch Doctor's Forebodings." *San Francisco Chronicle,* June 17, 1892; reprint edition, *University of California Anthropological Records* 15, No. 2 (1955): 155–156.

Possible evidence of the Ghost Dance.

1746. Guemple, D. L. "The Eskimo Ritual Sponsor: A Problem in the Fusion of Semantic Domains." *Ethnology* 8 (October 1969): 468–483.

A detailed analysis of the role of ritual sponsor as it is practiced by the Quqiktamiut Eskimo of the Belcher Islands.

1747. Handelman, Don. "The Development of a Washo Shaman." *Ethnology* 6 (October 1967): 444–464.

The life history of the last shaman among the Washo, Henry Rupert, 1885–present. Fascinating data, especially with respect to innovation.

1748. Harman, Robert. "Change in a Navajo Ceremonial." *El Palacio* 71 (Spring 1964): 20–26.

1749. Hawley, Florence. "The Keresan Holy Rollers: An Adaptation to American Individualism." *Social Forces* 5 (October-May 1947-49): 272–280.

1750. Hawley, Florence. "The Mechanics of Perpetuation in Pueblo Witchcraft." In *For the Dean, Essays in Anthropology in Honor of Byron Cummings on his 89th Birthday, September 20, 1950,* pp. 143–158. Tucson: Hohokam Museum Association, and Santa Fe: Southwest Monuments Association, 1950.

1751. Hendry, Jean. "Iroquois Masks and Maskmaking at Onondaga." *Bulletin 191, Anthropological Paper 74, Bureau of American Ethnology, Smithsonian Institution.* Washington, D.C.: Government Printing Office, 1964.

1752. Hodge, William H. "Navaho Pentecostalism." *Anthropological Quarterly* 37 (July 1964): 73–93.

A description and analysis of one episode centering around non-English speaking Navahos.

1753. Howard, James H. "Omaha Peyotism." *University of South Dakota Museum News* 11 (May 1950): 3–5.

Peyote has virtually replaced all of the other formal religions which the Omaha formerly possessed.

1754. Howard, James. "A Yanktonai Dakota Mide Bundle." *North Dakota History* 19 (April 1952): 132–139.

1755. Howard, James. "The Sun Dance of the Turtle Mountain Plains-Ojibwa." *North Dakota History* 19 (October 1952): 249–264.

1756. Howard, James, & Hurt, Wesley R., Jr. "A Dakota Conjuring Ceremony." *Southwestern Journal of Anthropology* 8 (Autumn 1952): 286–296.

1757. Howard, James. "Notes on Two Dakota 'Holy Dance' Medicines and Their Uses." *American Anthropologist* 55 (October 1953): 608–609.

1758. Howard, James. "An Oto-Omaha Peyote Ritual." *Southwestern Journal of Anthropology* 12 (Winter 1956): 432–436.

1759. Howard, James. "Mescalism and Peyotism Once Again." *Plains Anthropologist* 5 (1960): 84–85.

* 1760. Howard, James. "When They Worship the Underwater Panther: A Prairie Potawatomi Bundle Ceremony." *Southwestern Journal of Anthropology* 16 (Summer 1960): 217–224.

1761. Howard, James. "A Note on the Dakota Water Drinking Society." *American Indian Tradition* 7, no. 3 (1961): 96.

1762. Howard, James. "The Kenakuk Religion: An Early 19th Century Revitalization Movement 140 Years Later." *Museum News. University of South Dakota* 26 (November-December 1965).

1763. Howard, James H. "The Henry Davis Drum Rite: An Unusual Drum Religion Variant of the Minnesota Ojibwa." *Plains Anthropologist* 11 (1966): 117–126.

1764. Howard, James. "Half Moon Way: The Peyote Ritual of Chief White Bear." *Museum News. South Dakota Museum* 29, no. 1–2 (1967): 1–24.

Whitebear was of mixed black, Comanche and Kiowa descent.

1765. Howard, James H. "Bringing Back the Fire: The Revival of a Natchez-Cherokee Ceremonial Ground." *American Indian Crafts and Culture* 4 (January 1970): 9–12.

1766. Hurt, Wesley R., Jr. "Factors in the Persistence of Peyote in the Northern Plains." *Plains Anthropologist* 5 (1960): 16–27.

1767. Hurt, Wesley R., Jr. "The Yankton Dakota Church: A Nationalistic Movement of Northern Plains Indians." *Essays in the Science of Culture in Honor of Leslie A. White,* pp. 269–287. Edited by G. E. Dole and R. L. Carneiro. New York: T. Y. Crowell Co., 1960.

1768. Jacobson, Doranne. "Navajo Enemy Way Exchanges." *El Palacio* 71 (Spring 1964): 7–19.

1769. Jones, David. E. *Sanapia: Comanche Medicine Woman.* New York: Holt, Rinehart & Winston, 1972.

1770. Jones, J. A. "The Sun Dance of the Northern Ute." *Bulletin 157, Anthropological Paper 47, Bureau of American Ethnology, Smithsonian Institution.* Washington, D.C.: Government Printing Office, 1955.

The central theme of the paper is to determine what role the Sun Dance has played in Ute culture.

1771. Keech, Roy A. "The Pecos Ceremony at Jemez. August 2, 1932." *El Palacio* 36, nos. 17–18, (1934): 129–134.

1772. Kehoe, Alice B. "The Ghost Dance Religion in Saskatchewan, Canada." *Plains Anthropologist* 13 (1968): 296–304.

1773. Kew, John E. M. "Coast Salish Ceremonial Life: Status and Identity in a Modern Village." Ph.D. dissertation, University of Washington, 1970.

1774. Kilpatrick, Jack F., & Kilpatrick, A. G. "The Foundation of Life: The Cherokee National Ritual." *American Anthropologist* 66 (December 1964): 1386–1391.

Oklahoma Cherokee data.

1775. Kilpatrick, Jack F., & Kilpatrick, A. G. "Muskogean Charm Songs Among the Oklahoma Cherokees. *Smithsonian Contributions to Anthropology* 2, no. 3 (1967): 29–40.

1776. Kilpatrick, Jack F., & Kilpatrick, A. G. "Notebook of a Cherokee Shaman." *Smithsonian Contributions to Anthropology* 2, no. 6 (1970): 83–125.

1777. Kirby, Julia. "Traditional Practitioner Training Program (Navajo)." School of Journalism, University of Wisconsin, Madison, 1974. Mimeo.

1778. La Barre, Weston. "Religious Freedom of Indians Again Upheld." *American Anthropologist* 67 (April 1965): 505.

Peyote use by Indians for religious purposes supported in California.

1779. Lame Deer, John, & Erodes, Richard. *Lame Deer, Seeker of Visions. The Life of a Sioux Medicine Man.* New York: Touchstone, Simon and Schuster, 1972.

Interesting reading, especially when compared with Jones' Sanapia, the Comanche medicine woman.

* 1780. LaMere, Oliver. *Winnebago Calendar. 1920.* Privately printed.

    Excellent pictures and text.

1781. Landes, Ruth. "Potawatomi Medicine." *Transactions, Kansas Academy of Science* 66 (Winter 1963): 553-599.

    The Potawatomi near Mayetta, Kansas in the '30's.

* 1782. Laski, Vera. *Seeking Life. Memoirs of the American Folklore Society* 50 (1959).

    Esoteric ceremonial activity at San Juan Pueblo.

1783. Latorre, Dolores L., & Latorre, F. A. "The Ceremonial Life of Mexican Kickapoo Indians." *8th Congress of Anthropological and Ethnological Science.* Tokyo: 1968, pp. 268-270.

1784. Leviness, W. Thetford. "Christmas at Santa Clara." *New Mexico Magazine,* November-December, 1968, pp. 30-31.

    The artist Pablita Velarde talks about her pueblo at Christmas.

1785. Lewis, Thomas H., M.D. "The Oglala (Teton Dakota) Sun Dance: Vissicitudes of its Structures and Functions." *Plains Anthropologist* 17-55 (1972): 44-49.

1786. Liberty, Margot. "Suppression and Survival of the Northern Cheyenne Sun Dance." *Minnesota Archeologist* 27, no. 4 (1965): 121-143.

* 1787. Lieber, Michael D. "Opposition to Peyotism Among the Western Shoshone: The Message of Traditional Belief." *Man* 7 (September 1972): 387-396.

    Based on three months field research among the western Shoshone living on the Yomba reservation in Reese River and in the town of Austin, Nevada.

1788. McDowell, Edwin. "Navajo Medicine Men Are Busier Than Ever Bringing Peace of Mind." *The Wall Street Journal,* March 26, 1973.

1789. Mabe, Ruth A. "Rituals for the Christmas Season." *New Mexico Magazine,* November-December, 1968, pp. 6-9.

    "Pueblo Indians" of Tortugas near Las Cruces, New Mexico.

1790. Malan, Vernon. "The Dakota Indian Religion." *Bulletin 473,* Brookings: South Dakota State College, Agricultural Experiment Station, 1959.

    Describes and analyzes the differences in the value systems of the Dakota Indians and Western Civilization, and suggests a probable explanation for the religious practices of present day Pine Ridge Reservation residents.

1791. Margolies, Susan. "Powwows and Peyote Help Indians Adjust to Life in the Big City." *Wall Street Journal,* June 15, 1973, p. 10.

1792. Maring, Ester G. "The Religiopolitical Organization, Customary Law and Values of the Acoma (Keresan) Pueblo Indians: A Study in Acculturation and Social Control." Ph.D. dissertation, University of Indiana, 1969.

1793. Marriott, Alice, & Rachlin, Carol K. "The Dancing Feather." In *American Indian Mythology,* pp. 165–170. New York: Crowell, 1969.

1794. Meighan, C., & Riddell, F. *The Maru Cult of the Pomo Indians: A California Ghost Dance Survival.* Southwest Museum Papers 23, 1972.

1795. Merriam, Alan P. Review of *The Ghost Dance Religion and the Sioux Outbreak of 1890* by James Mooney. *Ethnomusicology* 10 (January 1966): 131.

1796. Miller, Virginia P. "The 1870 Ghost Dance on the Round Valley Indian Reservation: New Data and a New Look." Paper given at the American Anthropological Association meetings, 1974.

This paper adds archival evidence to previous accounts based on field evidence.

1797. Moore, John H. "A Study of Religious Symbolism among the Cheyenne Indians." Ph.D. dissertation, New York University, 1974.

1798. Nash, P. "The Place of Religious Revivalism in the Formation of the Intercultural Community on Klamath Reservation." In *Social Anthropology of North American Tribes,* pp. 375–442. Edited by Fred Eggan. Chicago: University of Chicago Press, 1955.

1799. Native American Church (Peyote). *NAC News.* Wittenberg, Wisconsin: May 8, May 22, 1974. Ditto.

Since this is a newsletter published by and for Winnebago people who follow the peyote road, it is difficult for an outsider to obtain copies. Extremely useful.

1800. Nurge, Ethel. "The Sioux Sun Dance in 1962." *XXXVI Congreso Internacional De Americanistas Separata del Vol. 3.* Sevilla 1966, pp. 105–114.

1801. Painter, Muriel T., & Sayles, E. B. *Faith, Flowers and Fiestas. The Yaqui Indian Year. A Narrative of Ceremonial Events.* Tucson: University of Arizona Press, 1962.

Good pictures, brief commentary.

1802. Pandey, Triloki Nath. "The Nature of Zuni Theocracy." In *Cambridge Papers in Social Anthropology, No. 8.* Edited by Meyer Fortes. Cambridge University Press (forthcoming).

1803. Pelletier, Wilfred, *et al. For Every North American Indian Who Begins to Disappear I Also Begin to Disappear. Being a Collection of Essays concerned with the Quality of Human Relations Between the Red and White Peoples of This Continent.* Toronto: Neewin Publishing Co., Ltd., 1971.

   The Canadian situation with emphasis on Indian-church relations.

* 1804. Petter, Rodolphe. "Some Reminiscences of Past Years in My Mission Service Among the Cheyenne." *The Mennonite (Mission Number)* 51 (November 1936): 1–18.

1805. Postal, Susan Koessler. "Hoax Nativism at Caughnawaga: A Control Case for the Theory of Revitalization" *Ethnology* 4 (July 1965): 266–281.

   Research done during the summer of 1963.

1806. Powell, Peter J. *Sweet Medicine. The Continuing Role of the Sacred Arrows, the Sun Dance, and the Sacred Buffalo Hat in Northern Cheyenne History. Volumes I and II.* Norman: University of Oklahoma Press, 1969.

   The best work of its kind.

* 1807. Radin, Paul. "A Sketch of the Peyote Cult of the Winnebago: A Study in Borrowing." *Journal of Religious Psychology* 7 (January 1914): 1–22.

* 1808. Richen, Marilyn C. "Leadership and Change in the Indian Shaker Church." Ph.D. dissertation, University of Oregon, 1974.

* 1809. Ridington, Robin. "The Medicine Fight: An Instrument of Political Process among the Beaver Indians." *American Anthropologist* 70 (December 1968): 1152–1160.

   The Beaver live in northeastern British Columbia. The medicine fight is "a style of discourse that defines the roles assumed in Beaver competition for the validation of supernatural power."

1810. Rough Rock Demonstration School (Navajo Reservation). *Appendix A. Board Meeting Held February 6, 1967. 8th Monthly Report of Rough Rock Demonstration School,* pp. 129–156.

   Concerns use of federal funds for training of singers.

1811. Rush, Emmy Matt. "The Indians of the Coachella Valley Celebrate Fiesta of the Choom-Ni." *El Palacio* 32, no. 1 (1932).

* 1812. Salter, Michael A. "An Analysis of the Role of Games in the Fertility Rituals of the Native North American." *Anthropos* 69 (1974): 494–504.

Of some contemporary relevance.

1813. Schaeffer, Claude E. "Blackfoot Shaking Tent." *Occasional Paper No. 5*. Glenbow-Alberta Institute, 1969.

1814. Schultz, John L., & Walker, Deward. "Indian Shakers on the Colville Reservation." *Commentary, Research Studies 35*, 1967. pp. 167–172.

1815. Schultz, John L. "Acculturation and Religion on the Colville Indian Reservation." Ph.D. dissertation, University of Washington, 1971.

1816. Shimkin, D. B. "The Wind River Shoshone Sun Dance." *Bulletin 151, Anthropological Paper 41, Bureau of American Ethnology, Smithsonian Institution.* Washington, D.C.: Government Printing Office, 1953.

"The purposes of this study of the Wind River Shoshone Sun Dance are to broaden existing knowledge of the past and present forms of the ceremony among these people, to trace its history, and to outline the social and psychological factors affecting the development of the institution or, conversely, stemming from it." p. 401. Fieldwork done in 1937–38.

1817. Sinclair, John L. "The Christmas Pueblo." *New Mexico Magazine,* November-December, 1963, pp. 7–9.

San Felipe at Christmas.

1818. Slotkin, J. S. "Menomini Peyotism. A Study of Individual Variation in a Primary Group with a Homogeneous Culture." *Transactions of the American Philosophical Society* 42, no. 4 (1952).

1819. Slotkin, J. S. "The Menomini Powwow. A Study in Cultural Decay." *Milwaukee Public Museum Publications in Anthropology* 4, 1957.

* 1820. Smith, David Merrill. "INKONZE: Magico-Religious Beliefs of Contact-Traditional Chipewan Trading at Fort Resolution, Northwest Territory, Canada." *Ethnology Division Paper No. 6, Mercury Series.* Ottawa: National Museum of Man, 1973.

1821. Spencer, Robert F. "Native Myth and Modern Religion Among the Klamath Indians." *Journal of American Folklore* 65 (1952): 217–226.

1822. Spindler, Louise S. "Witchcraft in Menomini Acculturation." *American Anthropologist* 54 (1952): 593–601.

Some useful case materials.

1823. Stearns, Mary Lee. "The Reorganization of Ceremonial Relations in Haida Society." Paper given at the American Anthropological Association meetings, 1974.

1824. Stevenson, Dorothy. "Shalako. Opera of the Gods." *New Mexico Magazine,* November-December, 1961, pp. 28 ff.

1825. Stevenson, Dorothy. "Song of the Deer." *New Mexico Magazine,* November-December, 1963, pp. 30–33.

    Tesuque Pueblo at Christmas-Deer Dance.

1826. Stevenson, Ian. "Culture Patterns in Cases Suggestive of Reincarnation among the Tlingit Indians of Southeastern Alaska." *Journal of the American Society for Psychical Research* 60 (March 1966): 229–243.

1827. Stewart, Kenneth M. "Witchcraft Among the Mohave Indians." *Ethnology* 12 (July 1973): 315–324.

1828. Stewart, Omer C. *The Native American Church and the Law with Description of Peyote Religious Services.* Reprinted from *Westerners Brand Book,* Vol. 17, 1961.

1829. Storm, Hyemeyohsts. *Seven Arrows.* New York: Harper & Row, 1972.

    Concerns ceremonial practice and world view of the Cheyenne. A very controversial book. The Northern Cheyennes have asked the publisher to withdraw it from sale.

1830. Sturtevant, William. "A Seminole Medicine Maker." In *In the Company of Man,* pp. 505–532. Edited by J. B. Casagrande. New York: Harper Torchbooks, 1960.

1831. Thomas, Prentice M., Jr. "Ecological and Social Correlates of Religious Movements among North American Indians." Ph.D. dissertation, Tulane University, 1972.

1832. Thomas, Robert K. "The Role of the Church in Indian Adjustment." *Kansas Journal of Sociology* 3 (Winter 1967): 20–28.

* 1833. Tooker, Elisabeth. *The Iroquois Ceremonial of Midwinter.* Syracuse: Syracuse University Press, 1970.

1834. Underhill, Ruth. "Religion Among American Indians." *The Annals of the American Academy of Political and Social Science* 311 (May 1957): 127–136.

1835. Valory, D. "The Focus of Indian Shaker Healing." Berkeley: *Kroeber Anthropological Society Papers* 35 (1966): 69–111.

1836. Voget, Fred W. "Current Trends in the Wind River Shoshone Sun Dance." *Bulletin 151, Anthropological Paper No. 42, Bureau of American Ethnology, Smithsonian Institution.* Washington, D.C.: Government Printing Office, 1953, pp. 485–499.

Discusses sponsorship and organization; preliminary dances; lodge construction; dance practices, and ideology.

* 1837. Vogt, Evon Z. "Study of the Southwestern Fiesta System as Exemplified by the Laguna Fiesta." *American Anthropologist* 57 (August 1955): 820–839.

An important paper, not only for the understanding of Laguna but for inter-cultural relations in the Southwest as well.

* 1838. Walker, Deward E., Jr. "Nez Perce Sorcery." *Ethnology* 6 (January 1967): 66–96.

1839. Walker, Deward E., Jr. *Conflict and Schism in Nez Perce Acculturation. A Study of Religion and Politics.* Pullman: Washington State University Press, 1968.

1840. Washburn, O. A., & Washburn, Eleanor. "Pueblo Christmas at Tesuque." *New Mexico Magazine,* November-December, 1969, pp. 4–5.

1841. Wilson, B. *Ukiah Valley Pomo Religious Life. Supernatural Doctoring, and Beliefs: Observations of 1939–1941.* University of California Archaeological Survey Reports 72, 1968.

1842. Wilson, Edmund. "The Zuni Shalako Ceremony." *Red, Black, Blond and Olive.* New York: Oxford University Press, 1956.

1843. Woodward, John A. "The Anniversary: a contemporary Diegueno complex." *Ethnology* 7 (January 1968): 86–94.

Observed in the 1960's.

* 1844. Wright, Barton. *Kachinas: a Hopi Artist's Documentary.* Flagstaff: The Northland Press, with the Heard Museum, 1973.

Reproduces 237 paintings of Hopi Kachinas by a single Hopi artist, Cliff Bahnimptewa. Brief descriptions of each are given with emphasis upon identification and function within the calendar of major esoteric ceremonies.

* 1845. Wyman, Leland C. *Blessingway. With Three Versions of the Myth Recorded and Translated from the Navajo by Fr. Berard Haile.* Tucson: University of Arizona Press, 1970.

An impressive work.

XXI. Health—Disease—Poverty

1846. Adair, John, *et al.* "Patterns of Health and Disease Among the Navahos." *The Annals of the American Academy of Political and Social Science* 311 (May 1957): 80-94.

1847. "Aging." *Trans-Action* 9, whole No. 72 (November-December 1971).

Brief consideration given to aged Navahos.

1848. Americans for Indian Opportunity. *Facts About American Indians in Wisconsin.* Prepared for Wingspread Conference on Issues and Concerns of Wisconsin Indians, convened by Great Lakes Resource Development Project of Americans for Indian Opportunity, Inc. in cooperation with the Johnson Foundation, September 21, 1973. Mimeo.

Brief summary of the history of the six tribes of contemporary Wisconsin. Some attention is also given to the "Major problems" of education, economic development, health, and welfare.

* 1849. Bahr, Donald Morris. "Psychiatry and Indian Curing." *Indian Programs* 2, no. 4 (1973): 1-9.

* 1850. Bahr, Donald M., *et al. Piman Shamanism and Staying Sickness* [*Ka:cim Mumkidag*]. Tucson: The University of Arizona Press, 1974.

Valuable ethnographic data.

1851. Bearn, L. F., & Wood, C. "The Crisis in Indian Health: A California Sample." *The Indian Historian* 2, no. 3 (1969).

1852. California. District Court of Appeals. *Acosta v. San Diego County, et. al.* 92 Cal., 272 Pac., 1954.

Welfare rights of reservation Indians.

1853. Chuculate, Richard. "American Indians and Social Welfare." *Cherokee Mental Health Project, School of Social Work.* Norman: University of Oklahoma, 1973. Mimeo.

Contains information about the University of Oklahoma social work program, a sampling of materials used in the course on American Indians and Social Welfare, and a bibliography of relevant articles.

1854. Dozier, E. P. "Problem Drinking Among American Indians. The Role of Sociocultural Deprivation." *Quarterly Journal of Studies of Alcohol* 27, no. 1 (1966): 72-87.

1855. Duin, Virginia Nolan. "The Problems of Indian Poverty: The Shrinking Land Base and Ineffective Education." *Albany Law Review* 36, no. 1 (1971): 143–181.

* 1856. Fairbanks, Robert A. "The Cheyenne-Arapaho and Alcoholism: Does the Tribe Have a Legal Right to a Medical Remedy?" *American Indian Law Review* 1 (Winter 1973): 55–77.

The Cheyenne-Arapaho have a legal right to medical care from the federal government. Over 75% of the tribe have an alcohol problem.

1857. Ferguson, Frances N. "A Community Treatment Plan for Navaho Problem Drinkers and a Few Words About the Role of Drinking in Navaho Culture." Paper given at the Southwestern Anthropological Association meetings, 1965. Mimeo.

1858. Ferguson, Frances N. "A Community Treatment Plan for Navaho Problem Drinkers. Results of the Project After Two Years in Operation." Address Presented at the 17th Annual Meeting of the North American Association of Alcoholism Programs. October, 1966. Mimeo.

1859. Ferguson, Frances N. "The Peer Group and Navaho Problem Drinking." Paper given at the Southern Anthropological Society meetings, 1966. Mimeo.

1860. Ferguson, Frances N. "Navaho Drinking: Some Tentative Hypotheses." *Human Organization* 27 (Summer 1968): 159–167.

1861. Ferguson, Frances N. "A Treatment Program for Navaho Alcoholics Results After Four Years." *Quarterly Journal of Studies on Alcohol* 31 (December 1970): 898–919.

1862. Ferguson, Frances N. "A Stake in Society: Its relevance to response by Navajo alcoholics in a treatment program." Ph.D. dissertation, University of North Carolina, 1972.

1863. Guidotti, T. L. "Health Care for a Minority: Lessons from the Modoc Indian Country in California." *California Medicine* 118 (1973): 98–104.

1864. Henderson, Norman B., project director. *Final Report of the Cooperative Program for Rehabilitation of the Disabled Indian.* Flagstaff: Northern Arizona University, June, 1967. Mimeo.

1865. Howell, Norma A. "Potawatomi Pregnancy and Child Birth." M.A. thesis, University of Kansas, 1970.

1866. Jenny, Martha R. *Menominee County Health Survey. A Profile of the Health Practices and Problems of the Indian Residents of Menominee County.*

Charitable, Educational and Scientific Foundation of the State Medical Society of Wisconsin. Racine: The Western Printing Company Foundation, 1964.

* 1867. Kupferer, Harriet J. "Health Practices and Educational Aspirations as Indicators of Acculturation and Social Class Among the Eastern Cherokee. *Social Forces* 41 (December 1962): 154-163.

1868. Levy, Jerrold, E. "Navajo Health Concepts and Behavior: The Role of the Anglo Medical Man in the Navajo Healing Process." *Tuba City Hospital Bulletin* 2, no. 2 (1961).

1869. Levy, Jerrold E. "The Influence of Social Organization on the Behavioral Response to a Health Activity: Ethnologist's Report, Tuba City Case Finding Program." *United States Public Health Service, Division of Indian Health, Window Rock Field Office*. Window Rock, Arizona, 1962.

1870. Levy, Jerrold ,E. "Some Trends in Navajo Health Behavior." Arizona Council for Research in Indian Education. Phoenix, Arizona, 1962.

1871. Levy, Jerrold E. "The Older American Indian." In *Older Rural Americans*. Edited by Grant Youmans. Lexington: University of Kentucky, 1967.

* 1872. Levy, Jerrold E. with Kunitz, S. F., & Everett, M. "Alcoholic Cirrhosis Among the Navajo." *Quarterly Journal of Studies on Alcohol* 30 (1969) 672-685.

* 1873. Levy, Jerrold E., & Kunitz, S. J. "Notes on some White Mountain Apache Social Pathologies." *Plateau* 42 (Summer 1969): 11-19.

* 1874. Levy, Jerrold E. with Kunitz, S. F. *et al.* "The Epidemiology of Alcoholic Cirrhosis in Two Southwestern Indian Tribes." *Quarterly Journal of Studies on Alcohol* 32 (1971): 706-720.

* 1875. Levy, Jerrold E., & Kunitz, Stephen J. *Indian Drinking. Navajo Practices and Anglo-American Theories.* New York: John Wiley & Sons, 1974.

1876. Littman, Gerard. "A Study of Alcoholism and Related Pathology Among American Indians in Transition." Manuscript, St. Augustine's Center for American Indians, December, 1968.

1877. Lurie, Nancy O. "A Suggested Hypothesis for the Study of American Indian Drinking." Unpublished paper, July, 1968.

1878. Lurie, Nancy O. "The World's Oldest On-Going Protest Demonstration: North American Indian Drinking Patterns." *Pacific Historical Review* 40 (August 1971): 311-332.

* 1879. Mason, Lynn. "Disabled Fishermen: Disease, and Livelihood among the Kuskowagamiut Eskimos of Lower Kalskay, Alaska." Ph.D. dissertation, University of California-Los Angeles, 1972.

1880. Maynard, Eileen, & Twiss, Gayle. "That These People May Live. Conditions Among the Oglala Sioux of the Pine Ridge Reservation." Pine Ridge, South Dakota: U.S. Public Health Service, 1969.

1881. Michigan. Interim Action Committee on Indian Problems. *Report on Indian Problems.* 1971. Mimeo of Primary Recommendations only.

1882. Parker, L. Mayland. "Observations Concerning the Causes of Poverty Among Reservation Indian People." Phoenix: OEO Office, 1968. Manuscript.

* 1883. Ritzenthaler, Robert E. "Chippewa Preoccupation with Health; Change in a Traditional Attitude Resulting From Modern Health Problems." *Bulletin, Public Museum of the City of Milwaukee* 19. December, 1953.

1884. Sears, William F., & Mariani, Eugene L. "Community Treatment Plan for Navajo Problem Drinkers. Sponsored by McKinley County Family Consultation Service, Inc." July, 1964, mimeo.

1885. Sessions, Frank Q. "Fairbanks Community Survey: A Profile of Poverty." *SEG Report No. 16.* December, 1967. College, Alaska: Institute of Social, Economic and Government Research, University of Alaska.

1886. Shumiatcher, Morris C. *Welfare: Hidden Backlash. A Hard Look at the Welfare Issue in Canada. What It Has Done to the Indian. What It could do to the Rest of Canada.* Toronto: McClelland and Stewart, Ltd., 1971.

1887. Sorkin, Alan. "Poverty and Dropouts. The Case of the American Indian." *Growth and Change. A Journal of Regional Development* 1 (July 1970): University of Kentucky, College of Business and Economics.

* 1888. Vogel, Virgil J. *American Indian Medicine.* Norman: University of Oklahoma Press, 1970; reprint edition, New York: Ballantine Books Inc., 1973.

    General, but a well written discussion with good pictures and a comprehensive bibliography.

1889. Wax, Murray L. "Poverty and Interdependency." In *The Culture of Poverty: A Critique,* pp. 338–344. Edited by E. B. Leacock. New York: Simon and Schuster, 1971.

    Concerns the Oglala Sioux of Pine Ridge, South Dakota.

1890. Weast, Don. "Problem Drinking Among Indians in an Urban Setting." January, 1967, mimeo.

  An outline for a Ph.D. dissertation in sociology from the University of Wisconsin in Madison.

* 1891. Weaver, Sally M. "Medicine and Politics Among the Grand River Iroquois. A Study of Non-Conservatives." *Publications in Ethnology No. 4.* Ottawa: National Museums of Canada, 1972.

* 1892. Willard, William. "The Community Development Worker in an Arizona Yaqui Project." Ph.D. dissertation, University of Arizona, 1970.

1893. Wisconsin. Subcommittee on Migrants and Indians. State Advisory Committee on Social Services. "Social Services to the Indian People." Madison: Wisconsin State Legislature, March, 1972. Mimeo.

XXII. Canadian Government Documents

1894. Barber, Lloyd I. "Statement made to the Standing Committee on Indian Affairs and Northern Development Concerning Indian Land Claims Policy in Canada, March 22, 1973." Revision No. 1. Mimeo.

1895. Briggs, Jean. *Utkuhikhalingmiut Eskimo Emotional Expression.* Ottawa: Northern Science Research Group 68-2: Department of Indian Affairs and Northern Development, 1968.

  Useful data also provided on kinship terminology and family composition.

* 1896. Brody, Hugh. *Indians on Skid Row.* Ottawa: Northern Science Research Group 70-2: Department of Indian Affairs and Northern Development, 1970.

1897. Canadian Council on Social Development. *Housing and People* 5 (Spring 1974): Ottawa.

1898. Canada. Committee Secretariat. Interdepartmental Committee on Financial Assistance to Voluntary Organizations. "Descriptive Analysis of the Phenomenon of New and Emerging Citizens Organizations and Their Relations with Departmental Field Offices." Ottawa: 1972, mimeo.

1899. Canada. Department of Citizenship and Immigration. Citizenship Branch. "Working Paper on Friendship Centres." Ottawa: 1965, mimeo.

  Attempts to arrive at a "conceptual framework for Friendship Centres."

* 1900. Canada. Department of Citizenship and Immigration. Indian Affairs Branch. *The Administration of Indian Affairs.* Ottawa: 1964, mimeo.

* 1901. Canada. Department of Citizenship and Immigration. Indian Affairs Branch. *Schedule of Indian Reserves and Settlements.* Part I. Prince Edward Island, Nova Scotia, New Brunswick, Quebec, Ontario, Manitoba, Saskatchewan, Alberta, Yukon and Northwest Territories. Revised to January 31, 1964. Mimeo.

1902. Canada. Department of Citizenship and Immigration. Indian Affairs Branch. *Summary of Submissions on the Indian Claims Bill C-130.* Ottawa. Mimeo.

1903. Canada. Department of Citizenship and Immigration. Library. *The Indian Act and Related Legislation from 1860 to (but not including) 1951.* Xerox copy.

1904. Canada. Department of Indian Affairs and Northern Development. *NAFC - National Association of Friendship Centres.* Printed directory, n.d.

1905. Canada. Department of Indian Affairs and Northern Development. "Indian Reserve Lands." *IAND Publications* QS-0272-000-EE-A-1.

1906. Canada. Department of Indian Affairs and Northern Development. *Indian Arts and Crafts.* Ottawa, n.d.

* 1907. Canada. Department of Indian Affairs and Northern Development. *Commentary on the Survey of the Contemporary Indians of Canada.* By H. B. Hawthorn *et al.* Mimeo, n.d.

1908. Canada. Department of Indian Affairs and Northern Development. "Canadian Eskimo Art Centres." (map) n.d.

1909. Canada. Department of Indian Affairs and Northern Development. Various miscellaneous papers (some on urban Indians).

1910. Canada. Department of Indian Affairs and Northern Development. "Frobisher Bay Eskimo Childhood." *IAND Publication No. QS-0006-051-EE-A-14.* By J. J. Hongimann and I. Hongimann. Ottawa, 1951.

1911. Canada. Department of Indian Affairs and Northern Development. Office Consolidation of the Indian Act R.S.C. 1952, c. 149 as amended by 1952–53, c. 41, 1956, c. 40, 1958, c. 19, 1960, c. 8, 1960–61, c. 9. Ottawa: The Queen's Printer, 1963.

1912. Canada. Department of Indian Affairs and Northern Development. "Outline for Chiefs and Councillors of the Reorganization of the Department of Indian Affairs and Northern Development." Ottawa, 1968.

* 1913. Canada. Department of Indian Affairs and Northern Development. *Choosing a Path. A Discussion Handbook for the Indian People.* Ottawa: Queen's Printer and Controller of Stationery, 1968.

Bland misdirection.

1914. Canada. Department of Indian Affairs and Northern Development. "The Government Policy on Indians. What is the Debate About?" A speech by The Honourable Jean Chretien, Minister of Indian Affairs and Northern Development to the Saskatchewan Women's Liberal Federation, Regina, Saskatchewan, 1969. Mimeo.

Native welfare is everyone's responsibility.

1915. Canada. Department of Indian Affairs and Northern Development. *Indian Policy. Government of Canada on Indian Policy.* 1969.

1916. Canada. Department of Indian Affairs and Northern Development. "Financing Indian Associations and Consultation." Prepared by William J. Fox, Policy Adviser, 1970. Mimeo.

"Draft for Discussion Only"

1917. Canada. Department of Indian Affairs and Northern Development. *Reference Book on Indian and Eskimo Program Information—Saskatchewan.* Ottawa, 1970. Mimeo.

* 1918. Canada. Department of Indian Affairs and Northern Development. "Responses by the Honourable Jean Chretien to Questions Submitted by the Student Newspaper of Sir George Williams University, December 15, 1970." Mimeo.

1919. Canada. Department of Indian Affairs and Northern Development. "What Are Eskimos?" *IAND Publication No. QS-2013-000-EE-A-11,* Ottawa, 1971.

1920. Canada. Department of Indian Affairs and Northern Development. *Annual Report Fiscal Year 1972-1973.*

1921. Canada. Department of Indian Affairs and Northern Development. "Canadian Indian Artists and Addresses." Ottawa, 1972. Mimeo.

1922. Canada. Department of Indian Affairs and Northern Development. "Northern Canada in the '70's." A Report to the Standing Committee on Indian Affairs and Northern Development on the Government's Northern Objectives, Priorities and Strategies for the '70's. Introductory Remarks by the Honourable Jean Chretien, Minister of Indian Affairs and Northern Development. 1972. Mimeo.

1923. Canada. Department of Indian Affairs and Northern Development. *About Indians. A Listing of Books.* 2nd edition. Ottawa: Information Canada, 1973.

Concerns materials devoted to the native peoples of the United States, Canada, and parts of Mexico. Many items are written for children.

1924. Canada. Department of Indian Affairs and Northern Development. *The Canadian Indian. A Brief Outline.* IAND Publication No. QS-0454-000-EE-A2. Ottawa, 1973.

* 1925. Canada. Department of Indian Affairs and Northern Development. *The Canadian Indian. Statistics.* Ottawa: Information Canada, 1973.

Contains statistics on Canada's Indian Population and information on various departmental programs.

* 1926. Canada. Department of Indian Affairs and Northern Development. "A Catalogue of Data in the Statistical Information Centre," Ottawa, 1973.

1927. Canada. Department of Indian Affairs and Northern Development. "History of Indian Policy, Background Paper 2." *IAND Publication No. QS-0344-000-EE-A1.* Ottawa, 1973.

1928. Canada. Department of Indian affairs and Northern Development. "North of 60. Eskimos of Canada." *IAND Publication No. QS-1206-000-BB-A2.* Ottawa, 1973.

1929. Canada. Department of Indian Affairs and Northern Development. *Tawow. Canadian Indian Cultural Magazine.* Ottawa.

1930. Canada. Department of Indian Affairs and Northern Development. "Economic Activity Summary and Economic Profile Evaluation, Walpole Island Band." Ontario, 1973. Mimeo.

1931. Canada. Department of Indian Affairs and Northern Development. *The Canadian Indian. Yukon and Northwest Territories.* Ottawa, 1974. Mimeo.

1932. Canada. Department of Indian Affairs and Northern Development. "Third International Symposium on Circumpolar Health." Abstracts of Papers. Yellowknife, Northwest Territories, 1974. Mimeo.

1933. Canada. Department of Indian Affairs and Northern Development. Education Branch. "Adult Education Relating Saskatchewan Newstart Research to Education for Indian Adults." 1971. Mimeo.

1934. Canada. Department of Indian Affairs and Northern Development. Education Branch. *Indian Education in Canada.* Ottawa, 1973.

* 1935. Canada. Department of Indian Affairs and Northern Development. Employment and Related Services Division. "University Graduates to December 1971." *IAND Publication No. QS-1110-000-EE-A-11.* Ottawa, 1972.

Lists native people by name, degree, university province and present employment.

1936. Canada. Department of Indian Affairs and Northern Development. Indian Affairs Branch. "Background Paper 1. Indian Status. What is the Present Law?" Ottawa, n.d.

1937. Canada. Department of Indian Affairs and Northern Development. Indian Affairs Branch. *Discussion Notes on the Indian Act.* Ottawa, reprinted 1968.

1938. Canada. Department of Indian Affairs and Northern Development. Indian Affairs Branch. "Local Government Survey, Alberta Region." 1969. Mimeo.

Official views on the development of "local government" in Indian communities in Alberta.

1939. Canada. Department of Indian Affairs and Northern Development. Indian Affairs Branch. *Linguistic and Cultural Affiliations of Canadian Indian Bands.* Ottawa, 1970.

Invaluable.

1940. Canada. Department of Indian Affairs and Northern Development. Indian Affairs Branch. "Indian Community Affairs Program." *IAND Publication No. QS-0604-000-EE-A-1.* Ottawa, 1972.

1941. Canada. Department of Indian Affairs and Northern Development. Indian Affairs Branch. "Indian Economic Development Program." *IAND Publication No. QS-0419-000-EE-A-1.* Ottawa, 1972.

1942. Canada. Department of Indian Affairs and Northern Development. Indian Affairs Branch. *Indian Education Program.* Ottawa, 1972. Mimeo.

1943. Canada. Department of Indian Affairs and Northern Development. Indian and Eskimo Affairs. *Personnel Distribution Study.* 1973. Mimeo.

A description of the Indian personnel distribution within the Indian and Eskimo Program.

1944. Canada. Department of Indian Affairs and Northern Development. Information Services. "Indian Policy—Where Does It Stand?" A speech by the Honourable Jean Chretien, P.C., M.P. Minister of Indian Affairs and Northern Development. Toronto, October, 1969. Mimeo.

1945. Canada. Department of Indian Affairs and Northern Development. Information Services. "Subject Categories for Newspaper Clippings." 1974. Mimeo.

1946. Canada. Department of Indian Affairs and Northern Development. Office of the Public Information Adviser. "Publications Catalogue." *IAND Publication No. QS-3019-000-BB-A1.* Ottawa, 1973. Mimeo.

* 1947. Canada. Department of Juctice. "A Consolidation of the British North America Acts 1867 to 1965." Prepared by E. A. Driedger, Q.C., B.A., LL.B., LL.D. Ottawa, 1965.

* 1948. Canada. Department of Regional Economic Expansion. Social and Human Analysis Branch. "Programs of Interest to Indians and Metis Administered by the Department of Regional Economic Expansion." Ottawa, 1970.

1949. Canada. Department of Citizenship and Immigration. Documentation Section, Canadian Citizenship Branch. "Report on the Consultation with the Canadian Indian Centre of Toronto." Ottawa, 1965. Mimeo.

There are no clear, over-all goals. There are difficulties in decision making; Indians do not have sufficient responsibilities in running the organization, etc.

* 1950. Canada. Department of Labour. Economics and Research Branch. "Main Patterns of Net Migratory Moves in Canada." *Labour Mobility—Study Paper No. 1.* Ottawa, 1965. Mimeo.

1951. Canada. National Government. "Organization of the Government of Canada. Section 3. Introduction to the Executive Branch." Ottawa, July, 1969.

1952. Canada. National Library. *Selective Bibliography of Works by Authors of Canadian-Indian and Eskimo Ancestry.* Ottawa, 1970. Mimeo.

1953. Canada. National Library. *Canadian Indian Arts & Crafts: Early Techniques of Traditional Indian Crafts; a selected bibliography.* Ottawa, 1973, mimeo.

General, Basketry, Bead and quillwork, Clothing, Dwellings, Dyes, Hairwork, Masks, Metal work, Ornaments and implements, Petroglyphs and pictographs, Pottery, Stone carving, Travel, Wampum, Weaving, Tanning and textiles, Wood carving and bark.

1954. Canada. National Library. *Woodland Indians.* Ottawa, 1973, mimeo.

Some contemporary material.

* 1955. Canada. Research Branch, Library of Parliament. *Indian Affairs: Some Perspectives on Recent and Current Matters of Issue.* Ottawa, 1973, mimeo.

Indian Identity and culture, Consultation and Self-determination, Rights and Treaties, Treaty Research, Indian Claims Commission, Hunting and Fishing Rights, Education, Economic Viability of Reserves, Urban Migration, The White Paper on Indian Policy, Indian Act, Political Aspirations.

1956. Canada. Trustee Act, Hospital Services Insurance Act, etc. "Between

Manitoba Hospital Commission and Kenneth D. Klein and Emma Spence, 1969." Mimeo.

1957. Chretien, Jean. "Statement Based on a Speech Delivered in Regina, October 2, 1969." Mimeo.

He really doesn't mean what he said in his "White Paper" of 1969.

1958. Chretien, Jean. "Statement of the Government of Canada on Indian Policy, 1969." Presented to the First Session of the Twenty-eighth Parliament by the Honourable Jean Chretien, Minister of Indian Affairs and Northern Development.

Controversial.

1959. Chretien, Jean. "The Unfinished Tapestry - Indian Policy in Canada." A speech by Chretien given at Queen's University March, 1971, as one of a series of lectures sponsored by The Dunning Trust Lecture Committee. Mimeo.

1960. The Commissioners of the Royal North-West Mounted Police. *Law and Order, Being the Official Reports to Parliament of the Activities of the Royal North-West Mounted Police Force from 1886-1887.* Ottawa: Maclean, Roger & Co., 1886-1887; reprint edition, Toronto: Coles Publishing Co., 1973.

1961. The Commissioners of the Royal North-West Mounted Police. *The New West, Being the Official Reports to Parliament of the Activities of the Royal North-West Mounted Police Force from 1888-1889.* Ottawa: Queen's Printer; reprint edition, Toronto: Coles Publishing Co., 1973.

1962. The Commissioners of the Royal North-West Mounted Police. *Opening Up the West, Being the Official Reports to Parliament of the Activities of the Royal North-West Mounted Police Force, from 1874-1881.* Ottawa: Maclean, Roger & Co.; reprint edition, Toronto: Coles Publishing Co., 1973.

1963. The Commissioners of the Royal North-West Mounted Police. *Settlers and Rebels, Being the Official Reports to Parliament of the Activities of the Royal North-West Mounted Police Force from 1882-1885.* Ottawa: Maclean, Roger & Co., 1882-1885; reprint edition, Toronto: Coles Publishing Co., 1973.

1964. Cumming, Peter A. "The State and the Individual (Indian Affairs). The 'New Policy' - 'Panacea' or 'Put-On.' " Ottawa, 1969, mimeo.

* 1965. Fields, D. B., & Stanbury, W. T. *The Economic Impact of the Public Sector Upon the Indians of British Columbia.* Report submitted to the Department of Indian Affairs and Northern Development. Vancouver: University of British Columbia Press, 1973.

* 1966. Haller, A. A. *Baffin Island-East Coast. An Area Economic Study.* Ottawa: Department of Indian Affairs and Northern Development, 1966.

* 1967. Hawthorn, H. B., editor. *A Survey of the Contemporary Indians of Canada. Economic, Political, Educational Needs and Policies. Parts I and II.* Ottawa: Indian Affairs Branch, Department of Indian Affairs and Northern Development, 1966 and 1967.

* 1968. Indian Act Consultation Meeting—1968-1969.

Sudbury, Ontario; Whitehorse, Yukon Territory; Edmonton, Alberta; Chilliwack, British Columbia; Prince George, British Columbia; Fort William, Ontario; Terrace, British Columbia; Kelowna, British Columbia; Nanaimo, British Columbia; Toronto, Ontario; (1969). Toronto, Ontario; La Maison Montmorency, Courville, Quebec; Quebec City, Quebec; Moncton, New Brunswick; Yellowknife, North West Territory; Regina, Saskatchewan; Terrace, British Columbia; Winnipeg, Manitoba (1968).

1969. Indian Act R.S.C. 1952, c. 149.

Office Consolidation.

1970. Indian Treaties (Canada). Blackfeet; Cree & Saulteaux; Ojibewa Indians of Lake Superior, Mississauga; Chippewa Indians; James Bay Treaty; Saulteaux & Swampy Cree; Chippewa & Cree; Saulteaux Tribe-Ojibbeway Indians. No. 8, 10, 11.

1971. Indian Affairs Branch. *Indians of Ottawa (An Historical Review).* Ottawa, January, 1966.

1972. Laing, A. *The Indian People and the Indian Act. Canadian Indians and the Canadian Government.* Ottawa: Department of Indian Affairs and Northern Development, n.d.

1973. Macpherson, N., Director of Education. "How I See Education for the Children of Canada's North." *News of the North,* May 29, 1974.

1974. Oswalt, Wendell H., & VanStone, James. "The Future of the Caribou Eskimos." pp. 19-34. *Northern Research and Coordination Centre.* Ottawa: Department of Northern Affairs and National Resources, 1960.

1975. Parsons, G. F. *Arctic Suburb: A Look at the North's Newcomers.* Ottawa: Mackenzie Delta Research Project, Northern Science Research Group, Department of Indian Affairs and Northern Development, 1970.

Fieldwork done in 1967 concerning white government employees living at Inuvik. Some data on native contact.

1976. T. J. Plunkett Associates Ltd. "Local Government on Indian Reserves. A Report." Toronto, 1967, mimeo.

Discusses a conference on "local government." Report made at the request of the Department of Indian Affairs and Northern Development.

1977. Smith, Derek. "Occupational Preferences of Northern Students," *Social Science Notes 5.* Ottawa: Northern Science Research Group, Northern Economic Development Branch, 1974.

Based on responses of 1,000+ high school students of all ethnic groups in the Mackenzie River delta, Yellowknife, Churchill, and Frobisher Bay.

1978. Stevenson, D. S. *Problems of Eskimo Relocation for Industrial Employment. A Preliminary Study.* Ottawa: Northern Science Research Group, Department of Indian Affairs and Northern Development, 1968.

Research conducted during 1967. Concerns families.

1979. Thomas, D. K., & Thompson, C. T. "Eskimo Housing As Planned Culture Change." *Social Science Notes 4.* Ottawa: Northern Science Research Group, Department of Indian Affairs and Northern Development, 1972.

Fieldwork conducted between 1967-1970 at Broughton Island, Frobisher Bay, Pangnirtung, Baker Lake and Cape Dorset.

1980. Thompson, Charles Thomas. *Patterns of Housekeeping in Two Eskimo Settlements.* Ottawa: Northern Science Research Group 69-1, Department of Indian Affairs and Northern Development, 1969.

Fieldwork conducted between August 1967 and July 1968, in Frobisher Bay, Baker Lake, and Cape Dorset.

* 1981. Usher, Peter J. *Fur Trade Posts of the Northwest Territories, 1870-1970.* Ottawa: Northern Science Research Group 71-4, Department of Indian Affairs and Northern Development, 1971.

Contains a list of all fur trade posts operating within the present boundaries of the Northwest Territories between 1870 and 1970. Brief outline of the development of the fur trade in the Northwest Territories is provided.

* 1982. Van Stone, James, & Oswalt, Wendell H. "The Caribou Eskimo Community of Eskimo Point." *Northern Research and Co-ordination Centre,* pp. 1-18. Ottawa: Department of Northern Affairs and National Resources, 1960.

1983. Van Stone, James, & Oswalt, Wendell H. "Three Eskimo Communities." *Anthropology Papers of the University of Alaska* 9, no. 1 (1960): 17-56.

1984. Wacko, William J. "Observations and Recommendations Respecting Alcohol and Drugs in the Northwest Territories." Prepared for the Department of Social Development, Government of Northwest Territories, 1973. Mimeo.

XXIII. United State Publications

This section, U.S. PUBLICATIONS, was very difficult to organize because of the quantity and diversity of the materials. The organization is done alphabetically by department, and by date (or occasionally by tribe if the material warranted it) within each category. To assist the reader to locate items, the section begins with an outline of the organization.

Two basic directories can be used to locate those documents listed below and other federal publications: the *Congressional Information Service*. Washington, D.C.: CIS Publisher, 1974, (item 11 in the bibliography), and the *Cummulative Subject Index to the Monthly Catalog of the United States Government Publications, 1900-1971*. Washington, D.C.: Carrollton Press, (Volume 1, 1973-   ).

Government publications are most likely to be found in Government Depository Libraries located throughout the country. Under the Depository Library Act of 1962, the depository list comprises all State Libraries, 2 libraries for each congressional district designated by the Representative from that district, 2 libraries to be designated in any part of the State by each Senator, the libraries of land-grant colleges etc. The address of the nearest Depository can be supplied by a local public library.

OUTLINE OF THE ORGANIZATION OF ALL U.S. PUBLICATIONS

1. U.S. Commission on Civil Rights (item 1985)
2. U.S. Comptroller General (items 1986-1989)
3. U.S. Congress. House and Senate Bills and Acts (items 1990-2044)

The first group of bills and acts, relating to Indians in general, is organized by date and number. The second group, relating to specific tribes, is classified by tribe and date alphabetically.

4. U.S. Congress. House. Committee on Appropriations. (items 2045-2053)
5. U.S. Congress. House. Committee of Education and Labor. (item 2054)
6. U.S. Congress. House. Committee on Interior and Insular Affairs. (items 2056-2097)

The first section, on general Indian topics, is organized by date. The second section, on individual tribes, is organized alphabetically by tribe, and by date within each tribe.

7. U.S. Congress. House. Committee of the Whole House on the State of the Union. (items 2098-2120)

The first section, on general topics, is organized by date. The second section, on individual tribes, is organized alphabetically by tribe.

8. U.S. Congress. House. Executive Documents. (items 2121-2124)
9. U.S. Congress. House. Miscellaneous Documents. (item 2125)
10. U.S. Congress. Joint Economic Committee. (items 2126-2128)
11. U.S. Congress. Senate. Bureau of Education. (item 2129)
12. U.S. Congress. Senate. Committee on Appropriations. (items 2130-2137)

The first section consists of Hearings on the Department of the Interior Appropriations. The second section consists of Mizen's reports on Federal facilities for Indians.

13. U.S. Congress. Senate. Committee on Interior & Insular Affairs. (item 2138-2189)

Section 1—Hearings on Interior Nominations.
Section 2—General topics organized by date.
Section 3—Hearings before the Subcommittee on Indian Affairs organized by date.
Section 4—Hearings before the Subcommittee on Minerals, Materials, and Fuels.
Section 5—Hearings before the Subcommittee on Public Lands.
Section 6—Hearings before the Subcommittee on Water and Power Resources.

14. U.S. Congress. Senate. (items 2190-2207)

These are reports *from* the Committee on Interior and Insular Affairs submitted to the whole Senate. They are organized by date and number.

15. U.S. Congress. Senate. Committee on the Judiciary. (items 2208-2210)
16. U.S. Congress. Senate. Committee on Labor and Public Welfare. (items 2211-2219)
17. U.S. Congress. Senate. Executive Documents. (items 2220-2221)
18. U.S. Congress. Senate. Senator . . . speaking (from Congressional Record). (items 2222-2223)
19. U.S. Department of Agriculture. (item 2225)
20. U.S. Department of Commerce. Bureau of the Census. (items 2226-2236)
    U.S. Department of Commerce News
    U.S. Department of Commerce. Economic Development Administration.
    U.S. Department of Commerce. U.S. Travel Service.
21. U.S. Department of Health, Education & Welfare. National Institute of Mental Health. (items 2237-2261)
    U.S. Department of Health, Education & Welfare. Public Health Service.

The first brief section is organized by date. The second section is organized by tribe.

U.S. Department of Health, Education & Welfare. Indian Health Service.
U.S. Department of Health, Education & Welfare. Social and Rehabilitation Service.
U.S. Department of Health, Education & Welfare. Social Security Administration.
22. U.S. Department of the Interior. Bureau of Indian Affairs. (items 2262-2388)

The first section is organized alphabetically by tribe or area. The second, general, section is organized by date.

U.S. Department of the Interior. Bureau of Reclamation.
U.S. Department of the Interior. Departmental Library.
U.S. Department of the Interior. Geological Survey.
U.S. Department of the Interior. Indian Arts & Crafts Board.
U.S. Department of the Interior. Office of Economic Analysis.

U.S. Department of the Interior. Office of the Secretary.
U.S. Department of the Interior. Office of the Solicitor.
23. U.S. Department of Labor. (item 2389)
24. U.S. Field Committee for Development Planning in Alaska. (items 2390–2391)
25. U.S. Indian Claims Commission. (items 2392–2394)
26. U.S. The National Archives. (items 2395–2397)
27. U.S. National Council on Indian Opportunity. (items 2398–2400)
28. U.S. Office of Economic Opportunity. (items 2401–2406)
U.S. Office of Economic Opportunity. Community Development.
29. U.S. Office of Management and Budget. (item 2407)
30. U.S. Office of the White House Press Secretary. (item 2408)
31. U.S. White House Conference on Ageing. (item 2411)

1985. U.S. Commission on Civil Rights. *Your Right to Indian Welfare. A Handbook on the BIA General Assistance Program.* Clearinghouse Publication No. 45. December, 1973.

1986. U.S. Comptroller General of the United States. *Effectiveness and Administration of the Community Action Program Administered by the White Earth Reservation Business Committee.* Washington, D.C.: Government Printing Office, July, 1969.

1987. U.S. Comptroller General of the United States. "Review of Certain Aspects of the Program for the Termination of Federal Supervision over Indian Affairs." BIA-DI. Report to the Congress of the U.S. March, 1961. U.S. General Accounting Office.

1988. U.S. Comptroller General of the United States. "Report to the Congress of the U.S. Examination into Policies for the Recovery of Government Expenditures Incurred in the Management and Operation of Indian Forest Enterprises." March, 1966.

1989. U.S. Comptroller General of the United States. "Report to the Congress of the U.S. Need for Effective Guidance of Navajo Tribe of Indians in Management of Tribal Funds." June, 1966.

---

* 1990. U.S. Congress. House. *A Bill to provide for the assumption of the control and operation by Indian tribes and communities of certain programs and services provided for them by the Federal Government.* H.R. 2377. 92nd Congress, 1st session, 1971.

1991. U.S. Congress. Senate. *A Bill to extend the life of the Indian Claims Commission.* S. 2408. 92nd Cong., 1st sess., 1971.

1992. U.S. Congress. House. *A Bill to provide for financing the economic development of Indians and Indian organizations.* H.R. 8063. 92nd Cong., 2nd sess., 1971.

1993. U.S. Congress. House. *A Bill to establish within the Department of the Interior the Indian business development program to stimulate Indian entrepreneurship and employment.* H.R. 8340. 92nd Cong., 1st sess., 1971.

* 1994. U.S. Congress. House. *A Bill to provide for the assumption of the control and operation by Indian tribes and communities of certain programs and services provided for them by the Federal Government.* H.R. 8796. 92nd Cong., 1st sess., 1971.

* 1995. U.S. Congress. House. *A Bill to establish within the Department of the Interior the Indian business development program to stimulate Indian entrepreneurship and employment.* H.R. 15322. 92nd Cong., 2nd sess., 1972.

* 1996. U.S. Congress. House. *A Bill to establish land use policy; to authorize the Secretary of the Interior, pursuant to guidelines issued by the Council on Environmental Quality, to make grants to assist the States to Develop and implement comprehensive land use planning processes; to coordinate Federal programs and policies which have a land use impact; to make grants to Indian tribes to assist them to develop and implement land use planning processes for reservation and other tribal lands; to provide land use planning directives for the public lands.* H.R. 10294. 93rd Cong., 2nd sess., 1973.

1997. U.S. Congress. House. *A Bill to authorize the Secretary of the Interior to make grants to assist the States and Indian tribes to develop and implement land use planning processes; to coordinate Federal programs and policies which have land use impact.* H.R. 11325, 93rd Cong., 1st sess., 1973.

1998. U.S. Congress. House. *An Act making appropriations for the Department of the Interior and related agencies for the fiscal year ending June 30, 1973.* Public Law 92–369, H.R. 15418, 92nd Cong., 1972.

1999. U.S. Congress. House. *A Bill to amend the Small Business Act to expand the definition of small business concern to include agri-businesses.* H.R. 12804. 93rd Cong., 2nd sess., 1974.

* 2000. U.S. Congress. House. *An Act to promote maximum Indian participation in the government and education of the Indian people; to provide for the full participation of Indian tribes in programs and services conducted by the Federal Government for Indians and to encourage the development of the human resources of the Indian people; to establish a program of assistance to upgrade Indian education; to support the right of Indian citizens to control their own educational activities; to train professionals in Indian education to establish an Indian youth intern program; and for other purposes.* S. 1017. 93rd Cong., 2nd sess., 1974.

2001. U.S. Congress. House. *A Bill to provide for the settlement of certain land claims of Alaska Natives.* H.R. 10367, 92nd Cong., 1st sess., 1971.

2002. U.S. Congress. House. An Act to provide for the settlement of certain land claims of Alaska Natives. Public Law 92-203, H.R. 10367. 92nd Cong., 1st sess., 1971.

2003. U.S. Congress. House. Alaska Native Claims Settlement Act. H. Conference Report No. 92-746 to accompany H.R. 10367. 92nd Cong., 1st sess., 1971.

Identical with S. Conference Report No. 92-581.

* 2004. U.S. Congress. House. *Providing for the Settlement of Land Claims of Alaska Natives.* H. Report No. 92-523. Together with a Dissenting View to Accompany H.R. 10367. 92nd Cong., 1st sess., 1971.

* 2005. U.S. Congress. Senate. *Alaska Native Claims Settlement Act of 1971.* S. Report No. 92-405 together with Additional and Supplemental Views to Accompany S. 35. 92nd Cong., 1st sess., 1971.

* 2006. U.S. Congress. Senate. *Alaska Native Claims Settlement Act.* S. Conference Report No. 92-581 to Accompany H.R. 10367. 92nd Cong., 1st sess., 1971.

2007. U.S. Congress. House. *Amending Section 28 of the Mineral Leasing Act of 1920, And To Authorize The Trans-Alaska Pipeline.* #93-617 Conference Report to accompany S. 1081. 93rd Cong., 1st sess., 1973.

2008. U.S. Congress. House. *An Act to provide for division and for the disposition of the funds appropriated to pay a judgment in favor of the Blackfeet Tribe of the Blackfeet Indian Reservation, Montana, and the Gros Ventre Tribe of the Fort Belknap Reservation, Montana, in Indian Claims Commission docket numbered 279-A.* S. 671. 92nd Cong., 1st sess., 1971.

2009. U.S. Congress. House. *A Bill to provide for division and for the disposition of the funds appropriated to pay a judgment in favor of the Blackfeet Tribe of the Blackfeet Indian Reservation, Montana, and the Gros Ventre Tribe of the Fort Belknap Reservation, Montana, in Indian Claims Commission docket numbered 279-A.* H.R. 9325. 92nd Cong., 1st sess., 1971.

2010. U.S. Congress. Senate. *An Act to declare that certain federally owned land is held by the United States in trust for the Lac du Flambeau Band of Lake Superior Chippewa Indians.* H.R. 2185. 92nd Cong., 1st sess., 1971.

2011. U.S. Congress. Senate. *An Act to provide for the disposition of funds arising from judgments in Indian Claims Commission dockets numbered 178 and 179, in favor of the Confederated Tribes of the Colville Reservation.* H.R. 6291. 92nd Cong., 2nd sess., 1971.

2012. U.S. Congress. Senate. *An Act to further the economic advancement and general welfare of the Hopi Indian Tribe of the State of Arizona.* H.R. 4869. 91st Cong., 1st sess., 1969.

2013. U.S. Congress. Senate. *An Act to authorize the sale of certain lands on the Kalispel Indian Reservation.* H.R. 8381. 92nd Cong., 1st sess., 1971.

2014. U.S. Congress. Senate. *An Act to approve an order of the Secretary of the Interior canceling irrigation charges against non-Indian-owned lands under the Modoc Point unit of the Klamath Indian irrigation project, Oregon.* H.R. 489. 92nd Cong., 1st sess., 1971.

2015. U.S. Congress. House. *A Bill to provide for the disposition of judgment funds on deposit to the credit of the pueblo of Laguna in Indian Claims Commission.* H.R. 10352. 92nd Cong., 1st sess., 1971.

* 2016. U.S. Congress. Senate. *An Act to repeal the Act terminating Federal supervision over the property and members of the Menominee Indian Tribe of Wisconsin as a federally recognized, sovereign Indian tribe; and to restore to the Menominee Tribe of Wisconsin those Federal services furnished to American Indians because of their status as American Indians.* H.R. 10717. 93rd Cong., 1st sess., 1973.

2017. U.S. Congress. Senate. *An Act to authorize the partition of the surface rights in the joint use area of the 1882 Executive Order Hopi Reservation and the surface and subsurface rights in the 1934 Navajo Reservation between the Hopi and Navajo Tribes, to provide for allotments to certain Paiute Indians.* H.R. 11128. 92nd Cong., 2nd sess., 1972.

2018. U.S. Congress. House. *A Bill to authorize the partition of the surface rights in the joint use area of the 1882 Executive Order Hopi Reservation and the surface and subsurface rights in the 1934 Navajo Reservation between the Hopi and Navajo Tribes, to provide for allotments to certain Paiute Indians.* H.R. 1193. 93rd Cong., 1st sess., 1973.

Provisions are different on this and related Bills.

2019. U.S. Congress. House. *A Bill to abolish the Joint Committee on Navajo-Hopi Indian Administration.* H.R. 4412. 93rd Cong., 1st sess., 1973.

2020. U.S. Congress. House. *A Bill to authorize the partition of the surface rights in the joint use area of the 1882 Executive Order Hopi Reservation and the surface and subsurface rights in the 1934 Navajo Reservation between the Hopi and Navajo Tribes, to provide for allotments to certain Paiute Indians.* H.R. 5647. 93rd Cong., 1st sess., 1973.

2021. U.S. Congress. House. *A Bill to provide for the mediation and arbitration of the conflicting interests of the Navajo and Hopi Indian Tribes in and to lands lying within the joint use area of the Hopi Reservation established by the Executive order of December 16, 1882, and to lands lying within the Navajo Reservation created by the Act of June 14, 1934, and for other purposes.* H.R. 7679. 93rd Cong., 1st sess., 1973.

2022. U.S. Congress. House. *A Bill to authorize the separation of the interests of the Hopi and Navajo Tribes in certain lands set aside by the Executive order of December 16, 1882, and to confirm to the Hopi Tribe exclusive rights in certain lands located within the exterior boundaries of the Navajo Reservation in Arizona as defined by Congress in 1934.* H.R. 7716. 93rd Cong., 1st sess., 1973.

2023. U.S. Congress. Senate. *An Act to abolish the Joint Committee on Navajo-Hopi Indian Administration.* S. 267. 93rd Cong., 1st sess., 1973.

2024. U.S. Congress. Senate. *A Bill to authorize the partition of the surface rights in the joint use area of the 1882 Executive Order Hopi Reservation and the surface and subsurface rights in the 1934 Navajo Reservation between the Hopi and Navajo Tribes, to provide for allotments to certain Paiute Indians.* S. 2424. 93rd Cong., 1st sess., 1973.

2025. U.S. Congress. Senate. *A Bill to provide for the efficient development of the natural resources of the Navajo and Hopi Reservations for the benefit of its residents, to assist the members of the Navajo and Hopi Tribes in becoming economically fully self-supporting, to resolve a land dispute between the Navajo and Hopi Tribes.* H.R. 3230. 93rd Cong., 2nd sess., 1974.

2026. U.S. Congress. Senate. *An Act to authorize the partition of the surface rights in the joint use area of the 1882 Executive Order Hopi Reservation and the surface and subsurface rights in the 1934 Navajo Reservation between the Hopi and Navajo Tribes, to provide for allotments to certain Paiute Indians, and for other purposes.* H.R. 10337. 93rd Cong., 2nd sess., 1974.

2027. U.S. Congress. House. *A Bill to provide for the efficient development of the natural resources of the Navajo and Hopi Reservations for the benefit of its residents, to assist the members of the Navajo and Hopi Tribes in becoming economically fully self-supporting, to resolve a land dispute between the Navajo and Hopi Tribes.* H.R. 14602. 93rd Cong., 2nd sess., 1974.

NAVAJO

2028. U.S. Congress. House. *An Act to determine the rights and interests of the Navajo Tribe and the Ute Mountain Tribe of the Ute Mountain Reservation in and to certain lands in the State of New Mexico.* S. 491. 90th Cong., 1st sess., 1967.

2029. U.S. Congress. Public Law 90-256. *An Act to determine the rights and interests of the Navajo Tribe and the Ute Mountain Tribe of the Ute Mountain Reservation in and to certain lands in the State of New Mexico.* S. 491. 90th Cong., 1968.

2030. U.S. Congress. Senate. *An Act to authorize grants for the Navajo Community College.* H.R. 5068. 92nd Cong., 1st sess., 1971.

2031. U.S. Congress. House. *A Bill to provide for the disposition of funds appropriated to pay a judgment in favor of the Navajo Tribe of Indians in Court of Claims case numbered 49692.* H.R. 7391. 93rd Cong., 1st sess., 1973.

2032. U.S. Congress. House. *A Bill to facilitate the exchange of school lands between the State of Utah and the Navajo Tribe.* H.R. 12803. 93rd Cong., 2nd sess., 1974.

2033. U.S. Congress. Senate. *A Bill to facilitate the exchange of school lands between the State of Utah and the Navajo Tribe.* S. 2270. 93rd Cong., 1st sess., 1973.

2034. U.S. Congress. House. *An Act to authorize the Secretary of the Interior to transfer franchise fees received from certain concession operations at Glen Canyon National Recreation Area in the States of Arizona and Utah.* S. 1384. 93rd Cong., 1st sess., 1973.

2035. U.S. Congress. Senate. *Authorizing the Secretary of the Interior to Transfer Franchise Fees Received From Certain Concession Operations at Glen Canyon National Recreation area, in the States of Arizona and Utah.* S. Report 93-169 to Accompany S. 1384. 93rd Cong., 1st sess., 1973.

OSAGE

2036. U.S. Congress. House. *A Bill to provide for the disposition of judgment funds of the Osage Tribe of Indians of Oklahoma.* H.R. 7093. 92nd Cong., 1st sess., 1971.

2037. U.S. Congress. House. *A Bill providing for the distribution of judgment funds of the Osage Nation of Indians.* H.R. 10213. 92nd Cong., 1st sess., 1971.

PAIUTE

2038. U.S. Congress. House. *A Bill to declare that certain public lands are held in trust by the U.S. for the Summit Lake Paiute Tribe.* H.R. 9702. 92nd Cong., 1st sess., 1971.

SALISH—KOOTENAI

2039. U.S. Congress. House. *A Bill to provide for the disposition of judgments, when appropriated, recovered by the Confederated Salish and Kootenai Tribes of the Flathead Reservation, Montana, in paragraphs 7 and 10, docket numbered 50233, United States Court of Claims.* H.R. 3333. 92nd Cong., 1st sess., 1971.

SHOSHONE

2040. U.S. Congress. House. *A Bill to provide for the apportionment of funds in payment of a judgment in favor of the Shoshone Tribe in consolidated dockets numbered 326-D, 326-E, 326-F, 326-G, 327-H, 366, and 367 before the Indian Claims Commission.* H.R. 10846. 92nd Cong., 1st sess., 1971.

SIOUX - FORT BELKNAP

2041. U.S. Congress. Senate. *An Act to declare that certain federally owned land is held by the United States in trust for the Fort Belknap Indian Community.* H.R. 10702. 92nd Cong., 1st sess., 1971.

TAOS

2042. U.S. Congress. Senate. *An Act to amend section 4 of the Act of May 31, 1933 (48 Stat. 108).* H.R. 471. 91st Cong., 1st sess., 1969.

Provides for the protection of the watershed within the Carson National Forest for the Taos Indians.

YANKTON SIOUX

2043. U.S. Congress. Senate. *An Act to provide for the disposition of funds to pay a judgment in favor of the Yankton Sioux Tribe in Indian Claims Commission docket numbered 332-A.* H.R. 7742. 92nd Cong., 1st sess., 1971.

YAVAPAI-APACHE

2044. U.S. Congress. Senate. *An Act to authorize the acquisition of a village site for the Payson Band of Yavapai-Apache Indians.* H.R. 3337. 92nd Cong., 1st sess., 1971.

2045. U.S. Congress. House. Committee on Appropriations. *Department of the Interior and Related Agencies Appropriations for 1967, Part 1.* Hearings Before a subcommittee of the House Committee on Appropriations, 89th Cong., 1967, pp. 13–410.

Consideration of Indian programs in the fields of health, arts and crafts, education.

* 2046. U.S. Congress. House. Committee on Appropriations. *Department of the Interior and Related Agencies Appropriations for 1970, Part 1.* Secretary of the Interior, etc. Hearings before a subcommittee of the House Committee on Appropriations, 91st Cong., 1st sess., 1970. pp. 29–66.

Overview of Indian areas of interest—interview with Secretary Hickel.

* 2047. U.S. Congress. House. Committee on Appropriations. *Department of the Interior and Related Agencies Appropriations for 1970, Part 2.* Bureau of Indian Affairs, etc. Hearings before a Subcommittee of the Committee on Appropriations, 91st Cong., 1st sess., 1970, pp. 1–300.

Interview with Robert Bennett *et al* about various Indian programs.

* 2048. U.S. Congress. House. Committee on Appropriations. *Department of the Interior and Related Agencies Appropriations for 1970, Part 3.* Indian Claims Commission, Indian Health Services and Facilities, National Council on Indian Opportunity, *et al.* Hearings before a subcommittee of the House Committee on Appropriations, 91st Cong., 1st sess., 1970.

* 2049. U.S. Congress. House. Committee on Appropriations. *Department of the Interior and Related Agencies Appropriations for 1972, Part 2.* Bureau of Indian Affairs *et al.* Hearings before a Subcommittee of the Committee on Appropriations, 92nd Cong., 1st sess., 1972. pp. 1057–1419.

* 2050. U.S. Congress. House. Committee on Appropriations. *Department of the Interior and Related Agencies Appropriations for 1972, Part 4.* Indian Health Services, National Council on Indian Opportunity, *et al.* Hearings Before a subcommittee of the House Committee on Appropriations, 92nd Cong., 1st sess., 1972, pp. 978–1126.

* 2051. U.S. Congress. House. Committee on Appropriations. *Department of the Interior and Related Agencies Appropriations for 1972, Part 5.* Indian Claims Commission *et al.* Hearings before a subcommittee of the House Committee on Appropriations, 92nd Cong., 1st sess., 1972. pp. 5–14.

2052. U.S. Congress. House. Committee on Appropriations. *Department of the Interior and Related Agencies Appropriations for 1972, Part 6.* Testimony of Members of Congress and other interested individuals and organizations. Hearings before a subcommittee of the House Committee on Appropriations, 92nd Cong., 1st sess., 1972.

Many witnesses speaking to various Indian programs.

2053. U.S. Congress. House. Committee on Appropriations. *Department of the Interior and Related Agencies Appropriations for 1974, Part 4.* Bureau of Indian Affairs, Indian Claims Commission, Indian Health Service, National Council on Indian Opportunity, Territorial Affairs. Hearings before a subcommittee of the House Committee on Appropriations, 93rd Cong., 1st sess., 1974.

2054. U.S. Congress. House. Committee of Education and Labor. *Extension of Elementary and Secondary Education Programs.* Hearings before the House Committee on Education and Labor, on H.R. 514. 91st Cong., 1st sess., 1969.

A bill to extend programs of assistance for elementary and secondary education, Part 1.

2055. U.S. Congress. House. Committee on Indian Affairs. *Reservation Counts of Indian Offenses.* Hearings before the House Committee on Indian Affairs on H.R. 7826. 69th Cong., 1st sess., 1926. Washington, D.C.: Government Printing Office, 1926.

2056. U.S. Congress. House. Committee on Interior and Insular Affairs. *Report with Respect to the House Resolution Authorizing the Committee on Interior and Insular Affairs to Conduct an Investigation of the Bureau of Indian Affairs.* H.R. 2503, 82nd Cong., 2nd sess., 1952.

Information available on the Cheyenne, Crow, Potawatomi, Stockbridge-Munsee, Winnebago, Koasati, Menominee tribes as well as cooperatives and tribal enterprises.

2057. U.S. Congress. House. Committee on Interior and Insular Affairs. *Indian Relocation and Industrial Development Programs.* Report of a Special Subcommittee on Indian Affairs of the Committee on Interior and Insular Affairs. H.R. 94, 85th Cong., 2nd sess., 1957.

2058. U.S. Congress. House. Committee on Interior and Insular Affairs. *Indirect Services and Expenditures by the Federal Government for the American Indian. Committee documents and information Relating to a Questionnaire Circulated to Various Federal Agencies on the Subject of Indirect Expenditures in the Field of Indian Affairs.* 86th Cong., 1st sess., 1959.

2059. U.S. Congress. House. Committee on Interior and Insular Affairs. *Indian*

Heirship Land Study. Analysis of Indian Opinion as expressed in Questionnaires. Vol. 1. 86th Cong., 2nd sess., 1960.

2060. U.S. Congress. House. Committee on Interior and Insular Affairs. *Indian Heirship Land Study. Tabulation of Questionnaires circulated to Various Indian Land Holders Concerning Heirship Problems. Vol. II.* 86th Cong., 2nd sess., 1960.

* 2061. U.S. Congress. House. Committee on Interior and Insular Affairs. *Indian Unemployment Survey. Part I. Questionnaire Returns. A Memorandum and Accompanying Information from the Chairman of the Committee on Interior and Insular Affairs to the Members of the Committee.* 88th Cong., 1st sess., 1963.

2062. U.S. Congress. House. Committee on Interior and Insular Affairs. *List of Indian Treaties. A Memorandum and Accompanying Information from the Chairman of the Committee on Interior and Insular Affairs, House of Representatives, to the Members of the Committee.* 88th Cong., 2nd sess., 1964.

2063. U.S. Congress. House. Committee on Interior and Insular Affairs. *Information on Removal of Restrictions on American Indians. A Memorandum and Accompanying Information from the Chairman of the Committee on Interior and Insular Affairs, House of Representatives, to Members of the Committee.* 88th Cong., 2nd sess., 1964.

* 2064. U.S. Congress. House. Committee on Interior and Insular Affairs. *Federal Opinion on the Need for an Indian Treaty Study. Report of the Committee on Interior and Insular Affairs pursuant to H.R. 80.* 89th Cong., 1st sess., 1965.

* 2065. U.S. Congress. House. Committee on Interior and Insular Affairs. *Federal Opinions on Treaty Study.* 89th Cong., 1st sess., 1965.

2066. U.S. Congress. House. Committee on Interior and Insular Affairs. *Lower Colorado River Basin Project. Hearing before the Subcommittee on Irrigation and Reclamation of the Committee on Interior and Insular Affairs on H.R. 4671 and similar bills.* 89th Cong., 1st sess., 1965.

2067. U.S. Congress. House. Committee on Interior and Insular Affairs. *Lower Colorado River Basin Project. Hearings before the Subcommittee on Irrigation and Reclamation of the Committee on Interior and Insular Affairs on H.R. 4671 and similar bills. Part II.* 89th Cong., 2nd sess., 1966.

* 2068. U.S. Congress. House. Committee on Interior and Insular Affairs. *Indian Fractionated Land Problems. Hearings before the Subcommittee on Indian Affairs of the Committee on Interior and Insular Affairs on H.R. 11113.* 89th Cong., 2nd sess., 1966.

To reduce the number of Fractional interests in trust and restricted allotments of Indian lands.

2069. U.S. Congress. House. Committee on Interior and Insular Affairs. *Accomplishments of the Committee on Interior and Insular Affairs of the House of Representatives during the 89th Congress.* 1966.

2070. U.S. Congress. House. Committee on Interior and Insular Affairs. *Indian Resources Development Act of 1967. Hearings before the Subcommittee on Indian Affairs of the Committee on Interior and Insular Affairs on H.R. 10560.* 90th Cong., 1st sess., 1967.

To provide for the economic development and management of the Resources of individual Indians and Indian tribes.

2071. U.S. Congress. House. Committee on Interior and Insular Affairs. *Policies, Programs, and Activities of the Department of the Interior Part II. Hearings before the Committee on Interior and Insular Affairs.* 90th Cong., 1st sess., 1967.

Briefing session with Commissioner of Indian Affairs and staff. Briefing on Indian Health and Sanitation.

2072. U.S. Congress. House. Committee on Interior and Insular Affairs. *Indian Claims Commission Act Extension and Enlargement. Hearings before the Subcommittee on Indian Affairs of the Committee on Interior and Insular Affairs on H.R. 2536.* 90th Cong., 1st sess., 1967.

To terminate the Indian claims commission.

* 2073. U.S. Congress. House. Committee on Interior and Insular Affairs. *Oil and Natural Gas Pipeline Rights-of-way. Part I. Hearings before the Subcommittee on Public Lands of the Committee on Interior and Insular Affairs on H.R. 9130.* 93rd Cong., 1st sess., 1973.

To amend section 28 of the Mineral Leasing Act of 1920, and to authorize a trans-Alaska oil and gas pipeline.

2074. U.S. Congress. House. Committee on Interior and Insular Affairs. *Regulation of Surface Mining. Part II. Hearings before the Subcommittee on the Environment and Subcommittee on Mines and Mining of the Committee on Interior and Insular Affairs on H.R. 3 and Related Bills.* 93rd Cong., 1st sess., 1973.

2075. U.S. Congress. House. Committee on Interior and Insular Affairs. *Indian Financing Act of 1973. Hearings before the Subcommittee on Indian Affairs of the House Committee on Interior and Insular Affairs on H.R. 6371, H.R. 6493, H.R. 9843.* 93rd Cong., 1st sess., 1973.

Some discussion as to what the federal government has done in this area in the past and might do in the future.

* 2076. U.S. Congress. House. Committee on Interior and Insular Affairs. *To Facilitate the Incorporation of the Townsite of Page, Arizona, As A Municipality. Part 1. Hearing before the Subcommittee on Water and Power Resources of the House Committee on Interior and Insular Affairs on H.R. 1194 and H.R. 9936.* 93rd Cong., 1st sess., 1973.

Urbanization in Navajo country.

AGUA CALIENTE

2077. U.S. Congress. House. Committee on Interior and Insular Affairs. *Agua Caliente Indians Conservatorships and Guardianships. Hearing before the Subcommittee on Indian Affairs of the Committee on Interior and Insular Affairs on H.R. 17273.* 90th Cong., 2nd sess., 1968.

ALASKA

* 2078. U.S. Congress. House. Committee on Interior and Insular Affairs. *Tlingit and Haida Indians of Alaska. Hearings before the subcommittee on Indian Affairs of the House Committee on Interior and Insular Affairs on H.R. 874.* 89th Cong., 1st sess., 1965.

To amend the act of June 19, 1935. Testimony of witnesses, written communications, data concerning the Tlingit and Haida Indian Central Council, map of Tlingit-Haida Territory, 1867.

2079. U.S. Congress. House. Committee on Interior and Insular Affairs. *Alaska Native Land Claims. Hearings before the House Subcommittee on Indian Affairs on H.R. 11213, H.R. 15049 and H.R. 17129.* 90th Cong., 2nd sess., 1968.

Contains texts of bills under consideration, the testimony of many witnesses, written communications to the subcommittee and pertinent additional information.

* 2080. U.S. Congress. House. Committee on Interior and Insular Affairs. Committee on Interior and Insular Affairs. *Alaska Native Land Claims Part I. Hearings before the House Subcommittee on Indian Affairs on H.R. 13142 and H.R. 10193.* 91st Cong., 1st sess., 1969.

Texts of bills, Department reports from Interior, Agriculture, Air Force, Civil Service Commission, Alaska Federation of Natives policy position, testimony of witnesses, written communications, map "System of Rectangular Surveys, May, 1969," pertinent additional information.

* 2081. U.S. Congress. House. Committee on Interior and Insular Affairs. *Alaska Native Land Claims Part II. Hearings before the House Subcommittee on Indian Affairs on H.R. 13142, H.R. 10193, and H.R. 14212.* 91st Cong., 1st sess., 1969.

Testimony of witnesses taken in Alaska, written communications including maps. An invaluable source of data with respect to land use and rights to resources.

* 2082. U.S. Congress. House. Committee on Interior and Insular Affairs. *Alaska Native Land Claims. Hearings before a subcommittee on Indian Affairs of the House Committee on Interior and Insular Affairs on H.R. 3100, H.R. 7039, and H.R. 7432.* 92nd Cong., 1st sess., 1971.

Texts of bills; testimony of witnesses; written comments; additional materials including native petitions and proposed amendments.

APOSTLE ISLANDS

* 2083. U.S. Congress. House. Committee on Interior and Insular Affairs. *Apostle Islands National Lakeshore. Hearing before the subcommittee on National Parks and Recreation of the House Committee on Interior and Insular Affairs on H.R. 555 and S. 621.* 91st Cong., 1st sess., 1969.

Statements to the effect that the local Indians do not favor the creation of a national park in their area since it would not contribute to their financial or social interests.

2084. U.S. Congress. House. Committee on Interior and Insular Affairs. *Apostle Islands National Lakeshore Part II. Hearing before the Subcommittee on National Parks and Recreation of the House Committee on Interior and Insular Affairs on H.R. 9306, and S. 621. 91st Cong., 2nd sess., 1970.*

More Indian protests against the creation of a national park encompassing most of the Apostle Islands area.

CALIFORNIA

2085. U.S. Congress. House. Committee on Interior and Insular Affairs. *Indian Tribes of California. Hearings before the Subcommittee of the Committee on Indian Affairs on H.R. 12788, the Raker Bill.* Washington, D.C.: Government Printing Office, 1920.

2086. U.S. Congress. House. Committee on Interior and Insular Affairs. *Hearing before the Subcommittee of the Committee on Indian Affairs. Part II.* 67th Cong., 2nd sess. Washington, D.C.: Government Printing Office, 1922.

Information gathering *re* K344.

2087. U.S. Congress. House. Committee on Interior and Insular Affairs. *Indian Tribes of California. Hearing before a Subcommittee of the Committee on Indian Affairs, on H.R. 8036 and H.R. 9497.* 96th Cong., 1st sess., 1926. Washington, D.C.: Government Printing Office, 1926.

Re K344.

2088. U.S. Congress. House. Committee on Interior and Insular Affairs. *A Review of California Indian Affairs. Hearings before the Subcommittee on Indian Affairs.* Washington, D.C.: Government Printing Office, 1963.

2089. U.S. Congress. House. Committee on Interior and Insular Affairs. *California Indians Judgment Fund, 1966. Hearings before the Subcommittee on Indian Affairs of the Committee on Interior and Insular Affairs on H.R. 8021.* 89th Cong., 2nd sess., 1966.

To provide for the disposition of funds appropriated to pay a judgment in favor of certain Indians of California.

2090. U.S. Congress. House. Committee on Interior and Insular Affairs. *To Provide for the Disposition of Funds Appropriated to Pay a Judgment in Favor of Certain Indians in California. Hearings before the Subcommittee on Indian Affairs.* Washington, D.C.: Government Printing Office, 1966.

Case K344—see Johnson 1966 below.

COLVILLE

* 2091. U.S. Congress. House. Committee on Interior and Insular Affairs. *Colville Termination. Hearings before the Subcommittee on Indian Affairs of the Committee on Interior and Insular Affairs on H.R. 6331, H.R. 5925 and S. 1413.* 89th Cong., 1st sess., 1965.

To provide for the termination of Federal supervision over the property of the Colville Tribe and individual members thereof, and to provide members of the Colville Confederated Tribes with full citizenship and to provide for vesting each tribal member with his equal cash share representing his equity in all reservation assets of the Colville Confederated Tribes in the state of Washington.

* 2092. U.S. Congress. House. Committee on Interior and Insular Affairs. *Colville Termination. Hearing before the Subcommittee on Indian Affairs of the Committee on Interior and Insular Affairs on H.R. 3051.* 90th Cong., 2nd sess., 1968.

Factionalism in the Colville Tribe.

KLAMATH AND MODOC

2093. U.S. Congress. House. Committee on Interior and Insular Affairs. *Disposition of Klamath and Modoc Judgment Funds. Hearings before the Subcommittee on Indian Affairs of the Committee on Interior and Insular Affairs on H.R. 907, H.R. 4964, and S. 664.* 89th Cong., 1st sess., 1965.

To provide for the disposition of judgment funds of the Klamath and Modoc Tribes and Yahooskin Band of Snake Indians.

MENOMINEE

* 2094. U.S. Congress. House. Committee on Interior and Insular Affairs. *Menominee Restoration Act. Hearings before a Subcommittee on Indian Affairs of the Committee on Interior and Insular Affairs on H.R. 7421.* 93rd Cong., 1st sess., 1973.

Vital to the understanding of the current Menominee situation.

NAVAJO AND HOPI

* 2095. U.S. Congress. House. Committee on Interior and Insular Affairs. *Partition of Navajo and Hopi 1882 Reservation. Hearings before the Subcommittee on Indian Affairs of the Committee on Interior and Insular Affairs on H.R. 11128, H.R. 4753, and H.R. 4754.* 92nd Cong., 2nd sess., 1972.

PAPAGO

* 2096. U.S. Congress. House. Committee on Interior and Insular Affairs. *Authorizing Long-Term Leases on the San Xavier and Salt River Pima-Maricopa Indian Reservation, Arizona. H. Report 1855 to accompany H.R. 7648.* 89th Cong., 2nd sess., 1966.

Relevant to Papago economic development.

TAOS

2097. U.S. Congress. House. Committee on Interior and Insular Affairs. *Taos Pueblo—Blue Lake. Hearings before the Subcommittee on Indian Affairs of the Committee on Interior and Insular Affairs on H.R. 471.* 91st Cong., 1st sess., 1969.

2098. U.S. Congress. House. Committee of the Whole House on the State of the Union. *Indian Higher Education. Report #1150 to accompany S. 876.* 90th Cong., 2nd sess., 1968.

2099. U.S. Congress. House. Committee of the Whole House on the State of the Union. *The American Indian. Message from the President of the United States transmitting a message relating to the problems of the American Indians.* Document 272. 90th Cong., 2nd sess., 1968.

2100. U.S. Congress. House. Committee of the Whole House on the State of the Union. *Providing for Loans to Indian Tribes and Tribal Corporations, and for other Purposes. Report 91–864 to accompany S. 227.* 91st Cong., 2nd sess., 1970.

2101. U.S. Congress. House. Committee of the Whole House on the State of the Union. *Establishing Within the Department of the Interior the Position of an Additional Assistant Secretary of the Interior. Report 92–166 to accompany H.R. 6993.* 92nd Cong., 1st sess., 1971.

CHEROKEE, CHICKASAW, CHOCTAW, SEMINOLE

2102. U.S. Congress. House. Committee of the Whole House on the State of the Union. *Providing for Disposition of Estates of Interstate Members of the Cherokee, Chickasaw, Choctaw, and Seminole Nations of Oklahoma Dying Without Heirs. Report 91–880 to accompany H.R. 4145.* 91st Cong., 2nd sess., 1970.

CHIPPEWA

2103. U.S. Congress. House. Committee of the Whole House on the State of the Union. *Providing for the Disposition of Judgment Funds of the Pembina Band of Chippewa Indians. Report No. 92–150.* 92nd Cong., 1st sess., 1971.

CHOCTAW

2104. U.S. Congress. House. Committee of the Whole House on the State of the Union. *Repealing the Act of August 25, 1959, with Respect to the Final Disposition of the Affairs of the Choctaw Tribe. Report No. 91–1151 to accompany H.R. 15866.* 91st Cong., 2nd sess., 1970.

HOPI

* 2105. U.S. Congress. House. Committee of the Whole House on the State of the Union. *Furthering the Economic Advancement and General Welfare of the Hopi Indian Tribe of the State of Arizona. Report No. 91–470.* 91st Cong., 1st sess., 1969.

HOPI AND NAVAJO

* 2106. U.S. Congress. House. Committee of the Whole House on the State of the Union. *Authorizing the Partition of the Surface Rights in the Joint Use Area of the 1882 Executive Order Hopi Reservation and the Surface and Subsurface Rights in the 1934 Navajo Reservation Between the Hopi and Navajo Tribes, Providing for Allotments to Certain Paiute Indians. Report No. 93–909 to accompany H.R. 10337.* 93rd Cong., 2nd sess., 1974.

IOWA TRIBES OF OKLAHOMA, KANSAS, AND NEBRASKA

2107. U.S. Congress. House. Committee of the Whole House on the State of the Union. *Providing for Disposition of Judgment Funds of the Iowa Tribes of Oklahoma and of Kansas and Nebraska. Report No. 92–149.* 92nd Cong., 1st sess., 1971.

NAVAJO AND UTE MOUNTAIN TRIBES

2108. U.S. Congress. House. Committee of the Whole House on the State of the Union. *Determining the Rights and Interests of the Navajo Tribe and Ute Mountain Tribe of the Ute Mountain Reservation in and to certain lands in the State of New Mexico. Report No. 1048 to accompany S. 491.* 90th Cong., 1st sess., 1967.

NAVAJO

2109. U.S. Congress. House. Committee of the Whole House on the State of the Union. *Amending the Act of June 13, 1962 (76 Stat. 96), With Respect to the Navajo Indian Irrigation Project. Report No. 91-1333 to accompany H.R. 13001.* 91st Cong., 2nd sess., 1970.

PIMA - PAPAGO

2110. U.S. Congress. House. Committee of the Whole House on the State of the Union. *Authorizing Long-Term Leases on the San Xavier and Salt River Pima-Maricopa Indian Reservations, Arizona. Report No. 1855 to accompany H.R. 7648.* 89th Cong., 2nd sess., 1966.

SALISH AND KOOTENAI

2111. U.S. Congress. House. Committee of the Whole House on the State of the Union. *Providing for the Disposition of a Judgment Recovered by the Confederated Salish and Kootenai Tribes of Flathead Reservation, Montana, in Paragraph II, Docket No. 50233, U.S. Court of Claims. Report No. 91-471.* 91st Cong., 1st sess., 1969.

SIOUX - FORT BELKNAP

2112. U.S. Congress. House. Committee of the Whole House on the State of the Union. *Authorizing the Transfer of the Brown Unit of the Fort Belknap Indian Irrigation Project on the Fort Belknap Indian Reservation, Montana, to the Landowners within the Unit. Report No. 91-1020.* 91st Cong., 2nd sess., 1970.

SNOHOMISH

2113. U.S. Congress. House. Committee of the Whole House on the State of the Union. *Providing for the Disposition of Judgment Funds of the Snohomish Tribe, the Upper Skagit Tribe, and the Snoqualmie and Skykomish Tribes. Report No. 92-148 to accompany H.R. 1444.* 92nd Cong., 1st sess., 1971.

SOBOBA BAND OF MISSION INDIANS

2114. U.S. Congress. House. Committee of the Whole House on the State of the Union. *Authorizing the Secretary of the Interior to Approve an Agreement*

Entered Into by the Soboba Band of Mission Indians Releasing a Claim Against the Metropolitan Water District of Southern California and Eastern Municipal Water District, California, and Providing for Construction of a Water Distribution System and a Water Supply for the Soboba Indian Reservation. Report No. 91–1017 to accompany H.R. 3328. 91st Cong., 2nd sess., 1970.

UMATILLA

2115. U.S. Congress. House. Committee of the Whole House on the State of the Union. *Providing for the Disposition of Judgment Funds of the Confederated Tribes of the Umatilla Indian Reservation. Report No. 91–472 to accompany H.R. 9477.* 91st Cong., 1st sess., 1969.

UTE

2116. U.S. Congress. House. Committee of the Whole House on the State of the Union. *Reimbursing the Ute Tribe of the Uintah and Ouray Reservation for Tribal Funds that were used to Construct, Operate, and Maintain the Uintah Indian Irrigation Project, Utah. Report No. 91–1152 to accompany H.R. 16416.* 91st Cong., 2nd sess., 1970.

2117. U.S. Congress. House. Committee of the Whole House on the State of the Union. *Providing for the Disposition of Funds Appropriated to Pay a Judgment in Favor of the Confederated Bands of Ute Indians in Court of Claims Case 47567, and a Judgment in Favor of the Ute Tribe of the Uintah and Ouray Reservation for and on Behalf of the Uncompahgre Band of Ute Indians in Indian Claims Commissions Docket Numbered 349. Report No. 91–1425 to accompany H.R. 16833.* 91st Cong., 2nd sess., 1970.

WASHOE

* 2118. U.S. Congress. House. Committee of the Whole House on the State of the Union. *Declaring That the United States Holds in Trust for the Washoe Tribe of Indians Certain Lands in Alpine County, California. Report No. 91–1149 to accompany H.R. 4587.* 91st Cong., 2nd sess., 1970.

YAKIMA

2119. U.S. Congress. House. Committee of the Whole House on the State of the Union. *Providing for the Disposition of Funds Appropriated to Pay Judgments in Favor of the Yakima Tribes in Indian Claims Commission Dockets Numbered 47–A, 162, and Consolidated 47 and 164. Report No. 91–1423 to accompany H.R. 15469.* 91st Cong., 2nd sess., 1970.

YAVAPAI

2120. U.S. Congress. House. Committee of the Whole House on the State of the

Union. *Amending the Act of August 9, 1955, to Authorize Longer Term Leases of Indian Lands at the Yavapai-Prescott Community Reservation in Arizona. Report No. 91-882 to accompany H.R. 12878.* 91st Cong., 2nd sess., 1970.

2121. U.S. Congress. House. Executive Document No. 296. *Indian Reservation in San Diego County, California.* 41st Cong., 2nd sess. Washington, D.C.: Government Printing Office, 1870.

Establishment of reservation in San Pasqual and Pala Valleys, 1870.

2122. U.S. Congress. House. Executive Document No. 91. *Mission Indians of Southern California by J. C. Ames.* 43rd Cong., 1st sess. Washington, D.C.: Government Printing Office, 1874.

Report on conditions of the neglected and abused Mission Indian tribes.

2123. U.S. Congress. House. Executive Documents No. 1, Pt. 5. 53rd Cong. *The Indian Exhibit at the Columbian Exposition.* Washington, D.C.: Government Printing Office, 1895.

* 2124. U.S. Congress. House. Executive Documents No. 319. *Relief of Certain Mission Indians in California.* 57th Cong., 1st sess. Washington, D.C.: Government Printing Office, 1902.

2125. U.S. Congress. House. Miscellaneous Document 340, Pt. 15. *Report on Indians Taxed and Indians Not Taxed in the U.S. (except Alaska) at the 11th Census: 1890.* Edited by Thomas Donaldson. Washington, D.C.: Government Printing Office, 1890.

2126. U.S. Congress. Joint Economic Committee. *Toward Economic Development for Native American Communities. A Compendium of Papers submitted to the Subcommittee on Economy in Government of the Joint Economic Committee. Vol. I.* 91st Cong., 1st sess., 1969.

Part I: Development Prospects and Problems.

* 2127. U.S. Congress. Joint Economic Committee. *Toward Economic Development for Native American Communities. A Compendium of Papers submitted to the Subcommittee on Economy in Government of the Joint Economic Committee. Vol. 2.* 91st Cong., 1st sess., 1969.

Part II: Development Programs and Plans.
Part III: The Resource Base.

2128. U.S. Congress. Joint Committee on Navajo-Hopi Indian Administration. *Legislation Concerning the Navajo Tribe. Hearing before the Joint Com-*

mittee on Navajo-Hopi Indian Administration, Congress of the United States. 86th Cong., 2nd sess., 1960.

* 2129. U.S. Congress. Senate. Bureau of Education. Special Report, 1888. *Indian Education and Civilization.* A Report Prepared in Answer to Senate Resolution of February 23, 1885, by Alice C. Fletcher. Washington D.C.: Government Printing Office, 1888; reprint edition, Millwood, New York: Kraus Reprint Co., 1973.

2130. U.S. Congress. Senate. Committee on Appropriations. *Senate Hearings Before the Committee on Appropriations. Department of the Interior and Related Agencies Appropriations, Parts 1 & 2. H.R. 17354.* 90th Cong., 2nd sess., Fiscal 1969, 1968.

2131. U.S. Congress. Senate. Committee on Appropriations. *Senate Hearings before the Committee on Appropriations on the Department of the Interior and Related Agencies Appropriations. H.R. 17619.* 91st Cong., 2nd sess., Fiscal 1971. Part 1: pp. 1–1217, Feb., 1970.

2132. U.S. Congress. Senate. Committee on Appropriations. *Senate Hearings before the Committee on Appropriations. Department of the Interior and Related Agencies Appropriations. H.R. 17619.* 91st Cong., 2nd sess., Fiscal 1971. Part 2, pp. 1219–2576, 1970.

2133. U.S. Congress. Senate. Committee on Appropriations. *Senate Hearings before the Committee on Appropriations. Department of the Interior and Related Agencies Appropriations. H.R. 17619.* 91st Cong., 2nd sess., Fiscal 1971. Part 3, pp. 2577–3644, 1970.

2134. U.S. Congress. Senate. Committee on Appropriations. *Senate Hearings before the Committee on Appropriations. Department of the Interior and Related Agencies Appropriations. H.R. 17619.* 91st Cong., 2nd sess., Fiscal 1971. Part 4, pp. 3645–4830, 1970.

* 2135. U.S. Congress. Senate. Committee on Appropriations. *Federal Facilities for Indians.* Report by Mamie L. Mizen. Washington, D.C.: Government Printing Office, 1965.

* 2136. U.S. Congress. Senate. Committee on Appropriations. *Federal Facilities for Indians. Tribal Relations with the Federal Government.* Report by Mamie L. Mizen. Washington, D.C.: Government Printing Office, 1966.

* 2137. U.S. Congress. Senate. Committee on Appropriations. *Federal Facilities for Indians. Tribal Relations with the Federal Government.* Report by Mamie L. Mizen. Washington, D.C.: Government Printing Office, 1967.

2138. U.S. Congress. Senate. Committee on Interior and Insular Affairs. *Interior Nomination. Hearing before the Committee on Interior and Insular Affairs on the Nomination of Robert LaFollette Bennett, of Alaska, to be Commissioner of Indian Affairs.* 89th Cong., 2nd sess., 1966.

2139. U.S. Congress. Senate. Committee on Interior and Insular Affairs. *Interior Nominations. Hearing before the Senate Committee on Interior and Insular Affairs on the Nominations of John Thomas Vance, Richard W. Yarborough, and Jerome K. Kuykendall to be Commissioners on the Indian Claims Commission.* 90th Cong., 1st sess., 1967.

2140. U.S. Congress. Senate. Committee on Interior and Insular Affairs. *Interior Nomination. Hearing before the Senate Committee on Interior and Insular Affairs on the Nomination of Margaret Hunter Pierce to be a Commissioner of the Indian Claims Commission.* 90th Cong., 2nd sess., 1968.

2141. U.S. Congress. Senate. Committee on Interior and Insular Affairs. *Interior Nomination. Hearing before the Committee on Interior and Insular Affairs on the Nomination of Louis R. Bruce, of New York, to be Commissioner of Indian Affairs.* 91st Cong., 1st sess., 1969.

2142. U.S. Congress. Senate. Committee on Interior and Insular Affairs. *Interior Nomination. Hearings before the Committee on Interior and Insular Affairs on the Nomination of Governor Walter J. Hickel, of Alaska, to be Secretary of the Interior.* 91st Cong., 1st sess., 1969. Parts 1 and 2.

2143. U.S. Congress. Senate. Committee on Interior and Insular Affairs. *Alaska Native Land Claims. Hearings before the Committee on Interior and Insular Affairs on S. 2906, S. 1964, and S. 2020.* 90th Cong., 2nd sess., 1968.

Contains texts of bills under consideration, the testimony of many witnesses, written communications to the committee and pertinent additional information.

2144. U.S. Congress. Senate. Committee on Interior and Insular Affairs. *Alaska Native Land Claims. Hearings before the Committee on Interior and Insular Affairs on S. 2906, S. 1964, S. 2690, S. 2020, and S. 3586. Related Bills. Part 2.* 90th Cong., 2nd sess., 1968.

Contains a text of S. 3586, Interior Department reports on S. 2690, S. 3586, testimony of witnesses and written communications.

2145. U.S. Congress. Senate. Committee on Interior and Insular Affairs. *Alaska Native Land Claims. Hearing Before the Committee of Interior and Insular Affairs on S. 1830.* 91st Cong., 1st sess., 1969.

Department reports from Agriculture, Budget, Interior, Treasury, a text of S. 1830, testimony of witnesses, written communications, pertinent additional information.

* 2146. U.S. Congress. Senate. Committee on Interior and Insular Affairs. *Alaska*

Native Land Claims Part III. Hearings before the Committee on Interior and Insular Affairs on S. 1830. 91st Cong., 1st sess., 1969.

Written communications and additional information including section-by-section analysis of bill, analysis of proposals for the settlement of Alaska Native land claims, and comparison of proposals of Federal Field Committee, Department of Interior, and Alaska Federation of Natives. Indispensable for an understanding of the question.

* 2147. U.S. Congress. Senate. Committee on Interior and Insular Affairs. *Alaska Native Claims Settlement Act of 1970. S. Report No. 91-925 to Accompany S. 1830.* 91st Cong., 2nd sess., 1970.

Recommends passage of bill with amendment. Summary statement of Native Claims problem provided under the following headings: I. Introduction; II. Background of Alaska Native Land Claims; III. Committee Recommendations; IV. History of Problem; V. Need; VI. Legislative History; VII. Costs and Benefits of Monetary Compensation; VIII. Section-by-section Analysis; IX. Executive Communications; Changes in Existing Law.

2148. U.S. Congress. Senate. Committee on Interior and Insular Affairs. *Alaska Native Land Claims. Hearings before the Committee on Interior and Insular Affairs on S. 35 and S. 835.* 92nd Cong., 1st sess., 1971.

Text of bills; Department reports from Indian Claims Commission, Interior, U.S. Court of Claims; testimony of witnesses; written communications; map, showing federal withdrawals, native villages, and state selected lands. Useful material.

2149. U.S. Congress. Senate. Committee on Interior and Insular Affairs. *Alaska Native Land Claims. Hearings before the Committee on Interior and Insular Affairs on S. 35, S. 835, and S. 1571. Part 2.* 92nd Cong., 1st sess., 1971.

Text of S. 1571; Department reports from Agriculture, Civil Service Commission, Interior; testimony of witnesses; written communications including critical analysis of S. 35 and a map of Tlingit and Haida territory.

2150. U.S. Congress. Senate. Committee on Interior and Insular Affairs. *Alaska Native Land Claims. Hearings before the Committee on Interior and Insular Affairs on S. 35, S. 835, and S. 1571. Part 3.* 92nd Cong., 1st sess., 1971.

Appendix containing written comments including the text of S. 1329, and Arctic Slope Native Association comments.

2151. U.S. Congress. Senate. Committee on Interior and Insular Affairs. *Hearings before the Committee on the Status of the Proposed Trans-Alaska Pipeline. Part 1.* 91st Cong., 1st sess., 1969.

Statements of witnesses. Most attention given to a physical description of the pipeline, and the safeguards necessary to protect other natural resources. Five brief paragraphs are devoted to admonition that natives should be trained and hired and not fired unless necessary. Map.

2152. U.S. Congress. Senate. Committee on Interior and Insular Affairs. *Hearings before the Committee on the Status of the Proposed Trans-Alaska Pipeline. Part 2.* 91st Cong., 1st sess., 1969.

Statements of witnesses, other communications for and against the pipeline. Positions taken are based upon beliefs as to whether or not economic benefits can be derived from the venture without seriously harming the present ecosystem. Map.

2153. U.S. Congress. Senate. Committee on Interior and Insular Affairs. *Hearings before the Committee on the Status of the Proposed Trans-Alaska Pipeline, Part 3.* 91st Cong., 1st sess., 1969.

Additional written communications concerning nature of proposed pipeline and nature and feasibility of proposed safeguards for natural environment. Map, chart.

2154. U.S. Congress. Senate. Committee on Interior and Insular Affairs. *Legislative Calendar.* 91st Cong., 1969–1970.

2155. U.S. Congress. Senate. Committee on Interior and Insular Affairs. *Policy Changes in the BIA.* December, 1970. 124 pages.

* 2156. U.S. Congress. Senate. Committee on Interior and Insular Affairs. *The Effects of Termination on the Menominee.* By Ada Deer, Laurel Otradovec, Lloyd Powless, James White, Georgianna Ignace. Testimony on Senate Concurrent Resolution 26, 1971. Mimeo.

2157. U.S. Congress. Senate. Committee on Interior and Insular Affairs. *Fort Belknap Indian Reservation and the Fort Belknap Builders, Inc. Staff Report of the Committee on Interior and Insular Affairs.* 92nd Cong., 2nd sess. Washington, D.C.: Government Printing Office, 1972.

2158. U.S. Congress. Senate. Committee on Interior and Insular Affairs. *Problems of Electrical Power Production in the Southwest. Report of the Committee pursuant to S. 45.* 92nd Cong., 1st sess., 1972.

2159. U.S. Congress. Senate. Committee on Interior and Insular Affairs. *Comprehensive Indian Education Act. Hearings before the Committee on S. 2724.* 92nd Cong., 2nd sess., 1972.

A Bill to Establish a National Indian Education Program by Creating a

National Board of Regents for Indian Education, Carrying Out of a National Indian Education Program, the Establishment of Local Indian School Boards.

2160. U.S. Congress. Senate. Committee on Interior and Insular Affairs. *Regulation of Surface Mining Operations. Hearings before the Committee on S. 425 and S. 923.* 93rd Cong., 1st sess., 1973. Part 1.

2161. U.S. Congress. Senate. Committee on Interior and Insular Affairs. *Regulation of Surface Mining Operations. Hearings before the Committee on S. 425 and S. 923. Part 2.* 93rd Cong., 1st sess., 1973.

2162. U.S. Congress. Senate. Committee on Interior and Insular Affairs. *Rights of Way Across Federal Lands. Hearings before the Committee on S. 1040, S. 1041, S. 1056, S. 1081. Part 1.* 93rd Cong., 1st sess., 1973.

Texts of bills, statements of witnesses, written communications. Federal government will not adequately protect native interests.

2163. U.S. Congress. Senate. Committee on Interior and Insular Affairs. *Rights of Way Across Federal Lands. Hearings before the Committee on S. 1040, S. 1041, S. 1056, S. 1081. Part 2.* 93rd Cong., 1st sess., 1973.

Statements of witnesses, written communications. Those commercial interests who stand to benefit immediately by the Alaska Pipeline favor its construction. Those who do not object to it.

2164. U.S. Congress. Senate. Committee on Interior and Insular Affairs. *Rights of Way Across Federal Lands: Transportation of Alaska's North Slope Oil. Hearings before the Committee on S. 970, S. 993, S. 1565. Part 3.* 93rd Cong., 1st sess., 1973.

Texts of bills, statements of witnesses, written communications. Data to the effect that the proposed Alaska Pipeline must be built immediately because it is the only economically and politically feasible means to relieve the "energy crisis." Necessary supporting material for viewing the native position.

2165. U.S. Congress. Senate. Committee on Interior and Insular Affairs. *Rights of Way Across Federal Lands: Transportation of Alaska's North Slope Oil. Hearings before the Committee on S. 970, S. 993, S. 1565, Part 4.* 93rd Cong., 1st sess., 1973.

Statements of witnesses, written communications. The impression is given that one of the reasons why the Pipeline will not be built through Canada is that Canadian natives are better organized to interfere with its construction and operation than are Alaskan natives.

* 2166. U.S. Congress. Senate. Committee on Interior and Insular Affairs. *Legislative Calendar.* 93rd Cong., 1973-1974.

* 2167. U.S. Congress. Senate. Committee on Interior and Insular Affairs. Subcommittee on Indian Affairs. *A Survey of the Conditions of the Indians in the U.S. Part II.* Washington, D.C.: Government Printing Office, 1929.

Includes hearings at San Francisco and Riverside in November, 1928, with verbatim transcript of testimony given by Indians and Indian welfare workers.

2168. U.S. Congress. Senate. Committee on Interior and Insular Affairs. Subcommittee on Indian Affairs. *A Survey of the Conditions of Indians in the U.S. Vol. II.* Washington, D.C.: Government Printing Office, 1932.

California is included.

2169. U.S. Congress. Senate. Committee on Interior and Insular Affairs. *Federal Indian Policy. Hearings before the Subcommittee on Indian Affairs of the Committee on S. 809, S. Cong. Res. 3, and S. 331.* 85th Cong., 1st sess., 1957.

Texts of bills, agency reports, statements of witnesses, additional supporting information. Appendix.

* 2170. U.S. Congress. Senate. Committee on Interior and Insular Affairs. *Taos Indians—Blue Lake. Hearings before the Subcommittee on Indian Affairs of the Committee on H.R. 3306, S. 1624, and S. 1625.* 90th Cong., 2nd sess., 1968.

2171. U.S. Congress. Senate. Committee on Interior and Insular Affairs. *Federal Lands in Trust for Tribes in Minnesota and Wisconsin. Hearing before the Subcommittee on Indian Affairs of the Committee on S. 1217 and S. 1230.* 92nd Cong., 1st sess., 1971.

To declare that certain federally owned lands within the White Earth Reservation, Minnesota, shall be held by the U.S. in trust for the Minnesota Chippewa tribe and lands in the Stockbridge-Munsee Community, Wisconsin, shall be held in trust for these Indians.

2172. U.S. Congress. Senate. Committee on Interior and Insular Affairs. *Indian Self-Determination. Hearing before the Committee o Indian Affairs of the Committee on S. 3157, S. 1583, S. 1574, and S. 2238.* 92nd Cong., 2nd sess., 1972.

2173. U.S. Congress. Senate. Committee on Interior and Insular Affairs. *Time Extension for Commencing Actions on Behalf of Indians. Hearing before the*

Subcommittee on Indian Affairs of the Committee on S. 3377 and H.R. 13825. 92nd Cong., 2nd sess., 1972.

2174. U.S. Congress. Senate. Committee on Interior and Insular Affairs. *Financing the Economic Development of Indians and Indian Organizations. Hearing before the Subcommittee on Indian Affairs of the Committee on S. 1341 and Related Bills.* 93rd Cong., 1st sess., 1973.

2175. U.S. Congress. Senate. Committee on Interior and Insular Affairs. *Indian Claims Commission Appropriations for Fiscal Year 1974. Hearings before the Subcommittee on Indian Affairs of the Commitee on S. 721.* 93rd Cong., 1st sess., 1973.

Includes data on completed and pending claims cases.

2176. U.S. Congress. Senate. Committee on Interior and Insular Affairs. *Partition of the Surface Rights of Navajo-Hopi Indian Land. Hearing before the Subcommittee on Indian Affairs of the Committee on H.R. 1193.* 93rd Cong., 1st sess., 1973.

2177. U.S. Congress. Senate. Committee on Interior and Insular Affairs. *Indian Judgment Funds Distribution Act of 1973. Hearing before the Subcommittee on Indian Affairs of the Committee on S. 1016.* 93rd Cong., 1st sess., 1973.

Concerns the formulation of a means for the government to pay land claims awards faster than extant legislation will permit.

2178. U.S. Congress. Senate. Committee on Interior and Insular Affairs. *Indian Trust Counsel Authority. Hearings before the Subcommittee on Indian Affairs of the Committee on S. 1012 and S. 1339.* 93rd Cong., 1st sess., 1973.

Partial deliberations concerning the possible creation of an agency to insure the proper use of natural resources owned by native peoples.

2179. U.S. Congress. Senate. Committee on Interior and Insular Affairs. *National Indian Goals and Progress Act. Hearing before the Subcommittee on Indian Affairs of the Committee on S. 1786.* 93rd Cong., 1st sess., 1973.

2180. U.S. Congress. Senate. Committee on Interior and Insular Affairs. *Indian Self-Determination and Education Program. Hearings before the Subcommittee on Indian Affairs of the Committee on S. 1017 and Related Bills.* 93rd Cong., 1st sess., 1973.

2181. U.S. Congress. Senate. Committee on Interior and Insular Affairs. *Establishment of the American Indian Policy Review Commission. Hearings before the Subcommittee on Indian Affairs of the Committee on Interior and Insular Affairs on S.J. Res. 133.* 93rd Cong., 1st sess., 1973.

Deliberations and testimony concerning an attempt by Congress and the Executive Branch to comprehensively deal with Indian problems and needs. Useful data, but Washington keeps to its position and the Indians to theirs.

2182. U.S. Congress. Senate. Committee on Interior and Insular Affairs. *Surface Mining. Hearings before the Subcommittee on Minerals, Materials, and Fuels of the Committee on Interior and Insular Affairs pursuant to S. Res. 45, a National Fuels and Energy Policy Study on S. 77, S. 630, S. 993, S. 1160, S. 1240, S. 1498, S. 2455, and S. 2777, Pending Surface Mining Legislation. Part 1.* 92nd Cong., 1st sess., 1971.

2183. U.S. Congress. Senate. Committee on Interior and Insular Affairs. *Surface Mining. Hearings before the Subcommittee on Minerals, Materials, and Fuels of the Committee on Interior and Insular Affairs Pursuant to S. Res. 45, a National Fuels and Energy Policy Study. Part 2.* 92nd Cong., 1st sess., 1971.

2184. U.S. Congress. Senate. Committee on Interior and Insular Affairs. *Surface Mining. Hearings before the Subcommittee on Minerals, Materials, and Fuels of the Committee on Interior and Insular Affairs Pursuant to S. Res. 45, a National Fuels and Energy Policy Study. Part 3.* 92nd Cong., 1st sess., 1972.

2185. U.S. Congress. Senate. Committee on Interior and Insular Affairs. *Lower Colorado River Land Claims. Hearings before the Subcommittee on Public Lands of the Committee on H.R. 10256.* 90th Cong., 2nd sess., 1968.

2186. U.S. Congress. Senate. Committee on Interior and Insular Affairs. *Wilderness Additions in Alaska, New Mexico, Oregon, and Washington. Hearings before the Subcommittee on Public Lands of the Committee on S. 3014.* 91st Cong., 1st sess., 1969.

2187. U.S. Congress. Senate. Committee on Interior and Insular Affairs. *Klamath Indian Forest. Hearing before the Subcommittee on Public Lands of the Committee on S. 3594, a Bill Providing for Federal Purchase of the Remaining Klamath Indian Forest.* 92nd Cong., 2nd sess., 1972.

2188. U.S. Congress. Senate. Committee on Interior and Insular Affairs. *Central Arizona Project. Hearings before the Subcommittee on Water and Power Resources of the Committee on S. 1004, S. 1013, S. 861, S. 1242, and S. 1409, Bills to Authorize the Construction, Operation, and Maintenance of the Central Arizona Project (Arizona-New Mexico); and Colorado River Project.* 90th Cong., 1st sess., 1967.

* 2189. U.S. Congress. Senate. Committee on Interior and Insular Affairs. *Navajo Indian Irrigation Project. Hearing before the Subcommittee on Water and Power Resources of the Committee on S. 203.* 91st Cong., 1st sess., 1969.

2190. U.S. Congress. Senate. *Service of Bureau of Indian Affairs Teachers.* Calendar No. 562, Report No. 91–567. 91st Cong. 1st sess., 1969.

ALASKA

2191. U.S. Congress. Senate. *Alaska Native Claims Settlement Act of 1970.* Calendar No. 926, Report No. 91–925. 91st Cong., 2nd sess., 1970.

2192. U.S. Congress. Senate. *Alaska Native Claims Settlement Act of 1971.* Calendar No. 403, Report No. 92-405. 92nd Cong., 1st sess., 1971.

FLATHEAD

2193. U.S. Congress. Senate. *Authorizing Disposition and Distribution of Judgments for Claims of Confederated Salish and Kootenai Tribes of the Flathead Reservation, Montana.* Calendar No. 325, Report No. 92-334. 92nd Cong., 1st sess., 1971.

LAGUNA

2194. U.S. Congress. Senate. *Providing for the Disposition of Judgment Funds on Deposit to the Credit of the Pueblo of Laguna in Indian Claims Commission, Docket Numbered 224.* Calendar No. 406, Report No. 92-409. 92nd Cong., 1st sess., 1971.

NAVAJO

2195. U.S. Congress. Senate. *Determining the Rights and Interests of the Navajo Tribe and the Ute Mountain Tribe of the Ute Mountain Reservation in and to Certain Lands in the State of New Mexico. Calendar* No. 440, Report No. 453. 90th Cong., 1st sess., 1967.

2196. U.S. Congress. Senate. *Amending the Act of June 13, 1962, with Respect to the Navajo Indian Irrigation Project.* Calendar No. 358, Report No. 91-363. 91st Cong., 1st sess., 1969.

2197. U.S. Congress. Senate. *Abolishing the Joint Committee on Navajo-Hopi Administration.* Calendar No. 18, Report No. 93-11. 93rd Cong., 1st sess., 1973.

2198. U.S. Congress. Senate. *Authorizing the Secretary of the Interior to Transfer Franchise Fees Received From Certain Concession Operations at Glen Canyon National Recreation Area, in the States of Arizona and Utah.* Calendar No. 162, Report No. 93-169. 93rd Cong., 1st sess., 1973.

NEW YORK

2199. U.S. Congress. Senate. *Providing for the Disposition of Funds Appropriated to Pay a Judgment in Favor of the Emigrant New York Indians in Indian Claims Commission Docket No. 75.* Calendar No. 521, Report No. 536. 90th Cong., 1st sess., 1967.

PAIUTE

2200. U.S. Congress. Senate. *Declaring that Certain Public Lands are Held in Trust by the U.S. for the Summit Lake Paiute Tribe.* Calendar No. 521, Report No. 92-540. 92nd Cong., 1st sess., 1971.

2201. U.S. Congress. Senate. *Declaring that Certain Federally Owned Lands are Held by the U.S. in Trust for the Paiute-Shoshone Tribe of the Fallon Reservation and Fallon Colony, Nevada.* Calendar No. 522, Report No. 92-541. 92nd Cong., 1st sess., 1971.

2202. U.S. Congress. Senate. *Declaring that Certain Federally Owned Lands in the State of Nevada are Held by the U.S. in Trust for Reno-Sparks Indian Colony.* Calendar No. 523, Report No. 92-538. 92nd Cong., 1st sess., 1971.

ROUND VALLEY

2203. U.S. Congress. Senate. *Round Valley Reservation Investigation* by Mr. Davies from the Committee on Indian Affairs. Report No. 1522. 48th Cong., 2nd sess., 1885.

SHOSHONE

2204. U.S. Congress. Senate. *Providing for the Apportionment of Funds in Payment of a Judgment in Favor of the Shoshone Tribe in Consolidated Dockets Numbered 326-D, 326-E, 326-F, 326-G, 326-H, 366, and 367 before the Indian Claims Commission.* Calendar No. 392, Report No. 393. 92nd Cong., 1st sess., 1971.

SOBOBA

2205. U.S. Congress. Senate. *Authorizing the Secretary of the Interior to Approve an Agreement Between the Soboba Band of Mission Indians and the Metropolitan and Eastern Municipal Water Districts and Providing for the Construction of a Water Supply System for the Soboba Indian Reservation.* Calendar No. 1401, Report No. 91-1387. 91st Cong., 2nd sess., 1970.

UMATILLA

2206 U.S. Congress. Senate. *Providing for the Disposition of Judgment Funds of the Confederated Tribes of the Umatilla Indian Reservation.* Calendar No. 564, Report No. 91-569. 91st Cong., 1st sess., 1969.

YAKIMA

2207. U.S. Congress. Senate. *Providing for the Disposition of Funds Appropriated to Pay Judgments in Favor of the Yakima Tribes in Indian Claims Commission Dockets Numbered 47-A, 162, and Consolidated 47 and 164.* Calendar No. 860, Report No. 91-857. 91st Cong., 2nd sess., 1970.

* 2208. U.S. Congress. Senate. Committee on the Judiciary. *Federal Protection of Indian Resources. Hearings before a Subcommittee of the Senate Committee on the Judiciary on Administrative Practices and Procedures Relating to*

Protection of Indian Natural Resources. Parts 1-7. 92nd Cong., 1st sess., 1971-1972.

* 2209. U.S. Congress. Senate. Committee on the Judiciary. *Constitutional Rights of the American Indian. Hearings before the Subcommittee on Constitutional Rights of the Committee on the Judiciary on S. 961, S. 962, S. 963, S. 964, S.* sess., 1961.

* 2210. U.S. Congress. Senate. Committee on the Judiciary. *Constitutional Rights of the American Indian. Hearings before the Subcommittee on Constitutional Rights of the Committee on the Judiciary on S. 961, S. 962, S. 163, S. 964, S. 965, S. 966, S. 967, S. 968, and S.J. Res. 40.* 89th Cong., 1st sess., 1965.

* 2211. U.S. Congress. U.S. Congress. Senate. Committee on Labor and Public Welfare. *Indian Education. Hearings before the Special Subcommittee on Indian Education of the Committee on Labor and Public Welfare. Part 1.* 90th Cong., 1st and 2nd sess., 1968.

Indian education in general, in the Southwest, and on the plains.

* 2212. U.S. Congress. Senate. Committee on Labor and Public Welfare. *Indian Education. Hearings before the Special Subcommittee on Indian Education of the Committee on Labor and Public Welfare. Part 2.* 90th Cong., 1st and 2nd sess., 1968.

Deals with the Oklahoma Cherokee.

* 2213. U.S. Congress. Senate. Committee on Labor and Public Welfare. *Indian Education. Hearings before the Special Subcommittee on Indian Education of the Committee on Labor and Public Welfare. Part 3.* 90th Cong., 1st and 2nd sess., 1968.

Education in the Southwest.

* 2214. U.S. Congress. Senate. Committee on Labor and Public Welfare. *Indian Education. Hearings before the Special Subcommittee on Indian Education of the Committee on Labor and Public Welfare. Part 4.* 90th Cong., 1st and 2nd sess., 1968.

Plains Indian education.

* 2215. U.S. Congress. Senate. Committee on Labor and Public Welfare. *Indian Education. Hearings before the Special Subcommittee on Indian Education of the Committee on Labor and Public Welfare. Part 5.* 90th Cong., 1st and 2nd sess., 1968.

Northwest.

* 2216. U.S. Congress. Senate. Committee on Labor and Public Welfare. *Indian Education, 1969. Hearings before the Subcommittee on Indian Education of*

the Committee on Labor and Public Welfare on Policy, Organization, Administration, and New Legislation Concerning the American Indians. Part 1. 91st Cong., 1st sess., 1969.

* 2217. U.S. Congress. Senate. Committee on Labor and Public Welfare. *Indian Education, 1969. Hearings before the Subcommittee on Indian Education of the Committee on Labor and Public Welfare on Policy, Organization, Administration, and New Legislation Concerning the American Indians. Part 2-Appendix.* 91st Cong., 1st session, 1969.

* 2218. U.S. Congress. Senate. Committee on Labor and Public Welfare. *The Education of American Indians. A Survey of the Literature.* Prepared for the Special Subcommittee on Indian Education of the Committee on Labor and Public Welfare by Brewton Berry. 1969.

   Invaluable.

2219. U.S. Congress. Senate. Committee on Labor and Public Welfare. *Indian Education: A National Tragedy—A National Challenge.* 1969 Report of the Committee on Labor and Public Welfare made by its Special Subcommittee on Indian Education. Washington, D.C.: Government Printing Office, 1969.

   A resolution authorizing an investigation into the problems of education for American Indians.

2220. U.S. Congress. Senate. Executive Document No. 95. *Indian Education and Civilization. A Report Prepared in Answer to Senate Resolution of February 23, 1885.* Bureau of Education, Special Report, 1888, by Alice C. Fletcher. 48th Cong., 2nd sess., 1888; reprint edition, Millwood, New York; Kraus Reprint, 1973.

* 2221. U.S. Congress. Senate. Document No. 121. *Memorial of the Northern California Indian Association* by C. E. Kelsey. 58th Cong., 2nd sess., Washington, D.C.: Government Printing Office, 1904.

   Asking for relief for landless Indians in northern California. Kelsey was Secretary of the Northern California Indian Association.

2222. U.S. Congress. Senate. Senator Fannin speaking on Lake Havasu City, a Prototype for Future Developments. 89th Cong., 1st sess., *Congressional Record* 21 October 1965.

2223. U.S. Congress. Senate. Senator Proxmire speaking on the Menominee Restoration Act and the Menominee Indians. 93rd Cong., 1st sess. *Congressional Record,* Vol. 119, 2 May, 1973.

* 2224. U.S. Court of Claims. *No. K-344, Decided October 5, 1942. The Indians of California, Claimants, by U.S. Webb, Attorney General of the State of California v. the United States.* Washington, D.C.: Government Printing Office, 1943.

2225. U.S. Department of Agriculture. *Rural Indian Americans in Poverty.* Agricultural Economic Report No. 167. Washington, D.C.: Government Printing Office, 1969.

* 2226. U.S. Department of Commerce. Bureau of the Census. *Indian Population in the United States and Canada, 1910.* Washington, D.C.: Government Printing Office, 1915; reprint edition, Millwood, New York, Kraus Reprint Co., 1973.

* 2227. U.S. Department of Commerce. Bureau of the Census. *The Indian Population of the United States and Alaska. Fifteenth Census of the U.S.: 1930.* Washington, D.C.: Government Printing Office, 1937; reprint edition, Millwood, New York: Kraus Reprint Co., 1973.

* 2228. U.S. Department of Commerce. Bureau of the Census. *Census of Population: 1970. Subject Reports. Final Report PC(2)-1F. American Indians.* Washington, D.C.: Government Printing Office, 1973.

* 2229. U.S. Department of Commerce. *Federal and State Indian Reservations and Indian Trust Areas.* Washington, D.C.: Government Printing Office, 1974.

2230. U.S. *Department of Commerce News.* "Census Shows Navajo Tribe is Indians' Largest." Washington, D.C., Jan. 22, 1973.

2231. U.S. *Department of Commerce News.* "Story of the First Americans Told in New Census Booklet for Students." Washington, D.C., September 13, 1973.

2232. U.S. Department of Commerce. Economic Development Administration. *Economic Development* 7, no. 12 (December 1970).

2233. U.S. Department of Commerce. Economic Development Administration. *Federal and State Indian Reservations. An EDA Handbook.* Washington, D.C.: Government Printing Office, January, 1971.

2234. U.S. Department of Commerce. Economic Development Administration. *Indian Economic Development. An Evaluation of EDA's Selected Indian Reservation Program. Vol. 1. Narrative.* Boise Cascade Center for Community Development, July, 1972.

2235. U.S. Department of Commerce. Economic Development Administration. *Indian Economic Development. An Evaluation of EDA's Selected Indian Reservation Program. Vol. 2. Individual Reservation Reports, Appendices.* Boise Cascade Center for Community Development, July, 1972.

* 2236. U.S. Department of Commerce. United States Travel Service. *Festival USA, 1973.* Washington, D.C.: Government Printing Office, 1973.

A listing of all National Festivals for the year 1973.

2237. U.S. Department of Health, Education and Welfare. National Institute of Health. *Nutrition, Growth and Development of North American Indian Children.* Edited by William Moore, Marjorie Silverberg, and Merrill Read. DHEW Publication No. (NIH) 72-26. Washington, D.C.: Government Printing Office, n.d.

2238. U.S. Department of Health, Education and Welfare. National Institute of Mental Health—Indian Health Service. *Suicide Among the American Indians. Two Workshops. Aberdeen, South Dakota, September 1967; and Lewistown, Montana, November 1967.* Public Health Service Publication No. 1903. June 1969.

2239. U.S. Department of Health, Education and Welfare. National Institute of Mental Health, Division of Special Mental Health Programs, Center for Studies of Crime and Delinquency. *Suicide, Homicide, and Alcoholism among American Indians: Guidelines for Help.* Publication No. (ADM) 74-42. Washington, D.C.: Government Printing Office, 1973.

2240. U.S. Department of Health, Education and Welfare. Office of Education. *Project Head Start in an Indian Community.* Bethesda, Maryland: ERIC Document Reproduction Service, The National Cash Register Company, 1965. By Alfonso Ortiz.

The pueblo (San Juan) could use a Head Start program provided that it could be adjusted to its particular socio-cultural situation.

2241. U.S. Department of Health, Education and Welfare. Public Health Service. *Some Trends in Navajo Health Behaviour* by Jerrold E. Levy. Window Rock, Arizona, 1962.

2242. U.S. Department of Health, Education, and Welfare. Public Health Service, *Indian Health Highlights.* 1966 Edition.

2243. U.S. Department of Health, Education and Welfare. Public Health Service. *Hospital and Medical Services. Fiscal Year 1968. Illness Among Indians and Alaska Natives Calendar Year 1967.*

2244. U.S. Department of Health, Education and Welfare. Public Health Service. *Washington Indian Vital Statistics, 1967.* Health Program Systems Center, 1967.

2245. U.S. Department of Health, Education and Welfare. Public Health Service. *Colorado Indian Vital Statistics, 1967.* Health Program Systems Center, 1968.

2246. U.S. Department of Health, Education and Welfare. Public Health Service. *Iowa Indian Vital Statistics, 1967.* Health Program Systems Center, 1968.

2247. U.S. Department of Health, Education and Welfare. Public Health Service. *New Mexico Vital Statistics, 1967.* Health Program Systems Center, 1968.

2248. U.S. Department of Health, Education and Welfare. Public Health Service. *North Carolina Indian Vital Statistics, 1967.* Health Program Systems Center, November, 1968.

2249. U.S. Department of Health, Education and Welfare. Public Health Service. *Utah Indian Vital Statistics, 1967.* Health Program Systems Center, 1968.

2250. U.S. Department of Health, Education and Welfare. Public Health Service. *Arizona Indian Vital Statistics, 1967.* Health Program Systems Center, 1969.

2251. U.S. Department of Health, Education and Welfare. Public Health Service. *North Dakota Indian Vital Statistics, 1967.* Health Program Systems Center, 1969.

2252. U.S. Department of Health, Education and Welfare. Public Health Service. *Oklahoma Indian Vital Statistics, 1967.* Health Program Systems Center, 1969.

2253. U.S. Department of Health, Education and Welfare. Public Health Service. *South Dakota Indian Vital Statistics, 1967. Health Program Systems Center, 1969.*

2254. *U.S. Department of Health, Education and Welfare. Public Health Service. South Dakota Indian Vital Statistics, 1967. Errata Notice.* Health Program Systems Center, 1969.

2255. U.S. Department of Health, Education and Welfare. *A Summary of the Initial System Design.* Health Program Systems Center, Indian Health Service, Tucson, Arizona, 1969.

2256. U.S. Department of Health, Education and Welfare. Public Health Service. *Indian Health Trends and Services. 1970 Edition.* Public Health Service Publication No. 2092.

2257. U.S. Department of Health, Education and Welfare. *Initial System Design (Summary).* Revised June 30, 1970. Office of Management Information Systems, Health Program Systems Center, Indian Health Service.

2258. U.S. Department of Health, Education and Welfare. *Indian Vital Statistics CY 1968. Navajo Area.* Indian Health Service, Health Program Systems Center, 1970.

2259. U.S. Department of Health, Education and Welfare. *Indian Vital Statistics CY 1968.* Phoenix Area. Indian Health Service, Health Program Systems Center, 1970.

2260. U.S. Department of Health, Education and Welfare. Social and Rehabilitation Service. *National American Indian Planning Project. Resources Directory.* Vermillion, South Dakota: n.d.

The National American Indian Planning Project is a program sponsored by the Association of American Indian Social Workers, Inc. Its purpose is to identify contemporary issues and problems facing the American Indian and to determine *Indian* priorities and recommendations for remedial and preventative programs.

2261. U.S. Department of Health, Education and Welfare. Social Security Adminstration. *Report on Wisconsin Winnebago Project Contribution of Community Development to the Prevention of Dependency* by Helen Miner Miller and Nancy O. Lurie. Washington, D.C.: 1963.

ALASKA

2262. U.S. Department of the Interior. Bureau of Indian Affairs. Alaska Power Administration. *Development of New Lands in Matanuska–Susitna Borough Alaska. Report of Study Team, February, 1970.*

This study shows that agriculture can flourish and contribute increasingly to development of both the Borough and the State.

2263. U.S. Department of the Interior. Bureau of Indian Affairs. *Alaskan Native Education: An Historical Perspective.* Research and Evaluation Report Series No. 18–A by Charles K. Ray. Albuquerque: Indian Education Resources Center, Division of Program Review and Evaluation, October, 1973.

CALIFORNIA

2264. U.S. Department of the Interior. Bureau of Indian Affairs. *A Report of Charles A. Wetmore Special U.S. Commissioner to the Mission Indians.* Washington, D.C.: Government Printing Office, 1875.

* 2265. U.S. Department of the Interior. Bureau of Indian Affairs. *Report on the Condition and Needs of the Mission Indians of California* by Special Agents Helen Jackson and Abbot Kinney to the Commissioner of Indian Affairs. Appendix XV, Report of the Commissioner of Indian Affairs for 1883.

2266. U.S. Department of the Interior. Bureau of Indian Affairs. *Report of the Special Agent for California Indians to the Commissioner of Indian Affairs.* by C. E. Kelsey. Carlisle Indian School Print, 1906.

Kelsey was made Inspector by the Secretary of Interior through an Act of Congress approved June 30, 1905 "to investigate . . . existing conditions of the California Indians and to report to Congress."

2267. U.S. Department of the Interior. Bureau of Indian Affairs. *California Rancheria Task Force Report.* BIA Sacramento Area Office, 1972.

2268. U.S. Department of the Interior. Commissioner of Indian Affairs. *Report of Special Agent John G. Ames in Regard to the Condition of the Mission Indians of California, with Recommendations.* Report of the Commissioner of Indian Affairs for 1873, Appendix A, pp. 29–40, 1874. Reprinted in *Reprints of Various Papers on California Archaeology, Ethnology and Indian History.* Edited by R. F. Heizer, Berkeley: Archaeological Research Facility, 1973.

CHEROKEE

2269. U.S. Department of the Interior. Bureau of Indian Affairs. *Indians. The Cherokees.* February, 1973.

COMANCHE

2270. U.S. Department of the Interior. Bureau of Indian Affairs. *Fort Sill ORBS Survey.* Research and Evaluation Report Series No. 19. Albuquerque: Indian Education Resources Center, July, 1973.

CROW

2271. U.S. Department of the Interior. Bureau of Indian Affairs. *Soil and Range Resources Inventory. Pryor Mountain Area. Crow Indian Reservation, Montana. 1968.* Missouri River Basin Investigations, Report No. 191.

2272. U.S. Department of the Interior. Bureau of Indian Affairs. *Soil and Range Resources Inventory. Garvin Basin. Crow Indian Reservation, Montana. 1969.* Missouri River Basin Investigations, Report No. 193.

EASTERN SEABOARD

2273. U.S. Department of the Interior. Bureau of Indian Affairs. *Indians of the Eastern Seaboard.* Washington, D.C.: Government Printing Office, 1969.

2274. U.S. Department of the Interior. Bureau of Indian Affairs. *Indians. Surviving Groups in Eastern and Southern States.* January, 1966.

FLATHEAD

2275. U.S. Department of the Interior. Bureau of Indian Affairs. *Potential for Intensive Timber Management on the Flathead Indian Reservation, Montana. 1967.*

FLORIDA

2276. U.S. Department of the Interior. Bureau of Indian Affairs. *An Approach to Planning for the Missosukee Tribe of Indians of Florida.* Report No. 208. Billings, Montana: Planning Support Group, March, 1973.

GULF COAST

2277. U.S. Department of the Interior. Bureau of Indian Affairs. *Indians of the Gulf Coast States.* Washington, D.C.: Government Printing Office, 1968.

LOWER PLATEAU

2278. U.S. Department of the Interior. Bureau of Indian Affairs. *Indians of the Lower Plateau.* Washington, D.C.: Government Printing Office, 1968.

Pamphlet on Indians in Nevada, Utah, and Colorado.

MONTANA & WYOMING

2279. U.S. Department of the Interior. Bureau of Indian Affairs. *Indians of Montana and Wyoming.* Washington, D.C.: Government Printing Office, 1968.

2280. U.S. Department of the Interior. Bureau of Indian Affairs. *The Montana—Wyoming Indian.* Billings Area Office, July, 1968.

NAVAJO

2281. U.S. Department of the Interior. Bureau of Indian Affairs. *You Asked About the Navajo!* Education, Health and Economic Problems of the Navajo. Lawrence, Kansas: Information Pamphlets About American Indians, Publications Service, Haskell Institute, n.d.

2282. U.S. Department of the Interior. Bureau of Indian Affairs. *Assisted Navajo Relocation—1952-1956.* Prepared by Robert M. Cullum, Gallup Area Relocation Specialist, October, 1957.

A study of the characteristics of Navajo PEOPLE who have relocated to a point away from the Navajo Reservation with BIA assistance.

2283. U.S. Department of the Interior. Bureau of Indian Affairs. *Need for Effective Guidance of Navajo Tribe of Indians in Management of Tribal Funds.* Report to the Congress of the U.S. by the Comptroller General of the U.S. June, 1966.

2284. U.S. Department of the Interior. Bureau of Indian Affairs. *Potential for Intensive Timber Management on the Navajo Indian Reservation, Arizona and New Mexico, 1967.*

2285. U.S. Department of the Interior. Bureau of Indian Affairs. *Navajo Indian Irrigation Project Phase I.* Section I: An Approach to Planning. Section II: The Status of Planning. Billings, Montana: Planning Support Group, Report No. 205, November, 1972.

* 2286. U.S. Department of the Interior. Bureau of Indian Affairs. *Navajo Indian Irrigation Project Phase II.* A Comprehensive Plan Framework. Billings, Montana: Planning Support Group, Report No. 211, 1973.

* 2287. U.S. Department of the Interior. Bureau of Indian Affairs. *Education for Cultural Adjustment. A Special Five-Year Program for Adolescent Indians.* Lawrence, Kansas: Haskell Institute, 1956.

   This pamphlet describes a special Navajo education program to help Navajo boys and girls 12 to 18 years old who have never been to school.

NORTH CAROLINA

2288. U.S. Department of the Interior. Bureau of Indian Affairs. *Indians of North Carolina.* Washington, D.C.: Government Printing Office, 1972.

OKLAHOMA

2289. U.S. Department of the Interior. Bureau of Indian Affairs. *Indians of Oklahoma.* Washington, D.C.: Government Printing Office, 1968.

SIOUX

* 2290. U.S. Department of the Interior. Bureau of Indian Affairs. *The Social and Economic Effects of Reservation Industrial Employment on Indian Employees and Their Families. Pine Ridge Indian Reservation, South Dakota.* Billings, Montana: Missouri River Basin Investigations Project, February, 1968.

* 2291. U.S. Department of the Interior. Bureau of Indian Affairs. *Oglala Irrigation Project—Cattle Enterprise. Pine Ridge Indian Reservation, South Dakota.* Billings, Montana: Missouri River Basin Investigations Project, April, 1969.

* 2292. U.S. Department of the Interior. Bureau of Indian Affairs. *The Fort Belknap Reservation Area. Its Resources and Development Potential.* Billings, Montana: A Missouri River Basin Study Conducted by the Missouri River Basin Investigations Project, Report No. 198, February, 1972.

* 2293. U.S. Department of the Interior. Bureau of Indian Affairs. *The Standing Rock Reservation. Its Resources and Development Potential.* Billings, Montana: Planning Support Group, January, 1973.

POTAWATOMI

2294. U.S. Department of the Interior. Bureau of Indian Affairs. *Preliminary Inventory of the Records of the Potawatomi Indian Agency.* BIA (Record Group 75). Compiled by Harry Svanda, April, 1965. General Services Administration, National Archives and Records Service, Region 6.

2295. U.S. Department of the Interior. Bureau of Indian Affairs. *The Sisseton Reservation Area. Its Resources and Development Potential.* Report No. 204, The Planning Support Group, BIA, Aberdeen Area Office, 1972.

2296. U.S. Department of the Interior. Bureau of Indian Affairs. *Resources of Sisseton Reservation Area—(Lake Traverse Reservation). History —Present—Potential.* Billings, Montana: Missouri River Basin Investigations Project, May, 1969.

2297. U.S. Department of the Interior. Bureau of Indian Affairs. *Spokane Indian Reservation. A Forest Inventory Analysis.* Denver: Indian Forestry Center, June, 1972.

2298. U.S. Department of the Interior. Bureau of Indian Affairs. *Preliminary Inventory of the Records of the Winnebago Indian Agency.* BIA (Record Group 75). Compiled by Harry Svanda, November, 1965. General Services Administration, National Archives and Records Service, Region 6.

* 2299. U.S. Department of the Interior. Office of Planning, Bureau of Indian Affairs. *The Zuni Indian Reservation. Its Resources and Development Potential.* Washington, D.C.: March, 1973.

Important data concerning social and cultural factors.

———————

2300. U.S. Department of the Interior. Office of Indian Affairs. *Subject Index of Indian Office Circulars, Nos. 160–1000. July 8, 1907–June 25, 1915.* Washington, D.C.: Government Printing Office, 1916.

2301. U.S. Department of the Interior. Bureau of Indian Affairs. *Annual Report of the Commissioner of Indian Affairs to the Secretary of the Interior.* Washington, D.C.: Government Printing Office, 1867–1932.

These are written by Indian Bureau officials.

2302. U.S. Department of the Interior. Bureau of Indian Affairs. *Annual Report of the Commissioner of Indian Affairs to the Department of the Interior.* Washington, D.C.: Government Printing Office, 1873–1934.

2303. U.S. Department of the Interior. Bureau of Indian Affairs. *Your Government and the Indian.* Washington, D.C.: Government Printing Office, n.d.

Very brief and general.

* 2304. U.S. Department of the Interior. U.S. Indian Service. *Ten Years of Tribal Government Under I.R.A.* by Theodore H. Haas, Chief Counsel, U.S. Indian Service. Haskell Institute Printing Service, 1947.

Effects of the Indian Reorganization Act.

* 2305. U.S. Department of the Interior. Bureau of Indian Affairs. "Placing Indians Who Live on Reservations: A Cooperative Program." *Employment Security Review* 26 (January 1959): 27–29.

A brief useful history of the program with respect to some of its phases.

2306. U.S. Department of the Interior. Bureau of Indian Affairs. *What Is Relocation? How Does It Work? Who Can Apply? Answers to Your Questions About Relocation Services.* Window Rock, Arizona: Navajo Agency, Branch of Relocation Services, September 5, 1959. Mimeo release.

2307. U.S. Department of the Interior. Bureau of Indian Affairs. *What Is Adult Vocational Training? How Does It Work? Who Can Apply? Answers to Your Questions about Adult Vocational Training.* Window Rock, Arizona: Navajo Agency, Branch of Relocation Services, September 5, 1959.

2308. U.S. Department of the Interior. Bureau of Indian Affairs. *Emotional Problems of Indian Students in Boarding Schools and Related Public Schools. Workshop Proceedings.* Albuquerque Indian School, April 11–13, 1960.

2309. U.S. Department of the Interior. Bureau of Indian Affairs. *Adult Vocational Training Services Activity.* Window Rock, Arizona: Navajo Agency, Branch of Relocation Services, October, 1960.

Mimeo release on schools and courses available.

2310. U.S. Department of the Interior. Bureau of Indian Affairs. *Fiscal Year 1961 Statistics Concerning Indian Education.* Lawrence, Kansas: Haskell Press, 1961.

2311. U.S. Department of the Interior. Bureau of Indian Affairs. *Report to the Secretary of the Interior by the Task Force on Indian Affairs.* July 10, 1961.

2312. U.S. Department of the Interior. Bureau of Indian Affairs. *The Bureau of Indian Affairs Voluntary Relocation Services Program.* Mimeo. distributed by Senator Alexander Wiley, 1961.

2313. U.S. Department of the Interior. Bureau of Indian Affairs. *Indian Administration in the United States.* Address by Philleo Nash, U.S. Commissioner of Indian Affairs, under the auspices of the School of Graduate Studies, University of Toronto, Toronto, Ontario, December 6, 1962.

2314. U.S. Department of the Interior. Bureau of Indian Affairs. *Answers to Your Questions on American Indians.* Washington, D.C.: 1962.

Small pamphlet with questions on education, health, land, citizenship, economic status, etc.

2315. U.S. Department of the Interior. Bureau of Indian Affairs. "The American Indians. Their Cultural Heritage, Their Contribution to the United States, Their Life Today." From *America Illustrated,* a publication of the U.S. Information Agency. 1962.

* 2316. U.S. Department of the Interior. Bureau of Indian Affairs. *United States Indian Population and Land. 1962.* Washington, D.C.: March, 1963.

2317. U.S. Department of the Interior. Bureau of Indian Affairs. *Annual Report 1962.* By Stewart L. Udall, Secretary. Washington, D.C.: Government Printing Office, 1963.

Report on the Bureau of Indian Affairs, Philleo Nash, Commissioner.

2318. U.S. Department of the Interior. Bureau of Indian Affairs. *Directory of Field and Central Offices, Bureau of Indian Affairs. July 1, 1963.*

2319. U.S. Department of the Interior. Bureau of Indian Affairs. *Progress in Employment Assistance* by Richard C. Davis. Mimeo, January, 1963. Reproduced by permission of "Indian Truth," published by the Indian Rights Association, Inc. Philadelphia, Pennsylvania: issue of September, 1962.

2320. U.S. Department of the Interior. Bureau of Indian Affairs. *Unemployment Among American Indians.* A statement by the BIA submitted to the Subcommittee on Employment and Manpower of the Committee on Labor and Public Welfare, U.S. Senate, September, 1963.

2321. U.S. Department of the Interior. Bureau of Indian Affairs. *The Economic Opportunity Act of 1964. Implications for American Indians.* Washington, D.C.: Government Printing Office, 1964.

2322. U.S. Department of the Interior. Bureau of Indian Affairs. *Employment Assistance Program.* Washington, D.C.: #134, February, 1964.

2323. U.S. Department of the Interior. Bureau of Indian Affairs. *Evolution of the*

Indian Industrial Development Program. Washington, D.C.: #134, March, 1964.

2324. U.S. Department of the Interior. Bureau of Indian Affairs. *Vocational Training Programs for American Indians.* Reprinted from December 1964 issue of Training Facts (Report No. 15), Office of Planning and Standards for Manpower Development, U.S. Department of Labor.

2325. U.S. Department of the Interior. Bureau of Indian Affairs. *Education—The Chance to Choose.* Remarks by Commissioner of Indian Affairs Philleo Nash at Fort Lewis College, Durango, Colorado, June 18, 1965. Washington, D.C.: Government Printing Office, 1965.

2326. U.S. Department of the Interior. Bureau of Indian Affairs. *American Indians and the American Society.* Remarks by Commissioner of Indian Affairs Philleo Nash, before the Institute on Human Relations, Fisk University, Nashville, Tennessee, June 29, 1965. Washington, D.C.: Government Printing Office, 1965.

2327. U.S. Department of the Interior. Bureau of Indian Affairs. *American Indians and the Federal Government.* Washington, D.C.: Government Printing Office, 1965.

Pamphlet outlining in brief the historic relationships between American Indians and the Federal Government and describing current programs of the BIA.

* 2328. U.S. Department of the Interior. Bureau of Indian Affairs. *Vacationing with Indians.* A Guide to Campgrounds and Tourist Attractions on Indian Reservations. Washington, D.C.: Government Printing Office, 1965.

2329. U.S. Department of the Interior. Bureau of Indian Affairs. *Answers to Questions about American Indians.* Washington, D.C.: Government Printing Office, 1965.

Useful data arranged under the topics: The Indian People; The Legal Status of Indians; The BIA; Indian Lands; The Economic Status of Indians; Indian Education; Indian Health; and including a suggested reading list.

2330. U.S. Department of the Interior. Bureau of Indian Affairs. *American Indian Calendar.* Washington, D.C.: Government Printing Office, 1965.

A listing by date of secular ceremonies, craft fairs, etc. of American Indians held in twenty-two states.

2331. U.S. Department of the Interior. Bureau of Indian Affairs. *Indian Affairs— 1965.* Washington, D.C.: Government Printing Office, 1966.

A Progress Report from the Commissioner of Indian Affairs, Philleo Nash.

2332. U.S. Department of the Interior. Bureau of Indian Affairs. *A Followup Study of 1963 Recipients of the Services of the Employment Assistance Program, Bureau of Indian Affairs.* October, 1966. Mimeo.

2333. U.S. Department of the Interior. Bureau of Indian Affairs. *Adult Vocational Training Services.* Washington, D.C.: Government Printing Office, 1966.

Small general pamphlet issued by the Branch of Employment Assistance, BIA.

2334. U.S. Department of the Interior. Bureau of Indian Affairs. *Report to the Congress of the U.S. by the Comptroller General of the U.S.* March, 1966.

Examination into policies for the recovery of Government expenditures incurred in the management and operation of Indian Forest Enterprises.

2335. U.S. Department of the Interior. Bureau of Indian Affairs. *Safety Progress Report 1968.* Washington, D.C.: Government Printing Office, 1968.

Topics covered are Fire Prevention; Safety Training and Education; Safety Awards and Commendations; Tribal Safety; Student Safety; Safety Promotion; Annual Tables of Accident Experience.

2336. U.S. Department of the Interior. Bureau of Indian Affairs. *Answers to your questions about American Indians.* [*May 1968*]. Washington, D.C.: Government Printing Office, 1969.

Useful. A wide variety of data arranged under the following topics: The Indian People; The Legal Status of Indians; The Bureau of Indian Affairs; Indian Lands; The Economic Status of Indians; Indian Education; Law and Order on Reservations; Indian Health. Reading lists and a directory of "Indian Museums" appended.

2337. U.S. Department of the Interior. Bureau of Indian Affairs. *Indian Affairs 1968.* Washington, D.C.: Government Printing Office, 1969.

A progress report from the Commissioner of Indian Affairs, Robert L. Bennett.

2338. U.S. Department of the Interior. Bureau of Indian Affairs. *American Indian Calendar.* Washington, D.C.: Government Printing Office, 1969.

Contents similar to *Calendar* of 1965.

2339. U.S. Department of the Interior. Bureau of Indian Affairs. Division of Credit and Financing. *Annual Credit and Financing Report, 1969.* Washington, D.C.: Government Printing Office, 1969.

Topics covered include: Indian economic development; sources of financing; authorizations and appropriations, etc.

2340. U.S. Department of the Interior. Bureau of Indian Affairs. *Federal Indian Policies.* 1969. Xerox Copy.

A summary of major developments from the pre-revolutionary period through the '60's.

2341. U.S. Department of the Interior. Bureau of Indian Affairs. *Adult Vocational Training Course Approval Under Public Law 959.* Mimeo, 1969.

2342. U.S. Department of the Interior. Bureau of Indian Affairs. Division of Credit and Financing. *Annual Credit and Financing Report, 1970.* Washington, D.C.: Government Printing Office, 1970.

Contents topically similar to 1969 report.

2343. U.S. Department of the Interior. Bureau of Indian Affairs. *American Indian Calendar, 1970.* Washington, D.C.: Government Printing Office, 1970.

A listing by month, approximate day, and location of secular events usually open to the public.

2344. U.S. Department of the Interior. Bureau of Indian Affairs. *A New Era for the American Indians.* 1970.

President Nixon's message to Congress on the American Indians, setting new Indian policies and goals, July 8, 1970.

2345. U.S. Department of the Interior. Bureau of Indian Affairs. *American Indian Know How!* An Invitation to Business and Industry.

A very small pamphlet on Indian industrial development.

2346. U.S. Department of the Interior. Bureau of Indian Affairs. *American Indian Calendar.* Washington, D.C.: Government Printing Office, 1971.

Contents topically similar to 1965 version.

2347. U.S. Department of the Interior. Bureau of Indian Affairs. *Information Needs to Support an Evaluation Process for BIA Educational Programs.* By James R. Jeffery. Research and Evaluation Report No. 16. Albuquerque: Indian Education Resources Center, December, 1972.

2348. U.S. Department of the Interior. Bureau of Indian Affairs. *Evaluation Report of the Special Scholarship in Law for American Indians.* University of New Mexico Law School. Research and Evaluation Report No. 12. Albuquerque: Indian Education Resources Center, 1972.

2349. U.S. Department of the Interior. Bureau of Indian Affairs. *Educational Needs Assessment in the BIA.* Research and Evaluation Report No. 9. Albuquerque: Indian Education Resources Center, June, 1972.

* 2350. U.S. Department of the Interior. Bureau of Indian Affairs. *Evaluation Report of the Center for the Study of Migrant and Indian Education, Toppenish, Washington.* By Paul R. Streiff. Research and Evaluation Report No. 8. Albuquerque: Indian Education Resources Center, 1972.

* 2351. U.S. Department of the Interior. Bureau of Indian Affairs. *The Haskell Transition Evaluation.* Research and Evaluation Report No. 7. Albuquerque: Indian Education Resources Center, 1972.

2352. U.S. Department of the Interior. Bureau of Indian Affairs. *Fiscal Year 1972 Statistics Concerning Indian Education.* Lawrence, Kansas: Haskell Indian Junior College, 1972.

2353. U.S. Department of the Interior. Bureau of Indian Affairs. *Indian Record.* December 1966-February 1972.

Copies of the newsletter issued by the BIA. Not all issues included between the dates given above.

2354. U.S. Department of the Interior. Bureau of Indian Affairs. *The States and Their Indian Citizens.* By Theodore W. Taylor. Washington, D.C.: Government Printing Office, 1972.

Chapters on early government-Indian relations; increased state involvement in the 1950's; termination; reappraisal in the '60's; relations between Indian citizens and states today; changing national policies; Federal obligations to Indians; viability of states; distribution of Indian Services; and the Indian potential.

* 2355. U.S. Department of the Interior. Bureau of Indian Affairs. *American Indians and Their Federal Relationship.* Plus a partial listing of other United States Indian Groups. Washington, D.C.: Government Printing Office, 1972.

Basic listing by state of all American Indian tribes, Eskimo, and Aleut groups for which the BIA has definite responsibility plus those tribes, bands, and groups terminated recently and those recognized for purposes of settling claims against the U.S. Government.

2356. U.S. Department of the Interior. Bureau of Indian Affairs. *Annual Credit Report, 1972.* Division of Credit and Financing, Bureau of Indian Affairs, 1972.

2357. U.S. Department of the Interior. Bureau of Indian Affairs. *Alaska Grass Baskets.* Personal communication by Richard P. Birchell, Superintendent, Bethel Agency, Bethel, Alaska. December, 1972.

An excellent description of how grass baskets are made in the Eskimo village of Tununak on Nelson Island, Alaska.

2358. U.S. Department of the Interior. Bureau of Indian Affairs. *Higher Education Evaluation. Student Characteristics and Opinions.* Research and Evaluation Report Seriees No. 20-A. Albuquerque: Indian Education Resources Center, June, 1973.

2359. U.S. Department of the Interior. Bureau of Indian Affairs. *Estimates of Resident Indian Population and Labor Force Status: by State and Reservation: March 1973.* Statistics, June, 1973. Mimeo.

2360. U.S. Department of the Interior. Bureau of Indian Affairs. *Indian Education: Steps to Progress in the '70's.* 1973.

Brief and very general.

2361. U.S. Department of the Interior. Bureau of Indian Affairs. *Indian Education Resources Center Bulletin* 1-present. Albuquerque: Indian Education Resources Center, 1973.

Some developments in federally sponsored Indian education discussed.

2362. U.S. Department of the Interior. Bureau of Indian Affairs. *Evaluation Report: Miccosukee Day School.* By Marie Monsen. Research and Evaluation Report Series No. 06-A. Albuquerque: Indian Education Resources Center, June, 1973.

2363. U.S. Department of the Interior. Bureau of Indian Affairs. *A History of Indian Policy.* By S. Lyman Tyler. Washington, D.C.: Government Printing Office, 1973.

2364. U.S. Department of the Interior. Bureau of Indian Affairs. *Indian Education Resources Center Bulletin* 1 (July 1973): reprint edition, October, 1973.

A synopsis of *To Live on This Earth* by Professor Robert J. Havighurst and Professor Estell Fuchs. This study, done between 1967 and 1971, is a landmark in American Indian education.

2365. U.S. Department of the Interior. Bureau of Indian Affairs. *Indian Education Resources Center Bulletin* 1 (September 1973).

Concerns re-alignment of Central Office Bureau of Indian Affairs.

2366. U.S. Department of the Interior. Bureau of Indian Affairs. *Indian Education Resources Center Bulletin* 1 (October 1973).

Includes Indian population by states.

2367. U.S. Department of the Interior. Bureau of Indian Affairs. *Indian Education Resources Center Bulletin* 2 (August 1974).

Johnson O'Malley Regulations.

2368. U.S. Department of the Interior. Bureau of Indian Affairs. *Indian Education Resources Center Bulletin* 2 (September 1974).

Various courses available for Indians.

2369. U.S. Department of the Interior. Bureau of Indian Affairs. *Indian Education Resources Center Bulletin* 2 (December 1974).

This issue is devoted entirely to the most significant Indian education legislation (Public Law 93–638) passed by the 93rd Congress.

2370. U.S. Department of the Interior. Bureau of Indian Affairs. *BIA Education Research Bulletin* 2 (January 1974).

2371. U.S. Department of the Interior. Bureau of Indian Affairs. *BIA Education Research Bulletin* 3 (September 1974).

Published periodically by the Division of evaluation, research and development for teachers and educators who are dedicated to improving Indian education.

2372. U.S. Department of the Interior. Bureau of Indian Affairs. *U.S. Office of Indian Affairs Annual Reports of the Commissioner of Indian Affairs for the Years 1824-1899.* New York: AMS Press, Inc., 1974.

2373. U.S. Department of the Interior. Bureau of Reclamation. *Livestock Industry in Alaska.* Alaska District Office, Juneau, Alaska, January, 1967.

Possibilities for an integrated feed production, livestock raising, livestock feeding and livestock processing industry in Soldotna-Kenai Peninsula—Kodiak Island—and Areas adjoining Kodiak Island, Alaska.

* 2374. U.S. Department of the Interior. Departmental Library. *Economic Development of American Indians and Eskimos 1930 through 1967. A Bibliography.* Compiled by Marjorie P. Snodgrass. Bibliography Series No. 10. Washington, D.C.: June, 1968.

* 2375. U.S. Department of the Interior. Geological Survey Professional Paper 567. *Dictionary of Alaska Place Names.* By Donald J. Orth. Washington, D.C.: Government Printing Office, 1967.

2376. U.S. Department of the Interior. Geological Survey, Albuquerque, New Mexico. *Site Study for a Water Well, Fort Wingate Army Ordnance Depot, McKinley County, New Mexico.* By John W. Shoemaker. Prepared by the U.S. Geological Survey in cooperation with Fort Wingate Army Ordnance Depot. Open-file report. April, 1968.

Developing a source of adequate well water is a difficult and expensive process.

2377. U.S. Department of the Interior. Indian Arts and Crafts Board. *Native American Arts* 1. Washington, D.C.: Government Printing Office, 1968.

2378. U.S. Department of the Interior. Indian Arts and Crafts Board. *Smoke Signals.* Various issues between 1951 and 1968.

Earlier issues up to 1961 were entitled "A Circular for Craftsmen" and were mimeographed. A magazine format with many pictures was adopted in the early 1960's.

2379. U.S. Department of the Interior. Indian Arts and Crafts Board. *Sources of Indian and Eskimo Arts and Crafts* 1 and 2. Washington, D.C., 1968.

2380. U.S. Department of the Interior. Indian Arts and Crafts Board. *The Sioux* by Stephen Feraca. 1969.

2381. U.S. Department of the Interior. Indian Arts and Crafts Board. *Source Directory 1 and 2.* February, 1974.

A listing of Indian and Eskimo owned and operated organizations marketing Native American arts and crafts.

2382. U.S. Department of the Interior. Indian Arts and Crafts Board. Brochure: *Museum of the Plains Indian and Crafts Center.* Billings: Northern Plains Indian Crafts Association, n.d.

2383. U.S. Department of the Interior. Office of Economic Analysis. *An Analysis of the Economic and Security Aspects of the Trans-Alaska Pipeline. Vols. 1–3.* December, 1971.

It is in the national interest to construct the pipeline. Constructing the trans-Alaska pipeline will not, in a major way, reduce the existing barriers to native employment. There will be a significant temporary growth in state personal income, but a probable increase in prices and cost of living in Alaska.

2384. U.S. Department of the Interior. Office of the Secretary. *Address of Secretary of the Interior Stewart L. Udall at Western Governors' Conference, Las Vegas, Nevada, April 26, 1966.*

An address on Indian development and the development of the natural resources of the West.

2385. U.S. Department of the Interior. Office of the Secretary. *President Nixon's Message to Interior.* Washington, D.C.: February 19, 1969.

2386. U.S. Department of the Interior. Office of the Secretary. *Remarks by Secretary of the Interior Walter J. Hickel before the National Congress of American Indians, Albuquerque, New Mexico, October 8, 1969.*

2387. U.S. Department of the Interior. Office of the Secretary. *Address by Commissioner of Indian Affairs Louis R. Bruce at the 25th Anniversary Convention of the National Congress of American Indians, Albuquerque, New Mexico, October 9, 1969.*

* 2388. U.S. Department of the Interior. Office of the Solicitor. *Federal Indian Law.* 2nd printing. New York: Association on American Indian Affairs, Inc., 1966.

_____

2389. U.S. Department of the Labor. Bureau of Labor Statistics. *Area Wage Survey. The Milwaukee, Wisconsin Metropolitan Area. April, 1969. Bulletin No. 1625-66.* Washington, D.C.: Government Printing Office, July, 1969.

_____

* 2390. U.S. Federal Field Committee for Development Planning in Alaska. *Alaska Natives and the Land.* Washington, D.C.: Government Printing Office, 1968.

_____

* 2391. U.S. Federal Field Committee for Development Planning in Alaska. *Estimates of Native Population in Villages, Towns, and Boroughs of Alaska.* Anchorage: January, 1969.

_____

2392. U.S. Indian Claims Commission. *Annual Report, 1968.* Washington, D.C.

2393. U.S. Indian Claims Commission. *Annual Report, 1969.* Washington, D.C.

* 2394. U.S. Indian Claims Commission. *Annual Report, 1973.* Washington, D.C.

A valuable document. Contains: Highlights; Efforts to Expedite the Work; Status of the Work; Number of dockets completed; Number of Dockets Complete by Awards; Appendices: Listing by Fiscal Years from 1947 to 1973 inc. of total of dockets completed and awards; Detailed list of awards by fiscal year; Summary of the status of final awards as of June 30, 1973; Compilation of the status of all cases as of June 30, 1973; Text of Public Law 92-265, extending the Indian Claims Commission; Chronological listing of the members of the Indian Claims Commission since its establishment; History of the Indian Claims Commission, and Nature of the Commissions' Work.

_____

2395. U.S. The National Archives. *Special Lists No. 13. List of Cartographic Records of the Bureau of Indian Affairs.* Compiled by Laura E. Kelsay. Washington, D.C.: National Archives and Records Service, General Services Administration, 1954.

2396. U.S. The National Archives. *Federal Explorations of the American West before 1880.* National Archives Publication No. 64-6. Washington, D.C.: National Archives and Records Service, General Services Administration, 1963.

2397. U.S. The National Archives. *Records of the Bureau of Indian Affairs.* Vols. 1

and 2. Compiled by Edward E. Hill. Publication No. 163. Washington, D.C.: National Archives and Records Service, General Services Administration, 1965.

2398. U.S. National Council on Indian Opportunity. Brief mimeographed fact sheet sent by Robert Robertson, Executive Director, March 10, 1970.

2399. U.S. National Council on Indian Opportunity. *Report.* National Council on Indian Opportunity, Office of the Vice President, Washington, D.C.: January 26, 1970.

2400. U.S. National Council on Indian Opportunity. *NCIO News.* Vol. 1 & 2 (Assorted Issues). Washington, D.C., 1971-1972.

2401. U.S. Office of Economic Opportunity. *Catalog of Federal Programs for Individual and Community Improvement.* December 15, 1965.

A description of governmental programs to help individuals and communities meet their own goals for economic and social development.

2402. U.S. Office of Economic Opporutnity. *A Summary of Indian Participation in OEO Programs.* Arizona State University, 1967.

2403. U.S. Office of Economic Opportunity. *Community Development.* "Phase 1—Initial Orientation for Community Development Aides." Washington, D.C.: September, 1967.

A curriculum guide for an Indian Community Action Training Program for the Three University Consortium (Arizona State, University of South Dakota, University of Utah).

2404. U.S. Office of Economic Opportunity. *Indian Community Action Project. Annual Report.* July 1966 through June 1967. Arizona State University.

* 2405. U.S. Office of Economic Opportunity. *American Indian Business Directory. A Working Handbook.* OEO Pamphlet 6164-3. Washington, D.C.: November, 1972.

2406. U.S. Office of Economic Opportunity. *Community Profiles.*

Profiles of the following Arizona Counties: Apache; Cochise; Coconino; Gila; Maricopa; Mohave; Navajo; Pima; Pinal; San Juan; Yavapai; and Yuma.

2407. U.S. Office of Management and Budget. *Update to the 1973 Catalog of Federal Domestic Assistance.* Washington, D.C.: Government Printing Office, 1974.

2408. U.S. Office of the White House Press Secretary. *Remarks of the President at Swearing-in of Robert L. Bennett as Commissioner of the BIA in the East Room.* April 27, 1966.

2409. U.S. Supreme Court. *Botiller v. Dominguez.* 130 U.S. 238, 1889.

Land title.

2410. U.S. Supreme Court. *Barker v. Harvey.* 181 U.S. 481, 1901.

Cula Expulsion order.

---

* 2411.U.S. 1971 White House Conference on Aging. *Report of the Special Concerns Sessions on The Elderly Indian.* Washington, D.C.: Government Printing Office, 1971.

XXIV. Current Newpapers, Newsletters, Magazines

PAN-INDIAN COVERAGE

2412. *Akwesasne Notes.* Mohawk Nation via Rooseveltown, New York. 13683.

The official publication of the Mohawk nation at Akwesasne. A militant newspaper published at irregular intervals. An Indian staff receives considerable support from white sources. Much of the contents are reprints from other newspapers.

2413. *The American Indian.* 1926-1931. Reprinted by Liveright Publishing Co. with index by J. M. Carroll. 51 issues, 1000 pp.

A newspaper of some historical interest, but often reflects the sentiments of its non-Indian sponsors.

2414. *American Indian Law Newsletter.* University of New Mexico Law School. 1968-

Poorly done, but of some value to gain a vague idea of Congressional activities concerning Indians.

* 2415. American Indian Press Association. *American Indian Media Directory.* 1974 edition. Washington, D.C.

2416. *AIS Newsletter.* American Indian Society of Washington, D.C. 519 - 5th Street, S.E., Washington, D.C. 20003.

Monthly.

2417. *The Amerindian.* American Indian Review. 1263 W. Pratt Blvd., #909, Chicago, Illinois, 60626.

A bi-monthly informational news bulletin about American Indians. Marion E. Gridley, Editor and Publisher.

2418. *Focus: Indian Education.* Indian Education Section, Capitol Square Building, 550 Cedar, St. Paul, Minnesota, 55101.

Written to provide current information on policies, programs, developments and educational opportunities involving Indian education on the state and local level.

2419. *Indian Affairs.* Newsletter of the Association on American Indian Affairs, Inc. 432 Park Avenue, South, New York, New York 10016.

Emphasis on happenings of major significance in current Indian affairs.

2420. *IERC Bulletin. Indian Education Resources Center.* U.S. Department of the Interior. Bureau of Indian Affairs. 123 4th Street S.W., P.O. Box 1783, Albuquerque, New Mexico 87103.

2421. *The Indian Historian.* American Indian Historical Society. 1451 Masonic Avenue, San Francisco, California 94117.

Published quarterly.

2422. *Indian Record.* U.S. Department of the Interior. Bureau of Indian Affairs. Washington, D.C.: Government Printing Office.

2423. *Indian Truth.* The Indian Rights Association. 1505 Race Street, Philadelphia, Pennsylvania 19102.

Contains news, articles, and book reviews about current Indian affairs.

2424. *Indian Viewpoint.* Motivation Through Communication. 217 N. 4th Avenue West, Duluth, Minnesota 55806.

Free newspaper issued monthly through a grant from the U.S. Office of Education, Department of Health, Education, and Welfare.

2425. *Journal of American Indian Education.* Published by the College of Education, Arizona State University, Tempe, Arizona.

2426. *Many Smokes.* National Indian Magazine. Western Printing and Publishing Company, Reno, Nevada.

May not be publishing now.

2427. *News Service.* American Indian Press Association. Room 206, 1346 Connecticut Avenue N.W., Washington, D.C. 20036.

An Indian owned and operated nonprofit corporation whose purpose is to develop and improve communications among Indian people and between Indians and the non-Indian public.

Medium Rare is the monthly newsletter published by this organization.

2428. *The Sentinel Bulletin.* National Congress of American Indians. Suite 312, 1346 Connecticut Avenue N.W., Washington, D.C. 20036.

Monthly newspaper.

* 2429. *Wassaja.* A National Newspaper of Indian America. The American Indian Historical Society. 1451 Masonic Avenue, San Francisco, California 94117.

A monthly newspaper which attempts to be comprehensive. Bias, where present, is obvious.

NORTHEAST: MAINE, NEW HAMPSHIRE, VERMONT, MASSACHUSETTS RHODE ISLAND, PENNSULVANIA, NEW YORK, WASHINGTON, D.C.

2430. *The Aroostook Indian.* Box 223, Houlton, Maine 04730.

Monthly mimeographed newsletter of the Association of Aroostook Indians.

2431. *CENA News.* Coalition of Eastern Native Americans. 927 15th Street, Washington, D.C. 20005.

CENA is a national Indian organization founded to assist in the economic, cultural and social advancement of Native Americans in the Eastern United States.

2432. *Maine Indian Newsletter.* P.O. Box 553,Old Town, Maine 04468.

Mimeographed newsletter.

2433. *Man in the Northeast.* P.O. Box 589, Center Harbor, New Hampshire 03226.

A publication dedicated to the study of The Anthropology of Northeastern North America. Published semi-annually.

* 2434. *Si Wong Geh.* Cattaraugus Indian Reservation Community Newspaper. P.O. Box 93, Irving, New York 14081.

Mimeo.

NORTHWEST: WASHINGTON, OREGON, IDAHO

2435. *Advocates for Indian Education.* The Northwest Tribes. E. 205 Boone Avenue, Spokane, Washington 99202.

Printed newsletter dealing with national Indian affairs.

2436. *Indian Voice.* Small Tribes Organization of Western Washington, Inc. 33324 Pacific Highway South, Federal Way, Washington 98002.

Printed newspaper featuring national and local events.

2437. *Kee Yoks.* Swinomish Community Action Program. P.O. Box 388, LaConner, Washington 98257.

Monthly mimeographed newsletter.

* 2438. *Lakota Oyate-Ki.* Oregon State Penitentiary. 2605 State Street, Salem, Oregon 97310.

Mimeographed booklet containing articles and events published at the Oregon State Penitentiary.

2439. *Northwest Indian News.* Seattle Indian Center Building, 619 Second Avenue, Seattle, Washington 98104.

2440. *Smoke Talk.* Brotherhood of American Indians. P.O. Box 500, Steilacoom, Washington 98388.

2441. *Tulalip See Yaht Sub.* The Tulalip Tribes. 6700 Totem Beach Road, Marysville, Washington 98270.

Mimeographed newsletter.

2442. *Yakima Nation Review 74.* The Yakima Tribe. Toppenish, Washington 98948.

Newspaper featuring local events.

CENTRAL: NORTH DAKOTA, SOUTH DAKOTA, NEBRASKA, MONTANA, KANSAS, MINNESOTA, WISCONSIN, MICHIGAN, IOWA, ILLINOIS, MISSOURI, INDIANA, OHIO

2443. *The Action News.* Community Action Program. Box 605, New Town, North Dakota 58763.

Mimeo.

* 2444. *A' Ses To.* "Blackfeet Camp Crier." Native American Programs Newspaper. Browning, Montana 59417.

Local and national news.

2445. *Becker County Record.* Detroit Lakes, Minnesota 56501.

General newspaper serving Becker County.

* 2446. *The Hunter.* North American Indian League of the Montana State Prison. Deer Lodge, Montana.

Mimeographed booklet containing articles, poetry, pictures.

2447. *The Indian in Michigan.* Michigan Commission on Indian Affairs. 454 Hollister Building, Lansing, Michigan 48902.

Printed booklet about the Indian groups and reservations in Michigan.

2448. *Indian Talk.* 457 Briarwood Avenue S.E., Grand Rapids, Michigan 49506.

2449. *Ko: Tta: Hilik.* Community Action Newsletter. Crow Agency, Montana.

Mimeographed.

2450. *Lutheran Church and Indian People.* 600 W. Twelfth Street, Sioux Falls, South Dakota 57104.

Published by the Lutheran Social Services of South Dakota.

2451. *Moccasin Telegraph.* Community Action Program. Grand Portage, Minnesota 56605.

Dittoed monthly newsletter featuring local news.

2452. *The Nishnawbe News.* Published for Indians of the Great Lakes Area by The Organization of North Amerian Indian Students. Marquette, Michigan 49855.

Monthly newspaper.

2453. *Onamia News.* Onamia, Minnesota 56359.

City newspaper.

2454. *Redlake Neighborhood Centers Newsletter.* Red Lake, Minnesota.

Mimeo.

2455. *Redletter.* Native American Committee, Inc. 1364 W. Wilson Avenue, Chicago, Illinois 60640.

Stress on education and health problems.

2456. *Shannon County News.* Kyle, South Dakota 57752.

News for Lakotas. (Name to be changed to reflect this.)

2457. *Standing Rock Star.* Standing Rock Sioux Reservation. Fort Yates, North Dakota 58538.

Monthly newspaper.

* 2458. *Tosan.* The Voice of the Tecumseh Confederacy. Editor: Jerry L. Pope. 318 N. Tacoma, Indianapolis, Indiana 46201.

   The Calumet. The Four-points Intertribal Council of Ohio, Inc. P.O. Box 283, Bellbrook, Ohio 45305.

   The New Phoenix. Jackson Blackfox, editor. Rt. 1, Box 201 N., South Point, Ohio.

   All these in one publication. Directed toward the Tecumseh Confederacy, Shawnee Nation, Choctaw Nation, Cherokee Nation, Creek Nation, United Remnant Bands.

2459. *Turtle Mountain Echo.* Box 432, Belcourt, North Dakota 58316.

   Published bi-weekly by the Turtle Mountain Band of Chippewas.

2460. *United Sioux Tribes Newsletter.* United Sioux Tribes of South Dakota Development Corporation. P.O. Box 1193, Pierre, South Dakota 57501.

   Bi-monthly—mimeo. Much national information.

2461. *The University of South Dakota Bulletin.* Institute of Indian Studies. Box 5, Vermillion, South Dakota 57069.

   Published eight times a year. South Dakota news.

2462. *Voice.* Great Lakes Indian Community. Box 5, Lac du Flambeau, Wisconsin 54538.

   Local news and general Indian information.

2463. *Warrior.* American Indian Center. 1630 W. Wilson, Chicago, Illinois 60640.

   Mimeo.

2464. *The Wig-I-Wam.* Division of Indian Work, Minneapolis Council of Churches. 3045 Park Avenue, Minneapolis, Minnesota 55407.

   Mimeo. Published monthly.

SOUTHEAST: FLORIDA, GEORGIA, SOUTH CAROLINA, NORTH CAROLINA, VIRGINIA, MARYLAND, WEST VIRGINIA, KENTUCKY, TENNESSEE, ALABAMA, MISSISSIPPI, LOUISIANA, ARKANSAS.

* 2465. *Alligator Times.* "The Newspaper of the Seminole Tribe of Florida." 6073 Stirling Road, Hollywood, Florida 33024.

   Monthly newspaper.

2466. *The Carolina Indian Voice.* P.O. Box 1075, Pembroke, North Carolina 28372.

Lumbee newspaper published each Thursday.

2467. *The Cherokee One Feather.* P.O. Box 501, Cherokee, North Carolina 28719.

Newspaper published weekly by the Tribal Council of the Eastern Band of Cherokee Indians.

2468. *Choctaw Community News.* Mississippi Band of Choctaw Indians. Tribal Office Building, Route 7, Box 21, Philadelphia, Mississippi 39350.

Monthly newspaper.

2469. *Newsletter.* Cherokee Boys Club, Inc. Box 507, Cherokee, North Carolina 28719.

2470. *The Uset Feathered Shaft.* News from United South-eastern Tribes Inc. 1970 Main Street, Wood Building, Sarasota, Florida 33577.

Temporarily discontinued until funding can be found as of August, 1974.

CALIFORNIA

2471. *California Indian Legal Services Newsletter.* 477 Fifteenth Street, Suite 200, Oakland, California 94612.

Mimeo.

2472. *Early American.* Newsletter of the California Indian Education Association. P.O. Box 4095, Modesto, California 95352.

Mimeo.

* 2473. *Five Feather News.* Tribe of Five Feathers. P.O. Box W, Lompoc, California 93436.

Mimeo. Local and national news written largely by Indians in prison.

2474. *The Indian Trader.* P.O. Box 404, La Mesa, California 92041.

Indian arts and crafts, history, shows, historical sites, museums, etc. Six issues per year.

2475. *Owens Valley Indian Education Center Newsletter.* P.O. 1648, Bishop, California 93514.

Mimeo.

2476. *Take Ten.* An Indian Newsletter. A Publication of the Indian Center of San Diego. 1623 Fifth Avenue, San Diego, California 92101.

Printed with pictures, articles, reviews.

2477. *The Tribal Spokesman.* Official newspaper of the Inter-Tribal Council of California, Inc. 2969 Fulton Avenue, Sacramento, California 95821.

Monthly.

2478. *United Indian Development Association Reporter.* 1541 Wilshire Boulevard, Los Angeles, California 90017.

"The Voice of American Indian Business."

2479. *Whispering Arrow.* Newsletter of the Northern Indian California Educational Project. 526 "A" Street, Eureka, California 95501.

SOUTHWEST: ARIZONA, NEW MEXICO, TEXAS, OKLAHOMA, COLORADO, UTAH, NEVADA

2480. *The American Indian Baptist Voice.* B. Frank Belvin, Indian Field Consultant. 1724 E. 9th Street, Okmulgee, Oklahoma 74447.

Published six times a year.

2481. *Canyon Shadows.* The Voice of the Havasupai. Supai, Arizona 86435.

Mimeo local newsletter.

2482. *CICSB Newsletter.* 811 Lincoln, Denver, Colorado 80203.

Printed by The Coalition of Indian Controlled School Boards, Inc.

2483. *DNA Newsletter.* P.O. Box 306, Window Rock, Arizona 86515.

Community Education—Preventive Law—Legal Services.

2884. *Fort Apache Scout.* Official Newspaper, White Mountain Apache Trive. Fort Apache Indian Reservation, Whiteriver, Arizona 85941.

2485. *Fort McDowell Indian Community News, Views, and Events.* A Community Newsletter. Route 1, Box 700, Scottsdale, Arizona 85256.

Mimeo.

2486. *Hopi Action News.* Winslow, Arizona.

Weekly newspaper published by the Hopi Action Program.

2487. *Indian Forerunner.* Eight Northern Indian Pueblos Newsletter. P.O. Box 927, San Juan Pueblo, New Mexico 87566.

2488. *Indian Times.* Published by the White Buffalo Council of American Indians. P.O. Box 4131. Santa Fe Station, Denver, Colorado 80204.

Published eight to twelve times a year. The White Buffalo Council welcomes all American Indian families to the Denver area and seeks to help them adjust to the city.

2489. *The Native Nevadan.* 98 Colony Road, Reno, Nevada 89502.

Published by the Inter-Tribal Council of Nevada.

2490. *Navajo Education Newsletter.* Window Rock, Arizona 86515.

Monthly publication of the Education Division, Navajo Area, Bureau of Indian Affairs.

2491. *The Navajo Times.* Window Rock, Arizona 86515.

Weekly official newspaper of the Navajo Tribe.

2492. *19 Pueblo News.* All Indian Pueblo Council, Inc. P.O. Box 6053, Albuquerque, New Mexico 87107.

Newspaper published twice a month.

2493. *OIO Newsletter.* Oklahomans for Indian Opportunity. 555 Constitution Avenue, Norman, Oklahoma 73069.

Published monthly "to tell the story of how Oklahoma's Indians are learning by doing."

2494. *Pima Maricopa Echo.* Gila River Indian Community. P.O. Box 185, Sacaton, Arizona, 85247.

2495. *The Quarterly of the Southwestern Association on Indian Affairs, Inc.* P.O. Box 1964. Santa Fe, New Mexico 87501.

Articles on past and present Indian life and culture.

* 2496. *Qua' Toqti.* Oraibi, Arizona 86039.

Hopi newspaper published weekly.

2497. *St. Christopher's Mission Newsletter.* Bluff, Utah 84512.

A mission of the Episcopal Church.

2498. *Smoke Signals.* Colorado River Indian Tribes. Parker, Arizona 85344.

Mimeo. Local newsletter.

2499. *The Southern Ute Drum.* Ignacio, Colorado.

Bi-weekly newspaper.

2500. *The Ute Bulletin.* Published by Ute Tribe. Fort Duchesne, Utah 84026. Newspaper.

ALASKA, CANADA

2501. *The Alaska Native Management Report.* 515 "D" Street, Anchorage, Alaska 99501.

A twice monthly publication of the Alaska Native Foundation.

2502. *Anica News Highlights.* 1306 Second Avenue, Seattle, Washington 98101.

Published monthly by the Manager and Staff of Alaska Native Industries Cooperative Association, Inc.

* 2503. *Eskimo.* P.O. Box 10, Chruchill, Manitoba, Canada.

Published twice a year by the Oblate Fathers of the Churchill-Hudson Bay diocese.

2504. *Native News.* BIA Bulletin.

Bureau of Indian Affairs, Box 3-8000, Juneau, Alaska, 99801.

2505. *River Times.* Owned and published by the Fairbanks Native Association. Fairbanks Native Center, 102 Lacey Street, Fairbanks, Alaska.

* 2506. *Tundra Times.* Box 1287, Fairbanks, Alaska, 99707.

Owned, controlled and edited by Eskimo, Indian, Aleut Publishing Co., a corporation of Alaska natives.

2507. *The Voice of Brotherhood.* 423 Seward Street, Juneau, Alaska 99801.

A monthly publication concerning the native population of Alaska.

XXV. Sources of an Informatin About American Indian Arts and Crafts and Music. These are Suppliers Not Only for Whites, but Also for Indians Themselves.

"NO EXCUSE NOW TO LOOK LIKE A DIRTY DUCE IN A CLEAN DECK. SHINE UP THOSE ARM BANDS, SCARF SLIDES, CONCHO BELTS AND PINS WITH SIMICHRONE POLISH." from Supernaw's Oklahoma Indian Supply Catalog, 1974-75.

2508. American Heritage Art Gallery. Dan Taulbee, owner and artist. 2706 Nettie, Butte, Montana 59701.

Don Taulbee, who is part Commanche Indian and was reared on the Flathead and Blackfeet Reservations in Montana, does work in oils, watercolours, and pen drawings.

2509. *American Indian Crafts and Culture.* Box 3638, Tulsa, Oklahoma 74152.

Magazine giving information on Indian costuming, craft articles, current Indian news, book and record reviews, features on Indians, groups, museums and artists, powwow information, Indian history. Good old Indian photos.

2510. American Indian Music for the Classroom from Canyon Records. 4143 North Sixteenth Street, Phoenix, Arizona 85016.

4 LP record or 4 cassette package includes teacher's guide, 20 study photographs, a set of spirit masters for each song, a bibliography and map. Overhead transparencies for each song may be ordered at additional cost.

2511. Awaxawi Arts and Crafts. 912 N. 17th Street, Bismarck, North Dakota 58501.

Indian craft items produced by local guilds in the Dakotas.

2512. The Bead Shaman. 400 San Felipe N.W. Albuquerque, New Mexico 87104.

A collection of trade beads and silversmith supplies.

2513. Blackbear's Great Plains Studios. 710 W. Douglas, Wichita, Kansas 67203.

No wholesale listing available.

2514. Catawba Indian Pottery of South Carolina by Sara Ayres. 1182 Brookwood Circle, W. Columbia, South Carolina 29169.

Custom made pieces, hand crafted pitchers, vases, ash trays, figures, planters, pipes, etc.

2515. Chahta Arts and Crafts. Box 371, Idabel, Oklahoma 74745.

Beadwork, baskets, weaving work, Indian dolls.

2516. Chitimacha Indian Craft Association. Route 2, Box 224, Jeanerette, Louisiana 70544.

Source of Chitimacha crafts, especially baskets of pine needles and river cane.

2517. Chippewa Cree Crafts of Rocky Boys Reservation. Box B, Havre, Montana 59501.

High quality beadwork, mocassins, Indian games.

2518. Choctaw Craft Association. Choctaw Indian Agency, Philadelphia, Mississippi 39350.

Choctaw baskets and other crafts.

2519. Dakotah Crafts. P.O. Box 103, Sisseton, South Dakota 57262.

Beadwork designed and handcrafted by Sisseton-Wahpeton Sioux Indians.

2520. Fine Apache Arts. George J. Stevens, owner. P.O. Box 57, San Carlos, Arizona 85550.

Apache baskets, cradle boards, jewelry, dolls.

2521. Four Winds Indian Trading Post. Preston E. Miller, trader. Route 1, St. Ignatius, Montana 59865.

Plains Indian crafts.

* 2522. Grey Owl Indian Craft Manufacturing Co. 150–02 Beaver Road, Jamaica, New York 11433.

Indian craft supplies.

2523. Holden, Patti. "The Language of Beads." *Illustrated London News,* Christmas, 1973.

Illustrations by Bill Holden of beadwork in Africa.

2524. Hopi Arts and Crafts Silvercraft. Cooperative Guild. Box 37. Second Mesa, Arizona 86043.

Jewelry, Kachina dolls, baskets, pottery.

2525. Indian Hills Trading Post. P.O. Box 229, Indian Hills Reservation. Petoskey, Michigan 49770.

Quill boxes, beadwork, black ash baskets, leather, barkwork, woodwork, etc.

2526. Indian Original. LaVern Heiter, Designer. 521 - 7th Street, Rapid City, South Dakota 57701.

Clothes tailored to fit.

2527. The Indian Shop. Escondido Mall. 1341 E. Valley Parkway, Escondido, California 92027. Leo and Monte Calac, owners.

Rugs, baskets, pottery, kachina dolls, paintings, moccasins, silver and turquoise jewelry.

* 2528. Iroqrafts. RR#2, Ohsweken, Ontario, Canada HOA 1MO.

Iroquois and Eskimo crafts.

2529. Jicarilla Museum. P.O. Box 126, Dulce, New Mexico 87528.

2530. Lone Bear Indian Craft Co. 5 Beekman Street, New York, N.Y. 10038.

Eastern woodland Indian craft work all hand made by American Indians.

2531. Marlinda Dolls. Marieita Wallace, Owner Manager. Box 611, Wrangell, Alaska 99929.

Marlinda dolls, ladies cloth parkas made by Alaskan Indians of the Tlinget Tribe.

2532. Navajo Arts and Crafts Enterprise. Drawer A, Window Rock, Arizona 86515.

Owned and managed by the Navajo tribe to help Navajo craftsmen market their wares at a fair price, to improve the quality of their work, and to preserve traditional native skills.

2533. Nizhonie Fabrics, Inc. 810½ N. Broadway, Box 729, Cortez, Colorado 81321.

Indian owned and operated. Authentic historical Indian designs on fabrics.

2534. Oklahoma Indian Arts and Crafts Cooperative. Box 966, Anadarko, Oklahoma 73005.

Represents some of the most talented Indian artists and craftsmen in Oklahoma.

2535. Pipestone Indian Shrine Association. Pipestone National Monument. Box 727, Pipestone, Minnesota 56164.

Site of the famed pipestone quarries of Minnesota. Pipes, catlinite articles, and books are sold in the display and sales shop located in the Indian Cultural Center.

* 2536. Plume Trading and Sales Co., Inc. 155 Lexington Avenue, New York, New York 10016. Office and Mail Order Division: P.O. Box 585, Monroe, New York 10950.

Supplies for making Indian Crafts.

* 2537. Supernaw's Oklahoma Indian Supply. "Indian owned and operated." Box 216, Skiatook, Oklahoma 74070.

Major supplier of craft materials and finished items to the powwow world. Trade directed primarily to American Indians.

2538. Tatanka Sapa Trading Post. P.O. Box 23, Lombard, Illinois 60148.

Indian craft supplies, finished articles from Indian co-ops, custom work on special order.

2539. Tipi Shop - Halley Park. P.O. Box 1270, Rapid City, South Dkota 57701.

Beadwork, quillwork, pipestone, stationery, raw materials.

2540. Toksook Bay Arts and Crafts. Nelson Island, Toksook Bay, Alaska 99637.

Source of Eskimo crafts. Basketry, dance fans, spears and harpoons, beadwork, wood and ivory carving, etc.

2541. Touching Leaves Indian Crafts. Lenape (Delaware) Handicrafts. 929 Portland, Dewey, Oklahoma 74029. Nora Thompson Dean, owner.

The main purpose is to promote the Lenape people and culture.

2542. Treasure-House of Worldly Wares. 1880 Lincoln Avenue, Calistoga, California 94515.

Southwestern crafts, beadwork.

2543. Treaty Oak Trading Post. 5241 Lexington Avenue, Jacksonville, Florida 32210.

Many raw materials. Seminole handicrafts, Indian records and tapes, books.

2544. Wana-Tua Designs, Inc. 1210 North Hudson, Oklahoma City, Oklahoma 73102.

Original fashions designed by Mabel Harris in ribbonwork patterns of the woodlands Indians.

2545. Winnebago Public Indian Museum. Box 441, Wisconsin Dells, Wisconsin 53965. Roger Little Eagle, owner, operator.

Moccasins, deerskin accessories, smoked moose items, beadwork, wood carvings, Winnebago baskets, Southwestern items.

2546. Warpath. Indian Jewelry and Artifacts. Indian owned and operated. 4711 Monroe, San Diego, California 92115.

They also carry Indian records.

2547. Winona Indian Trading Post, Pierre Bovis. P.O. Box 324, Santa Fe, New Mexico 87501.

Books, supplies, crafts of many tribes. Professional appraisal service offered by mail or personally for large collections.

2548. The Zuni Craftsmen Cooperative Association. Zuni, New Mexico 87327.

Large stock of Zuni jewelry for sale to wholesalers.

XXVI. Some Museums Having Displays/Publications Concerned with American Indians—Prehistory, History, and Contemporary Periods (See Item 28.)

2549. Campbell River and District Historical Society. P.O. Box 101, Campbell River, British Columbia V9W 4Z9.

2550. Carnegie Museum of Natural History. 4400 Forbes Avenue, Pittsburgh, Pennsylvania 15213.

2551. Center for the Study of Man. Smithsonian Institution, Washington, D.C. 20560.

* 2552. The Florida State Museum. Museum Road, University of Florida, Gainesville, Florida 32601.

2553. Garvies Point Preserve and Museum. Barry Drive, Glen Cove, Long Island, New York 11542.

* 2554. The Heard Museum. 22 E. Monte Vista Road, Phoenix, Arizona 85004.

2555. Huron Indian Village. Little Lake Park, Midland, Ontario, Canada.

2556. Illinois State Museum. Springfield, Illinois.

2557. Indiana University Museum. Student Building 107, Bloomington, Indiana 47401.

* 2558. Logan Museum of Anthropology. Beloit College, Beloit, Wisconsin.

2559. Robert H. Lowie Museum of Anthropology. University of California, 103 Kroeber Hall, Berkeley, California 94720.

2560. *Malki Museum.*

   A new museum created by and for the Indians of Southern California.

2561. Manitoba Museum of Man and Nature. 190 Rupert Avenue, Winnipeg R3B ON2.

* 2562. Milwaukee Public Museum. 800 West Wells Street, Milwaukee, Wisconsin 53233.

2563. Museum of Anthropology. University of Kansas, Lawrence, Kansas 66044.

* 2564. Museum of Anthropology. University of Michigan, University Museums Building, Ann Arbor, Michigan 48104.

2565. Museum of New Mexico. P.O. Box 2087, Sante Fe, New Mexico 87501.

* 2566. Museum of Northern Arizona. P.O. Box 1389, Flagstaff, Arizona 86001.

* 2567. National Museums of Canada. 360 Lisgar Street, Ottawa, Ontario. K1A OMB.

2568. Nevada State Museum. Carson City, Nevada 89701.

2569. New Brunswick Museum. 277 Douglas Avenue, Saint John, New Brunswick.

2570. Newfoundland Museum. Duckworth Street, St. John's, Newfoundland.
Discussions for a publications series have been initiated, but it is not functioning as yet.

2571. New York State Museum and Science Service. Albany, New York 12224.

2572. Ohio Historical Society. Columbus, Ohio 43211.

* 2573. Peabody Museum of Archaeology and Ethnology. Harvard University, 11 Divinity Avenue, Cambridge, Massachusetts 02138.

2574. Pennsylvania Historical and Museum Commission. Harrisburg, Pennsylvania.

2575. Provincial Museum of Alberta. 12845 - 102 Avenue, Edmonton, Alberta, Canada T5N OM6.

2576. Provincial Museum. Victoria, British Columbia, Canada.

2577. The Rochester Museum and Science Center. 657 East Avenue, Rochester, New York 14603.

* 2578. Royal Ontario Museum. 100 Queen's Park, Toronto, Ontario, Canada M5S 2C6.

* 2579. San Diego Museum of Man. 1350 El Prado, Balboa Park, San Diego, California 92101.

2580. Saskatchewan Museum of Natural History. Wascana Park, Regina, Saskatchewan, Canada.

* 2581. State Historical Society of Wisconsin. 816 State Street, Madison, Wisconsin 53706.

2582. Treganza Anthropology Museum. San Francisco State University, San Francisco, California 94132.

* 2583. University of Missouri-Columbia, Museum of Anthropology Publications, 100 Swallow Hall, Columbia, Missouri 65201.

2584. University of Nebraska State Museum. 14th and U Streets, Lincoln, Nebraska, 68506.

* 2585. University Museum. Southern Illinois University at Carbondale, Carbondale, Illinois 62901.

XXVII. Maps

* 2586. *The American Heritage Pictorical Atlas of the United States.* Edited by Hilde H. Kagan. New York: McGraw-Hill Book Co., 1966.

   A good general treatment.

* 2587. *The Atlas of American Agriculture.* Washington, D.C.: U.S. Department of Agriculture, 1936.

   Considers a wide range of variables.

* 2588. *Canada Showing Location of Indian Bands with Linguistic Affiliations 1968.* Ottawa: Indian Affairs Branch, Department of Indian Affairs and Northern Development.

   Some overlap with "Indian Lands and Languages" in the *National Atlas of Canada,* but the scale is much larger and additional supporting information is supplied. Scale: 1:6,336,000.

* 2589. *Indian Lands and Related Facilities as of 1971.* Washington, D.C.: Bureau of Indian Affairs, Department of the Interior.

   Contains information on Federal Indian Reservations, Former Reservations in Oklahoma, Existing Tourist Complexes, Planned Tourist Complexes, Interstate Highways, National Forests, National Parks, National Wildlife Refuges, State Reservations, Indian Groups Without Trust Land, Federally Terminated Tribes and Groups, BIA area and agency offices. The best available.

* 2590. *Indians of North America Before Columbus.* Supplement to *National Geographic* 146 (December 1972). Washington, D.C.: Cartographic Division, National Geographic Society.

Extremely general, but done in an attractive fashion. William Sturtevant and Gordon Willey were the principal consultants.

* 2591. *The National Atlas of Canada.* Fourth Edition. Ottawa: Surveys and Mapping Branch, Department of Energy, Mines and Resources, 1973.

The best available single source. Of special interest are maps concerning Indian Lands and Languages and the Indian and Eskimo Population. Four maps are devoted to exploration and one to the posts of the Canadian fur trade. All maps are supported by text.

* 2592. *The National Atlas of the United States.* Washington, D.C.: U.S. Geological Survey, 1955–1972.

An authoritative source containing an extensive array of information.

* 2593. *Northwest Territories and Yukon Territory.* Ottawa: Department of Mines and Technical Surveys, Surveys and Mapping Branch, 1959.

Contains information on: highways, motor roads, winter tractor roads, railways, post offices, trading posts, hospitals, nursing stations, schools, industrial homes, Royal Canadian Mounted Police Posts, airfields, seaplane anchorages, wireless stations, meterological stations, elevations in feet and glaciers or icecaps. Scale: 1:4,000,000.

* 2594. Paullin, Charles D. *Atlas of the Historical Geography of the United States.* Washington, D.C.: Carnegie Institution of Washington and the American Geographical Society of New York, 1932.

A valuable source. Contents consist of: The Natural Environment; Cartography, 1492–1867; Indians, 1567–1930; Indian Tribes and Linguistic Stocks, 1650; Indian Battles, 1521–1700, 1701–1800, 1801–1845, 1846–1890; Indian Reservations 1840, 1875, 1900, 1930; Indian Missions, 1567–1861; Explorations in the West and Southwest, 1535–1852; Lands 1603–1930 (includes Indian Cessions 1750–1890); Settlement, Population and Towns, 1650–1790; States,Territories and Cities 1790–1930; Population 1790–1930 by ethnic group; Colleges, Universities, and Churches, 1775–1890; Boundaries, 1607–1927; Political Parties and Opinion, 1788–1930; Political, Social and Educational Reforms, 1775–1931; Industries and Transportation, 1620–1931; Foreign Commerce, 1701–1929; Distribution of Wealth, 1799–1928; Plans of Cities, 1775–1803; Military History, 1689–1919; Possessions and Territorial Claims of the United States; Also Certain Military Operations and Grounds Formerly Frequented (ca. 1815–1860) by American Whalers.

Index